Forgotten Horrors

FORGOTTEN HORRORS

Early Talkie Chillers from Poverty Row

George E. Turner   **Michael H. Price**

SOUTH BRUNSWICK AND NEW YORK: A. S. BARNES AND COMPANY
LONDON: THOMAS YOSELOFF LTD

A. S. Barnes and Co., Inc.
Cranbury, New Jersey 08512

Thomas Yoseloff Ltd
Magdalen House
136-148 Tooley Street
London SE1 2TT, England

Library of Congress Cataloging in Publication Data

Price, Michael H.   1947
   Forgotten horrors.

   Includes index.
   1. Horror films—Dictionaries. I. Turner,
George, 1925-   II. Title.
PN1995.9.H6P7 1979   791.43'7   78-69636
ISBN 0-498-02136-X

PRINTED IN THE UNITED STATES OF AMERICA

Contents

AMORE E MORTE
TANGLED DESTINIES
THE MIDNIGHT WARNING
STRANGE ADVENTURE
SAVAGE GIRL
SECRETS OF WU SIN
THE DEATH KISS
THE INTRUDER
TOMBSTONE CANYON

1933   *78*

THE HORROR
THE WHISPERING SHADOW
THE VAMPIRE BAT
VOODO
SUCKER MONEY
THE THREE MUSKETEERS
A SHRIEK IN THE NIGHT
A STUDY IN SCARLET
THE FLAMING SIGNAL
THE SPHINX
TOMORROW AT SEVEN
STRANGE PEOPLE
CORRUPTION
SAVAGE GOLD
THE AVENGER
TARZAN THE FEARLESS
DEVIL'S MATE
THE DELUGE
THE EMPEROR JONES
THE WOLF DOG
JAWS OF JUSTICE

1934   *110*

BIG CALIBRE
MYSTERY LINER
THE LOST JUNGLE
THE HOUSE OF MYSTERY
PICTURE BRIDES
DRUMS O' VOODOO
THE MYSTIC HOUR
MURDER IN THE MUSEUM
FIFTEEN WIVES
RANDY RIDES ALONE
GREEN EYES
THE STAR PACKER
JANE EYRE
THE MOONSTONE
MANIAC
THE RETURN OF CHANDU
THE RETURN OF CHANDU (Feature Version)
CHANDU ON THE MAGIC ISLAND
THE GHOST WALKS
MYSTERY MOUNTAIN
MURDER ON THE CAMPUS

1935   *146*

MYSTERIOUS MR. WONG

Preface

The fact of obscurity is justification enough for this collection, which takes for granted that the follower of cinema will have better than a nodding acquaintance with the *major* studios' milestones in horror and weird mystery.

For obscurity—more so than however well they inspire tension and dread—links the films discussed here. The appearance of virtually any of them on television or in a theatre would amount to a discovery. Only a fraction of these pictures made from 1929 through 1936 (a period popularly known as the Golden Age of the talkie "horror" film) will have any sort of reputation today in comparison with attention accorded the likes of *Frankenstein* and *Dracula*. The present writers call belated notice to these forgotten chillers without segregating them into such categories as Western, whodunit, spooky comedy, jungle or piracy adventure, or outright horror melodrama. The criterion is that the film convey a strange menace. H. P. Lovecraft, the brilliant writer of pulp-magazine horrors, applied such a standard to literature, holding that some of the most worthy examples of weird fiction may be found as elements of tales which have an entirely different tone overall. We would be remiss not to treat movies similarly.

Likely *The Vampire Bat* and *White Zombie* will strike a responsive chord, but many of their companions produced outside the major studios are so little known as to have escaped the notice of even the trade journals. Who remembers *Murder at Dawn, Fifteen Wives, Condemned To Live, Maniac, Drums of Jeopardy,* or *Sinister Hands*? While such sparse notice is often unjustified, it hardly defies explanation.

Poverty Row status contributes strongly to the obscurity. The term POVERTY ROW is not altogether accurate in its connotation of categorically cheap production, but it does serve to designate the films herein as separate from the works of major studios. Most independents aimed for what *Variety* terms "the shirtsleeve audience," losing any expectations of notice from the stylishly critical press.

Although the talkie "horror" tradition is widely supposed to have begun with Universal's *Dracula* and *Frankenstein* in 1931, these two actually are turning points on a road whose paving was initiated in 1928 with the second all-talking feature, Warners' serio-comic *The Terror.* This and most other pioneer talkies of the *genre* were built along the lines of popular Broadway "mystery farces" such as *The Cat and the Canary, The Gorilla,* and *The Bat,* all of which were successful as silents and which were reprised as talkies by 1930.

Talkies in 1929 were for the most part anything but satisfactory. Arguments raged whether disk or optically reproduced sound-on-film would be the standard and, indeed, whether the "novelty" of sound would last. Some producers were thrilled to make talking dramas while others could hardly wait to return to the silents they felt the public ultimately would demand. Silent-era stars were doomed by inappropriate voices, thick foreign accents, "mike fright," or the inability to memorize dialogue. Actors and off-scenes personnel trekked in from New York, some of them destined to become leaders in the new medium, others as unable to adapt to "canned" drama as many silent picture craftsmen were unable to adapt to sound.

What studios could bear the cost installed sound equipment and built sound stages while insiders pondered noisily whether the "fad" would endure. Larger studios still made both silent and sound versions of most pictures, meantime adding music, sound effects, and sprinklings of dialogue to pictures completed as silents. Many small-town and neighborhood theatres continued to show silent films, but a non-talkie hadn't a chance to open in a big-city downtown house.

Poverty Row programs often found their way onto screens behind such curtains as this. The promotional messages on the curtain helped offset economic stringencies of the Depression years.

Because the majors were making full use of their limited sound facilities, independent companies were unable to obtain sound stage space or equipment even if they could afford it. Some independents employed "bootleg" soundtracks to avoid a licensing fee of $500 a reel for sound-on-film. Still others doggedly kept making silent pictures for a vanishing market, and most died with the silent era.

Independents that remained during the Great Depression of the 'thirties were of several general types.

The true Poverty Row outfits obtained financing, rented studio space as needed, avoided retakes and special effects, and commissioned only necessary lab work. They produced on shoestring budgets and fast schedules, often shooting a feature for as little as $8,000 to $10,000 in as few as four to ten days. Typical are Monogram, Mascot, Majestic, Puritan, Invincible-Chesterfield, Reliable, and Progressive. Most dealt largely in low-budget Westerns for the rural and Saturday matinee trade. Their non-Western product was designed for the bottom of the double bills programmed by most urban theatres.

A second category of independent production has but a few exponents. A related group comprising Tiffany, Sono Art, Educational, and World Wide had its own studio and produced some pictures comparable to those of the majors. Monogram and Mascot later established their own studios.

Yet another class, including such producers as Samuel Goldwyn, Harold Lloyd, Roland West, Twentieth Century, and Reliance, transcends the Poverty Row stereotype; prestige pictures from these sources enjoyed substantial financial backing and standing release agreements with major firms. For unabashedly proud reasons, Mr. Goldwyn might well have preferred that his well-heeled sector of Hollywood independence be—to borrow a "Goldwynism"—"included out" of a discussion on Poverty Row. So be it.

Efforts of the true Poverty Row companies are best appreciated by an open mind willing to forego more fashionable fare. Few of the shows played Broadway; most, therefore, were not reviewed outside the trade press. The few that were reviewed for the general public were treated as a rule with unwarranted contempt. Even within the confines of the "horror" *genre* they delivered such rewards as an all-Technicolor, all-talking feature early in 1930 *(Mamba);* the first screen depiction of Haitian magic *(White*

10

Zombie); the first serial with sound *(King of the Kongo);* a late example of the vanishing art of hand-colouring *(The Death Kiss);* an ancestor of the Bob Hope school of wisecracks in counterpoint with scary doings *(The House of Mystery);* and worthy adaptations of literary classics including *Jane Eyre, The Moonstone,* and *A Study in Scarlet.*

They boast brilliant acting from such bypassed favorites of the silent era as H. B. Walthall, Francis X. Bushman, Phillips Smalley, and Conway Tearle; high-calibre performances from actors bound for stardom, such as Ginger Rogers, Walter Brennan, Boris Karloff, George Brent, and Rita (Cansino) Hayworth. And they showcase many inimitable portrayals by superb players who were not "stars" — money could not buy better acting than was provided by Lionel Atwill, Reginald Owen, Sidney Blackmer, or Jean Hersholt, to name but a few. Here too are the late works of such fine silent film directors as Fred Newmeyer and William Nigh, as well as the fledgling work of future major directors like Richard Thorpe, Edwin Marin, and Bruce Humberstone. The use of dependable actors and off-screen personnel was a necessity in independent production, for retakes were an unaffordable commodity.

Inventiveness flourished on Poverty Row. Poetic fantasy pervades the melodrama of *White Zombie.* Vampire legendry is given unique twists through the suggestion of prenatal influence in *Condemned To Live* and an infusion of science fiction in *The Vampire Bat.* Standard Western fare is coupled with horror in *Tombstone Canyon. The Deluge* is one of the few pre-World War II films to address an end-of-the-world theme. *Maniac* represents an attempt to transpose Poe's writings into erotic subject matter. Much of the sophisticated stunt work essential to action pictures was developed at Mascot and Monogram.

Obscurity of certain of these films can be traced to exhibitor embarrassment because of their treatment of ethnic groups. Minority contributions to these films cannot be ignored, however, accusations of racism notwithstanding. Art must be viewed as a product of its time; no observer can reasonably expect a film of 1930 to reflect the tastes of the present decade, yet one of the most steadfastly fashionable components of retrospective criticism is to term a picture "dated." This unrealistic approach becomes an absurd reaction when an individual of the enlightened present pretends to expect an early talkie to apply up-to-date attitudes toward racial or national minorities.

Films of the period discussed here often featured black actors as superstitious servants and Oriental actors as practitioners of the fearsome "yellow peril." The likes of Willie Best, Clarence Muse, Richard Loo, and Jimmy Wang were striving to portray their races in a medium whose audiences could barely imagine a minority representative in anything but a subordinate or threatening role. The best black players — Muse, Stepin Fetchit, Best, and Mantan Moreland — in fact managed to parody the stereotypes which white-supremacy advocates applied to them. The very appearance of a black comedian was a breakthrough in cinema aimed at white audiences; many such parts in silent films — *The Lost World* (1925), for example, and *One Exciting Night* (1922) — were assigned to white actors in blackface. A viewer with a sensitive — not a thin-skinned — attitude will accept comedy by blacks or villainy by Orientals as a product of a bygone age and appreciate the beginnings of an inclination to let minorities interpret themselves on screen.

Rewards enjoyed by *Dracula, Frankenstein,* and Paramount's *Dr. Jekyll and Mr. Hyde* sent the Poverty Row impresarios scrambling onto the bandwagon. Independently made horror films flooded the market during 1932 and '33, most continuing in the old-fashioned traditions of Broadway and early Vitaphone but with interesting variations. The old-house comedy-thriller is married to scientific horror in *Murder at Dawn* and to a Poe theme in *The Monster Walks.* The independents produced surprisingly few unadulterated horror films of the Universal school; there are *White Zombie, The Vampire Bat,* and, years later, *Condemned To Live.* As the Depression wiped out most small-time producers, other short-lived but ambitious companies took their places.

In 1934 the dwindling independents maintained a large output, but none of the Poverty Row product was comparable to that of the majors. A group of small companies formed Republic Pictures, which hovered between major and minor status. The old Monogram had entered this venture along with Mascot, Liberty, and Majestic, and shortly thereafter a new Monogram was organized.

Then 1936 saw a pronounced slackening of the "horror" cycle among both the majors and the independents, brought on partially through increasing censorship demands. Most of the old Poverty Row companies had vanished or were soon to do so. Then a European horror ban administered the *coup de grace.* Three years later the genre rose from the grave for another go at it — which is another story.

Acknowledgments

The authors acknowledge with gratitude these sources of vital information, encouragement, and assistance:

Mr. Les Adams
Mr. Robert Armstrong (dec.)
Mr. Mischa Auer (dec.)
Mr. Vince Barnett (dec.)
Mr. Granville Bates (dec.)
Mr. Spencer Gordon Bennet
Mr. Charles Bickford (dec.)
Mr. Robert Bloch
Mr. David Bowser
Mr. Charles D. Broun (dec.)
Mr. Bob ("Tracy") Burns
Mr. Ray Charles
Mr. Chester Clute (dec.)
Mr. Ray Corrigan (dec.)
Mr. Buster Crabbe
Mr. Frankie Darro (dec.)
Mr. Reginald Denny (dec.)
Mr. August W. Derleth (dec.)
Mr. Melvyn Douglas
Mr. Linwood G. Dunn, A. S. C.
Mr. John Gallaudet
Dr. Orville Goldner, O.B.E.
Mr. George T. Grader
Mr. Bob Hope
Mr. Arthur Housman (dec.)
Mr. I. Stanford Jolley
Mr. Boris Karloff (dec.)
Mr. Sam Katzman (dec.)
Mr. Tom Keene (dec.)
Mr. Cy Kendall (dec.)
Mr. Edgar Kennedy (dec.)

Mr. Donald Kerr
Mr. Richard Kidwell
Mr. Fuzzy Knight (dec.)
Mrs. Jane Marshall
Mr. Thom Marshall
Mr. Kermit Maynard
Mr. John P. McCarthy, Jr.
Mr. Jerry McDonough
Miss Susan Metcalf
Mr. Don Moore
Mr. Earl Moseley
Mr. William Pawley (dec.)
Mr. Samuel A. Peeples
Mr. Nat Pendleton (dec.)
Miss Barbara Pepper (dec.)
Mr. Roland C. Price (dec.)
Mr. Lucien Prival (dec.)
Dr. Bill G. ("Buck") Rainey
Mr. Duncan Renaldo
Mrs. Tex Ritter (Dorothy Fay)
Mr. Reb Russell
Miss Vivian Salazar
Mr. J. Ben Sargent
Mr. Harry Semels (dec.)
Mr. Johnny Sheffield
Mr. Anthony Slide
Mr. James Stephenson (dec.)
Miss Judy Tolk
Mr. Fred Tripp (dec.)
Mrs. Mary Kate Tripp
Mr. Richard Tucker (dec.)

Mr. Allan R. Turner
Mr. King Vidor
Mr. Theodore von Eltz (dec.)
Mrs. Jean Wade
Mr. George WaGGner

Mr. Pierre Watkin (dec.)
Mr. John Wayne
Mr. Grant Withers (dec.)
Miss Fay Wray
Mr. Carleton Young

The Academy of Motion Picture Arts & Sciences

The American Society of Cinematographers (A. S. C.)

The American Society of Composers, Authors & Publishers (A. S. C. A. P.), Sara Kerber, Index Department

Cable Films of Kansas City, Missouri, Herbert Miller, Vice President in Charge of Marketing

Film Favorites of Canton, Oklahoma

The Hoblitzelle Theatre Arts Library, Humanities Research Center, University of Texas at Austin, Edwin Neal, Research Assistant

The Learning Resources Center of Amarillo (Texas) College

The Library of Eastern New Mexico University at Portales

The Library of West Texas State University at Canyon

The Mary E. Bivins Memorial Library and Municipal

Library Facilities, Amarillo, Texas

Movie Wonderland of Goleta, California

The Radio-Television Production Department of Amarillo (Texas) College, Allen Shifrin, past Director

The Samuel French Company of New York City

The Screen Directors Guild

The Screen Writers Guild

The Southern Music Publishing Company, Incorporated, of New York City

The Texas Commission on the Arts & Humanities, Maurice Coats, past Executive Director

Total Television of Amarillo, Texas, Chuck Christiansen, General Manager

Forgotten Horrors

"It is kept in mind, I hope, that I don't make these things up. I just report them."

—Les Adams [letter to the authors, August 1977]

Amen.

—The Authors

1929

BLACK WATERS (1929)

*(British & Dominion Films, Ltd. –
World Wide Pictures, Incorporated)*

Directed by Marshall Neilan; *produced by* Herbert Wilcox; *based upon the play,* FOG, *by* John Willard; *continuity and dialogue by* John Willard; *photographed by* David Kesson; *dialogue director,* Frank Reicher; *film editor,* Rose Smith; Western Electric *sound on film and disk; produced at* Metropolitan Studio; *running time in Great Britain,* 90 minutes, *in United States,* 81 minutes; *released in U. S.* April 14, 1929, *through* Educational Film Exchanges.

PLAYERS: *The Reverend Mr. Eph Kelly,* James Kirkwood; *Eunice,* Mary Brian; *Charlie,* John Loder; *Jimmy Darcy,* Robert Ames; *Randall,* Frank Reicher; *Chester,* Hallam Cooley; *Temple,* Lloyd Hamilton; *Jeelo,* Noble Johnson; *Olaf,* Ben Hendricks.

Synopsis

Charlie and Eunice, in evening dress, are watching a cabaret show in San Francisco when they receive a note asking them to come to a deserted wharf at midnight, to attend a houseboat party. They see a ghostly sailing ship moored at the wharf. An old watchman, Olaf, warns them not to go aboard. They hear a weird drumming, which Olaf attributes to "Larrabee's blackbird – a cannibal, 'e is, a Voodoo cannibal that does Larrabee's dirty work." Others gather: a grim-faced older man named Randall, bent on revenge, because the mysterious and allegedly crazed sea captain, "Tiger" Larrabee, stole Randall's wife and then abandoned her; Chester, a young man-about-town who was Eunice's lover; Temple, a stuttering valet; and the Reverend Eph Kelly, a grotesque waterfront character who describes himself as "just a poor servant of the Lord, come to save souls." The group boards the ship and meets the mute

giant, Jeelo, who appears as savage as Olaf described him. They find a prisoner, Jimmy Darcy, who identifies himself as a newspaper reporter who had "been tipped to watch 'Tiger' Larrabee, and I managed to get aboard, but they got me and tied me up."

A voice over the radio warns the guests they will all be dead before dawn. They try to leave but find that the ship is drifting to sea, its mooring hawser cut. One by one, Chester, Randall, Temple, and Darcy disappear overboard in the darkness, killed by Jeelo's blowgun or by the mysterious host. At last only Charlie, Eunice, and the Reverend Mr. Kelly remain, locked in the cabin under the baleful eye of Jeelo. Kelly is revealed as the insane Larrabee, who, in his madness, beats Jeelo until the man is near death. Larrabee declares he has a motive for killing all of them, saying, "Damn you all! I'm giving a party in Hell, and you're all coming with me *now!*" He has placed a bomb aboard, set to explode in five minutes. Larrabee is killed by the dying Jeelo. Charlie finds an axe and smashes the cabin door. He finds the bomb and throws it overboard an instant before it explodes. There is a romantic ending for Charlie and Eunice.

Notes

It's a significant curiosity that the first talking feature produced by an English company was made in the United States. Herbert Wilcox, commissioned by the British & Dominion Films, Ltd., to make an all-talking picture, was unable to obtain suitable equipment in the English studios so he went to America and filmed *Black Waters* in association with World Wide Pictures and the Western Electric Company. The director was an American, the brilliant Marshall Neilan, whose career – already hurt by a flippancy toward producers – was being destroyed by

100% all-talking. Early March Release

They won't need eyes at all to thrill at this startling story of the Frisco docks and Tiger Larrabee's death ship. A beautiful girl and her rival lovers; the gristly midnight fog through which an unseen fiend launches silent, invincible death bolts; a scared-to-death stuttering valet for comedy relief; the hissing creeping black waters that carry the ship and its frantic freight down-bay until—

Recreating, improving its original, the Broadway stage hit "Fog" by John Willard, author of "The Cat and the Canary."

WESTERN ELECTRIC
SYSTEM
BOTH FILM AND DISC

The cast includes:

James Kirkwood	Robert Ames
John Loder	Lloyd Hamilton
Mary Brian	Frank Reicher
Hallam Cooley	Ben Hendricks
Noble Johnson	

'Black Waters'
The Sensational All-Talking Feature
Marshall Neilan Production

The First International Talking Film
Produced in Hollywood by
British and Dominions Films, Ltd.

WORLD WIDE
PICTURES

Physical Distribution thru Educational

A pre-release publicity montage. Top: John Loder, Frank Reicher, Ben Hendricks. Center: James Kirkwood, Mary Brian. Bottom: Robert Ames, Lloyd Hamilton, Noble Johnson.

Mary Brian.

Robert Ames.

alcoholism. The cast is American, with the exception of English leading man John Loder.

Advertisements for the film (announced at first as *Fog,* title of the reasonably successful Broadway play on which *Black Waters* was based) reflected the "talkie craze" atmosphere of the times: "They don't need eyes! The dialogue is *that* good — but the photography is great too." The acting is in fact superior, in comparison with most of that encountered in the earlier talkies; the photography is exquisite; and there are certainly distinct contributions to sound technique. But still, *Black Waters* was not very popular on either side of the Atlantic. This lack of acceptance can be traced to long stretches of dialogue which slow the action and weaken the suspense. Alfred Hitchcock's *Blackmail* (1930), which came along a short time later as the first talking film produced in England, gained a great deal of attention, virtually eclipsing its Anglo-American predecessor.

Neilan seemed unable to adapt to the talkies. A fine Theatre Guild actor and director, Frank Reicher, was brought in to play a role in *Black Waters* and to assist in the handling of dialogue, but the halt-and-go effect of action interrupted by speeches keeps the film from achieving its potential. There are, nevertheless, some noteworthy performances, particularly those of James Kirkwood as the demonic madman and Noble Johnson as his fearsome servant. Lloyd Hamilton, a popular comedian of the silent films, doffed his trademark, a checkered bill cap, in favor of a bowler hat, to make his talkie debut as a stuttering valet. The result is not as humorous as was anticipated, although youngsters enjoyed imitating Hamilton's gimmick of whistling in order to stop stammering.

What appears to be an innovative use of sound occurs at the climax. The camera leaves the unmasked killer as he does his "mad scene," the rambling voice coming over while other action is being shown. Another highly dramatic use of the soundtrack has Hallam Cooley being dragged to his doom in the darkness, crying, "Hang on to me, Charlie — something's got me by the legs. Oh, damn it, pull!" The scene is much more terrifying than it would have been in silent technique, with an inserted dialogue title.

Fog, the play, is the work of John Willard, whose *The Cat and the Canary* (filmed four times) is the definitive 'twenties-style farce-mystery. Oddly enough, in view of the playwright's popularity and esteem within the industry, *Fog* seems never to have been published.

THE HOUSE OF SECRETS (1929)

(Chesterfield Motion Picture Corporation)

Presented by George R. Batcheller; *directed by* Edmund Lawrence; *based on the novel by* Sydney Horler; *scenario and dialogue by* Adeline Leitzbach; *photographed by* George Webber, Irving Browning, George Peters, *and* Lester Lang; *film editor,* Selma Rosenbloom; RCA Photophone *sound; running time,* 71 minutes; *released* May 26, 1929.

PLAYERS: *Margery Gordon,* Marcia Manning; *Barry Wilding,* Joseph Striker; *Dr. Gordon,* Elmer Grandin; *Joe Blake,* Herbert Warren; *Sir Hubert Harcourt,* Francis M. Verdi; *Bill,* Richard Stevenson; *Wharton,* Harry M. Southard; *Wu Chang,* Edward Roseman; *Home Secretary Forbes,* Walter Ringham.

Synopsis

Barry Wilding, a globetrotting young American, arrives in London and learns he has inherited a country estate, *The Hawk's Nest.* He must sign a paper declaring he will never sell the property. Barry and his detective friend, Joe Blake, encounter some dangerous trespassers at the estate, where the beautiful Margery Gordon seems disturbed by Barry's presence. The behavior of Margery's supposed father is eccentric. Barry is menaced by two American gangsters, Wharton and Bill, and a Chinese named Wu Chang skulks about the premises.

Margery demands that Barry leave her and her father alone at the estate for at least six months. Barry seeks help from Home Secretary Forbes in an attempt to fathom the happenings, but he is refused. Finally he learns that Margery's purported father is Sir Hubert Harcourt, a scientist who has suffered a mental breakdown while working in seclusion at the *Nest* to develop a poison gas for the government.

Bill and Wharton imprison Barry, Margery, Sir Hubert, and Joe. The hoodlums are seeking a pirate treasure concealed at the estate. Forbes arrives in time to rescue everybody. Sir Hubert regains his senses. Barry and Margery decide to share the *Nest.*

Notes

Chesterfield produced about a dozen features a year from 1925 until early 1937. Most of its movies were made on sets and stages rented at Universal and Pathé. Key production personnel varied little; Lon Young was production supervisor, M. A. Anderson was chief cameraman, Edward Jewell was art director, and such directors as Phil Rosen, Richard Thorpe, Frank Strayer, and Charles Lamont stayed busy for long periods of non-stop activity.

The exception to this continuity was *The House of Secrets,* filmed in New York with a pick-up crew. Sound stages and equipment available for rental were makeshift affairs at best. Although *Secrets* was made only as a talkie (when most major companies were releasing both silent and talkie versions of their product), Chesterfield continued to make silent features for about a year after this initial foray into sound. Edmund Lawrence, credited as director, evidently made no other pictures; the name may have been a pseudonym. Chief cameraman George Webber photo-

A faded scene from a forgotten picture, with forgotten stars Marcia Manning, Joseph Stryker.

graphed most of Allan Dwan's pictures for Fox, as well as many products of Paramount's Astoria, Long Island, studio.

Marcia Manning was a pretty ingenue who appeared in many Pathé comedies. Joseph Striker, a slim and athletic New Yorker, is best known for his portrayal of John the Baptist in Cecil B. DeMille's *The King of Kings* (1927). *Secrets'* other cast members are actors from the stage who seldom made pictures.

Though a landmark as one of the earliest sound-on-film productions by an independent company, *The House of Secrets* drew little attention. Chesterfield remade the story property, a 1926 novel, in 1936.

KING OF THE KONGO (1929)

(Mascot Pictures Corporation)

Produced by Nat Levine; *directed by* Richard Thorpe; *a serial in 10 chapters; length, silent version,* 18,760 *feet; released* August 9, 1929.

Synchronized Version

Musical score and song, "Love Thoughts of You," *by* Lee Zahler; Victor *sound on disk; running time,* 212 minutes.

PLAYERS: *Diana Martin,* Jacqueline Logan; *Larry Trent,* Walter Miller; *Chief of Secret Service,* Richard Tucker; *Scarface Macklin,* Boris Karloff; *Jack Drake,* Larry Steers; *Commodore,* Harry Todd; *Prisoner,* Richard Neill; *Trader John,* Lafe McKee; *Priest,* J. P. Leckray; *Mooney,* William Burt; *Derelict,* J. Gordon Russell; *Native Chief,* Robert Frazer; *Poppy,* Ruth Davis; *Gorilla,* Joe Bonomo.

Chapter Titles

1) Into the Unknown; 2) Terrors of the Jungle; 3) The Temple of the Beasts; 4) Gorilla Warfare; 5) Danger in the Dark; 6) The Fight at the Lion Pit; 7) The Fatal Moment; 8) Sentenced to Death: 9) Desperate Chances; 10) Jungle Justice.

Synopsis

Larry Trent, a Secret Service agent, is sent to a little-known part of the Congo to investigate a gang of ivory thieves, and to look into the disappearance of another secret agent, Larry's brother. Natives warn him to avoid the ruins of an old temple, which a gorilla known as the king of the Congo guards. Larry explores around the temple and finds a golden trinket whose presence suggests that treasure may be hidden in the vicinity. When he returns to the trading post he meets the ward of a priest, Diana Martin, whose father had left her a trinket matching the one found at the temple. Diana is searching for her father, who disappeared when she was a child.

The temple is a hideout for the gang. There is a mysterious prisoner, from whom the ruffians are trying to force the secret of the treasure. The ringleader appears to be an enigmatic character, Scarface Macklin.

Escaping several encounters with the gang, the gorilla, and other jungle dangers, Larry saves his brother from the hoodlums and reveals Macklin as Diana's father. The real gang boss proves to be an unsuspected "friend."

Notes

Serials with sound were late in coming. Chapter plays' popularity waned during the late 'twenties; to compound the ill fortune, attempts to record sound outdoors were handicapped by distortion and extraneous noise, but such efforts could not be avoided. Few fans would tolerate a product without outdoor action, and moviegoers were beginning to demand sound. Henry MacRae tried for two years to convince Universal that he could produce a successful dialogue serial, but neither Universal nor the other serial leader, Pathé, would free precious sound facilities for a class of production in which studio heads were losing interest.

A small outfit, Mascot, which at that time made nothing *but* serials, proved its "Blazing the Trail" slogan by making the first sound serial, *King of the Kongo*. A theme song, a synchronized score, sound effects, and occasional dialogue were recorded on disks. The composer was Lee Zahler, whose old-fashioned but sometimes effective music accompanied dozens of films well into the 'forties. Nat Levine personally carried the wax masters to the Victor Talking Machine Company for processing, flying in a Ford Tri-Motor "tin goose" from Los Angeles to Kansas City and travelling thence by train to Camden, New Jersey. Levine — to whom a buck was a dollar — was taking no chances, for the recordings had accounted for about $5,000 of the $40,000 spent on production.

A minor part of the budget was salary for a veteran character actor, Boris Karloff, who drew $75 a week during the three-week schedule. The stars were Jacqueline Logan, a former Ziegfeld Follies beauty from Texas, well known at Pathé and for her portrayal of Mary Magdalene in Cecil B. DeMille's *The King of Kings* (1927); and Pathé's leading serial hero, Walter Miller. Levine got these popular players

Jacqueline Logan.

23

at affordable prices because Pathé was in dire financial straits.

Director Richard Thorpe, like Karloff, was on his way to bigger and better things. A former vaudeville comic from Hutchinson, Kansas, he was the Rollo Thorpe in the *Torchy* comedies before he became a prolific director of silent Westerns and serials for the independents. He continued in the small time until the middle 'thirties, when he blossomed suddenly with M-G-M's *Night Must Fall* (1936). During a long career with M-G-M he directed all but two of the big-budget *Tarzan* films (1936-1942) and *Huckleberry Finn* (1939), *White Cargo* (1942), *Ivanhoe* (1952), and *The Prisoner of Zenda* (1952) among many, many others.

King of the Kongo was a big success for Levine. It also was released in silent form with subtitles and received wide distribution on a states' rights basis. Typical of Mascot, it boasts plenty of action, mostly staged in a convincing jungle set with a ruined temple that was built originally for a silent epic. Stock footage of Angkor gives the set dramatic sweep. Joe Bonomo, famed strongman star of silent pictures, receives frequent camera attention in his gorilla suit. As the show's "red herring" (one who appears too guilty to be the real villain), Karloff is impressive, but his acting in 1929 had no more taken on the subtleties of his post-*Frankenstein* work than Thorpe's direction suggested *Night Must Fall.*

UNMASKED (1929)

(Artclass Pictures)

A Weiss Brothers *production; directed by* Edgar Lewis; *based on a story by* Arthur B. Reeve; *scenario by* Albert Cowles; *dialogue by* Bert Ennis *and* Edward Clark; *photographed by* Thomas Malloy, Buddy Harris, *and* Irving Browning; *edited by* Martin G. Cohn; DeForest Phonofilm *sound; running time,* 62 minutes; *released* Dec. 15, 1929.

PLAYERS: *Craig Kennedy,* Robert Warwick; *Prince Hamid,* Milton Krims; *Mary Wayne,* Susan Conroy; *Billy Mathews,* Sam Ash; *Inspector Collins,* Charles Slattery; *Larry Jamieson,* Lyons Wickland; *Franklin Ward,* William Corbett; *Cafferty,* Roy Byron; *Mrs. Brookfield,* Marie Burke; *Madam Ramon,* Kate Roemer; *Mrs. Ward,* Helen Mitchell; *Gordon Hayes,* Waldo Edwards; *Imposter,* Clyde Dillison.

Synopsis

While visiting at the Brookfield estate, scientific detective Craig Kennedy tells of an unsolved case:

Kennedy relates as to how he was called into investigate the murder by poison of Mrs. Franklin Ward. The police suspected Mary Wayne, but Kennedy had reason to suspect Hamid, an East Indian mystic who was seeking to contact Mrs. Ward's dead son. Kennedy explains that he exposed Hamid's spiritualistic paraphernalia and learned that while Miss Wayne did indeed administer the lethal draught, she did so while hypnotized by Hamid. The killer managed to

The talkies' first Craig Kennedy — Robert Warwick.

escape. Kennedy and Miss Wayne became engaged, the detective adds in finishing his story.

At this point, Kennedy reveals that Hamid is among Mrs. Brookfield's guests, incognito, and that he can be identified by a scar on his forearm. The supposed Count Sebastian Domingo de Navarre is revealed as the former Hamid, and this time he does not escape.

Notes

Brothers Max, Louis, and Adolph Weiss branched from the lamp business into phonographs and early in the movie business bought a small store-theatre at Avenue A and Fourth Street in New York. An interstate chain of fifteen theatres developed, and in about 1917 they began to make their own pictures. Output grew to from ten to fourteen features per year during the nineteen-twenties, plus serials and shorts.

For a year Louis Weiss managed the DeForest Phonofilm Studios for Lee DeForest, the famed inventor and sound-film manufacturer-producer. In 1929 he arranged to produce *Unmasked* — the first feature to be made in DeForest Phonofilm — at the DeForest New York plant, where the inventor himself had made more than a thousand talking short subjects with his process since 1923. *Unmasked* is one of Arthur B. Reeve's tales of Craig Kennedy, "the scientific detective," a character who had gained a wide following among serial fans, via such efforts as *Exploits of Elaine* (1915) and *The Radio Detective* (1926).

The first feature to deal with Kennedy toned down the action and concentrated on mystery, romance, and an abundance of dialogue. *Unmasked,* as such, moves slowly in comparison with the frantic pacing of the serials, although it is not so unimaginative as some other early talkies. The deadening effect of long takes and much dialogue is lessened by the film's construction, unusual for the time, which embraces a long flashback resolved only after a return to the framing story.

Robert Warwick, veteran stage and film star, is a stern and deep-voiced Kennedy. Most of the other players are unknowns. Director Edgar Lewis, a writer and stage actor from Missouri, was a pioneer action director for Pathé, Fox, and Selznick, among other concerns. He had just completed a two-year series of Westerns at Universal when he made *Unmasked,* after which he directed romantic dramas for Chesterfield.

1930

THE VOICE FROM THE SKY (1930)

(Ben Wilson Productions)

Produced by Ben Wilson Productions; *directed by* Ben Wilson; RCA *sound; a serial in* 10 chapters *of* two reels each; *distributed as a states'-rights release by* G. Y. B. Productions, Hollywood, *in* January of 1930.

PLAYERS: Wally Wales, Jean Delores.

Chapter Titles

1) Doomed; 2) The Cave of Horror; 3) The Man From Nowhere; 4) Danger Ahead; 5) Desperate Deeds; 6) Trail of Vengeance; 7) The Scarlet Scourge; 8) Trapped by Fate; 9) The Pit of Peril; 10) Hearts of Steel.

Synopsis

A scientific genius known only as "The Man From Nowhere" knows how to suspend all energy in the earth's atmosphere. The voice of the hooded madman booms from the sky, warning the populace of a large city that they will be destroyed unless they meet his terms. A young detective and his sweetheart thwart the scheme and unmask the villain.

Notes

In October of 1930, Universal's talking serial, *The Indians Are Coming*, opened at The Roxy on Broadway to tremendous acclaim. Will Hays, president of the Motion Picture Producers & Distributors Association, wrote to Universal president Carl Laemmle, "The entire motion picture industry owes you a debt of gratitude for *The Indians Are Coming*. It brought 20,000,000 children back to the theatre."

The *first* "all talking and sound" serial with soundtrack on film (as opposed to disk) was produced about a year earlier, but it was ignored and seems to exist today only in the form of hazy memory. Produced independently by Ben Wilson, *The Voice From the Sky* was not registered for copyright and never was reviewed by the trade magazines. An advertisement in the *Film Daily Yearbook* for 1930 announced that the serial was "Now available for state rights market," but the release must have been extremely limited. Another ad describes it as "A story of a scientist that invented a secret formula that can destroy the world. Come and learn the secret."

The star was Wally Wales, then a well-known hero of independent Westerns, who later played character roles as Hal Taliaferro. In a letter of October 6, 1974, Wales told film historian Bill G. ("Buck") Rainey what he remembered of *The Voice From the Sky:*

"It was about a mad inventor who could (by some

means) throw his voice in the air so a whole city could hear it. He then threatened the officials and people that if they didn't change their rotten ways he would destroy them and all they had. The film was made in Hollywood — at the very beginning of sound when no one knew how to make sound pictures. I doubt very much if it was ever released. It must have been pretty BAD! No one seemed to know what they were doing. Everyone in the early days of sound was experimenting. It was a very bad time for all of us."

Producer-director Ben Wilson was the leading man in the first American serial, Edison's *What Happened to Mary* (1912). Later, he and Neva Gerber were teamed in nine silent serials, several of which Wilson directed. He was unable to gain a foothold in the talkies.

INGAGI (1930)

(Congo Pictures, Ltd.)

Presented by Nathan M. Spitzer; *produced by* William Alexander; *directed by* William Campbell; *photographed by* Harold Williams, George Summerton, Ed Joyce, Fred Webster, *and* L. Gillingham; *edited by* Grace McKee; *screen adaptation by* Adam Hull Shirk; *musical score by* Edward Gage; *narrated by* Louis Nizor; *running time,* 75 minutes; *previewed* March of 1930; *released* March 15, 1931, *by* Radio-Keith-Orpheum Distributing Corporation.

PLAYERS: *Themselves,* Sir Hubert Winstead, Daniel Swayne; *Gorilla,* Charles Gemora.

Synopsis

Winstead and Swayne lead an expedition into Africa to investigate legends of a gorilla-worship tribe. They survive a lion attack, trap a leopard and a giant phython, and hunt hippos. They find a reptile so venomous it cannot be brought to civilization.

Rumour has it that gorillas larger than any known to science have depopulated a village. The explorers find the sought-after colony and witness the sacrifice of a virgin, who is carried away by a huge ape. The safari discovers the tribe of gorillas and several wild women who live with the apes. The gorillas attack, and the expeditioners kill a six hundred-pound specimen. One of the women mourns the death of what apparently was her lover. The safari returns to civilization with pictorial evidence of incredible discoveries.

Notes

Although credit titles state frankly that *Ingagi* was written by Adam Hull Shirk, whose stage melodramas furnished plotlines for several movies about gorillas, the presentation suggests the picture is an authentic record of a scientific expedition. Advertising amplified the suggestion: "GIANT GORILLAS! WILD WOMEN! AMAZING DISCOVERIES OF JUNGLE LIFE! THE SCIENTIFIC MARVEL OF THE AGE!" Such claims were the stock-in-trade of Nat Spitzer, an old-time circus impresario.

Much footage is silent-vintage expeditionary film from Africa. Some such scenes are quite good; others are so blurred as to induce ocular pain. The off-screen voice explains that the film was affected by unbearable tropical heat and also emphasizes the explorers' constant peril.

Intercut are fictional episodes filmed in California. The "venomous reptile" is a leopard tortoise decked with the armour of a pangolin (a scaly anteater) and laminated bird wings. Prehensile-tailed monkeys unique to tropical Ameri-

Charlie Gemora does his stuff with a "native girl" in Darkest California.

27

ca gambol about the jungle, and an armadillo — also peculiar to the New World — is seen. An alligator, still another product of the Americas, is shown nesting among eucalyptus leaves, which grow in profusion in California but not at all in Africa. Scenes of African tribesmen alternate with shots of much paler American blacks in clothing better suited to the cottonfield than the Congo.

Members of the California preview audience in early 1930 recognized the "native girl" abducted by the gorilla as a bit player well known at Central Casting. The costume she wears when left alone in the jungle inexplicably changes before the gorilla abducts her. The monster, shown only in medium and long shots, is Charlie Gemora, leading portrayer of gorillas, who at the time was working at M-G-M with Lon Chaney in *The Unholy Three.* Close-ups of a real ape show not a gorilla but an orang-outan, native to Borneo and Sumatra. Gemora, in traditional movie style, navigates upright instead of on all fours, as is the wont of the gorilla.

Effective advertising and press emphasis on the controversy over *Ingagi* made it a tremendous commercial success. Cries of outrage — ("It is not only the greatest movie hoax . . . , but the most offensive," wrote the editor of *Screenland*) — only increased the crowds.

The American Society of Mammalologists, at a meeting in New York City, drew up a formal resolution of protest which was announced by Dr. William K. Gregory of the American Museum of Natural History:

"That in accordance with the facts brought out in the discussion of the film *Ingagi,* which has been viewed by many of our members, the American Society of Mammalologists hereby expresses its utter disapproval of this film, which grossly misrepresents the natural history of Africa, while pretending to be a truthful record of a scientific expedition. The American public should understand that certain animals shown in the film have never been found in the wild state in Africa. Also that a man made up as a gorilla is represented as carrying off a native woman. In response to many protests and letters, certain members . . . who have done field work in Africa have viewed the film and are unanimous in deploring its numerous fictitious features which are misleadingly mingled with genuine natural history records."

The Society queried the British Embassy and was informed there was no such Englishman as Sir Hubert Winstead.

State and local censor troubles plagued *Ingagi,* both because of the "hoax" accusations and because the "virgin sacrifice" was played topless. The Ohio director of education forbade showing of the picture in that state, and several large theatre circuits pulled it from their schedules after the New York Better Business Bureau on June 2, 1930, issued a report that the gorilla scenes were faked. In some areas Congo Pictures secured a release by the insertion of a foreword admitting dramatization of the gorilla scenes.

In July the producers were brought before Federal Judge William Bondy in New York and ordered to show cause why they should not be enjoined from distributing *Ingagi.* This order resulted from a plagiarism suit filed by attorney Louis Nizer in behalf of Byron P. Mackenzie, described as "son of Lady Mackenzie, the African game hunter." Allegations were that about half the footage was taken from Lady Mackenzie's *Heart of Africa,* for which she shot 20,000 feet of film in 1914. In November, Federal Judge Alfred C. Coxe awarded the Lady Mackenzie Film Company a $150,000 judgment against Congo Pictures and made permanent a temporary injunction restraining the defendants from disposing of any assets.

Despite entanglements, *Ingagi* went into national release again on March 15, 1931. It was refused a New York license for "nature faking," but in November it was cleared for a profitable run at the Central Theatre in New York City. The picture eventually grossed a reported $4,000,000.

Another scathing indictment, from the American Nature Association of Washington, D. C., termed *Ingagi* "an imposition on the public, a blot on the moving picture industry, and a serious threat to the usefulness of moving pictures . . ." Admitting it to be "good entertainment," the group worried of "the danger that the public will accept all its 'revelations' as scientific truth" and as "factual substantiations for the ancient and hoary legends of the jungle."

Seldom has there been such noise over so little. Gemora said he hired the black actress and staged his part of the picture for $5,000 and sold it to Spitzer for $7,000. *Ingagi* made so much money that other fast-buck producers were inspired to give the world such women-love-apes operas as *Forbidden Adventure in Angkor* and *Love Life of a Gorilla.* The ruckus went on for quite some time, and while its notoriety lasted *Ingagi* became one of the first "household words" to emerge from talkie cinema. Even comedy producer Hal Roach, whose characteristic avoidance of topical humor helped create a wealth of timeless films, saw fit to devote a gag to *Ingagi* in a 1932 *Our Gang* short

Forbidden Adventure in Angkor (1937), inspired by big-boxoffice returns of Ingagi.

Son of Ingagi (1940), a sequel in name only.

subject, "A Lad an' a Lamp." The story deals with the seeming transformation of Stymie Beard's kid brother into a chimpanzee. A helpful cop asks for a description of the youngster, and Stymie reports, "Well, he used to look like me — but now he looks like Ingagi!"

MAMBA (1930)

(Color Art Production – Tiffany Pictures, Incorporated)

Directed by Albert S. Rogell; *story by* Ferdinand Schumann-Heink *and* John Reinhardt; *continuity and dialogue by* Tim Miranda *and* Winifred Dunn; *photographed in* Techicolor *by* Charles Boyle; *art director,* Andre Chautin; *sound recording by* Louis J. Myers; *music by* James C. Bradford; *RCA Photophone sound; also disc sound; filmed at* California Tiffany Studios; *running time,* 78 minutes; *released* March 10, 1930.

PLAYERS: *August Bolte,* Jean Hersholt; *Helen von Linden,* Eleanor Boardman; *Karl von Reiden,* Ralph Forbes; *Count von Linden,* Josef Swickard; *Major Cromwell,* Claude Fleming; *Cockney,* Will Stanton; *Major von Schultz,* William von Brincken; *Hassim,* Noble Johnson; *Hassim's Daughter,* Hazel Jones; *Guido,* Andres de Segurola; *British Soldier,* Arthur Stone; *German Soldier,* Torben Meyer; *Fullerton,* Edward Martindel.

Synopsis

The richest man in Neu Posen, a German settlement in East Africa, is a cowardly planter, August Bolte. The natives call him Mamba, the name of a deadly snake. Among the settlers and the German and British military, Bolte can communicate only with his Cockney manservant, whose presence seems to prove Bolte's belief that he can buy anything he wants. The year is 1914, and rumors of war abound.

A letter from Count von Linden, facing disgrace and imprisonment in Germany, requests of Bolte a loan of $100,000. The Count offers his daughter, Helen, as a wife for Bolte, who departs for Germany. To save her father from ruin, Helen agrees to marry the coarse Bolte.

Bound for Africa, Bolte and his frau meet Karl von Reiden, a young officer appointed to command at Neu Posen. Helen and Karl meet often on deck. Upon arrival, Bolte flaunts his bride.

Bolte stages a lavish reception to introduce his bride to the community. His exploitation of Helen angers von Reiden and Major Cromwell, the British commander. The celebration is interrupted by a native girl whom Bolte has wronged. Later, Bolte flies into a rage and is about to lash Helen when Karl arrives, humbles Bolte, and takes Helen in his arms. Hassim, a native leader, accuses Bolte of the death of his daughter.

War is declared between Germany and England. Bolte, failing to bribe his way out of military conscription, flees into the jungle and meets Hassim's natives, who are in revolt. Bolte fires on the natives and turns, only to be captured by another tribal band. Bolte begs for his life to no avail.

The natives attack the Bolte plantation. Karl is wounded when he comes to Helen's aid. Just as it appears the Germans will be overwhelmed, they are rescued by Cromwell's soldiers.

Notes

Had there existed a Villain of the Year trophy, Jean Hersholt could have won it hands-down for 1930. In rapid succession he terrorized Eleanor Boardman in *Mamba,* Lupe Velez in *Hell Harbor,* and Helen Twelvetrees in *The Cat Creeps;* he also played the Chinese menace opposite Lupe Velez in *East Is West,* but his scenes were redone with Edward G. Robinson upon the realization that Hersholt's Danish accent clashed with the pidgin-English lines assigned him. In silent films Hersholt created such memorable heels as Marcus in *Greed* (1924) and Ed Munn in *Stella Dallas*

(1925). His villains were lustful, vulgar brutes as a rule, with beady eyes and thick, wet lips, and yet each had a distinct and well-rounded personality. The real Hersholt was a kind and charitable man who won awards for his portraiture at the Academy of Arts in Copenhagen, directed stage plays, played hockey, collected stamps, and was a director of several California banks. The Academy of Motion Picture Arts & Sciences named its Humanitarian Award in his honor.

As the hated Mamba, Hersholt superbly sets forth one of his most despicable creatures and remains central throughout — the show's only genuinely convincing character. Eleanor Boardman and Ralph Forbes are appealing, but they and the stodgy Britishers and the restless natives are little more substantial than stock characters out of romantic fiction. There are strong minor characters nonetheless, such as Noble Johnson's imposing Hassim, Will Stanton's scrawny sycophant, and Josef Swickard's shabby aristocrat.

Mamba is a landmark, one of the most ambitious features ever attempted by a small studio. Costuming is elaborate, construction of the settlement is realistic, and spectacle is seen in the uprising and in a banquet at which a procession of natives carries in an astonishing array of foods.

Most remarkable, the use throughout of Technicolor was a formidable undertaking at a time when even the use of sound offered serious problems. Natural color filming was hardly the simple matter it is today, and even major companies seldom attempted a complete feature in color, although color sequences (usually musical numbers) were not uncommon in early talkies.

Technicolor then was a two-color process which extracted a surprising range of hues from red and green. *Manba's* jungle scenes are properly garish, with lush greens and deep, flickering shadows. Flesh tones are remarkably accurate.

Director Albert Rogell, of Oklahoma City, entered the industry in 1916 and performed almost every conceivable job — carpenter, prop man, electrician, cameraman, cutter, and titler. He directed eight features a year for Universal during the 'twenties and made some of the excellent Ken Maynard Westerns at First National. He proved a versatile director at various majors in the talkie era and became one of the first big names to enter television production. Rogell was a thoroughgoing professional, one of those men who produce enormous amounts of good work without quite bringing the critics to attention. Rogell's dynamic handling of *Mamba* is complemented ideally by James C. Bradford's elaborate musical score, a great asset to the atmosphere of the picture. In addition to dramatic agitatos and *misteriosi*, there is widespread use of German, Arabic, and English marches and themes.

Mamba is a highlight of all its principals' careers, deserving of continuing attention for its content and exposition and for its status as a breakthrough in cinema technology.

1931

THE PHANTOM OF THE WEST (1931)

(Mascot Pictures Corporation)

Produced by Nat Levine; *directed by* D. Ross Lederman; *story by* Ford Beebe; *photographed by* Benjamin Kline; *music by* Lee Zahler; Disney Film Recording Company *sound; a serial in* 10 chapters, 21 reels; *released* January 1, 1931.

PLAYERS: Jim Lester, Tom Tyler; *Mona Cortez*, Dorothy Gulliver; *Martin Blain*, William Desmond; *Bud Landers*, Tom Santschi; *Oscar*, Tom Dugan; *Royce Macklin*, Philo McCullough; *Keno*, Joe Bonomo; *Peter Drake*, Kermit Maynard; *Francisco Cortez*, Frank Lanning; *Sheriff Ryan*, Frank S. Hagney; *Stewart*, Dick Dickinson; *Ruby Blain*, Hallee Sullivan; *Deputy*, Al Taylor.

Chapter Titles

1) The Ghost Rides; 2) The Stairway to Doom; 3) The Horror in the Dark; 4) The Battle of the Strong; 5) The League of the Lawless; 6) The Canyon of Calamity; 7) The Price of Silence; 8) The House of Hate; 9) The Fatal Secret; 10) Rogue's Roundup.

Synopsis

Jim Lester allows an escaped convict, Francisco Cortez, to hide at his ranch. Two deputies from nearby Rawton tell Jim that Cortez is serving a life term for murder, and that it was he who killed Jim's father. Cortez overhears and escapes, leaving a note claiming that he is innocent and that seven men in Rawton know the identity of the real murderer. Soon afterward, the town is terrorised by a ruthless gang called the League of the Lawless, which takes orders from the mysterious Phantom. Notes left around town warn that unless one of the seven men reveals the name of the murderer, all seven will die.

Jim aligns himself with Mona Cortez, daughter of the convict, in an attempt to get the truth. Suspicion falls upon Blain, Landers, Macklin, Keno, Drake, and Sheriff Ryan. Jim also is framed and becomes a suspect. Several of the men crack under the strain and try to reveal the killer, but they are slain by the Phantom.

At last Jim finds the clues that clear himself and Cortez. A town "character" known as Oscar proves to be the Phantom.

Notes

Mascot's first all-talking, sound-on-film serial, *The Lone Defender* (1930), allowed the public to hear the great dog star, Rin Tin Tin, snarl and bark for the first time. The next Mascot serial, *The Phantom of the West,* was the first talkie in which Tom Tyler, a popular FBO silent Western star, appeared. At liberty after FBO changed ownership to become RKO-Radio Pictures, Incorporated, and at a time when outdoor films were suddenly passé, Tyler was one of the few Western types to make a successful transition to sound. He worked steadily in pictures for another eighteen years, both as a cowboy hero and as a character actor (Tyler was Kharis, the mummy, in Universal's *The Mummy's Hand* [1940]), until crippling arthritis forced him into retirement. The director, D. Ross Lederman, had been prominent at the Warner Brothers lot during the silent era but was having trouble breaking into the talkies. His only serial paved the way to continuance of his career at Columbia and Warners for another twenty years.

Like other Mascot masked villains, the Phantom appears to be almost everybody in the cast except Tom Dugan, who handles comedy relief until the last half of the last chapter. The flitting shadow of the fiend is that of another actor who neither looks nor sounds like the raspy-voiced comedian.

Producer Nat Levine's approach to serials was such that the addition of sound did not slow the action as was the case in many pictures of the time. The scenery, mostly in the area of Kernville, California, and the excellent stunt work compensate for some crudities of production. Some fine character players appear in supporting roles.

KING OF THE WILD (1931)

(Mascot Pictures Corporation)

Produced by Nat Levine; *directed by* Richard Thrope; *screenplay by* Wyndham Gittens *and* Ford Beebe; *photographed by* Benjamin Kline *and* Edward J. Kull; *musical director,* Lee Zahler; *assistant directors,* Theodore Joos *and* Lionel Backus; *sound recording by* George Lowerre, Disney Sound Recording Company; *a serial in* 12 chapters — Chapter Number One contains three reels, Chapters Two through Twelve comprise two reels each; *total running time,* 248 minutes; *released* March of 1931.

PLAYERS: *Robert Grant,* Walter Miller; *Muriel Armitage,* Nora Lane; *Mrs. LaSalle,* Dorothy Christie; *Harris,* Tom Santschi; *Mustapha,* Boris Karloff; *Bimi,* Cyril MacLaglen; *Tom Armitage,* Carroll Nye; *Peterson,* Victor Potel; *Mrs. Colby,* Martha Lalande; *Dakka,* Mischa Auer; *Officer,* Lafe McKee; *and* Otto Hoffman, Fletcher Norton, Albert De Warton, Merrill McCormick, Earle Douglas, Larry Steers, Eileen Schofield, Walter Ferdna, Norman Feusier, Dick La Reno, *and* Floyd Shackelford.

Chapter Titles

1) Man Eaters; 2) The Tiger of Destiny; 3) The Avenging Horde; 4) Secret of the Volcano; 5) The Pit of Peril; 6) The Creeping Doom; 7) Sealed Lips; 8) Jaws of the Jungle; 9) The Door of Dread; 10) The Leopard's Lair; 11) The Fire of the Gods; 12) Jungle Justice.

Synopsis

Soldier of fortune Robert Grant is blamed for the murder of an Indian Rajah when actually the crime was committed by a man named Dakka. Harris, an unscrupulous dealer in wild animals, also is involved in the killing, as is an African Sheik, Mustapha. A letter revealing the truth, known only to Mustapha, has been written in invisible ink. Grant escapes from an Indian prison and disguises himself, securing passage on a ship on which Harris and his ape-like servant, Bimi, are returning with a cargo of beasts. Also aboard is Mrs. LaSalle, whom Harris has hired to seek the location of a diamond field. She is killed by a mysterious gunman, and accusations are levelled against Grant, Harris, and Secret Service agent Peterson. A typhoon wrecks the steamer off Africa, and the tigers and leopards escape.

Mustapha's men find young Tom Armitage delirious with fever and bring him to their desert camp. Armitage reveals knowledge of the diamond field but does not disclose its location. Mustapha plans to torture the information from him. A tiger from the ship attacks some of Mustapha's followers, killing a camel, and is trapped in a pit. Armitage, refusing to reveal the location of the diamond field, is cast into the pit but escapes.

Mustapha gives Harris a forgery of the invisible-ink letter. Grant rescues Mustapha from a leopard but is kept from obtaining the genuine letter by the arrival of Mustapha's minions. Grant is aided in his investigation by Armitage's sister, Muriel, and by a Secret Service agent disguised as an old woman. A mystery man wearing black glasses also is interested in the case.

Grant learns the diamond field is in the crater of the volcano. He is under attack from Mustapha when government troops rout the Sheik's henchmen and capture Mustapha. Harris flees on horseback with the letter but is killed as the frightened horse throws him from a cliff. Bimi finds the broken body of his master. Grant's name is cleared.

Notes

Nat Levine saw an opportunity to benefit from M-G-M's

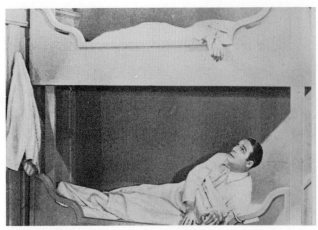

Walter Miller learns the disadvantages of being cuffed to a lower bunk.

Cyril McLaglen as Bimi.

giant publicity campaign in connection with the African expedition which was making *Trader Horn* (1930). He contracted with *Horn's* leading players, Harry Carey and Edwina Booth, for three serials. When the actors returned to the States, Levine was ready to begin shooting, but then M-G-M called Carey and Booth back for extensive retakes. Levine went ahead into production with Walter Miller and Nora Lane as leads.

For *King of the Wild*, Levine gathered an excellent supporting cast including Tom Santschi, a favorite heavy from silent pictures; Arthur McLaglen, one of Victor McLaglen's husky brothers; Mischa Auer as an East Indian assassin; and Boris Karloff, who was but a few months away from stardom with *Frankenstein*. Karloff is effective as the Sheik except for a broadly conceived French-Arab accent.

The serial emerged as exciting but overly complex, possessed of a primitive charm typical of the Mascot product. It boasts striking photography of the desert outside Yuma, Arizona, and of Levine's favorite outdoor

location, Bronson Canyon, a massive stone quarry conveniently situated in North Hollywood. Interiors were made at Tec-Art Studios in Los Angeles. Well-conceived touches are evident throughout, such as the scene in which Walter Miller wakes aboard ship to see a bloody hand dangling from the upper berth. Particularly effective is the last shot in the twelfth episode, wherein the ape-man carries the corpse of his master over a hill into the sunset.

DRUMS OF JEOPARDY (1931)
a.k.a. MARK OF TERROR (in reissue)

(Tiffany Pictures, Inc.)

Directed by George B. Seitz; *continuity and dialogue by* Florence Ryerson; *photographed by* Arthur Reed; *film editor,* Otto Ludwig; *sound,* Corson J. Jowett; *art direction,* Ralph M. DeLacy; *costumes,* Elizabeth Coleman; *properties,* Eddie Boyle; *musical director,* Val Burton; *filmed at* California Tiffany Studios; RCA *recording; running time,* 68 minutes; *released* March 2, 1931.

PLAYERS: *Boris Karlov,* Warner Oland; *Kitty Conover,* June Collyer; *Prince Nicholas Petrov,* Lloyd Hughes; *General Petrov,* George Fawcett; *Prince Ivan,* Ernest Hilliard; *Prince Gregor,* Wallace MacDonald; *Martin Kent,* Hale Hamilton; *Anya Karlov,* Florence Lake; *Piotr,* Mischa Auer; *Aunt Abbie,* Clara Blandick; *Tazia,* Ann Brody; *Stephens,* Murdoch MacQuarrie; *Henchman,* Harry Semels; *Detective Brett,* Edward Homans; *Girl,* Ruth Hall.

Wallace MacDonald eludes Mischa Auer on the dock at San Pedro.

Synopsis

In Czarist Russia, scientist Boris Karlov learns his daughter, Anya, has attempted suicide following betrayal by a lover. She refuses to disclose the man's identity, but Karlov finds a clue: a necklace known as the Drums of Jeopardy, property of the aristocratic Petrov family.

The Petrov patriarch, his son Ivan, and Ivan's two

Lloyd Hughes fights two Bolsheviks.

nephews, Nicholas and Gregor, are entertaining an American criminologist, Martin Kent. Old Petrov tells the story of the Drums, which his great-grandfather stole from an Eastern empress. He asks Gregor to bring the necklace from a vault, but Gregor claims to have forgotten the combination. Nicholas gets the necklace box, which proves to the empty. The dying Anya runs in and approaches Gregor. Karlov follows, demanding to know who wronged his daughter. He threatens to kill them all, whereupon he is seized and disarmed. He exclaims that "a man of the people" has no recourse against the misdeeds of the aristocracy. As he leaves, carrying Anya, Karlov threatens to return the Drums, one pendant at a time, as tokens of revenge. Legend holds that a person who receives a Drum is marked for death.

In 1930, Karlov intercepts a letter from Ivan to Kent telling that Karlov, since the Revolution, has gained eminence as a Bolshevik and has made life miserable for the Petrov family, even to the slaying of old General Petrov. Ivan and his nephews are coming to America for protection.

On a foggy night as the ship nears New York, the Petrovs receive a message reading, "Welcome to America — Karlov." A man claiming to be Kent's agent enters to say the Petrovs must go ashore by launch. Other "detectives" throw the family's servant overboard. The leader of the "detectives" is Piotr, Karlov's assistant. Aboard the launch, Karlov himself greets the Russians.

Nicholas and Gregor escape when the launch docks. Nicholas, who has suffered a head wound, climbs a fire escape and stumbles into a penthouse. The resident, Kitty Conover, covers Nicholas with a gun; he asks her to 'phone Kent and then collapses. Kitty sends her Aunt Abbie to fetch a doctor. The old lady meets Piotr and sends him for the doctor. He goes to a nearby building where Karlov holds Ivan captive.

"I hate to part with you until I have your nephews to keep me company," Karlov tells Ivan.

"Look here," Ivan replies. "If you will let my nephews go, you may do anything you want with me. I swear, I won't even cry out."

Karlov chuckles. "But I *want* you to cry out," he says before he strangles Ivan. Piotr enters, with word of Nicholas' whereabouts, and Karlov orders, "Get my hat and coat and the bag — eh, the *black* bag."

Posing as a doctor, Karlov accompanies Piotr and another thug to the Conover apartment. He is about to administer a lethal injection to Nicholas when Kent and his men arrive. Karlov and Piotr escape; the other henchman is wounded and dies in a fall. Thinking he sees Karlov in another building, Nicholas shoots a figure which proves to be the propped-up corpse of Ivan. It is decided that Nicholas and Gregor will be hidden at Aunt Abbie's country home.

Next evening Kent receives word that Karlov has died in an explosion following his betrayal by an underling. Leaving a detective to guard the home, Kent goes with a supposed policeman to identify Karlov's body. He is seized outside and taken to an old watermill. Karlov greets him cordially.

"Good evening, Doctor," Kent responds. "I see the reports of your death have been considerably exaggerated . . . I suppose it was the traitor who was found dead in your place?"

"Right. Just before the bomb exploded, I changed clothes with him and escaped under the very noses of your men." Karlov offers Kent a cigarette, laughing, "If you're not afraid to try one."

"Oh, no, not at all. I don't believe you'd be so unoriginal as to —," Kent breaks the suggestion off in a laugh.

"Oh, no, no, no."

"I don't need to ask how your men got hold of that letter from headquarters."

"No, I fancy it's quite obvious. The body of their messenger ought to show up at the top of the mill pond in, say, four or five days. I figured the code letter would keep you from suspecting my man, but still I'm disappointed in you, Mr. Kent. I didn't think you would walk into my trap quite so blindly."

"Would it make you any happier to know I *saw* the trap and walked into it *deliberately?*" Kent asks triumphantly. "When I heard the body was unrecognizable I knew you were still alive, and in hopes of preventing further killings, I let your man lead me to you so that I could do *this!*" Kent draws a concealed revolver and empties it into Karlov's chest. Karlov laughs heartily.

"Ah, an excellent shot, all of them over the heart. But fortunately, in Russia, I acquired the habit of wearing a bulletproof vest . . . But didn't it occur to you that you might fail, and that the consequences might not be — pleasant?"

"Naturally," Kent replies clamly.

Lloyd Hughes faints in June Collyer's art-deco apartment.

"You should have been a Russian, Mr. Kent," Karlov exclaims with an admiring laugh. "You would have been a great help to me."

"Hardly. You see, I consider you a madman."

"Because I kill people? Yesterday you killed my man. Just now you tried to kill me. Do you consider yourself a madman?"

At the refuge, romance is shaping between Nicholas and Kitty. Nicholas decides he and Gregor should leave the estate because their presence endangers the women. The conniving Gregor scribbles a note to Karlov and, planting it on Abbie, tricks her into the hands of the criminals. She is taken to the mill where Karlov reads the note: Gregor will name Anya's seducer if Karlov "will not touch" Gregor. Allowing himself to be taken to the mill, Gregor, in fact the betrayer of Anya, blames Nicholas. True to his word, Karlov does not touch Gregor. He hurls a vial of poison gas into the room where Gregor is imprisoned.

Detective Brett, guarding Nicholas and kitty, is killed. Karlov agents take Nicholas and Kitty to the mill. Karlov puts Nicholas in the cellar and lights both ends of a candle. By the time the candle has burned out, Karlov dictates,

Nicholas must have killed the girl he loves. Then Kitty is forced into the cellar.

The actual plan, Karlov boasts to Kent, is for Nicholas and the girl to seek an escape. Nicholas finds some loose stones and tries to dig out. Water from the surrounding stream rushes in.

Kent's men have trailed the killers. In a gun battle all the thugs are killed but Piotr and Karlov. Kent takes a revolver from a fallen hoodlum and fells Piotr. Karlov is at bay.

As Nicholas and Kitty are saved from the rushing waters, Karlov uncorks a vial of poison gas, but Aunt Abbie pushes him off balance before he can throw it. He falls into the cellar and sinks to his death.

Notes

In 1923, M. H. Hoffman filmed an adaptation of Harold McGrath's popular horror novel, *The Drums of Jeopardy,* with Wallace Beery as the vengeful Bolshevik, Karlov. Tiffany's all-talking remake, completed at the beginning of 1931, features the wonderful Warner Oland as the arch villain. Florence Ryerson's script differs greatly from both

36

the book and the silent film, but there is no modernizing of the venerable tale. The talkie version, in fact, is delightfully old-fashioned and unrestrained in its melodramatic action. It is as illogical as a Pearl White serial, and fully as exciting. The choice of director was appropriate: George B. Seitz, greatest of the silent serial masters.

Oland, a classical stage actor from Sweden, specialised at the time in the portrayal of Oriental villains. He had just played Fu Manchu in three highly successful films at Paramount, carrying on in a role similar to many he played while menacing Pearl White and Juanita Hansen in Pathé serials. He had broadened his scope somewhat by essaying one sympathetic character — Al Jolson's father in *The Jazz Singer* (1927) — along with some non-Oriental villains in *Don Juan* (1926) and *The Big Gamble* (1930). Following completion of *Drums of Jeopardy,* Oland landed the role he was born to play, the title character of Fox's *Charlie Chan Carries On* (1931). So identified did he become with the genial Chinese detective that his years of villainy were virtually forgotten. From then until his death in 1938, Oland starred in seventeen Chan pictures, making only occasional detours into evildoing.

Oland is at his best in *Drums,* deftly underplaying throughout to project a brooding malevolence. The handsome team of June Collyer and Lloyd Hughes provides the romantic moments. Wallace MacDonald — later a producer at Columbia — does well as Hughes' treacherous brother. Hale Hamilton is capital as a gutsy detective. The young Russian actor, Mischa Auer, who for several years had been portraying eccentric characters in films, scores as Oland's viciously dedicated sycophant. A secondary henchman is Harry Semels, like Oland a celebrated villain of the Pathé silent serials.

More than comedy relief is contributed by Clara Blandick in her specialty as a snippy maiden aunt, a role she also provided for two versions of *Tom Sawyer.* A beautifully executed exchange between Blandick and Oland is useful in illustrating Karlov's impatient monomania:

"I've been waitin' to get at you for a long time," Aunt Abbie tells Karlov, who replies graciously that he is flattered. "Well, you *won't* be so flattered — you'll be *flattened* when I get through," she rages. "I been itchin' to give you a piece of my mind. Now don't try to talk because it won't do you a bit of good 'til I've had my say. I know your sort, makin' jokes about everything, even murder. I've seen 'em born and I've seen 'em grow up, pullin' wings off flies when they're babies, huntin' robins with slingshots and drownin' tomcats when they're boys, shootin' and murderin' when they're men. And where are they now?"

Karlov has listened patiently to this harangue, interjecting a gentle "But, my dear . . ." and an amused "Booo!" Now he replies, "Why I'm sure I don't know. Where are they?"

"Hung, that's what!" Abbie snaps. "Every mother's son of 'em, hung! And mark my words, my man, you'll end on

a scaffold yourself with your samovars and your vodkas!"

Here Karlov's manner changes abruptly: "Take this woman away, she annoys me. Stop her mouth." As Abbie is dragged away she has the last word:

"All I got to say is I *never did* like caviar."

The production has an expensive look, reminiscent of the costly production values M-G-M employed. Lavish settings include the palatial Petrov home, an art deco apartment, an ocean liner, a spooky old mansion, and a mill that bears comparison with the one in *Frankenstein.* The sound effects of wind, gunshots, and thunder — all of which had to be faked to register on the primitive equipment used in 1930 — sound pretty artificial. Occasional undercranking of the camera gives a few scenes a silent-picture quality. Lighting makes imaginative use of shadows and the effect of lightning on windows.

Seitz proved as able a director for the talkies as he had been for the silent era. His later work included the excellent *Last of the Mohicans* (1953) and all but three of M-G-M's sixteen *Hardy Family* pictures.

MURDER AT MIDNIGHT (1931)

(Tiffany Productions, Incorporated)

Produced by Phil Goldstone; *directed by* Frank R. Strayer; *story by* W. Scott Darling *and* Frank R. Strayer; *dialogue by* W. Scott Darling; *photography by* William Rees; *art director,* Ralph M. DeLacy; *edited by* John Rawlins; *musical director,* Val Burton; *costumes by* Elizabeth Coleman; RCA *recording; filmed at* California Tiffany Studios; *running time,* 69 minutes; *released* Sept. 1, 1931.

PLAYERS: *Mrs. Kennedy,* Aileen Pringle; *Millie Scripps,* Alice White; *Montrose,* Hale Hamilton; *Inspector Taylor,*

Robert Elliott; *Aunt Mildred,* Clara Blandick; *Lawrence,* Brandon Hurst; *Grayson,* Leslie Fenton; *Colton,* William Humphrey; An English Guest, Tyrell Davis; *Maid,* Aileen Carlisle; *Mr. Kennedy,* Kenneth Thomson; *Channing,* Robert Ellis.

Synopsis

As a man and a woman embrace, there appears the woman's husband, gun in hand. He fires, and the suitor falls. "You killed him — my ideal!" cries the woman. "Well," returns the husband, "there *lies* your *ideal.*"

The sound of applause proves the murder to have been a charade. The guests conjecture as to what pun the skit represents. Montrose, a criminologist, has the solution: *Ideal* plus *lies* equals *idealise.* But then it is found that the "victim," host Kennedy's secretary and friend, is in fact dead; there had been a bullet in the charade-gun fired by Kennedy. Horrified, Kennedy opens the gun and finds another live shell. Montrose takes charge pending arrival of the police, and Kennedy goes to his study.

Inspector Taylor arrives and demands to see "the other body." Someone had phoned headquarters, saying *two* persons were dead.

In his study, Kennedy is confronted by the murderer, whom he knows and suspects. There is a shot, and Kennedy slumps forward. Before he dies, he tells the killer he has left a revealing letter. The murderer arranges the body to appear a suicide. The inspector, having heard the shot, rushes upstairs and finds Grayson, brother of Kennedy's wife, in a room nearby. Unnoticed, a gloved hand reaches in and hides an envelope behind a painting. The police have discarded a murder-suicide theory because Kennedy and his amaneunsis are known to have been close friends. But the ominous-looking butler, Lawrence, insists he heard the two victims arguing during the morning.

Lawrence catches Millie Scripps in a lie. She loves Grayson, the law learns, but nothing can be discerned about

Clara Blandick.

her relationship to the case. The police learn of a quarrel over Kennedy's new will — now missing — which would disinherit Mrs. Kennedy.

Millie finds the envelope behind the picture and makes an appointment with the police. When the investigators arraive, she is found murdered. Lawrence, next to find the envelope, phones the police. The wire goes dead, he jiggles the receiver, and he dies. Montrose shows that the butler was wounded by a diabolical contraption: a needle fitted into the telephone.

Mrs. Kennedy's Aunt Mildred finds the envelope and prepares to take it to Montrose. As Mildred leaves, Mrs. Kennedy phones Montrose, and it becomes plain that an affair exists between them. Awaiting the aunt, Montrose equips his phone with the same sort of device that killed the butler. Mildred balks at showing Montrose the papers, and he depresses a foot switch which rings a bell. He tells her it must be Inspector Taylor calling for her. She picks up the phone and, getting no answer, prepares to jiggle the cradle when the inspector enters. Taylor knows that Montrose is the killer. Again Montrose rings the bell. Taylor takes the receiver and hands it to Montrose, telling him the call is for him. Montrose puts the receiver to his ear, depresses the hook, and falls dead.

Notes

"It isn't murder, but an epidemic," says Inspector Taylor during *Murder at Midnight.* W. Scott Darling's ingenious screenplay, a collaboration with director Frank R. Strayer, allows for five violent deaths and yet contains so many clever twists and turns as to keep the viewer amused as well as horrified.

The story's durability is illustrated in that Darling used it again in 1939 for *The Mystery of Mr. Wong* and yet again in 1947 for *The Chinese Ring.* The intelligence of the dialogue includes some engaging comic interludes with Clara

Hale Hamilton and Brandon Hurst offer their cooperation.

Hale Hamilton, done in by his own satanic device. Clara Blandick is amazed; Robert Elliott is sorrowful.

Blandick, in her usual grouchy maiden aunt role, and Tyrell Davis as an effeminate Englishman. The opening of the show is a double surprise: An apparent murder proves to be part of a game of charades, then it is found that the play victim actually *has* been murdered. The ending is equally surprising, with the disclosure of the murderer's identity catching most viewers very much off-guard.

Hale Hamilton and Robert Elliott are first-rate as the sleuths interested in the case, Alice White gives a saucy performance as the maid Millie, Aileen Pringle works well as the wife of the second victim, and Brandon Hurst is impressive as the (as always) innocent but suspicious-looking butler.

Tiffany provided its usual solid production values, particularly in obtaining William Rees from Warner Brothers to handle the photography. Strayer's direction is noteworthy for its avoidance of the heavy-handedness that could easily have turned a pleasing mystery into a morbid affair.

CHINATOWN AFTER DARK (1931)

(Action Pictures Corporation)

Presented by Ralph M. Like; *directed by* Stuart Paton; *supervised by* Cliff Broughton; *story by* Betty Burbidge; *photographed by* Jules Cronjager; *film editor,* Viola Roehl; *art director,* Ben Dore; *musical director,* Lee Zahler; *recording supervisor,* James Stanley; *assistant director,* Wilfred E. Black; RCA *sound; produced at* International Film Corporation Studios; *running time,* 59 minutes; *released* October 15, 1931.

PLAYERS: *Jim Bonner,* Rex Lease; *Lotus,* Barbara Kent; *Lee Fong,* Edmund Breese; *Madame Ying Su,* Carmel Myers; *Ralph Bonner,* Frank Mayo; *Horatio Dooley,* Billy Gilbert; *Captain of Detectives,* Lloyd Whitlock; *Ming Fu,* Laska Winter; *Varanoff,* Michael Visaroff; *Cop,* Charles Murphy; *Servants,* James B. Leong *and* Willy Fung.

Synopsis

An American saves the life of Prince Lee Fong — at the cost of his own — during an uprising in China. Lee Fong

39

RALPH M. LIKE presents

CHINATOWN AFTER DARK

with
BARBARA KENT – REX LEASE
CARMEL MYERS – EDMUND BREESE
directed by STUART PATON

See what happens in the under world dens after dark!

pledges to take the man's infant daughter to America and care for her. As the girl, Lotus, reaches womanhood, Lee Fong realizes he must leave his house and gain acceptance among her own race. Appealing to his family in China for money to provide for Lotus, he is informed that an American, Ralph Bonner, will bring him his inheritance.

Bonner arrives in San Francisco bearing an antique dagger, a Chinese artifact which has been the object of several attempts at theft by a gang of highbinders. The leader of the ruffians enlists the aid of Madame Ying Su. Disguised as a crew member, Ralph goes to the apartment of his brother, Jim, who agrees to accompany him to the house of Lee Fong. Jim waits outside while Ralph delivers the dagger, which proves to contain in its handle a priceless ruby. The lights are extinguished suddenly, a scream is heard, and Jim enters to find Lee Fong dead, a faded poppy beside the body. No sign is to be found of Ralph or the dagger. Jim tells Lotus he will return after he searches for his brother.

Outside his apartment, Jim finds Madame Ying Su, who claims to have come into the hallway to gain shelter from the rain. She tries to detain Jim, who finally goes to his rooms. He finds Ralph lying in a pool of blood, seemingly near death. Again there is a faded poppy. The telephone wires have been cut. Jim goes to summon a doctor; when he returns, Ralph has disappeared. Jim goes to Chinatown the following evening to call upon Madame Ying Su, whom he suspects, upon learning she is called "the Poppy."

Horatio Dooley, the detective in charge of the case, believes Jim is the killer, but Lotus refuses to listen to him. Jim returns to spy on Madame Ying Su and is captured by her men. He is imprisoned in her apartment. Dooley, insisting to Lotus that Jim is a member of Madame's gang, takes the girl to Madame's tea room. While Dooley is searching for Jim, Lotus is abducted by Madame's henchmen. Jim asks permission to question the girl about the dagger; Madame consents but leaves a man to spy on them. Jim overcomes the spy and finds a secret passage leading to the street. He sends Lotus for help.

Dooley goes to Lee Fong's home and finds it has been ransacked. From the ceiling falls the missing dagger, narrowly missing the detective. Dooley returns to Madame's house with a squad of policemen. Madame Ying Su and her men are overcome. Ralph is found, still alive, imprisoned in a secret passage. Ralph explains that when he was attacked, he threw the dagger into the ceiling.

Notes

Sometimes suspenseful, but fast-moving and interesting throughout, Action's *Chinatown After Dark* is a pleasing melodrama. It has a smooth performance (with moments of cheesecake) by Carmel Myers as a dragon lady who will stop at nothing to obtain a valuable jewel. Barbara Kent (who was the leading lady in Harold Lloyd's first talkie, *Welcome Danger* [1929]), is a charming heroine. Frank Mayo and Rex Lease are adventurous brothers, a team that along with Billy Gilbert's comical, cigar-chomping detective and Edmund Breese's elderly Chinaman helps lift the picture above the usual "quickie" level. The otherwordly atmosphere of Chinatown is well sustained, and the direction, by a big-timer of the silent era, Stuart Paton, is strong on pace and characterization.

Rex Lease, James Leong, Jewel Carmen.

THE LIGHTNING WARRIOR (1931)

(Mascot Pictures Corporation)

Produced by Nat Levine; *directed by* Armand Schaefer *and* Benjamin Kline; *photographed by* Ernest Miller, William Nobles, *and* Tom Galligan; *supervising editor,* Wyndham Gittens; *story by* Wyndham Gittens, Ford Beebe, *and* Colbert Clark; *film editor,* Ray Snyder; *music by* Lee Zahler; *sound engineer,* George Lowerre; *sound system,* Cinephone *by* Disney Sound Recording Co.; *a serial in twelve chapters; running time,* 250 minutes; *released* Dec. 1, 1931.

An
ALL TALKING
SERIAL IN TWELVE
THRILLING CHAPTERS

Nat Levine
presents

RIN-TIN-TIN in the LIGHTNING WARRIOR

PLAYERS: *Jimmy Carter*, Frankie Darro; *Jimmy's Father*, Hayden Stevenson; *Alan Scott*, George Brent; *Sheriff*, Pat O'Malley; *Dianne*, Georgia Hale; *Pierre Lafarge*, Theodore Lorch; *John Hayden*, Lafe McKee; *Angus Macdonald*, Frank Brownlee; *Wells*, Bob Kortman; *Adams*, Dick Dickinson; *Ken Davis*, Yakima Canutt; *Indian George*, Frank Lanning; *Woman*, Helen Gibson; *Man*, Kermit Maynard; *Rinty the "Lightning Warrior,"* Rin Tin Tin.

Chapter Titles

1) The Drums of Doom; 2) The Wolf Man; 3) Empty Saddles; 4) Flaming Arrows; 5) The Invisible Enemy; 6) The Fatal Name; 7) The Ordeal of Fire; 8) The Man Who Knew; 9) Traitor's Hour; 10) The Secret of the Grave; 11) Red Shadows; 12) Painted Faces.

Synopsis

A cloaked madman, the Wolf Man, instigates a wave of Indian terrorism. Amidst the panic, rumors persist of a lost tribe in the nearby hills. The Sheriff of the mining community deputizes Wells and Adams to investigate the legend.

An arrow fells Jimmy Carter's father as he and the boy travel downriver to their gold mine. Jimmy drags his father ashore. Pierre Lafarge is in a cabin close by, as is the corpse of William Scott, an investigator of the Indian uprising. As Lafarge flees on horseback, Scott's dog, Rin Tin Tin, attacks. The Wolf Man captures Jimmy. The Sheriff and deputies arrive and take Lafarge to the cabin. They find the body and free Jimmy.

The Wolf Man has erased a message Scott left, telling where identification of the Wolf Man could be found. The fiend orders Wells and Adams to get the information, reputedly hidden in the dog's collar. Alan Scott, brother of the slain investigator, arrives to carry on in his brother's stead.

Dianne, whom the Sheriff claims is his daughter, is really the daughter of Lafarge, who by now has been released. The settlers repel an Indian attack at the Carter mine. Foreman Angus Macdonald suggests that John Hayden — who holds notes on many of the mines — head a vigilante crew, but Hayden declines the honor, having been accused by the Sheriff of being the Wolf Man.

Alan finds Hayden in the mine, unconscious and cloaked in the garb of the Wolf Man. Hayden says the mine belongs to him because Jimmy's slain father had been in arrears. In another questionable disclosure, Lafarge tells Dianne that Hayden is behind the Indian attacks.

Jimmy, unconscious following a hairbreadth escape, is carried up a cliff by Indian George. Rinty gives chase, but George causes the dog to fall.

Alan is accused of agitating the Indians. Meantime, Rinty enables Jimmy to escape. Indian George is clubbed unconscious. In George's pockets, Lafarge finds the message from Alan's brother. Alan escapes his accusers but is trapped in a milling machine by Lafarge. Dianne saves Alan and leaves with Lafarge.

Rinty, under fire from Wells, Adams, and Martin, doubles back to push the men into a lagoon. The Wolf Man kills Martin, then instructs Wells and Adams to kill Jimmy. Believing this task accomplished, they join Macdonald's

George Brent loses the advantage to Bob Kortman in the Wolf Man's cave. Rin Tin Tin will turn the tables.

crew, which has captured Alan — now accused of Jimmy's apparent death. Rinty has rescued Jimmy, whose appearance saves Alan. Alan captures Indian George, whose clothing yields the message of the Wolf Man's identity. Lafarge grabs the note before it can be read, writes Hayden's name on it, and places it where Alan, Macdonald, and the Sheriff can find it. Alan and Rinty chase Hayden, who reaches safety despite appearances that he has died in a fall.

At the Wolf Man's orders, Indians capture Lafarge. New terrorism commences. Hayden sneaks the identity message from the Sheriff's quarters; the Wolf Man steals it from him. Next the message shows up, inexplicably, in Indian George's possession. Alan is captured and tied to a stake with Lafarge. Jimmy frees them, and they survive an Indian attack.

Alan captures Hayden. From afar he hears the Wolf Man's eerie wail. Alan and Macdonald seek Indian George. The Wolf Man seizes Dianne, but Lafarge frees her. The Wolf Man later captures Macdonald and Jimmy, but they escape, only to be imprisoned by Indian George and a war party. Hayden meantime frees himself from a cell, and in a struggle the jailhouse catches fire. The elusive report of the Wolf Man's identity continues to change hands.

Finally Alan exposes the Wolf Man as Macdonald, who has hired outlaws to pose as Indians to scare away the villagers. The genuine Indians, led by George, rout the imposters and head back to their hideaway in the hills. Lafarge and Jimmy become allies, and Alan and Dianne start talking marriage.

Notes

Jack L. Warner once said his favorite actor was Rin Tin Tin, a German Shepherd dog whose starring films during the late 'twenties helped keep Warner Brothers solvent. Rinty was a war dog, brought back from a French battlefield by trainer Lee Duncan, who made and spent a fortune by exploiting the animal's uncanny ability to express emotions for the camera. Audiences were enchanted by Rinty's performances, which remain unsurpassed by those of any imitators. When he made *The Lightning Warrior* he was fourteen and becoming lame. His condition necessitated use of doubles for the more violent action, but Rinty still had the power to charm. Shortly after completion of the serial, Rinty leapt into his master's arms and died.

Rinty's supporting cast included Frankie Darro, a spunky twelve-year-old who could ride like a miniature stunt veteran; Georgia Hale, once a leading lady for Chaplin and von Sternberg and victim of a collapsed career with the talkies' advent; and George Brent, a handsome Irish adventurer and Broadway leading man making his screen debut. Outstanding among the "heavies" is a Mascot regular, the malevolent-featured Bob Kortman.

First director Armand Schaefer, who had directed the Red Grange serial, *The Galloping Ghost* (1930), was adept at the tight methods necessary to Mascot production. Co-director Benjamin Kline was a noted cameraman.

Arguably the company's best, *The Lightning Warrior* unreels at a breathtaking pace. Stunting is superb. Scenery is impressive. The town of Sainte Suzanne is the oft-used Western village at the Prudential Studio near Kernville. The Wolf Man's lair is a tunnel in Bronson Canyon. A few indoor scenes were done on rented stages at Universal and Tec-Art. The entire production cost $45,000.

The identity of the Wolf Man, typical of Mascot, is a well-kept secret. Evident here is the cheating Levine employed to confuse audiences: The Wolf Man is impersonated by Ted Lorch, who also plays a key suspect, until another less sinister-looking character is unmasked.

Tinny even by 1931 standards, sound is nonetheless used creatively to heighten the sense of hovering menace. Incessant drumming — inspired, Levine said, by the native drumming in *Trader Horn* (1930) — lends atmosphere to several sequences. Wind likewise contributes to the tension, howling mournfully through the cave of the Wolf Man. Music is heard only during the titles.

TERROR BY NIGHT (1931)
a. k. a. THE SECRET WITNESS

(Famous Attractions Corporation)
Produced by Famous Attractions Corporation: *directed by* Thornton Freeland; *screenplay by* Samuel Spewack, *based on his novel,* MURDER IN THE GILDED CAGE: *photographed by* Robert Planck; *recording engineer,* Corson Jowett; *film editor,* Louis H. Sackin; *running time,* 68 minutes; *previewed and tradeshown as* TERROR BY NIGHT *by* Famous Attractions, October 1931; *released* December 12, 1931, *as* THE SECRET WITNESS *by* Columbia Pictures Corporation.

PLAYERS: *Lois Martin,* Una Merkel; *Arthur Jones,* William Collier, Jr.; *Bella,* Zasu Pitts; *Captain McGowan,* Purnell Pratt; *Larson,* Clyde Cook; *Lewis Leroy,* Ralf Harolde; *Tess,* June Clyde; *Sylvia Folsom,* Rita La Roy; *Herbert Folsom,* Hooper Atchley; *Brannigan,* Paul Hurst; *Gunner,* Nat Pendleton; *Moll,* Greta Grandstedt; *Building Engineer,* Clarence Muse.

Synopsis

Philandering Bert Folsom finds it convenient to be separated from his wife, Sylvia, but not divorced. When he refuses her a divorce, Sylvia storms from his penthouse apartment voicing threats. Then Folsom argues with his bodyguard, a thug named Gunner, whom he turns over to the police because of an alleged theft. Young and beautiful Tess Jones, Folsom's paramour, leaps to her death from his penthouse terrace when she learns he is married. Brannigan, a stupid cop, listens in on a telephone conversation between Folsom and his friend, Lewis Leroy, who asks Folsom to tune in his radio speech at ten o'clock. Brannigan goes to

somebody has ripped out the master light switch. Police send for the building engineer who, mistakenly thinking he has been brought in for questioning, almost hysterically denies his guilt. There is a shot in the dark, and when the lights are restored the engineer is found to be dead. A smoking gun is clutched in the hands of Folsom's ape, apparently placed there by the killer.

McGowan arrests "Casey" and dismisses everybody else. Lois is convinced that the wrong man has been arrested. She steals down to the basement apartment of the engineer and there is seized by the throat by some unseen person. Escaping, she pursues other clues and again almost succumbs to the killer. Using herself as a decoy, Lois tricks Leroy into admitting the crime as he stands near an open telephone. The murder gun was triggered when Folsom turned on the radio.

Notes

Splendid direction by Thornton Freeland, a well-written script by Sam Spewack, beautiful photography by Robert Planck, and first-class work by a notable cast lifted Famous Attractions' *The Secret Witness* well above the usual small company standard. A Hollywood preview garnered such good reviews ("... audience in a turmoil of tense excitement and laughter ...") that Columbia Pictures bought the film outright.

Such a rotter is the first victim, as played by Hooper Atchley, that one is hard-put at first to consider his killer a villain. Atchley two-times his wife, drives a young girl to suicide (and jokes over the telephone with a friend a few minutes later!), and accuses his valet-bodyguard of a crime the servant did not commit. The later actions of the murderer, however, prove him to be as despicable as his victim.

Una Merkel, as a spunky girl who puts her life on the line to solve the case, does well with the best role in the show. Zasu Pitts, as a nosey and jittery telephone operator, and Paul Hurst, as a thickheaded cop, provide clever comedy relief. Hurst directed some 340 silent pictures but turned his stage forté to an acting career when talking pictures were introduced. "Buster" Collier — who had just received acclaim for his work in King Vidor's *Street Scene* — is good as the persecuted hero, Purnell Pratt is a convincing detective, and a young veteran of the stage, Ralf Harolde, makes a dapper suspect an interesting character. Nat Pendleton, champion Olympics wrestler, the Australian comedian Clyde Cook, and the black singer-actor Clarence Muse stand out in a competent supporting cast.

Freeland was noted for his light "touch" as director of such delightful comedies as *Three Live Ghosts* (1929), *Whoopee!* (1930), *Six Cylinder Love* (1931), *Flying Down to Rio* (1933), and *George White's Scandals* (1935). In this rare excursion into suspense and murder, Freeland maintains an enviable balance, in which the dark shadows of

talk to Folsom and finds him dying from a bullet wound. Folsom gasps, "Casey ..." and dies, mourned by his pet ape.

Lois Martin, who lives in the apartment below the penthouse, is thrust into the case when the police arrest a young man who has entered her window during the night, carrying a gun. The police are suspicious of Lois because she tried to shield the youth, who proves to be Arthur ("Casey") Jones, brother of the dead Tess. Jones admits that he had come to kill Folsom, only to find his intended victim lying on the floor, and he says he fled when Brannigan knocked on the door. Police Captain McGowan takes charge of the case, sending for Mrs. Folsom and Leroy. Mrs. Folsom is in love with Leroy, but when questioned she maintains she loved her husband deeply. Leroy and Mrs. Folsom suspect one another; both deny complicity. Gunner is brought in, handcuffed, vehemently denying both the murder and the theft. Gunner attempts to escape. Suddenly the building is plunged into darkness;

mystery are contrasted with sprightly comic interludes. The result is highly satisfactory.

LAW OF THE TONGS (1931)

(Willis Kent Productions)
Produced by Willis Kent; *directed by* Lewis D. Collins; *story by* Oliver Drake; *photographed by* William Nobles; *running time,* 56 minutes; *released* December 15, 1931.

PLAYERS: *Joan,* Phyllis Barrington; *Charlie Wong,* Jason Robards; *Doug,* John Harron; *Madame Duval,* Dorothy Farley; *Mother McGregor,* Mary Carr; *Yuen Lee,* Frank Lackteen; *Captain McGregor,* William Mahlen; *Davy Jones,* Richard Alexander.

Synopsis

Joan, a dance-hall hostess, meets Doug, a seemingly destitute young man, who convinces her she should not be working in such a sordid atmosphere. Quitting her job, Joan wanders the streets, unable to find work. She is befriended and taken in by Charlie Wong, a tong leader engaged in the smuggling of aliens into the United States. Wong treats the girl as he would a daughter, and when he learns she is worried about Doug, takes her to a Salvation Army branch where she finds him. Joan is horrified to learn that Doug is a government agent sent to get evidence against Wong.

Doug is captured by tong leaders, who condemn him to death. Joan enters the tong headquarters in an attempt to save Doug, thus violating the law of the tongs; the rule demands the life of any infidel who trespasses upon tong territory. Through a bold move, Wong rescues Joan, who escapes. The vengeful Yuen Lee kills Wong as the police, led by Joan, return in time to save Doug from his captors.

Notes

Probably the best of Willis Kent's low-budget productions, *Law of the Tongs* is a pretty good chiller which has a stronger "heart" interest than most other action films in its class. Jason Robards, a First National leading man whose career was taking a nosedive from which it failed to recover, is excellent as a Chinese gang boss who goes soft over a

young girl. The Turkish actor, Frank Lackteen, provides a menacing presence. The other players do good work, particularly Phyllis Barrington. Director Lew Collins manages well both the scary and the sentimental aspects of the story, and the Oriental atmosphere is properly threatening.

The "yellow peril" closes in on Phyllis Barrington and John Harron.

Phyllis Barrington, John Harron, Frank Lackteen.

1932

THE SHADOW OF THE EAGLE (1932)

(Mascot Pictures Corporation)

Produced by Nat Levine; *directed by* Ford Beebe; *additional direction by* B. Reeves Eason; *supervised by* Nat Lewis; *story by* Ford Beebe, Colbert Clark, *and* Wyndham Gittens; *photographed by* Benjamin Kline *and* Victor Scheurich, IATSE; *musical score,* Lee Zahler; *film editor,* Ray Snyder; *supervising editor,* Wyndham Gittens; *stunt supervisor,* Yakima Canutt; *sound engineer,* George Lowerre; *sound system,* Powers Cinephone *by* Disney Sound Recording Company; *a serial in* 12 chapters *with a total running time of* 250 minutes; *released* Feb. 1, 1932.

PLAYERS: *Craig McCoy,* John Wayne; *Jean Gregory,* Dorothy Gulliver; *Danby,* Walter Miller; *Ward,* Kenneth Harlan; *Evans,* Richard Tucker; *Ames,* Pat O'Malley; *Boyle,* Yakima Canutt; *Clark,* Edmund Burns; *Gardner,* Roy D'Arcy; *Clown,* Billy West; *Nathan Gregory,* Edward Hearn; *Green,* Lloyd Whitlock; *Midget,* Little Billy; *Strong Man,* Ivan Linow; *Ventriloquist,* James Bradbury, Jr.; *Kelly,* Ernie S. Adams; *Moore,* Bud Osborne; *Policeman,* Monty Montague.

Chapter Titles

1) The Carnival Mystery; 2) Pinholes; 3) The Eagle Strikes; 4) The Man of a Million Voices; 5) The Telephone Cipher; 6) The Code of the Carnival; 7) Eagle of Vulture? 8) On the Spot; 9) When Thieves Fall Out; 10) The Man Who Knew; 11) The Eagle's Wings; 12) The Shadow Unmasked.

Synopsis

Skywriting messages from a pilot called the Eagle threaten an aircraft company. Police accuse Nathan Gregory, who had been known by such a name while a war ace. Gregory admits only that he hates the corporate officers, because their success is the result of an invention stolen from him. Another suspect is Craig McCoy, stunt pilot for Gregory's carnival. Craig, whose duties include skywriting, is in love with Gregory's daughter, Jean.

Upon learning that the plans of a Gregory invention have been stolen, Craig pursues Green, a corporate director who is seen fleeing the carnival gorunds. Billy, a carnival midget, hitches a ride on the back of a car carrying Eagle henchmen Boyle and Moore. He sees Green enter a 'phone booth and call a directors' meeting. As Boyle shows Green the stolen plans, Craig races past on his motorcycle and snatches the plans. Back at the carney, Jean's father has disappeared.

Told of the directors' meeting, Craig breaks in and tries unsuccessfully to convince the board of Gregory's innocence. A plane is heard, and all watch as the unmarked craft writes the name of a director, Clark, then draws a line through it. The lights go out, a sepulchral voice proclaims that the Eagle has struck, and a shot is heard. Clark has been murdered.

Gregory has returned to the carnival. Directors Evans, Ames, Ward, Danby, and Green arrive and accuse Gregory. The loyal carney hands sound the emergency cry of "Hey, Rube!" and in the commotion Gregory seeks to escape by plane. Jean also rushes toward the plane, but a masked man dressed like Gregory pushes her aside, leaps into the cockpit, and starts the plane. The craft bears down on Craig and Jean, who narrowly escape. Gregory has vanished.

Examination of a note from Jean's father shows certain letters emphasized with pinpricks, forming a coded message that he is a captive in an asylum. Jean subsequently is taken prisoner, but she obtains a pistol and holds the Eagle's agents at bay while phoning the directors for help. Craig tries to go, but is held by the directors. The shadow of the Eagle appears, and in the resulting consternation Craig escapes, pursued by the directors. Accompanied by the

NAT LEVINE PRESENTS

the SHADOW of the EAGLE

starring

JOHN WAYNE
DOROTHY GULLIVER
KENNETH HARLAN
WALTER MILLER

John Wayne and Dorthy Gulliver try to halt the Eagle's escape. In a typical Mascot subterfuge, the Eagle looks suspiciously like Roy D'Arcy, who isn't the Eagle at all.

carney strong man, Craig goes to the sanatorium. Disguised in a smock and mask, he searches for Jean.

The strong man protects Jean and carries her atop a scaffolding as Craig takes on the attackers. In a car crash, the scaffolding is smashed. An accomplice spirits Jean away. The strong man overtakes the accomplice, who is about to reveal the Eagle's identity when he is killed by a bullet ostensibly from nowhere.

Eagle agent Gardner steals Gregory's plans but is overtaken by Craig. The men fight in a Ferris wheel gondola, and Craig, thrown out toward certain death, saves himself by catching onto the framework.

At length, Craig proves Danby is the Eagle. The master criminal is killed when he tries to escape.

Notes

"We worked so hard on those Mascot serials we didn't have time to think," John Wayne told the authors recently. "We would put twenty-five reels in the can in sixteen to twenty-three days of shooting — and that's nights, too. A working day was from twelve to twenty hours. They didn't hire you for acting, they wanted endurance. You had to be able to last through it. We didn't have much dialogue, and we didn't fool with retakes, which is okay with me because your first take is your most natural and spontaneous anyway. I loved it; I had a wonderful time."

Wayne had been groomed for stardom as the hero of Raoul Walsh's expensive Fox Western, *The Big Trail* (1930). From this premature peak his career plummeted. Agent Al Kingston brought Wayne to Nat Levine, who was looking for a "Lindberg type" to play an aviator in three serials.

The youthful, lanky Wayne was delighted to get the job at $2,000 for all three serials. Through these and a string of Warner Brothers and Monogram "quickie" Westerns, he became a star in the eyes of the Saturday matinee habitués long before he achieved exalted status with the mainstream audiences.

At four a.m. the day after he signed the contract, Wayne travelled with Levine in the producer's chauffeured Packard to Antelope Valley, changing into costume and applying makeup — (Levine thought Wayne looked too young) — during the three-hour drive. Arriving on location at sun-up, he was put immediately to work. Sixteen hours later the sun was down, and work was halted until next daybreak. Location work was no picnic. Work was hard, conditions were primitive (no tents), and meals were sandwiches.

"We had only one interior set," Wayne recalled, "So we had to suggest changes of scene by changing our clothes. I got damn' tired of gettin' in and out of my clothes all the time." While at work on this serial Wayne met Yakima Canutt, who became his lifelong friend and associate.

Eagle was the directorial debut of Ford Beebe, a pioneer screenwright and "film doctor." After several days of wet-weather work, Beebe fell ill. Action specialist B. Reeves ("Breezy") Eason was brought in to direct on alternate days, and this new system — letting one director prepare for a day's shooting while another was on the set — proved so efficient as to become standard serial procedure.

To support the new star, Levine gathered his usual remarkable cast of meaningful "names," many of whom had been stars or leads in the silents. Typically Mascot, the script is overcomplicated but contains some excellent action. Stunting by Canutt, Monty Montague, and Wayne himself is first-rate. Photography is good in view of the hectic pace (with eighty-odd camera set-ups a day!). There are primitive special effects; the skywriting scenes, for example, are obvious cartoon animation. There is carnival music but no dramatic underscoring. Chapter prologues have off-screen narration.

Dorothy Gulliver and John Wayne turn Lloyd Whitlock over to the police. The cop at right is stuntman Monty Montague.

THE MONSTER WALKS (1932)

(Action Pictures, Incorporated)
Produced by Ralph M. Like; *directed by* Frank R. Strayer; *supervised by* Cliff Broughton; *photographed by* Jules Cronjager; *edited by* Byron Robinson; *art director,* Ben Doré; *set decorations,* Ralph Black; *sound supervision,* George Hutchins; *musical director,* Lee Zahler; RCA *sound system; produced at* International Film Corporation, Ltd.; *running time,* 60 minutes; *released* Feb. 10, 1932.

PLAYERS: *Ted Clayton,* Rex Lease; *Ruth Earlton,* Vera Reynolds; *Robert Earlton,* Sheldon Lewis; *Hanns Krug,* Mischa Auer; *Mrs. Krug,* Martha Mattox; *Herbert Wilkes,* Sidney Bracy; *Exodus,* Sleep 'n' Eat (Willie Best).

Synopsis

Home from Europe, Ruth learns of the death of her scientist father. She and her fiancé, Ted, brave a mountain storm to be present at the bier. They are greeted by Robert, Ruth's uncle, and Wilkes, the family lawyer. Robert, a paralytic, has been dependent on his brother, Ruth's father.

Ruth views the body with Mrs. Krug, the housekeeper, while Mrs. Krug's son Hanns attends to the baggage and puts away the car. Ruth is to inherit the estate, which would revert to Robert in the event of her death.

A fierce cry is heard from Yogi, a great ape which Ruth's father had kept caged as a pet in the cellar. Ruth's concern mounts, for her soujourn in Europe had stemmed from her fear of the ape. Ruth even fears the house itself, with its hidden passageways.

The half-wit, Hanns, complains of the unfairness of the will. He claims the servants deserve some reward for their long silence (whose purpose has yet to be disclosed).

A scream from Ruth's room attracts Ted, Mrs. Krug, and Wilkes. Ruth claims the ape had attacked her, but Wilkes assures her the creature is securely locked away. Without the knowledge of the rest of the household, Mrs. Krug decides to spend the rest of the night in Ruth's room.

Hanns denies knowledge of any passageways. As Ted and Wilkes go to question Robert, they hear Ruth's door open. In Ruth's bed is the corpse of Mrs. Krug. Ted realizes the killer must have meant to do away with Ruth instead. Robert is the only logical suspect in view of the will; yet Robert is paralysed.

Hanns tells Ted that Robert is calling for him. Ted finds Robert near death. The uncle confesses he devised the plan which caused Hanns, while attempting to kill Ruth, to strangle his own mother; that Hanns is Robert's son by Mrs. Krug; and that the plotters had hoped to gain the fortune and let the blame rest with the ape.

Hanns has tethered Ruth to a post and is lashing the ape into a fury. The ape grabs the lash, whose wrist-hold Hanns cannot let go. Ted finally breaks into the cellar and rescues Ruth just as the ape crushes Hanns' throat.

Notes

The establishing scenes of *The Monster Walks* would do credit to some German "Golden Age" classic: A shrouded corpse lies in a candle-lit room while lightning flashes beyond the window, winds howl, and thunder rumbles. In a moment there enters the movies' most sinister housekeeper — the sharp-featured Martha Mattox, who established the role in Universal's *The Conflict* (1921) and gave it its most celebrated exposition in *The Cat and the Canary* (1927). Meantime, another veteran of gooseflesh, Sheldon Lewis, confers with his gaunt servant, Mischa Auer, elsewhere in the house. Their connivances are interrupted by another disturbing sound: the scream of a maddened ape.

The rest of the show fails to attain such power. One failing is that the script (by Robert Ellis, who wrote many of the Fox *Charlie Chan* films) is so clearly derivative of *The Cat and the Canary* that familiarity blunts the edge of such hackneyed devices as thunderclaps and skulking servants. Another is that the ape proves to be a chimpanzee — in reality a dangerous creature which may weigh as much as 150 pounds and have superhuman strength, formidable teeth, and an impulsive, vitriolic temper. The public, however, considers any chimp "cute" because of the frequent appearance of young chimps as affectionate pets in comedies and jungle pictures. Even so able a director as Frank Strayer was hard-put to overcome these handicaps.

Among occasional good touches, Auer plays an off-key rendition of Brahms' *Lullaby,* a noteworthy inclusion in that the actor was a grandson of violin virtuoso Leopold Auer. Rex Lease is stolid, and the petite Vera Reynolds, a former Cecil B. DeMille star on her decline, performs well, but does not appear as young and innocent as the character

Mischa Auer, Sidney Bracy, Rex Lease.

is scripted (by her husband, incidentally). The black actor, Willie Best, gives a hilarious parody of the "frightened manservant" stereotype. Bob Hope, who worked with Best in *The Ghost Breakers* (1940), called him "the best actor I know."

Production took place at International Film Corporation on Sunset Drive in Los Angeles, the former Charles Ray Studio, which Ralph M. Like converted into a sound studio after acquiring it in 1927. Action Pictures became part of Mayfair Pictures, Incorporated, shortly after completion of *The Monster Walks.*

MURDER AT DAWN (1932)

(Big 4 Productions)

Produced by John R. Freuler; *supervised by* Burton King; *directed by* Richard Thorpe; *story and screenplay by* Barry Barringer; *photographed by* Edward S. Kull; *film editor,* Fred Bain; *sound by* Earl Crane; *electrical effects by* Kenneth Strickfaden; *running time,* 61 minutes; *released* February 15, 1932.

PLAYERS: *Danny,* Jack Mulhall; *Doris,* Josephine Dunn; *Gertrude,* Marjorie Beebe; *Freddie,* Eddie Boland; *Henry,* Mischa Auer; *Housekeeper,* Martha Mattox; *The Stranger, Arnstein,* J. Crauford Kent; *Judge Folger,* Phillips Smalley; *Goddard,* Al Cross; *Dr. Farrington,* Frank Ball.

Synopsis

Judge Folger accuses two Wall Street wolves of unlawful stock-market manipulations, executed through their knowledge of an invention being perfected by Professor Farrington. Folger decides to investigate.

Danny, and Farrington's daughter, Doris, decide to go to Farrington's mountain hideaway, *The Crag,* to seek consent to their marriage. As chaperones they take along a madcap married couple, Freddie and Gertrude. None of the frightened townsfolk will take them to the forbidding mansion. Finally they get a frightened old Negro to drive them, but he flees at sight of a "ghost" — a suit of long underwear flapping on a clothesline.

Farrington is at work among his weird machinery, tended by his sinister-looking housekeeper and her no less spooky son, Henry. Folger arrives and discusses with the professor the DXL Accumulator, with which Farrington expects to harness solar power. Someone switches off the lights and enters, carrying a blinding beacon. Doris and company arrive to find that Folger has been killed. Farrington has disappeared.

In a secret passageway, Freddie encounters a keg of bootleg whiskey with predictable consequences. In another room he finds the body of the professor and, in a closet, the body of Henry. Freddie goes to fetch Danny, but by the time they return, both corpses have vanished.

Jack Mulhall, Josephine Dunn, Marjorie Beebe, Eddie Boland, Martha Mattox.

A distinguished stranger arrives and takes charge of the search. A mysterious figure is seen to hurl Henry's body into a pool, but in the darkness it is impossible to recover the body.

Henry and the professor actually are alive, the servant having imprisoned Farrington in an adjoining tower. Henry has assembled a duplicate of Farrington's accumulator, but it can be perfected only with a formula known only to Farrington. Henry wires the professor to the machine, warning him that the rising of the sun will activate the device unless the formula is revealed.

Henry drags Doris to the hidden laboratory and attaches her to the accumulator. Danny sees Henry emerge from a secret doorway. They fight, but Henry breaks free and climbs to the tower. Danny catches Henry just before dawn and topples him from the roof to his death. Danny smashes the accumulator just as the sun begins to activate it.

A detective employed by Folger appears, dragging a mannequin of Henry which had been used to mislead the others. He also exposes the stranger as Arnstein, one of the Wall Street wolves whom Folger was trying to expose and who had hired Henry to steal Farrington's invention.

Notes

John R. Freuler started the Theatre Comique in Milwaukee in 1905 and five years later organized the American Film Company. In January of 1930 he set up Big 4 Productions to supply small-town theatres with low-budget, all-talking Westerns. Principal stars were Buzz Barton and Bob Custer. *Murder at Dawn* was the first and last non-Western to carry the Big 4 brand. The mystery proved sufficiently profitable that Freuler Film Associates was formed for the production of Monarch Melodramas. Eighteen of these were announced along with six Tom Tyler Westerns. The company went out of business in 1933 after delivering part of the ambitious program.

Barry Barringer was an Alabama newspaperman who acted in silents opposite such early stars as Mary Fuller and Dorothy Phillips. By 1917 he had established himself as a screenwright and remained in that field well into the 'thirties. His script for *Murder at Dawn* is a curiosity, in its combination of the standard "old-house" comedy/mystery with a science fiction theme.

Uninspired direction shows that Richard Thorpe's potential had yet to be realized. This weakness and a small budget failed to provide much of a showcase for so intriguing an idea. Unusual sets and shadowy photography, however, allow for some creepy moments. There are pleasant performances by Jack Mulhall and Josephine Dunn (both demoted from Warner Brothers), Phillips Smalley, Frank Ball, and Crauford Kent. Kent, a gentleman of dignity, specialised in portrayals of the unsuspected culprit in innumerable mystery films; his approach was of the "Heh-heh. You must be joking, Inspector" sort. Some lowbrow comedy is at times effective, and the element of menace is handled in the best sinister housekeeper/sneaky handyman tradition by Martha Mattox and Mischa Auer, virtually repeating their roles from *The Monster Walks*. The film's "DXL Accumulator" device was designed by Kenneth Strickfaden, the electronics wizard from Santa Monica who created the fantastic equipment used in *Frankenstein*.

SINISTER HANDS (1932)

(Willis Kent Productions)

Produced by Willis Kent; *directed by* Armand Schaefer; *screenplay by* Norton Parker, *from his novel,* THE SEANCE MYSTERY; *adapted by* Oliver Drake; *photographed by* William Nobles; *produced at* Talisman Studios; *running time,* 65 minutes; *released* February 22, 1932.

PLAYERS: *Detective Captain Devlin,* Jack Mulhall; *Ruth Frazer,* Phyllis Barrington; *Judge McLeod,* Crauford Kent; *Swami Yomurda,* Mischa Auer; *Watkins,* Jimmy Burtis; *Richard Lang,* Phillips Smalley; *Nick Genna,* Louis Natheaux; *Betty Lang,* Gertrude Messenger; *John Frazer,* Lloyd Ingraham; *Vivian Rogers,* Helen Foster; *Mrs. Lang,* Lillian West; *Lefty Lewis,* Fletcher Norton; *Mary Browne,* Bess Flowers; *Tommy Lang,* Russell Collar.

Synopsis

The elderly Lang is murdered during a séance at his mansion. The weapon, an Oriental dagger, was wielded by a left-handed person. Investigators Denham and Watkins learn that everyone persent is a suspect.

The fake swami was disliked by Lang and had been victimizing Lang's wife; Mrs. Lang hated her husband and is romantically entangled with one of the guests; Lang and his daughter were at odds because of her relationship with a former gangster, also a guest; a judge seems to have shared some secret with Lang; a crippled, elderly neighbor had threatened Lang because of the deceased's interest in the neighbor's young wife; Lang's secretary has been stealing from her employer; the butler is an ex-convict called Lefty Lewis.

The weapon vanishes and reappears in the body of Lewis, who had been about to tell Denham the killer's identity.

Denham proves that only the judge had the opportunity to commit both murders. The guilty man confesses he bore a grudge against Lang. As he is about to be taken away, the judge swallows poison concealed in this ring.

Notes

A typical mystery of the period, with the added weirdness of a séance killing, *Sinister Hands* was among a handful of "indoor pictures" made by Willis Kent, who specialized in the "quickie" Western. The old mansion here was a sufficiently impressive rental set at Talisman Studios in Hollywood. Jack Mulhall's Irish pep and Mischa Auer's menace are well exploited; Kent, in fact, must have considered Auer's money-grubbing Swami Yomurda character as deserving of more than red-herring status, for Auer recreated the role in a Kent production of 1933, *Sucker Money,* discussed elsewhere in the present volume. Director

Jack Mulhall.

Armand Schaefer, a colorful and hard-working Canadian who grew up in the film industry, joined the Mack Sennett Studio in 1924, working as electrician, set dresser, and prop man. For a while he was prop master for Mary Pickford, then he joined Action Pictures as an assistant director, working in this capacity on fifty-odd Westerns starring Buffalo Bill, Jr., Wally Wales, and Buddy Roosevelt. He was free-lancing as an assistant director in 1931 when Willis Kent gave him his first directing job, *Reckless Rider,* a Lane Chandler Western. Schaefer, later a director and associate producer for Mascot, also produced Gene Autry's Republic and Columbia features and was president of Autry's television producing company, Flying A.

The economies of *Sinister Hands* sidestep many of the atmospheric touches necessary to the maintenance of suspense. Jimmy Burtis as the obligatory dimwit detective provides some comedy. Phillips Smalley, a top star and director for Universal in the silent days, gives a brief but effectively nasty performance as the first victim.

The identity of the murderer holds no surprise for the viewer, who has learned to suspect the least suspicious member of the cast — in this instance, a cast which is collectively suspect, as witness the play-on-words title in view of each household member's being a southpaw. Even the detective hero mentions that the guilty person is "above suspicion" — a sure tip-off.

STRANGERS OF THE EVENING (1932)

(Tiffany Pictures Corporation)

Directed by H. Bruce Humberstone; *produced by* Sam Bischoff; *adapted from the book,* THE ILLUSTRIOUS CORPSE, *by* Tiffany Thayer; *adaptation and dialogue by* Stuart Anthony *and* Warren B. Duff; *photographed by* Arthur Edeson; *settings by* Ralph M. DeLacy; *film editor,* Dave Berg; *supervising editor,* Martin G. Cohn; *sound,* Corson Jowett; *costumes,* Elizabeth Coleman; *properties,* Eddie Boyle; *music director,* Val Burton; RCA *recording; filmed at* California Tiffany Studios; *running time,* 71 minutes; *released* May 15, 1932.

PLAYERS: *Sybil,* Zasu Pitts; *Brubacher,* Eugene Pallette; *Frank Daniels,* Lucien Littlefield; *Robert Daniels,* Tully Marshall; *Ruth,* Miriam Seegar; *Dr. Everette,* Theodor von Eltz; *Chandler,* Warner Richmond; *Tommy,* Harold Waldridge; *Nathan Frisbee,* Mahlon Hamilton; *Sutherland,* Alan Roscoe; *First Man,* Charles Williams; *Second Man,* William Scott; *Nolan,* James Burtis; *Roberts,* Francis Sayles; *Policeman,* Hal Price.

Synopsis

Frank Daniels becomes irate when he learns of his daughter Ruth's plan to elope with Dr. Raymond Everette. Everette has a laboratory in Chandler's Undertaking Parlours where, some short while later, a corpse represented as that of Frank Daniels is brought. Still later, Tommy, a

51

"SNOOKIE, TELL ME WHAT HAPPENED?"

"WELL, THE COPS SAID
I KILLED A MAN—AND
THEY GOT MAD WHEN
I ASKED THEM, DID I?"

Strangers
of the
Evening

presented by
TIFFANY PRODUCTIONS

Horror and Hilarity, Mystery and
Mirth, Capering Corpses and
Tangled Loves!

with

SAZU PITTS
LUCIEN LITTLEFIELD
Eugene Pallette
Theodor von Eltz

Based on the novel, "The Illustrious Corpse,"
by TIFFANY THAYER

novice assistant, flees in horror at sight of what must be a horrible apparition.

Detective Brubacher investigates Daniels' death. Ruth, Everette, and Tommy are nowhere to be found. Then an amnesiac wanders in and tells Brubacher he knows where a murder has been committed. The police book him as "Richard Roe."

Everette determines to solve the murder of his new father-in-law. He surprises undertaker Chandler in the act of disposing of a bloodied suit of clothing. Through Sybil, a domestic slavey who has befriended "Richard Roe," Everette locates Tommy.

Frank Daniels has been seen alive. Exhumation shows his casket contains what Chandler identifies as the remains of Clark C. McNaughton, a politico. McNaughton had been shot during a disagreement at Chandler's home after McNaughton had accused a henchman, Jack King, of a double-cross. King has died in an auto accident.

Everette and Tommy head for the McNaughton vault, where hoodlums are transferring the casket to a truck. Everette and Tommy appropriate the truck and speed away with the casket. Chandler has hired the thugs to steal the coffin, Everette learns, whereupon he confronts the undertaker and his pals. After a round of fisticuffs, Everette and Tommy take the gang to Brubacher.

Chandler admits the body in Daniels' casket is really that of Jack King. He explains the body-switching was an attempt to prevent a political scandal.

Finally Ruth recognizes "Richard Roe" as her father. It seems that Daniels, having argued with Everette over the elopement plans, was accosted by hoodlums and left for

dead. Then two well-meaning men had taken him to the funeral parlour, where, after a snooze on a slab, he got up and walked away. It was the sight of the supposedly dead Daniels that had sent Tommy running.

Daniels is pleased after all with his daughter's marriage. The McNaughton murder is cleared up. And Sybil has won Daniels.

Notes

The blackly funny *Strangers of the Evening* anticipated a trend which persists today. Its depiction of comic occurances in an undertaking establishment was attacked as tasteless in 1932; today the film seems, in light of macabre comedies more recently in vogue, a product of impeccable taste.

Strangers was the first directorial assignment for H. Bruce ("Lucky") Humberstone, who from age nineteen had worked at various studios as a script clerk, assistant cameraman, assistant director, and actor. During apprenticeship Humberstone assisted thirty-six leading directors, concerning himself with a study of the techniques and tricks of each. *Strangers* attracted sufficient attention to establish Humberstone as a formidable talent; his career developed into the direction of dozens of major productions, among them, *If I Had a Million* (1932), *King of the Jungle* (1933), *I Wake Up Screaming* (1942), *Wonder Man* (1945), and *Fury at Furnace Creek* (1948).

Tiffany borrowed for *Strangers of the Evening* one of the great cameramen, Arthur Edeson, whose films include *The Thief of Baghdad* (1924), *The Lost World* (1925), *The Bat* (1926), *All Quiet on the Western Front* (1931), *Frankenstein* (1931), *The Old Dark House* (1932), *The Invisible Man* (1933), *Mutiny on the Bounty* (1935), *The Maltese Falcon* (1941), and *Casablanca* (1943). Edeson's mastery of lighting and composition combine with the

The "corpse," Lucien Littlefield, warms up to romance with Zasu Pitts.

tasteful direction to create a smooth visual flow seldom seen outside the major studios.

"The more ingenuity a cameraman has," Edeson said, while *Strangers* was in production, "the more opportunity he will find for getting effects in a 'mystery' story. All cameramen have artistic aspirations, and the setting of a mystery story is obviously the most perfect medium for experiment with strange camera angles and tricky lighting effects."

Zasu Pitts stands out among the players, fluttering wide-eyed through exquisitely dialogued scenes with the distinctive mannerisms that convulsed audiences and once prompted W. C. Fields to admonish a little girl who wanted to quit her studies with, "Do you wanta grow up to be like Zasu Pitts?" Erich von Stroheim called Miss Pitts "the ablest dramatic actress on the screen" and cast her strikingly in tragic roles in the monumental *Greed* (1925) and *The Wedding March* (1929). The public preferred her in humorous roles, however, and these dominated her long career.

Lucien Littlefield, the perennial pipsqueak, is a splendid foil for Miss Pitts. The robust Eugene Pallette is fine as a grouchy detective, and Harold Waldridge provides amusement as an undertaker's helper scared green by the disturbing goings-on.

WHITE ZOMBIE (1932)

(Halperin Productions)

Directed by Victor Halperin; *produced by* Edward Halperin; *story and dialogue by* Garnett Weston; *cinematographer,* Arthur Martinelli; *assistant director,* William Cody; *editor,* Harold MacLernon; *RCA sound by* Clarco; *settings by* Ralph Berger *and* Conrad Tritschler; *special effects by* Howard Anderson; *makeup artists,* Jack P. Pierce *and* Carl Axcelle; *second assistant director,* Herbert Glazer; *dialogue director,* Herbert Farjeon; *production assistant,* Sidney Marcus; *musical arrangements,* Abe Meyer; *original music,* Guy Bevier Williams *and* Xavier Cugat; *additional music by* Nathaniel Dett, Gaston Borch, Hugo Riesenfeld, Leo Kempenski, H. Herkan, *and* H. Maurice Jacquet; *produced at* Universal City *and* RKO Pathé Studios; *running time,* 69 minutes; *released* July 28, 1932, *through* United Artists.

PLAYERS: *Murder Legendre,* Bela Lugosi; *Madeline Short,* Madge Bellamy; *Neil Parker,* John Harron; *Dr. Bruner,* Joseph Cawthorn; *Charles Beaumont,* Robert Frazer; *Driver,* Clarence Muse; *Silver,* Brandon Hurst; *Pierre,* Dan Crimmins; *Chauvin,* John Peters; *Von Gelder,* George Burr McAnnan; *Zombies,* John Printz, Claude Morgan, *and* John Fergusson; *Maids,* Annette Stone *and* Velma Gresham.

Synopsis

Along a desolate road in the Haitian mountains, a carriage bearing Neil Parker and Madeline Short encounters a funeral in which the body is being interred in the

roadway. The driver explains that such practice is widespread in Haiti; it protects the body from theft by ghouls. Further down the road the coach stops again at sight of a man of satanic appearance (later to be identified as one called Murder Legendre). Six human shapes step forth. The coachman cries, "Zombies!" and whips the horses down the path at breakneck speed. The stranger pulls a scarf from about Madeline's neck.

Later, the driver explains the creatures on the road were zombies, resurrected from death through witchcraft, and the stranger is their sorcerous master. Silhouettes of the monsters are seen to stalk across a nearby hilltop, evoking terror which overcomes the coachman's dignified composure.

Dr. Bruner, a missionary, has been summoned to the Beaumont mansion to marry Neil and Madeline. Neil, a bank employee in Port au Prince, has summoned his fiancée from America; she met the wealthy Beaumont aboard ship. Beaumont has insisted the wedding take place on his plantation. Bruner is uneasy about Beaumont's lack of scruples and penchant for debauchery, but he cannot voice his suspicions because of the loyal presence of Beaumont's servant, Silver. Beaumont's interest in Madeline is patently more than platonic.

The roadway burial.

Beaumont, summoned to a coach driven by one of the hulking creatures, is taken to a huge sugar mill where numerous zombies labor. One of them stumbles and topples into a cane-crushing machine and is ground to bits by his heedless fellows. Beaumont finally is brought to the office of the man called Murder, who still carries Madeline's scarf. Beaumont has tried to hire Murder to kidnap Madeline, but the master of zombies maintains such action will not bring about the desired result. He tells Beaumont the only way to win Madeline is to make a zombie of her. Beaumont argues he can gain her affections otherwise, but Murder insists, "There *is* no other way." He instructs Beaumont to put the merest "pinpoint" of a potion on a flower or in a glass of wine to be given Madeline.

Back at the mansion the lovesick Beaumont pleads with Madeline to reconsider her marriage plans. She refuses. He gives her a rose — a rose tainted with Murder's potion. Neil and Madeline's wedding takes place and a banquet follows. Meantime, Murder appears outside the house and takes a candle from a lamp. This he carves into the shape of a

woman and wraps it in the scarf he took from Madeline. As Madeline looks into her wine glass she sees the face of Murder. "I see —," she says, "I see death." Outside, Murder melts the effigy, and Madeline crumples to the floor. She is pronounced dead by the doctor.

Neil's mind almost snaps. He becomes a drunken derelict, seeing Madeline's pale form in every shadow. He stumbles down the road, calling her name, in the black of night.

Murder and Beaumont, accompanied by the six zombie bodyguards, disinter the body of Madeline. Neil arrives and finds the crypt empty.

Neil and Dr. Bruner set out into the jungle to seek the lair of the zombie-master.

At Murder's clifftop castle, Beaumont realizes his rash action has made Madeline a mechanical, soulless creature. Beaumont pleads with Murder that "She must be gay and happy again," but Murder poisons Beaumont's drink and, following a sardonic toast, tells him the potion will turn him into a zombie. The bodyguards throw Silver to his doom in an underground river.

An old witch-doctor, Pierre, tells Neil and Bruner of Murder and his castle: "A cloud of vultures always hovers

Robert Frazer is appalled at Bela Lugosi's suggestion that the woman Frazer loves could become a zombie like John Peters.

Madeline's "death." John Harron, Madge Bellamy, Robert Frazer.

Robert Frazer, Bela Lugosi, and company remove Madge Bellamy from the tomb. In the film itself, the zombies carry her out in her casket.

over the house of the living dead." They reach the beach, where vultures hover and screech. Bruner leaves the feverish Neil and goes to reconnoiter the castle.

By some mystic reaction to the nearness of her lover, Madeline goes out onto a balcony. Neil is drawn to the castle, where he wanders aimlessly until he collapses at the top of a staircase. Murder orders Madeline to stab her husband but must summon all his willpower to make her strike. Before the blade can fall, her hand is stayed by a hooded figure, and now Murder cannot force her to kill. She runs to a verandah and is about to leap to her death, but Neil recovers and stops her. Murder and his zombies crowd Neil to the edge of the precipice. Neil fires on the creatures, but bullets have no effect. The hooded figure — unmasked as Dr. Bruner — fells Murder with an iron rod.

Neil flings himself to the floor as the zombies shamble over the edge. Madeline recovers her wits momentarily but lapses back into coma when Murder wakes.

Murder, seeking to escape, turns at the head of the stairs and hurls a gas grenade; the gas, combined with black magic, could make living corpses of Neil and Bruner. Beaumont, struggling to overcome his paralysis, appears on the parapet and grapples with Murder. The sorcerer falls over the cliff to be dashed on the rocks. Beaumont, too, falls to his death.

Madeline wakes and says, "Neil, I — I dreamed."

Notes

The word *zombie* was introduced to the American reading public in 1929 in William B. Seabrook's book on Haitian Voodoo, *The Magic Island,* and to the dramatic stage in Keneth Webb's New York play, *Zombie,* which opened in February of 1932. In March of that year Webb brought suit against movie producers Edward and Victor Hugo Halperin, who had announced their intention of

Bela Lugosi carves an effigy in wax of the half-paralyzed Robert Frazer while expressing regret that Frazer is unable to describe his symptoms.

A posed gathering of all the principals on the verandah of the "house of the living dead." In the film, a glass shot expands the scope of the set to gigantic propotions.

making a movie titled *White Zombie.* The Halperin brothers won the case and completed their movie for summer release, thereby introducing the zombie to motion pictures. The film had a box office star, Bela Lugosi, fresh from his successes in *Dracula* and *Murders in the Rue Morgue,* and the prestige of a United Artists release — quite an honor for an outside producer in those days.

Filming was done at the RKO-Pathé lot in Culver City, where the Garden of Gesthemane set from Cecil B. DeMille's *The King of Kings* (1927) was transformed into the mountaintop verandah of a sorcerer's castle, and at Universal City, where the magnificent interiors of the castle were assembled out of parts of the big sets from *Dracula* and *Frankenstein.* With much pre-production planning, the Halperins were able to produce their film with speed and economy and yet achieve a spectacular quality through utilization of large sets and imaginative special effects.

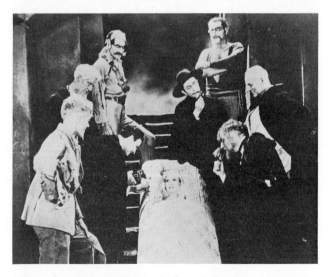

After the cameras stop grinding following a successful "take," the cast assumes a less foreboding attitude.

Lugosi later said bitterly that the Halperins offered him only $500 for a week's work in the picture (he did the job, he said, for $900). The leading lady, blonde and lovely Madge Bellamy, a prominent silent star, had been out of pictures for two years studying stage technique, and was intent upon re-establishing herself in cinema. She failed, however, to regain her following.

No movie ever has received a more thorough critical scourge than *White Zombie,* yet more recently it has gained notice as an outstanding film of the 'thirties. This belated acknowledgement is hardly as paradoxical as it seems, for in 1932 the fashion among critics was to take a condescending view toward genre films, especially horror pictures. Critics had been kind to *Dracula, Frankenstein,* and *Dr. Jekyll and Mr. Hyde* a few months earlier, but once a "horror fad" was established, the honeymoon ended.

White Zombie suffered even more than other such pictures because of an embarrassingly outmoded, silent-film style of acting — a failing of the Halperins, who nearly a decade later continued to insist upon heavy, pantomimic performances. Miss Bellamy's painted Cupid's-bow mouth suggests 1926 more than 1932.

Critics failed to note *any* of the elements that raise *White Zombie* above such handicaps. If the Halperins were unable to adjust to the talkies' new acting techniques, they certainly were ahead of their contemporaries in mastering sound as a dramatic device at a time when many directors were unable to reconcile the possibilities of a mix of sight and sound without sacrificing one to the other.

The brothers, who came from Chicago in the early 'twenties and set up their own production company, were continually theorizing and experimenting to find a scientific approach to moviemaking. They made graphs analyzing successful films in an effort to establish foolproof structural formulae. By the time they embarked upon *White Zombie,* they were in their mid-thirties and had made some thirty features. Having thoroughly studied available talking pictures, they reached the accurate conclusion that most contained too much talk and not enough action. They decided to hold dialogue to fifteen per cent — only what was necessary to advance the story. Just as a good artist will follow through with a planned design, the Halperins stuck with their decision, even though it meant they must prune pages from the script. The result is a rapid and smooth continuity. The longest stretch of dialogue, filmed in one exceedingly long "take," is Dr. Bruner's explanation of zombies, incorporating Article 249 of the Haitian Penal Code: "Also shall be qualified as attempted murder the employment of drugs, hypnosis or any other occult practise which produces lethargic coma, or lifeless sleep, and if the person has been buried it shall be considered murder no matter what result follows."

Sparseness makes dialogue all the more striking. Lugosi has the best lines, delivering them in his rich Hungarian accent with demonic intensity. His zombies, he boasts,

"work faithfully; they're not worried about long hours." Lugosi tells Robert Frazer he cannot hope to win the girl: "Not in a month nor even a year. I've looked into her eyes. She is deep in love — but not with you." After the girl has been made a zombie, Lugosi hears Frazer despairingly tell her that he must take her back; he interrupts with a smirking, "Back to the grave, *Monsieur?"* Lugosi seems evil incarnate as he introduces his gaunt servants: "In life they were my enemies. Latour, the witch-doctor, once my master; the secrets I tortured out of him! Von Gerde, the swine, swollen with riches; he fought against my spell even to the last. Victor Trisher, Minister of the Interior; Scarpia, the brigand chief. Marquis, Captain of the Gendarmerie. And this — this is Chauvin, the high executioner, who almost executed *me!"* When Frazer realizes his wine has been drugged, Lugosi explains, "I have taken a fancy to *you,* Monsieur." Harron, trapped by the zombies at the frantic climax, asks Lugosi who they are. He is told, "To you, my friend, they are the angels of death."

Lugosi's gusto complements the Gothic fairytale context, and better than adequate performances are delivered by Frazer, Joseph Cawthorn, Clarence Muse, and Brandon Hurst. Miss Bellamy is dynamic in pantomime, an inappropriate voice only occasionally marring her delicately rendered characterization. John Harron fares not so well. The convincingly cadaverous zombie makeups are the work of Carl Axcelle and Universal's remarkable Jack Pierce, who transformed Boris Karloff for such works as *Frankenstein* (1931) and *The Mummy* (1933). The sight of bullets thudding into the bared chest of the giant Chauvin without halting his advance or drawing blood is as frightening a moment as any film can offer.

Many scenes of strong depth are framed through trees and such architectural details as quatrefoils on the Castle Dracula staircase. The castle's gigantic main room is made to appear more so by glass shots in which artwork expands the scope. There are cavernous corridors (including the basement of Castle Frankenstein) where the characters must walk along narrow pathways to avoid a torrent of water. A balcony, from the set of the 1923 *Hunchback of Notre Dame,* hangs precariously over a chasm, and the clifftop verandah (also created by a blend of a huge set with glass paintings) exudes danger. The sugar mill is a dizzying mass of girders, catwalks, and huge windlasses. The Beaumont mansion and the crypt are no less impressive. Outdoor locations are used for the cemetery, lonely roads, and the jungle. Great shadows reminiscent of those in *The Bat Whispers* (1931) hover over many scenes. Memorable optical effects are a scene of the lovers' carriage with Lugosi's eyes superimposed and a diagonally split screen showing the mesmerized girl and her distraught husband. Transitional wipes and slow dissolves are used artfully. The opening of *White Zombie* anticipates a practice which has become widely used during the past three decades, with the scene of the roadway burial commencing before the

George Burr McAnnan, Joseph Cawthorn, Bela Lugosi.

titles appear. Long opening sequences, before the appearance of titles, are common today.

Fine use is made of long silences punctuated with sudden noises and occasional bursts of music. In this respect, *White Zombie* proves an ancestor of the unusual handling of sound in the Val Lewton productions *The Cat People* (1942) and *I Walked with a Zombie* (1943). The music was arranged by Abe Meyer, a silent picture maestro who, unable to get a musical directorship with any of the major studios after theatre orchestras became obsolete, undertook to supply scores for most of the independents. The native drumming and chants were composed by Guy Bevier Williams. Also commissioned for the film was a Spanish *jota* by Xavier Cugat; this work is properly unnerving in sequences where Harron pursues the vision of his lost bride. An unusually weird effect is produced by the tragic spiritual, "Listen to the Lamb," as hummed by alternating male and female choruses. Some action is underscored by appropriate agitatos from silent films.

Its flaws notwithstanding, *White Zombie* remains one of the most interesting and haunting of all horror films, largely because of the presence of the cruelly underrated Lugosi as its pivotal character. Sources close to the production have indicated Lugosi took charge of part of the writing and direction, perhaps intent on making the picture fit himself instead of sublimating his talents to fit the picture as was usually the case.

THE THIRTEENTH GUEST (1932)

(Monogram Pictures Corporation)

Produced by M. H. Hoffman; *directed by* Albert Ray; *from the book by* Armitage Trail; *continuity by* Francis Hyland; *adaptation by* Arthur Hoerl; *dialogue by* Armitage Trail; *production manager,* Sidney Algier; *Photographed by* Harry Neumann *and* Tom Galligan; *film editor,* Leete R. Brown; *art director,* Gene Hornbostel; *assistant director,* Gene Anderson; RCA *sound: filmed at* RKO-Pathé *Studio; running time,* 69 minutes; *released* Aug. 30, 1932.

PLAYERS: *Marie Morgan/Lela,* Ginger Rogers; *Phil Winston,* Lyle Talbot; *Captain Ryan,* J. Farrell Macdonald;

Detective Grump, Paul Hurst; *Harold "Bud" Morgan,* James C. Eagles; *Thor Jensen,* Eddie Phillips; *John Adams,* Erville Alderson; *Marjorie Thornton,* Frances Rich; *Joan Thornton,* Ethel Wales; *Captain Brown,* William B. Davidson; *Dick Thornton,* Phillips Smalley; *Dr. Sherwood,* Crauford Kent; *Detective Carter,* Tom London; *Policeman,* Al Bridge; *Winston's Date,* Adrienne Dore; *Marie's Father,* Charles Meacham; *Marie's Mother,* Isobel LeMall; *John Barksdale,* Robert Klein; *Cab Driver,* Harry Tenbrook; *John Morgan,* John Ince; *Wayne Seymour,* Allan Cavan; *Jail Sergeant,* Henry Hall; *Mike (Jailer),* Tiny Sandford; *Prisoner,* Kit Guard; *Prisoner,* Lynton Brent; *Photographer,* Bobby Burns.

J. Farrell MacDonald watches as Lyle Talbot examines Ginger Rogers for surgical scars.

Synopsis

Late at night a cab halts in front of the big, empty house at 122 Old Mill Road. The blonde passenger tells the driver to wait while she unlocks the front door. Meantime, a man's shadowy figure enters the back door. Inside, the young woman plays a flashlight over the sheet-covered furnishings and finds telephones in service. She dials the operator and demands to know why phones are connected in a house that has been vacant thirteen years. In the dining room she finds rats crawling among the decayed remains of a banquet. She draws from her purse an envelope on which is written, "To be handed to my daughter Marie Morgan on her twenty-first birthday," and which contains a message: "13-13-13." She envisions the persons who occupied the thirteen chairs thirteen years ago: her father, herself, her mother, lawyer Barksdale, aunt Lucille, uncle John, brother Harold, her childhood sweetheart Thor Jensen, her bratty cousin Marjorie, uncle Dick, aunt Joan, and uncle Wayne. The thirteenth chair was reserved for a secret guest who never arrived. At the sound of footfalls, she turns to flee. Outside, the cabbie hears a woman's scream, a gunshot, and maniacal laughter. The driver summons Police Captain Ryan and his bumbling helper, Detective Grump.

Private investigator Phil Winston's date with a pretty girl is interrupted by a call from Ryan. Winston arrives and is shown the body of a blonde, apparently Marie Morgan, seated at the table in the abandoned house. The coroner ascribes death to electrocution, but the chair is not wired. Ryan explains that Morgan, Sr., died at dinner thirteen years ago and that his wife closed the house that night, and "all these folks have been waiting for their dinner ever since." Morgan's will left the bulk of his fortune to the mysterious thirteenth guest. Ryan learns that Barksdale had the electricity and telephones restored. A dragnet is ordered for the lawyer. Ryan's car is stolen.

Next evening, Grump falls asleep while guarding the house. Barksdale steals inside. A hooded figure, watching from a secret room through a slot, presses a button and the 'phone rings. Barksdale picks up the receiver. The hidden figure closes an electrical circuit and Barksdale falls, twitching as the current courses through his body. Grump, wakened by the hideous scream, hurries to the police station. Ryan and Winston return with Grump, who defends his having abandoned his post by attempting to imitate the shriek and asserting that it sounded like "Tarzan . . . an' the devil, . . . an' a couple o' hyeenees throwed in!" They find the body of Barksdale at the table. Two policemen bring in Marie Morgan, very much alive. After someone had fired a shot at her the first night, she hid in the basement and later fled in Ryan's car. Winston reveals he had noticed scars around the dead girl's face, suggesting plastic surgery, and learned that her face had been remade to resemble Marie's by a Dr. Sherwood. Ryan suspects Barksdale, but Winston asks, "Then who killed the gentleman on your right?"

Winston gathers Marie and the six surviving guests at his apartment. Harold and Thor seem normal enough, but Dick and Joan seem ruthless; their daughter Marjorie is an overt nymphomaniac, and Adams is a rascally type. Uncle Wayne is believed to be in Japan. "Someone is determined to kill every person who attended that dinner thirteen years ago," says Winston. ". . . As Captain Ryan so elegantly describes it, 'The murderer intends to line that table with stiffs'." Winston, angered by the family's bickering, arranges for them all to be jailed as material witnesses.

The corpse of Wayne is found in the old house. Winston finds that all the suspects are still jailed. He orders that they be freed but followed. Wayne's body is in the library, pulsing with electricity from the phone clutched in hand. The killer has left the switch on, claiming another victim while in jail. The wires are cut, and it is found that the telephone is made of steel.

Dr. Sherwood names Thor as the man who arranged for surgery on the murdered girl. A call purportedly from Winston advises Marie to go the house. There, the masked man rings the telephone, but as she reaches for it the real phone in the receiving room rings. She sets down the steel phone an instant before the hooded man closes the switch. Winston is on the other line, warning her to get out, but before she can leave, the hooded man captures her.

59

The mystery man and the murder switch. (Frame enlargement.)

At the house, Winston and Harold confront Thor with the evidence. Thor confesses he and Barksdale hired a girl named Lela to impersonate Marie. Someone else, mistaking Lela for Marie, killed her after Thor frightened Marie away.

In a room below the killer's hideaway, the hooded man tries to force Marie to tell him the combination of a vault. At last she tells him: 13-13-13. The police break in just as the killer gets the safe open. Marie locks him in the vault. Unmasked, he proves to be Adams. The safe contains $1,000,000 in securities and a note from Marie's father, explaining that he did not trust his in-laws and made his curious will to give them time to kill each other before Marie would inherit the fortune. Winston decides not to let Marie's wealth stand in the way of his courtship.

Grump has meantime become intimate with Marjorie. As Ryan glares, the klutzy detective offers an excuse: "Well, you told me to tail her."

Notes

Outstanding by any standards, *The Thirteenth Guest* gave star billing for the first time to Ginger Rogers, a vivacious song-and-dance girl from Broadway who had attracted favorable attention at several major studios; and to Lyle Talbot, a second-string leading man at Warners. Both players justified this faith with thoroughly professional performances. They were destined for long and successful careers.

Monogram was started in 1931 by a group of veteran independents, including W. Ray Johnson and Trem Carr, with headquarters at Talisman Studios. M. H. Hoffman was a member for a short time; he preferred to work with his own production crew at Pathé, and after completing *The Thirteenth Guest* he withdrew to continue under his Allied brand. The film was a profitable item which Monogram kept in release for years on the strength of Miss Rogers' burgeoning popularity. In 1943 Monogram remade it as *The Mystery of the Thirteenth Guest*, unfortunately losing much of the charm of the original.

The story, by *Scarface* author Armitage Trail, invites atmospheric treatment. In the original screen interpretation, the exterior of the old house is real, and the Pathé interiors are properly weird. The hooded killer, who could have stepped from the cover of one of the era's pulp mystery magazines, seems part of the setting. The murderer's devilish methods are presented so graphically that the scenes of electrocution would not have passed the stronger censorship regulations instituted in 1934. Nor would some of the gags and an angry "Damn!" muttered by the hero.

Among support, J. Farrell Macdonald registers well as the apoplectic policeman. Paul Hurst, who alternated successfully between comic and villainous roles, provides much amusement as a dim-witted detective. Ethel Wales and Phillips Smalley are splendid as a ruthless society couple (understandably favored as a target of Poverty Row producers during the Depression!), and Erville Alderson does a clever job of depicting a personable rogue who proves to be a fiend.

Unusual comedy bits are well written and well performed. Particularly good is the sequence in which the wealthy members of the family, dressed in their finery, are cast into jail with an assortment of low-lifes. Funnier yet is Hurst's loud-mouthed attempt to demonstrate how the killer's howl sounded.

Photography is notable for its uncharacteristic use of changes in focus during scenes and for some striking night effects. The only music is a portion of Brahms' *Academic Festival Overture* at the opening.

THE HURRICANE EXPRESS (1932)

(Mascot Pictures Corporation)

Produced by Nat Levine; *directed by* Armand Schaefer *and* J. P. McGowan; *story by* Colbert Clark, Barney Sarecky, *and* Wyndham Gittens; *adaptation and dialogue by* Wyndham Gittens, Colbert Clark, Barney Sarecky, Harold Tarshis, George Morgan, *and* J. P. McGowan; *photographed by* Ernest Miller *and* Carl Wester, IATSE; *film editor,* Ray Snyder; *supervising editor,* Wyndham Gittens; *sound engineer,* George Lowerre; *music by* Lee Zahler; *sound,* Disney Recording Company; *a serial in* 12 chapters, 25 reels; *also released in a* feature version *running* 80 minutes; *released* August 15, 1932.

PLAYERS: *Larry Baker,* John Wayne; *Gloria Martin (Stratton),* Shirley Grey; *Edwards,* Tully Marshall; *Stevens,* Conway Tearle; *Jim Baker,* J. Farrell MacDonald; *Jordan,* Matthew Betz; *Hemingway,* James Burtis; *Walter Gray,* Lloyd Whitlock; *Mathews,* Joseph Girard; *Stratton,* Edmund Breese; *Jim,* Glenn Strange; *Sandy,* Al Ferguson; *Porter,* Snowflake (Fred Toomes); *Co-Pilot,* Eddie Parker.

Chapter Titles

1) The Wrecker; 2) Flying Pirates; 3) The Masked Killer; 4) Buried Alive; 5) Danger Lights; 6) The Airport Mystery; 7) Sealed Lips; 8) Outside the Law; 9) The Invisible Enemy;

who vows to avenge his father's murder. L&R officials suspect Gray is the Wrecker because of rivalry. Also under suspicion is Stratton, former railroad president, who has escaped from prison where he was sent for an alleged embezzlement. Gloria meets the vengeful Stratton, her father, at an isolated cabin.

L&R manager Edwards and lawyer Stevens interrogate persons involved in the collision. Carlson, who signalled No. 57, says he saw the engineer, Jordan, in the cab. Jordan is discharged and threatens to get even. Edwards and Stevens receive a warning tapped out in Morse code over the telephone that the *Express'* gold cargo will not go through. Stratton, Gloria, Gray, and Jordan, are all aboard the *Express* when it leaves. Larry finds Carlson bound. Wrecker henchmen Barney, Mike, Jim, and Sandy attack Larry, who leaps through a window and escapes in an auto with the heavies in pursuit. Meantime, the *Express* conductor is waylaid and in a moment apparently emerges from the room into which he was dragged. He steals the key to the gold car, shoots the fireman and guard, and knocks the engineer unconscious. Ahead, henchmen have placed a boxcar across the tracks. Larry pulls alongside the speeding train and leaps to the engine, fighting with the "conductor." The man fells Larry and climbs to the roof, where he removes the conductor's cap and jacket, then discards a lifelike mask of the conductor! A biplane lowers a rope ladder, and the Wrecker escapes.

Larry wakes in time to slow the train before it hits the boxcar. Stratton uncouples the train and escapes with the engine and gold car. Gloria and Larry board the engine and reason with Stratton, who wants the gold as a lever to make the L&R officials clear him of the false charge that sent him to prison. One of Gray's transport planes rakes the *Express* with machine gun fire, forcing Larry, Gloria, and Stratton to leap for their lives. The henchmen load the gold into the plane, which then is commandeered by Larry and his

John Wayne slugs it out with Ernie Adams, Glenn Strange, Lloyd Whitlock, Charles King, and Al Ferguson on a precarious freight-loading platform.

10) The Wrecker's Secret; 11) Wings of Death; 12) Unmasked.

Synopsis

When the L&R Railroad's No. 57 is ordered to a siding to permit passage of the famed *Hurricane Express,* a mystery man known only as the Wrecker strikes down the engineer of No. 57. Gloria Martin, secretary to the L&R manager, is a passenger on one of Walter Gray's airliners when she sees the *Hurricane* heading for collision with No. 57. She warns pilot Larry Baker, whose father Jim is engineer of the *Hurricane.* Against Gray's orders, Larry lands near a switch, smashes the lock, and routes No. 57 almost in time, but the *Express* smashes into the rear of the other train. Jim Baker dies in the crash. Gray fires Larry, friends. Disabled by machine gun fire, the plane crashes in flames as its occupants parachute to safety.

Larry borrows a car from a farmhouse while Stratton hides the gold. Larry tries to retrieve the gold but is attacked by the Wrecker's men. He escapes when a train demolishes the heavies' car. Gloria is kidnapped when she returns and imprisoned in a shack in the railroad yard. Then appears the Wrecker, who seemingly is Gray. Larry finds the hideout and rescues Gloria as the Wrecker escapes, leaving behind a mask of Gray. As Larry fights the henchmen, he is knocked from a platform onto the tracks. A train rushes over him, but he is unscathed because he lies between the tracks.

Stratton arranges to meet with Edwards to return the gold in exchange for proof of his innocence. Edwards arrives at the rendezvous, a deserted mine, but Gloria appears and declares the Wrecker is Edwards. Larry arrives with railroad detectives Hemingway and Matthews, but the Wrecker escapes after touching off a dynamite blast. A mask of Edwards is found. The Wrecker reappears later as Larry, and again as Edwards. The real Edwards overpowers the imposter and tears off the mask, but is killed before he can reveal the Wrecker's identity.

Tricking the Wrecker gang into a trap at the mine, Stratton and Larry are ambushed by a machine-gunning henchman. Matthews and Hemingway come to the rescue, killing the gunner. The Wrecker and his men escape. Stratton returns the gold, which Stevens orders shipped on the *Express.* Disguised as Jordan, the Wrecker prepares to stop the train at a point where his men are posted. Gray, who has been held by the gang, escapes to warn Larry and Gloria. Larry and Stratton get the drop on the henchmen, and Larry pursues the *Express* by car, transferring to the cab to battle the Wrecker, who now seems to be Gray. Shot by his own gun in the struggle, the Wrecker is carried from the train. When the real Gray appears, it becomes plain that

the Wrecker again is in disguise. The dying man proves to be Stevens.

The Wrecker admits he framed Stratton for his own thefts, made it appear Edwards was responsible, and murdered Edwards to gain control of the L&R. The wrecks were staged to bring down the value of the line. He planned to buy the company with stolen gold, frame Gray as the Wrecker, and in the same stroke eliminate airline competition.

Stratton regains leadership of the L&R and enters into negotiations with Gray to combine their operations. Larry becomes chief pilot and wins Gloria's hand.

Notes

John Wayne's second Mascot serial is in every way an improvement over *The Shadow of the Eagle.* The story is almost logical, and a great gimmick is introduced by having the mystery villain disguise himself as most of the principals at different times, making identification even more difficult than usual. This was not only a scary touch but also a clever economy move which made it possible for whichever cast members happened to be available on a given day to do double duty as the villain! Most of the filming was done in the San Fernando Valley and at Bronson Canyon. There are only occasional lapses of quality in the miniature work involving trains and aircraft.

The cast, as usual, consists of real pros whose presence gives the proceedings a touch of class. Nearly all the male principals, from the boyish Wayne to the doddering Tully Marshall, get a chance to do a Jekyll-Hyde characterization as the master criminal. Wayne obviously does a lot of his own stunt work, with Eddie Parker doubling some of the more harrowing action. Sniveling little Ernie Adams does a good job as the "brains" of the heavies.

Mascot regular Armand Schaefer co-directed with J. P. McGowan, whose name is indelibly associated with railroad melodramas. In 1914 McGowan directed the serial that started the trend, *The Hazards of Helen,* and his subsequent work included the railroad films *The Girl and the Game* (1915), *Whispering Smith* (1916), *The Lost Express* (1917), *The Railroad Raiders* (1917), *The Train Wreckers* (1925), *The Open Switch* (1926), *Peril of the Rail* (1926), *Red Signals* (1927), and *The Lost Limited* (1927). An Australian, McGowan directed at least 131 features and serials and played roles in many of them. He died in 1952.

In addition to the railroad action, *The Hurricane Express* features much footage of Ford Tri-Motor aircraft.

THE PHANTOM EXPRESS (1932)

(Majestic Pictures Corporation)

Charles King, John Wayne, Al Ferguson in Episode Six.

Produced by Irving C. Franklin *and* Donald M. Stoner;

written and directed by Emory Johnson; *photographed by* Ross Fisher; *film editor,* S. Roy Luby; *sound system,* RCA Photophone; *running time,* 70 minutes; *released* September 15, 1932.

PLAYERS: *Smoky Nolan,* J. Farrell MacDonald; *Bruce Harrington,* William Collier, Jr.; *Carolyn Nolan,* Sally Blane; *President Harrington,* Hobart Bosworth; *Axel,* Axel Axelson; *and* Lina Basquette, Huntley Gordon, Claire McDowell, Eddie Phillips, Jack Pennick, Robert Ellis, Carl Stockdale, David Rollins, Tom Wilson, Alan Forrest, Alice Dahl, Tom O'Brien, Brady Kline, Jack Mower, Jack Trent, *and* Bob Littlefield.

Synopsis

Smoky Nolan, a respected veteran engineer, is at the throttle of a locomotive speeding through the black of a moonless night. Signals tell him the track is clear, but suddenly the headlight of another train looms directly ahead. Smoky grinds the train to a halt, and it lurches from the tracks, pulling much of the consist with it. Although Smoky survives this, his first wreck, many others on board are killed in the disaster. There is no collision, however; the phantom locomotive which caused the accident vanishes without a trace.

Smoky, accused of negligence in the crash, appears before the railroad president, Harrington. While the engineer's daughter, Carolyn, awaits her father, she chances to meet Bruce Harrington, playboy son of the line's president. Bruce abruptly undergoes a change of character, having fallen for Carolyn; he astounds his father, who had considered Bruce a hedonistic sort, by asking for a job with the railway.

In particular, Bruce wants the assignment of investigating reports of a phantom express train which has caused a long series of wrecks leading up to the one involving Smoky's train. President Harrington agrees, and Bruce goes to live at the Nolan residence, at the far end of the line, under an assumed name.

The railroad president has heretofore resisted efforts to convince him to sell the line. But now, under pressure of the wrecks, he specifies a date on which he will make a decision.

Bruce's investigation has turned up much that invites suspicion, but he still cannot fathom the mystery of the disappearing train.

Smoky has, in the meantime, been dismissed in disgrace from the road. The news comes on his birthday, and he breaks down when he arrives home to find that Bruce and the Nolan family have prepared a party for him. Convinced that Smoky is innocent in the accident, Bruce continues the probe. From the pocket of one of the trainyard workmen, Bruce finds a letter threatening him. He and Axel, Smoky's fireman, follow this man. Elsewhere, hoodlums kidnap Carolyn and a friend who is posing as Bruce and lock them in a deserted barn.

Rescue follows, and Bruce overcomes the gang that is responsible for the wrecks. He has unearthed the secret of the phantom express — which in fact is not a train, but a low-flying airplane rigged with locomotive lights. The aircraft has been used to frighten engineers into derailment, then has soared away before it could collide with the train wreckage.

Upon revealing that the phantom "train" was the axis of a plot to force sale of the railroad, Bruce realizes that if he cannot reach his father within the hour, the sale will have been consummated. His father is ninety miles away, and a storm has destroyed all lines of communication. The only hope of getting through is by train, and Smoky is the only engineer who can make the run in time.

Smoky, glad for the opportunity to redeem himself, takes the throttle, and in a mad ride over crumbling bridges and through washouts and landslides he reaches President Harrington in time to save the railroad.

Notes

One of the better independent pictures of 1932 is Majestic's *The Phantom Express.* The film successfully combines a hint of the supernatural and a genuinely baffling mystery angle with the traditional railroad chase thriller, a popular hangover from silent days. Its story bears a strong resemblance to the Mascot serial, *The Hurricane Express,* which was released a month earlier, but a wide gulf separates the two in terms of quality. Writer-director Emory Johnson provided *The Phantom Express* with well-paced performances, snappy dialogue, and action sequences of a high order. By securing the cooperation of the Southern Pacific Railroad, the producers could achieve spectacular qualities quite beyond the scope of the usual independent production.

Many scenes were filmed in and around the machine shops and roundhouse of the Southern Pacific headquarters in Los Angeles, with about 125 steam locomotives appearing in the background. A wreck was staged in the Mojave Desert, utilizing an old locomotive, a tender, and several passenger coaches. The train was given a three-mile start and was travelling sixty miles per hour when the engineer and firemen leaped to safety, a moment before the engine struck a section of track that had been weakened. The train is seen to surge from the tracks and plough through the ground as the coaches pile up.

Although Johnson specialized in action pictures — his best known being *Westbound Limited* (1923) and *The Third Alarm* (1930) — he invested *The Phantom Express* with a great deal of atmosphere in its night scenes, setting dramatic lighting effects against stark blackness, and with some unnerving storm effects.

"Buster" Collier and Sally Blane (sister of Loretta Young) are appealing in the romantic leads, but the players are dominated by J. Farrell MacDonald and Hobart Bosworth, two fine character actors. Axel Axelson and Tom O'Brien provide comedy relief.

OUT OF SINGAPORE (1932)
a. k. a. GANGSTERS OF THE SEA

(Goldsmith Productions, Ltd.)

Produced by Ken Goldsmith; *directed by* Charles Hutchison; *screenplay by* John S. Natteford; *story by* Fred Chapin; *photographed by* Edward S. Kull; *film editor,* S. Roy Luby; *sound recording,* Freeman Lang; *assistant director,* Melville DeLay; *running time,* 61 minutes; *released* September 24, 1932.

PLAYERS: *Woolf Barstow,* Noah Beery; *Concha,* Dorothy Burgess; *Mary Carroll,* Miriam Seegar; *Scar Murray,* Montagu Love; *Steve Trent,* George Walsh; *Bloater,* Jimmy Aubrey; *Captain Carroll,* William Moran; *Bill,* Olin Francis; *Second Mate Miller,* Ethan Laidlaw; *Wong,* Leon Wong; *Captain Smith,* Horace B. Carpenter; *Snowball,* Snowflake (Fred Toomes); *Sailor,* Ernest Butterworth.

Synopsis

Old Captain Carroll is hard-put to find a first mate for his three-masted cargo ship, the *Marigold,* bound for Manila and Singapore. At last he signs on Woolf Barstow, whose loss of three ships has earned him an unsavory reputation. With Barstow is his scheming boatswain, Scar Murray. These two plot to gain control of the ship. Barstow also has designs upon Mary, the captain's pretty daughter. Barstow commences to poison the captain, causing him to fall ill of what appears to be some disease. Miller, the second mate, overhears the plotting of Barstow and Murray when the ship is in harbor at Singapore. The conspirators overpower Miller and drown him.

Barstow goes to a saloon operated by his friend, Wong, a Chinese merchant who has arranged to ship a fake cargo insured for a large sum aboard the *Marigold.* He also meets his old sweetheart, Concha, who is now a dancer at Wong's. Although many men desire her, Concha has remained true to her first love, Barstow. When Barstow spurns her in her dressing-room, Concha tries to knife him, but Barstow hurls her aside and walks out. To replace the missing second mate, Barstow hires Steve Trent, a derelict who is handy with his fists. Steve's pal, Bloater, ships on as cook.

Nearing death, Captain Carroll learns that Barstow plans to blow up the ship before it reaches Manila with Wong's mythical cargo. The old man struggles with Barstow, who mortally injures him. Barstow's show of kindness and concern fools Mary, but the plotter in fact seethes with rage, because he perceives that love is developing between Mary and the regenerated Trent.

Concha has come aboard as a stowaway. She and Mary

Noah Beery, Dorothy Burgess.

64

become friends, and at last the dancer convinces Mary of Barstow's villainy. Mary learns too late, however, for Barstow and Murray are beginning to work their scheme. Trent is overpowered during a fight with Barstow and is locked in the forepeak. Barstow informs Mary that she, Barstow, and Murray will be the only survivors of the ship and that she will be taken to a nearby island before the explosion.

He issues the stores of whiskey to the crew members, who soon become a drunken mob. To keep the men occupied, Barstow throws Concha to them. Concha escapes to find Barstow lighting the explosives. By a ruse she locks him in a room out of reach of the dynamite. Concha frees Mary and Trent, who in turn rescue the drunken Bloater. Steve kills Murray, and the three launch a lifeboat. Concha, meantime, has donned her most seductive costume and dances for the crewmen, who make sufficient noise to drown out Barstow's cries for help. Concha's sensuous dance of death ends as the ship is blown to bits.

Noah Beery, Dorothy Burgess.

Notes

Not only was Jack London's *The Sea Wolf* filmed several times, it also inspired a number of imitative pictures. One of the most entertaining of these is a Poverty Row product directed by the erstwhile serial daredevil, Charles Hutchison, for producer Ken Goldsmith, *Out of Singapore.* Much of the charm of this elemental tale derives from the presence of two of the screen's greatest portrayers of villainy, Noah Beery and Montagu Love. Truly an unprincipled pair, Beery and Love slowly slowly poison an elderly man, steal a ship in order to destroy it with all hands lost so they can collect on a non-existent but heavily insured cargo, beat and drown a ship's officer, kidnap the murdered captain's daughter, and throw Beery's former paramour to a

drunken crew. Dorothy Burgess is equally impressive as the vengeful dancing girl, appearing in revealing costumes that would not have been acceptable to the stringent Production Code Administration of two years later. George Walsh and Miriam Seegar do not fare well with the sound medium, she being too old-fashioned an ingenue and he lacking the vocal ability to match his splendid appearance; both had been notables of the pre-sound 1920s. Jimmy Aubrey and Snowflake (Fred Toomes) provide some welcome comic bits.

Goldsmith, a meticulous producer who later worked at Universal, gets a great deal out of a small budget, and Edward Kull's photography is up to par.

THE CROOKED CIRCLE (1932)

(World Wide Pictures)

Presented by E. W. Hammons; *produced by* William Sistrom; *directed by* H. Bruce Humberstone; *screenplay by* Ralph Spence; *additional dialogue by* Tim Whelan; *photographed by* Robert B. Kurrle; *sound recording,* William Fox; *art director,* Paul Roe Crawley; *film editor,* Doane Harrison; *music director,* Val Burton Western Electric *sound; running time,* 70 minutes; *released* September 25, 1932, *by* Fox Film Corporation.

PLAYERS: *Brand Osborne,* Ben Lyon; *Nora,* Zasu Pitts;

Crimmer, James Gleason; *Thelma,* Irene Purcell; *Yoganda,* C. Henry Gordon; *Harmon,* Raymond Hatton; *Harry,* Roscoe Karns; *Colonel Wolters,* Berton Churchill; *Kinny,* Spencer Charters; *The Stranger,* Robert Frazer; *Yvonne,* Ethel Clayton; *Rankin,* Frank Reicher; *Dan,* Christian Rub; *and* Tom Kennedy, Paul Panzer.

Synopsis

"To do for each other, to defend any brother — a fight to the knife and a knife to the hilt!" Such is the pledge of the Crooked Circle as voiced by its leader, Rankin, while the five hooded members touch a human skull at the centre of a round table. The group's enmity has been aroused by activities of the Sphinx Club, an amateur detective organization. The wealthy Brand Osborne has announced his resignation from the Sphinx Club at the behest of his fiancée, Thelma Parker. The members gather to meet Brand's successor, a Hindu named Yoganda, who is introduced by Colonel Wolters, senior member.

Yoganda, claiming psychic power, warns of imminent peril. The club recesses to meet later at Wolter's mansion,

Melody Manor. This is a weird place where "Something always happens to somebody," as Nora, the housekeeper, puts it. Old Dan, a retainer, reveals that strange violin music is heard at times, followed by disaster. The clock sometimes strikes thirteen. A hermit who resides nearby predicts odd occurrences.

Wolters disappears. A woman screams for help, and Brand recognizes the voice as that of Thelma. Neither person can be found. Patrolman Crimmer, having followed Brand's car to the manse, chances upon a hidden spring in the library, and a bookcase slides open, disclosing the body of Wolters. A violin string is about the neck. The unnerved cop disappears down a chute which leads from a chair in the house, threading its way outside between two graves.

Brand, who had been late in arriving because a man detained him at home, is surprised by the same man, who emerges from a large clock. As Brand gets the drop on the intruder, the butler, Rankin, intrudes and the stranger takes the chair exit. Rankin knocks Brand unconscious.

Brand accuses Yoganda of the trickery. Yoganda, however, leads the group to a wall panel, behind which he

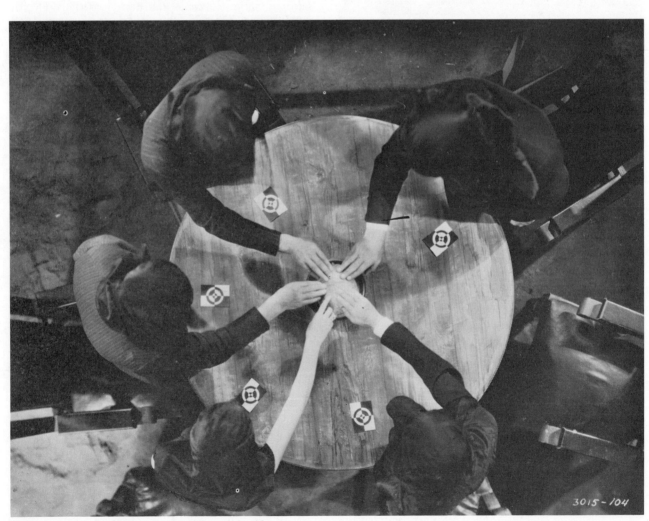

The meeting of the Circle at the opening of the film.

Zasu Pitts, James Gleason.

The villains are captured by C. Henry Gordon, Irene Purcell, and Ben Lyon. The Circle members are Robert Frazer, an unidentified player, Paul Panzer, and Frank Reicher.

reveals the Crooked Circle — with Thelma among the members.

The Hindu proves to be a Secret Service agent. Thelma is his assistant. Wolters appears, and Yoganda explains he placed the colonel in a suspended state, to keep the Circle from harming him. Soon all the mysteries are explained, and Crimmer is left to take credit for solving a case about which he knows nothing.

Notes

"Lucky" Humberstone's rare gift for balancing drama with comedy to showcase the best aspects of each was effectively demonstrated in his first directorial effort, *Strangers of the Evening.* His second, *The Crooked Circle,* is an even better example of farce-mystery, one which brought considerable prestige to World Wide, then the most consistently able of the small companies. The screenplay is an original by Ralph Spence, who wrote the hit play, *The Gorilla.* Spence was one of the best title writers for silent films and was a noted "picture doctor" who rescued many a pretentious flop after all else had failed. Here Spence alternates gags and scares about one-for-one with scintillating dialogue, avoiding dullness. *The Crooked Circle* defies classification; it opens with weird horror, then becomes a crook melodrama, develops into light comedy, and then returns to mystery. Somehow, it works.

The notable mixed comedy team of James Gleason and Zasu Pitts was introduced in this picture. The tough, easily exasperated Gleason and the quavering, graceful Miss Pits, opposites in every imaginable way, complement one another perfectly. The first-class cast also includes Ben Lyon, lead of the spectacular *Hell's Angels* (1930); pretty Irene Purcell, leading lady of Paramount's classic comedy, *Million Dollar Legs* (1932); the master of pomposity, Berton Churchill; Raymond Hatton, who is wonderfully eccentric as a sneaky hermit; C. Henry Gordon, in a good red herring role; Roscoe Karns, who adds neat comic touches; and Frank Reicher, the fine Munich-born actor from Broadway's Theatre Guild.

William Sistrom, a Fox producer, gathered for his first independent production a top-drawer crew. The splendid sets were designed by Paul Roe Crawley, of *The Bat Whispers* (1932). Photographer Robert Kurrle was one of Warners' best. The film editor was Doane Harrison, of Paramount. Reviewers and the public were enthusiastic.

AMORE E MORTE (1932)

(Aurora Film Corporation)

Directed by Cav. Rosario Romeo; *story and dialogue by* Cav. Rosario Romeo; *photographed by* Alfred Gandolfi *and* Nicholas J. Rogalli; *produced by* The Aurora Film Corporation of New York; *running time,* 94 minutes; *released* October 6, 1932.

PLAYERS: *Ruggiero de Agro,* Cav. Rosario Romeo; *Barbara,* Carmelina Romeo; *Mauro,* Antonio Ruggieri; *Lucia,* Ada Ruggieri; *Sylvestro,* Raffaele Bongini; *Chiara,* Clara Diana; *Minico,* Angelo Gloria; *Gennarino,* Guglielmo Onofri; *and* G. Perez, P. Perez, J. Busacco, A. Fratellone, *and* F. Colombo.

Synopsis

Indiscretions of its men have brought a curse upon the Agro family. Ruggiero de Agro, as ladies' man of a little farming community near Mount Etna in Eastern Sicily, neglects his wife and small children to such an extent that the wife must steal to survive. One of Agro's lovely victims, Chiara, dies after confessing her plight, and her grieving father sets out for revenge during the *festa de raccolta.* He is about to kill Agro when a terrific storm intervenes. The family curse is fulfilled with Agro's destruction by lightning.

A strange and compelling picture, the only production of Aurora Film Corporation of New York City, is *Amore e Morte (Love and Death)*. Adapted from a classic tragic drama of the *teatro dialatelle siciliano* and enacted by a cast of Sicilian-Americans, the production was filmed in the stony farmlands near Watchung Mountain in New Jersey. Its players, costumes, and props — including donkeys, ancient farm implements, and a Sicilian *caretto* drawn by a plumed horse — were for the most part taken from the Teatro d'Arte, a Sicilian theatrical troupe headed by Commander Giuseppe Sterni. A lonely stone farmhouse — complete with vineyards, orchards, and an isolated barn — is an appropriate setting for much of the action. Dialogue is Sicilian, Italian, and Italo-American, without subtitles.

Maintaining throughout an air of conviction and playing the family curse for full impact — particularly in a festival sequence with authentic singing and dancing, and during a climactic thunderstorm — the picture is superior to similar productions made in Italy at the time.

Rosario Romeo and his cast seem to have been known only to ethnic audiences; they perform with a professionalism which would justify substantially more widespread attention. The cameramen were well known in New York studios. Alfred Gandolfi photographed that remarkable and tragic expedition picture, *The Viking* (1931), and Nick Rogalli's many films include D. W. Griffith's last picture, *The Struggle* (1932). (The latter, a story of a drunkard's reformation, was so unpopular that United Artists withdrew it from circulation after a few showings.)

TANGLED DESTINIES (1932)

(Mayfair Pictures Corporation)

Presented by George W. Weeks; *produced by* Ralph M. Like; *directed by* Frank M. Strayer; *story and continuity by* Edward T. Lowe; *supervised by* Cliff Broughton; *film editor,* Byron Robinson; *photographed by* Jules Cronjager; *art director,* Ben Dore; *musical director,* Lee Zahler; *assistant director,* Vernon Keays; International *sound recording; produced at* International Studios; *running time,* 64 minutes; *previewed* October 18, 1932.

PLAYERS: Vera Reynolds, Glenn Tryon, Lloyd Whitlock, Doris Hill, Sidney Bracy, Gene Morgan, Ethel Wales, Syd Saylor, Mona Lindley, James B. Leong, William Burt, Henry Hall, and William Humphrey.

Synopsis

An airliner makes a forced landing at night in the desert. Through a dense fog a deserted house is seen. The passengers, the pilot, and the co-pilot — nine men and four women — take refuge in the house. A small power plant is put into service, and the thirteen are settling down for the

False priest Henry Hall covers the survivors. The victim on the floor is Ethel Wales. Beside her is Vera Reynolds. Others shown are Syd Saylor (left), James B. Leong, Gene Morgan, Mona Lindley, Glenn Tryon, Doris Hill, William Humphrey, and Sidney Bracy.

night when the lights go out. A shot is heard. When electricity is restored, it is discovered that one of the passengers has been murdered. Another passenger reveals himself to be a detective assigned to guard the victim, who was carrying a bag of diamonds. The bag is found, but the gems it contains are false.

The detective and a lawyer interrogate the survivors, all of whom become panicky save for an elderly woman — who tends to her knitting as though nothing were wrong — and a parson, who tries to calm the others. There is a second murder: The detective has come too close to the truth. Suspicion falls upon everybody before it becomes evident that the old lady has possession of the real jewels. She is killed by the supposed minister, a notorious jewel thief in disguise. The killer is overcome as the night of terror ends.

Henry Hall, Glenn Tryon, Syd Saylor, Ethel Wales, William Humphries, Lloyd Whitlock, Mona Lindley.

Although the title suggests a marital drama, *Tangled Destinies* in fact is a well-written, neatly played murder mystery with the perfect setting for a small-scale reign of terror: a desolate old house. The superiority of the dialogue and plotting, along with the professionalism of the thirteen players (all veterans of the stage and of silent pictures), easily diverts attention from the fact that the sets and lighting aren't quite up to the quality of the major-studio products. Suspense is present throughout, with dialogue well employed to keep the plot moving. Clever deployment of suspicion makes it virtually impossible to pick the real murderer out of the crowd, except by making a lucky guess. Apart from the aircraft sequence at the beginning, action is confined to the forbidding farmhouse, but the quality of direction keeps things moving. The acting is more than adequate, with Syd Saylor providing some well-timed brash humor, and Ethel Wales contributing a splendid portrait of a quiet lady with a Madonna's smile and a bag of priceless gems.

THE MIDNIGHT WARNING (1932)

(Mayfair Pictures Corporation)

Directed by Spencer Gordon Bennet; *story by* Norman Battle; *screenplay and dialogue by* John Thomas Neville; *photographed by* Jules Cronjager; *film editor,* Byron Robinson; *musical director,* Lee Zahler; *sound recording,* Homer Ackerman; Western Electric *sound; running time,* 63 minutes; *released* November 15, 1932.

PLAYERS: *William Cornish,* William (Stage) Boyd; *Enid Van Buren,* Claudia Dell; *Mr. Gordon,* Huntley Gordon; *Erich,* John Harron; *Dr. Stephen Walcott,* Hooper Atchley; *Rankin,* Lloyd Whitlock; *Dr. Brown,* Phillips Smalley; *Adolph Klein,* Lloyd Ingraham; *Dr. Barris,* Henry Hall; *and* Lon Poff *and* Art Winkler.

Synopsis

Just back from the Orient, Enid Van Buren returns to the hotel where she and her brother had checked in only a few hours before. None of the hotel personnel admits to remembering her brother, and when she examines the hotel register she finds it appears she came to the hotel alone. Doctors suggest that she is insane, explaining that the orphaned girl had no brother. Aided by her boyfriend, Erich, and a private detective, William Cornish, Enid sets out to learn what became of her brother. Cornish sifts the ashes of the hotel incinerator and finds a small piece of cartilage, which he explains to Erich is from a human ear. Enid, meantime, is driven near madness by what she believes to be the voice of her brother. A confrontation in a

Hooper Atchley and William (Stage) Boyd come to the assistance of Claudia Dell.

mortuary reveals that the hotel owners have conspired to destroy the missing man's body and all knowledge of his existence, because he died of bubonic plague in the hotel. Cornish and Erich rescue Enid from her tormentors.

Notes

A well-known story which seems to have originated during the Chicago World Fair of 1893 is the basis for *The Midnight Warning,* a low-budget film from Mayfair Pictures, successor to Action Pictures. Alexander Woolcott once wrote the parent tale for *The New Yorker* magazine, calling it "The Most Maddening Story in the World." As recently as 1951 it was used as the basis for a major English film, *So Long at the Fair,* with Jean Simmons and Dirk Bogarde.

William (Stage) Boyd's hard-bitten performance as an efficient private detective is one of the good things about *Warning.* The were two William Boyds in pictures at the time. The blond-haired Pathé-DeMille and RKO-Radio star became Bill Boyd for several years while the tough-talking Broadway star of *What Price Glory?* was billed as William (Stage) Boyd. Both men were hard drinkers, and each was continually being embarrassed by being blamed for the other's escapades. The death of (Stage) in 1935 resolved the problem, whereupon Bill, whose career was waning due to bad publicity, retrieved his full monicker and embarked upon a lucrative new career at Paramount as the star of the long-lived *Hopalong Cassidy* pictures.

Another mark of quality in *Warning* is the use of such unusual touches as having Boyd, watching from across the street, read the lips of a suspect entering a taxicab. In another scene he digs through ashes in search of a clue to a man's disappearance and finds some telling evidence: a piece of ear cartilage which, he explains, is more difficult to destroy than bone. The use of spectral voices to terrorize the girl into madness, and a grisly sequence in a morgue provide some memorable moments. Among the conspirators, Huntley Gordon, Hooper Atchley, Phillips Smalley, and Lloyd Whitlock stand out. Both sound and photography vary in quality.

Spencer Gordon Bennet began directing Pathé serials in 1920 and was a leading specialist in this form for thirty-seven years. His ability to work fast and shave production costs by "editing in the camera" made him a much-in-demand craftsman on Poverty Row, but this rare talent cheated him of the opportunity to display often the creative touches of which he was capable.

STRANGE ADVENTURE (1932)

(Monogram Pictures Corporation)

Produced by I. E. Chadwick; *supervised by* Trem Carr; *directed by* Phil Whitman *and* Hampton Del Ruth; *photographed by* Leon Shamroy; *story by* Arthur Hoerl; *adapted by* Lee Chadwick; *length,* seven reels; *released* November 20, 1932.

PLAYERS: *Lieutenant Mitchell,* Regis Toomey; *Toodles,* June Clyde; *Mrs. Sheen,* Lucille LaVerne; *Silas Wayne,* William V. Mong; *Dr. Bailey,* Jason Robards; *Claude Wayne,* Eddie Phillips; *Robert Wayne,* Dwight Frye; *Sarah Boulter,* Isabelle Vecki; *Stephen Boulter,* Alan Roscoe; *Gloria,* Nadine Dore; *Jeff,* Snowflake (Fred Toomes); *Coroner,* William J. Humphrey; *Officer Kelly,* Harry Myers; *Policeman,* Eddy Chandler.

Synopsis

A police cruiser lurches to a halt before the old, dark Wayne mansion, and two law officers are met at the door by the butler, Jeff. In the sitting-room of old Silas Wayne,

Jason Robards, Regis Toomey.

the policemen are told that someone will be arrested before the night ends. Wayne calls for a family assembly downstairs and tells the relatives he intends to read his will so as to let them know how much each member will benefit from his death. As Wayne commences to read he pitches forward. Dr. Bailey approaches to administer treatment; a knife is found in the oldster's heart. The police put everyone under house arrest and call Lieutenant Mitchell.

Mitchell, assisted by a pretty girl reporter called Toodles, questions the aged housekeeper Mrs. Sheen, the physician Bailey, and survivors, including nephew Robert Wayne, niece Sarah Boulter and her husband Stephen, and Silas Wayne's ward Gloria. Boulter seeks to direct suspicion toward Robert and Claude Wayne, cousins who are said to have quarreled over the beauteous Gloria. Mitchell locks Robert away, but a packed bag is the only trace he can find of Claude. Mitchell and Toodles leave the house; he returning to headquarters and she driving into an alley and reentering the Wayne place, flashlight in hand. Frightened by a hooded figure, she hides in an attic closet and suddenly bursts out, screaming for help. Claude is found dead in the closet.

Suspicion points to Boulter, Mitchell considers, but Mrs. Sheen's actions also are questionable. Then Gloria is captured by the hooded man, tied to her bed, and threatened with a dagger. Mitchell captures the assailant in a furious battle. Dr. Bailey is revealed to be the killer, having slain old Wayne while pretending to minister to him.

Notes

I. E. Chadwick was a leading independent producer who, during the 'twenties, established his own studio on Sunset Drive in Hollywood. His silents include the 1925 version of *The Wizard of Oz,* with Larry Semon as the Scarecrow and Oliver Hardy as the Tin Woodsman. Struggling to survive in the early talkie era, Chadwick joined W. Ray Johnson, Trem Carr, and other independents in establishing Monogram Pictures. An early Chadwick-Monogram effort, *Strange Adventure*, is a rather good variation on the then-popular theme of the gathering of heirs at an old mansion to hear the reading of a will. There are some effective scares, comedy by a couple of inept policemen and a frightened servant played by the expressive Fred ("Snowflake") Toomes, romance, and a hooded killer. The killer's costume, incidentally, did double duty in *The Thirteenth Guest* a few months earlier.

Regis Toomey is a pleasantly efficient detective and June Clyde a brazen reporter. William V. Mong snarls his way effectively through the role of the hated rich man. Jason Robards, Dwight Frye, and Alan Roscoe are the kind of suspects any mystery film should have, and Lucille LaVerne (D. W. Griffith's favourite villainess) is grimly present as the granite-faced housekeeper. Leon Shamroy's photography sets the menacing tone very well.

SAVAGE GIRL (1932)

(Freuler Film Associates – Monarch Pictures – Commonwealth Pictures Company)

Produced by Henry R. Freuler; *directed by* Harry S. Fraser; *story and screenplay by* N. Brewster Morse; *photographed by* Edward S. Kull; *film editor,* Fred Bain; *sound recording,* Homer Ackerman; *music by* Lee Zahler; *International sound recording; length,* six reels; *released* December 5, 1932.

PLAYERS: *The Goddess,* Rochelle Hudson; *The Scientist,* Walter Byron; *The Millionaire,* Harry F. Myers; *The Valet,* Theodore Adams; *The German,* Adolph Milar; *The Chauffeur,* Floyd Shackleford; *The Gorilla,* Charles Gemora.

Walter Byron, Adolph Milar, and Harry Myers meet the jungle girl, Rochelle Hudson.

Synopsis

A young scientist approaches a millionaire playboy for financing of an African expedition to find a legendary white goddess. Under influence of drink, the eccentric financier decides to make the trip himself and take along his valet and his sports car.

Quarreling develops among the safari. A villainous German finds the "goddess," who lives in the protection of a gorilla. Desiring the girl for himself, the German foments a native uprising. The scientist faces death by fire in a savage ritual when the millionaire and his servant drive through and rout the natives.

The German, in a fight which follows, clouts the scientist unconscious. Before a killing blow can be delivered, the gorilla intrudes and crushes the German. All ends in romance for the scientist and his "goddess."

Rochelle Hudson, Walter Byron.

Notes

Despite its imposing number of production companies, *Savage Girl* is strictly small-time, with but little claim to fame. It did give Rochelle Hudson her first leading role, which led to better things at RKO and Fox. It is interesting also for its casting of Harry Myers in a role similar to his unforgettable drunken millionaire of Chaplin's *City Lights* (1931). Also in the competent cast are Walter Byron, British romantic actor; Adolph Milar, specialist in portrayals of World War I villains; and Ted Adams, usually a heavy in Westerns but effective here in a light comedy part. The script, possibly suggested by Universal's *Lorraine of the Lions* (1925), is an early instance of the jungle-girl type film popularized some years later by Dorothy Lamour and Maria Montez. Instead of a sarong, Miss Hudson is fetchingly clad in a brief leopard-skin outfit. Harry Fraser, who usually directed Westerns, handled the picture in a straight melodramatic style. The photography is expertly done.

SECRETS OF WU SIN (1932)

(Invincible Pictures Corporation)

Presented by Maury M. Cohen; *produced by* George R. Batcheller; *directed by* Richard Thorpe; *adaptation by* William McGrath; *story by* Basil Dickey; *continuity by* Betty Burbridge; *photographed by* M. A. Anderson; *art director,* Edward C. Jewell; *film editor,* Roland C. Reed; *musical director,* Abe Meyer; *sound engineer,* Pete Clark; *assistant director,* Melville Shyer; *produced at* Universal City; *distributed by* Chesterfield Motion Pictures Corp.; RCA *sound; running time,* 65 minutes; *released* December 15, 1932.

PLAYERS: *Nona Gould,* Lois Wilson; *Jim Manning,* Grant Withers; *Margaret King,* Dorothy Revier; *Roger King,* Robert Warwick; *Miao Lin,* Toschia Mori; *Eddie Morgan,* Eddie Boland; *Wu Sin,* Tetsu Komai; *Charlie San,* Richard Loo; *Luke,* Luke Chan; *Wang,* Jimmy Wang; *Minister,* Lafe McKee; *Informant,* Henry Hall.

Synopsis

Undercover in Chinatown to investigate coolie-smuggling, *Tribune* managing editor Jim Manning foils a suicide try by Nona Gould, a writer, and gives her a job with his newspaper. Realizing suspicion, Manning relinquishes the investigation to reporter Eddie Morgan. Manning refuses Nona permission to help.

Eddie is served a drugged drink while visiting a shady restaurant with Wang, a hireling of Wu Sin. Nona trails a Wu Sin underling to where he meets two white men at a truck. She overhears plans to unload coolies from a speedboat linked to the ship *Hirondelle*.

Eddie is thrown out of the restaurant. By feigning sleep, he has heard details of the smuggling. Manning decides to hold the story until he learns who is behind the racket. Nona learns the *Hirondelle* is owned by Roger King, father of Manning's jealous fiancée, Margaret. Margaret denounces Nona, who admits her affection for Manning. King assures his daughter that Nona's charges are without foundation but later secretly meets Wu Sin and orders that Manning be silenced. Among the Tong, the lot of Manning's murder falls to Charlie San, lover of Wu's granddaughter, Miao Lin. Charlie refuses the assignment, but Wu sways him by offering Miao Lin as the prize for the deed.

Miao Lin, unaware that Manning is the intended victim, confides in Nona. When Manning learns of King's alliance with Wu Sin, and ignores Margaret's pleas to shield her father, she breaks the engagement.

Charlie San wounds Manning. Nona wins Manning's leniency for Charlie, by explaining the circumstances. The newspaper exposé breaks. Wu Sin commits suicide. King and Margaret sail aboard the *Hirondelle*. Charlie San is paroled and marries Miao. Manning and Nona marry.

Notes

Maury Cohen's Invincible Pictures joined George Batcheller's venerable Chesterfield Motion Picture Corporation in 1932. The merger created an aggressive little company which in its heyday turned out a picture a month. Most of the team's product was filmed on rented sets at Universal in North Hollywood, the remainder being made at RKO-Pathé in Culver City. Strangely enough, the company made numerous mystery films, a couple of all-out horror yarns, and many romantic society dramas — but no Westerns. Most of its 1932-'33 product was directed by Richard Thorpe.

The popular "yellow peril" theme surfaced in *Secrets of Wu Sin,* a fanciful original by Basil Dickey, author of dozens of serials from the Pearl White epics into the 'forties. Continuity is engineered by Betty Burbridge, equally noted for a stream of silent and talkie Western scripts. The picture has pace, action, and a nice atmosphere of menace, and it showcases Thorpe's evolving command of direction.

Acting is good for the most part, with well-cast principals. The Japanese Tetsu Komai's evil Chinese, Wu Sin, strikes a sharp contrast with his best-remembered role, that of the doggedly faithful manservant to Charles

Laughton in *Island of Lost Souls* (1932); Komai has kept active in television into this decade. *Secrets* also boasts the presence of authentic Chinese actors Richard Loo, Luke Chan, and Jimmie Wang. Within a decade a long procession of World War II movies found them specializing in portrayals of Japanese war criminals. Another Japanese, Toschia Mori, has a Chinese part in *Secrets*.

Use of standing sets, and Universal City's magnificent collection of authentic Oriental properties give *Secrets* a substantial appearance well beyond what the budget otherwise would have permitted. The film's only music is a delicate Oriental theme played under the credits.

THE DEATH KISS (1932)

(World Wide Pictures, Incorporated)

Presented by E. W. Hammons; *produced by* KBS *at* California Tiffany Studios; *executive producers,* Burt Kelly, Samuel Bischoff, *and* William Saal; *directed by* Edwin L. Marin; *from the novel by* Madelon St. Dennis; *screenplay by* Barry Barringer *and* Gordon Kahn; *photographed by* Norbert Brodine; *film editor,* Rose Loewinger; *supervising editor,* Martin G. Cohn; *art director,* Ralph M. DeLacy; *sound engineer,* Hans Weeren; *musical director,* Val Burton; Western Electric *sound system; running time,* 75 minutes; *released* December 24, 1932, through Fox Films.

PLAYERS: *Franklyn Drew,* David Manners; *Marcia Lane,* Adrienne Ames; *Joseph Steiner,* Bela Lugosi; *Detective Lt. Sheehan,* John Wray; *Officer Gulliver,* Vincent Barnett; *Leon Grossmith,* Alexander Carr; *Tom Avery,* Edward Van Sloan; *Howell,* Marold Minjir; *Hilliker,* Wade Boteler; *Assistant Director,* Al Hill, *Script Clerk,* Barbara Bedford; *Chalmers,* Alan Roscoe; *Mrs. Avery,* Mona Maris; *Brent,* Edmund Burns; *Hill,* Jimmy Donlin; *Clerk,* Harold Waldridge; *Todd,* Lee Moran; *Doorman,* Wilson Benge; *Mechanic,* Eddy Chandler; *Gaffer,* Harry Strang; *Bill,* Eddie Boland; *Cop,* Frank O'Connor; *and* Forrest Taylor, Paul Porcasi.

Synopsis

As Myles Brent leaves a palatial night spot, a beautiful woman suddenly embraces and kisses him, then hurries inside. The kiss is a signal to gangsters parked nearby, and Brent falls in a volley of gunfire.

The camera pulls away to reveal that the scene has taken place on a sound stage where a movie called *The Death Kiss* is being filmed. Tom Avery, the director, calls for a retake,

telling Brent, "When you die this time let's have less gymnastics, and don't spin like a top when you fall." A moment later it is discovered that Brent actually has been shot to death. Avery notifies Leon Grossmith, head of Tonart Studio, who cries, "Oy! That's gonna cost me a fortune!" Steiner, the general manager, calls the police and tries to establish order.

Detective Lt. Sheehan finds a note on Brent that implicates his former wife, Marcia Lane, the actress who delivered the "death kiss" in the fatal scene. Then Franklyn Drew, author of the screenplay, butts in with the suggestion that Sheehan should "pin the murder on the murderer, if that's not against the rules." Drew, who is in love with Marcia and is anxious to clear her, points out that she was on the other side of the set from where the gunfire took place. The possibility is explored that one of the guns used by the players may have fired a real bullet, but it is found that these guns are .45-calibre, whereas the slug that killed Brent was a .38. Gulliver, a dimwitted studio cop, brings in a suspect, Chalmers, an extra, who is carrying a loaded .38. Chalmers admits he had considered using the gun on Brent, who had him discharged, but it has not been fired. Despite his protestations of "Oy, what a calamity" Grossmith also had a motive for killing Brent, for in a tense scene, he reveals that he is in love with Marcia.

A print of the murder scene is received, and everybody gathers in the projection room to see what the film will reveal. Before the crucial footage can appear on screen, the film bursts into flame. The operator has been clubbed, and a cigarette with a rouged tip was used to start the fire. As plans are made to order another print, the lab reports that the negative has been destroyed with acid. Sheehan's suspicion is aroused by the makeup director's statement that only Marcia uses the kind of rouge found on the cigarette.

Prowling the darkened stage, Drew finds a .38-calibre pistol planted in a spotlight and rigged so that it will fire when the spot is turned on. A distorted reflection appears in the lamp, and Drew is clubbed down. When Gulliver awakens him, the gun has disappeared. Drew and Gulliver go to see Chalmers, who was the studio's head electrician before he became a hopeless alcoholic. They find Chalmers dead in his bungalow, poisoned by acid. A suicide note under Chalmers' right hand includes a confession to the murder of Brent, but Drew notes that Chalmers' watch is on his right wrist, indicating that he was left-handed. Someone poisoned Chalmers' gin by reaching through the delivery service door of the ice box. This murder further implicates Marcia, in Sheehan's estimation, when the detective finds tire marks from Marcia's roadster outside Chalmers' house and learns that the poison was battery acid from the same car.

Drew learns that Brent took his many paramours to the Cliffside Inn and finds a love letter signed "Agnes." Sheehan finds Marcia in Steiner's office and arrests her on suspicion. Drew notices a photograph of Steiner's wife, signed "Agnes" in the same handwriting as was on the letter. A visit to the Cliffside Inn and a chat with a gossipy bellboy reveal to Drew that Brent was there with a dark-haired woman on the previous evening and that another man arrived and was beaten up by Brent after an altercation.

At the studio, Steiner decides to re-shoot the death scene on the standing set using a double for Brent, thus enabling the studio to finish the picture and make good its $239,351 investment. Marcia arrives in Sheehan's custody, and Avery arrives with his wife and sets to work. Drew hurries in with the information he found at the Cliffside Inn, and Sheehan finds this interesting but not conclusive. Then Drew learns that .38-calibre guns were ordered for the murder scene and the .45-calibre weapons were sent by accident. Sheehan agrees that the person who ordered the guns did so with knowledge of the .38 concealed in the lamp. Drew and Sheehan are standing near an open microphone, and their conversation is overheard.

Abruptly the lights are doused. There are shots and screams. Electricians man the spotlights and pick out a figure hiding in the catwalks overhead. As the police close in, the killer leaps toward another platform, misses, and falls to his death. Sheehan turns the body over as Mrs. Avery comes through the crowd. Looking down at the dead face of her husband, Mrs. Avery, the woman at the Cliffside Inn, snarls, "He's dead, yes! Well, I'm glad."

Notes

"Mine dear Mr. Little," dictates Leon Grossmith, president of Tonart Pictures, as his simpering secretary takes a letter, "Since I read your scenario I have come to the absolutely conclusion that your name . . . fits you something beautiful. And furthermore and yet besides . . ." As played by Alex Carr, the veteran co-star of Samuel

Goldwyn's silent *Potash and Perlmutter* series, Mr. Grossmith is a recognizable early Hollywood type: the powerful but uneducated immigrant executive. Later, when a hard-headed police detective fails to recognize a Tonart star, Grossmith wails, "Over a million dollars we spend advertising her and he . . . do'know who is Marcia Lane."

There are other recognizable — if slightly caricatured — types at Tonart, the big studio actually played by little Tiffany Studios in *The Death Kiss*. Bela Lugosi's Joseph Steiner, the studio manager, is almost fatherly — except in one scowling confrontation. Grossmith's secretary, portrayed by Harold Minjir, minces and flutters. Edward Van Sloan, as a noted director, is curt and cutting on the sound stage but warm and chatty off. The assistant director is a tough guy, played by real-life ex-gangster Al Hill. Barbara Bedford, as a script clerk, epitomizes cool efficiency. A matinee idol, played by Edmund Burns, is a cad. His beautiful co-star, Adrienne Ames, seems appropriately haughty, yet likeable. Of Alan Roscoe, as a down-and-outer who formerly had a good job at the studio, it is said that he "would drink anything that wasn't too thick to chew." A cold-blooded publicist, Jimmy Donlin, works hard at projecting a nice-guy image to harassing newspapermen. The grips, electricians, cameramen, and other artisans go about their tasks with wise-cracking coolness.

From such characters comes much of the charm of *The Death Kiss,* a well-made murder yarn that presents a more honest and entertaining view of the goings-on about a movie studio than is customary in pictures of this kind. The assumption by moviemakers that the public is entirely ignorant of the workings of a movie company has been demonstrated as recently as *Won Ton Ton, the Dog That Saved Hollywood* (1976), in which a chase supposed to be happening on a movie lot during the silent era was filmed among rows of sound stages. By respecting the viewer's intelligence, *The Death Kiss* touches upon many of the related functions of the studio personnel from top to bottom, without interrupting the progression of the story.

The murder investigation is more conventional: The police are apoplectic and hard-headed, becoming understandably nettled when the scriptwriter-hero regales them with such lines as, "I was beginning to be afraid that you might say something sensible." At one point John Wray, in charge of the investigation, moans that he can remember "when murders were nice, clean, simple things done with machine guns and meat axes, but *this* case . . ."

Although the presentation of the crime-solving script writer differs little from that of the crime-solving reporter of innumerable movies, David Manners speaks better English, his deductions are always logical, and he has a vested interest in the case rather than being merely a "buttinsky." Manners generally is considered a "Tennis, anyone?" sort of hero because of his mild-mannered characterizations in *Dracula* (1931), *The Mummy* (1935), *The Black Cat* (1934), and *The Mystery of Edwin Drood*

(1935), popular Universal horror films. In *The Death Kiss* he delivers a snappy performance far more winning than those for which he is better known. Comedy relief is offered by an incredibly stupid studio security guard played by Vince Barnett, who had just scored heavily as Paul Muni's sycophant in *Scarface* (1932).

An interesting touch is the use of hand-coloring, an effect seldom employed in talkies. When the murder film is being projected and suddenly catches fire, the screen turns red. During the climactic chase scenes there are yellow spotlights and red flashes of gunfire.

At thirty, Edwin L. Marin, who had been an assistant director since 1919, received his first solo assignment in *The Death Kiss*. Marin soon graduated to the majors, where he was considered one of Hollywood's more versatile and dependable directors. He died in 1951, having directed fifty-six features including *Bombay Mail* (1934), *A Christmas Carol* (1938), *A Gentleman After Dark* (1942), *Tall in the Saddle* (1944), *Johnny Angel* (1945), *Nocturne* (1946), and *Fort Worth* (1951).

The lurid title, an advertising campaign which depicted Lugosi ogling Adrienne Ames' throat, and the presence of three of the leading players from *Dracula* — Lugosi, Manners, and Van Sloan — led the customers to expect further vampiric delights. Such misleading ballyhoo alienated the horror fans, but the picture delighted the critics, who responded with enthusiastic reviews.

THE INTRUDER (1932)

(Allied Pictures Corporation, Ltd.)

Produced by M. H. Hoffman; *associate producer,* M. H. Hoffman, Jr.; *directed by* Albert Ray; *story and screenplay by* Frances Hyland; *photographed by* Harry Neumann *and* Tom Galligan; *art director,* Gene Hornbostel; *film editors,* Mildred Johnston *and* Leete R. Browhn; *gowns by* Alfreda; *sound recording,* Homer C. Ellmaker; *musical director,* Abe Meyer; *production manager,* Ray Culley; *RCA Victor recording; produced at* RKO-Pathé Studio; *running time,* 66 minutes; *released* December 25, 1932.

PLAYERS: *John Brandt,* Monte Blue; *Connie Wayne,* Lila Lee; *Daisy,* Gwen Lee; *Reggie Wayne,* Arthur Housman; *Valet,* Sidney Bracy; *Wild Man,* Mischa Auer; *Cramer,* Harry Cording; *Samson,* William B. Davidson; *Mr. Wayne,* Wilfred Lucas; *Purser,* Lynton Brent; *Hanson,* Jack Beek; *Captain,* Allen Cavan.

Synopsis

A passenger aboard the S. S. *Intruder* is murdered. John Brandt assists the captain in trying to solve the mystery, but before much headway is made, the ship is wrecked in a storm. The survivors reach a desert island, where they are terrorized by weird sounds from the jungle and by fear that the killer will strike again. A cave containing several

Monte Blue wonders what the tipsy Arthur Housman is up to.

skeletons is found. Brandt is accused of being the murderer, but another killing occurs. The captain and two girls, Connie and Daisy, flee into the jungle to escape the mysterious killer. They encounter a fanatical wild man, but are rescued by Brandt, who then exposes and captures the man who committed the second murder. The group is rescued by a passenger ship. Before they reach port, Brandt reveals the identity of the first victim's killer.

Notes

A creation of the same writer-producer-director team responsible for the better-known *The Thirteenth Guest* and *A Shriek in the Night, The Intruder* is wilder and funnier than either. Extravagant and unpredictable, this curious mystery-adventure yarn would rank among the more engaging thrillers of its time if not for some obvious miniature effects and an unevenness of photographic style. The studio photography (mostly shipboard scenes) is of a consistently high quality; not so with some of the island night scenes. There are two murders, a jungle wild man (played to the hilt by Mischa Auer), a shipwreck, skeletons, an inebriated playboy (the best "drunk" impersonator of his day, Arthur Housman), and plenty of suspects — all of which keep things rolling for an hour-and-then-some with hardly a pause. Monte Blue is a stalwart hero, mature and assertive, and Lila Lee — despite ill health — a delightful leading lady.

TOMBSTONE CANYON (1932)

(World Wide Pictures, Inc.)

Presented by E. W. Hammons; *a* K-B-S *production filmed at* California Tiffany Studios; *directed by* Alan James; *photographed by* Ted McCord; *executive producers,* Burt Kelly, Sam Bischoff, *and* William Saal; *story by* Claude Rister;

continuity by Earle Snell; *film editor,* Dave Berg; *supervised by* Irving Starr; *settings by* Ralph M. DeLacy; *sound supervision,* Hans Weeren; *musical director,* Val Burton; *costumes,* Elizabeth Coleman; *set decorations,* Eddie Boyle; RCA *recording; running time,* 62 minutes; *released* Dec. 25, 1932.

PLAYERS: *Ken Mason,* Ken Maynard; *Jenny Lee,* Cecilia Parker; *The Phantom,* Sheldon Lewis; *Alf Sikes,* Frank Brownlee; *Sheriff,* Bob Burns; *Clem,* George Gerring; *Colonel Lee,* Lafe McKee; *Henchmen,* Jack Clifford, Edward Peil, Sr., *and* George Chesebro; *Himself,* Tarzan the Wonder Horse.

Synopsis

Cowpuncher Ken Mason, who has reason to wonder about his parentage, receives a note from Luke Waley promising to tell who Ken "really is," along with instructions that he come to Tombstone Canyon. At the entrance to the Canyon, a burst of gunfire greets Ken. He is rescued by Jenny Lee, daughter of a neighboring rancher to Luke,

who has sent her to meet Ken. They hear a shrill cry — the scream of a phantom killer who is terrorising the locality.

Luke has been shot and dies before he can give Ken the promised information. Ken and the Sheriff decide that whoever killed Luke must be intent upon keeping Ken from learning his own background. They connect the Phantom with the death.

Ken goes to work for Colonel Lee, and he and Jenny decide to marry. Alf Sikes, owner of the Lazy S Ranch, is the only person besides Luke to know of Ken's arrival, and Ken decides Alf will be able to tell something of the questioned identity. He is convinced of this when the Sheriff arrives with a warrant for Ken's arrest — sworn out by Sikes.

Masquerading as the Phantom, Ken forces Alf to admit that he killed Luke and that he knows the names of Ken's parents. Before the rancher can tell, his son Clem and several Lazy S hands return, forcing Ken and Jenny into an abrupt departure. One of Sikes's men is killed by the Phantom. Convinced that Ken is the Phantom, the ranch-hands ride to town to organize a posse. Ken narrowly escapes a lynch mob before the Sheriff can take him into protective custody. Sikes and his men overhear Ken and the Sheriff discussing a plan to arrest Sikes for the murder of Luke. They free Ken through a ruse and murder the Sheriff under circumstances that implicate Ken.

Ken escapes to Tombstone Canyon, where he captures some of the posse members and ties them up in a cave. The Phantom finds the bound men, killing such of them as are Lazy S hands and promising to free the others when he finds Sikes.

The Phantom gets the drop on Alf and Clem, and then he identifies himself as Alf's brother, Matt, whom Alf had many years ago left for dead after trampling his face to make it unrecognizable. The Phantom asks the whereabouts of his son, and Alf is forced to admit that the son is alive — that, in fact, he is working for Colonel Lee. Ken rushes out of hiding, and the Phantom shoots him. Alf tells the Phantom he has shot his own son.

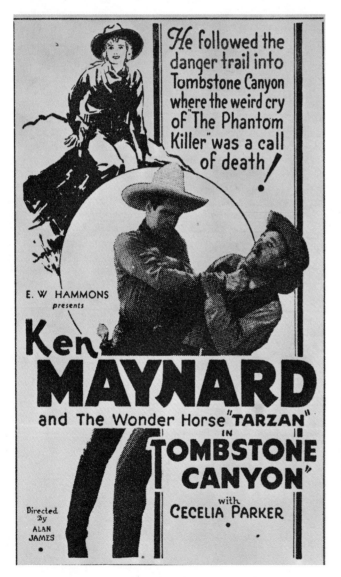

Ken Maynard and Cecilia Parker hear the cry of the Phantom. Photographed in the Red Rock Canyon in the Mojave Desert.

Alf is thrown from the cliff to his death. The Phantom shoots Clem, who is trying to force Ken off the cliff. As Clem wounds the Phantom, Colonel Lee and Jenny arrive. The Phantom, dying, begs Ken not to think harshly of him.

Notes

Ken Maynard's early-'thirties Westerns were so popular that he had his choice of scripts, directors, and support. Many of the screen stories, in fact, were written by Maynard, who seldom took credit. He also wrote music and shot second-unit secnes for many of his pictures. *Tombstone Canyon* is one of several good Maynard productions made at Tiffany, during a period of estrangement from his home studio, Universal. Maynard had an explosive temperament and had displeased Carl Laemmle, Jr., Universal's production chief.

Superb horsemanship and athletic abilities and virile good looks, along with a lighthearted air, more than compensated for Maynard's limitations at acting. He often mingled a liking for bizarre themes with the expected outdoor action. The blend of weird mystery with hard riding and gunplay rescued his films from the stereotype and made them the most memorable of the genre.

Maynard's Universal team handled direction and photography on *Tombstone Canyon.* Exteriors were filmed in Red Rock Canyon in the Mojave Desert, an area of unusual rock formations which has figured prominently in such diverse productions as *The Mummy,* the *Flash Gordon* serials, *Planet of the Apes* (1968), and *Apache Drums* (1951).

Tombstone Canyon contains enough killings, both cold-blooded and hot-blooded, to rival the Italian Westerns of forty years later, as well as chases, gunfights, and combat atop a cliff. The really striking feature, however, is the grotesque Phantom, who haunts the region like some Shakespearean ghost. The role is played by the grand old villain of silent pictures, the Clutching Hand himself, Sheldon Lewis. Lewis applies here the same intensity he poured into his 1920 version of *Dr. Jekyll and Mr. Hyde.* Old-fashioned histrionics and a horrific makeup of his own creation make Lewis' Phantom one of the strangest characters in any film. One of the many luminaries of the silents who had fallen upon lean times since the talkie surge, Lewis uses his voice most effectively here, contriving to make it sound grating and mechanical. He even supplies the Phantom's weird cry and, for the climax, a hair-raising death-rattle.

Cecilia Parker, a popular matinee ingenue who became a *Hardy Family* co-star, is an appealing heroine. The Arkansas comedian, Bob ("Bazooka") Burns, is the Sheriff. In a reissue of *Tombstone Canyon,* after Burns had become a star at Paramount, Burns' name was moved up to the co-starring spot originally occupied in the main title by Tarzan, Maynard's Palomino horse.

1933

THE HORROR (1933)

(Bud Pollard Productions, Incorporated)

COMPANY PERSONNEL: *producer-director,* Bud Pollard; *camera,* Dal Clawson; *art director,* Lester; *set decorations,* John Alsteadt; *assistants to producer,* Joe Banon *and* Frank Passar; *musical director,* William David; *sound supervisor,* Jerre Barton; *produced at* Bud Pollard Studios, Grantwood, New Jersey; *distributed by* Stanley Distributing Corporation.

Notes

Bud Pollard (whom researchers sometimes confuse with Universal's distinguished director, Harry Pollard) was an admitted producer of exploitation pictures, operating his own studio in New Jersey. Little is known of his product, for the films were roadshown at specialty houses rather than being released in the conventional manner.

For the 1933 season, Pollard announced a lineup including three films whose titles suggest they belong in this book. One is *The Horror.* The latter two, *Lunatic at Large* and *The Green Jade,* are likely suspects, but whether these were produced is a question we have been unable to resolve.

The Horror, however, definitely went into production, as evidenced by existing stills and posters. While these show a great deal — a "mystery mansion" setting, an apparent madman, Eastern mystics, an ape-like creature — they actually reveal little. One player's resemblance to Lon Chaney, Sr., has prompted speculation that the makeup was an attempt to capitalize on the popularity of the "man of a thousand faces," but this serves little more purpose than to slur Pollard's marketing savvy; Chaney had died three years earlier. We have been unable to identify any of the players, and we have yet to discover anybody who has seen *The Horror.*

BUD POLLARD

DIRECTOR

◆

1933-1934 RELEASES

SIX EXPLOITATION FEATURES

"THE HORROR"

"DANCE HALL DAMES"

"LUNATIC AT LARGE"

"METROPOLITAN MURDERS"

"FRAMED"

"THE GREEN JADE"

◆

723 SEVENTH AVENUE

Telephone BRyant 9-2180   New York City

Bud Pollard's tradebook advertisement for the '33-'34 season.

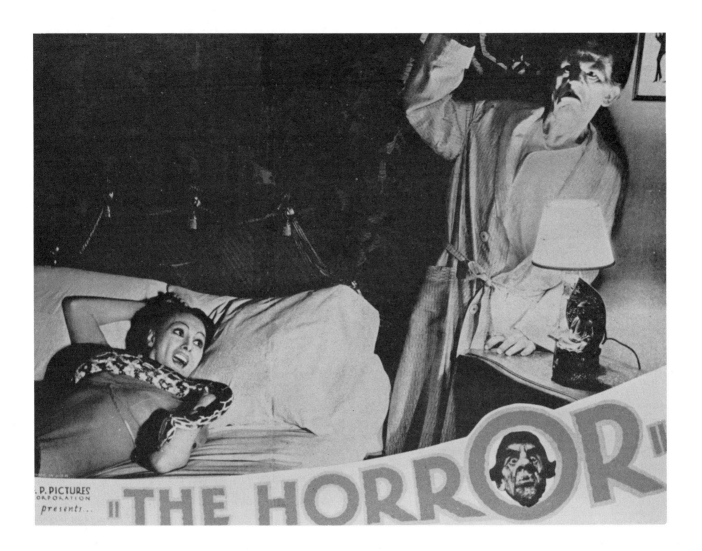

THE WHISPERING SHADOW (1933)

(Mascot Pictures Corporation)

Produced by Nat Levine; *directed by* Albert Herman *and* Colbert Clark; *supervising editor*, Wyndham Gittens; *story by* Barney Sarecky, George Morgan, Norman S. Hall, Colbert Clark, *and* Wyndham Gittens; *photographed by* Ernest Miller *and* Edgar Lyons, IATSE; *film editors*, Ray Snyder *and* Gilmore Walker; *sound engineer*, Homer Ackerman, International Recording Engineers; *production manager*, Larry Wickland; *associate producer*, Victor Zobel; *continuity*, Howard Bimberg; *cameraman*, Victor Scheurich; *assistant directors*, George Webster *and* Theo ("Doc") Joos; *cutter*, George Halligan; *sound supervisor*, Terry Kellum; *musical director*, Abe Meyer; *a serial in* 12 chapters, 25 reels; *also released in a* six-reel feature version; *released* January 15, 1933.

PLAYERS: *Professor Strang*, Bela Lugosi; *Vera Strang*, Viva Tattersall; *Jack Foster*, Malcolm McGregor; *President Bradley*, Henry B. Walthall; *Detective Raymond*, Robert Warwick; *The Countess*, Ethel Clayton; *Steinbeck*, Roy D'Arcy; *Sparks*, Karl Dane; *Young*, Lloyd Whitlock; *Slade*, Bob Kortman; *Jerome*, Lafe McKee; *Bud Foster*, George J. Lewis; *Williams*, Jack Perrin; *Kruger*, Max Wagner; *Foreman*, Kernan Cripps; *Driver*, Eddie Parker; *Detective*, Gordon DeMain; *Mitchell*, George Magrill; *Dupont*, Tom London; *Jarvis*, Lionel Backus; *Deane*, Norman Feusier.

Chapter Titles

1) The Master Magician; 2) The Collapsing Room; 3) The All-Seeing Eye; 4) The Shadow Strikes; 5) Wanted for Murder; 6) The Man Who Was Czar; 7) The Double Room; 8) The Red Circle; 9) The Fatal Secret; 10) The Death Warrant; 11) The Trap; 12) King of the World.

Synopsis

Trucks of a transport-storage firm are being wrecked by agents of the Whispering Shadow, a gang boss who can project his voice and his shadow anywhere. Drivers are slain and cargoes robbed. Each attack is heralded by failure of the radio apparatus in a laboratory atop the warehouse. The Shadow's identity is unknown even to his men, who are fearfully aware that disobedience means death. He can see and hear through walls, and he can electrocute men by remote control. Raymond, a criminologist, is hired to investigate.

When driver Bud Foster is killed, his brother, Jack, gets on the Shadow's trail and soon receives warning that he is doomed. Jack determines that each hijacked truck had carried a box destined for The House of Mystery, a wax museum run by Professor Strang. A magician and sculptor, Strang makes lifelike figures that move and speak. Jack is clubbed down by Strang, who places the blame on an animated caveman statue. Jack becomes interested in Strang's pretty daughter, Vera.

Kruger, a Shadow henchman, is captured by Jack. When police question him, he is electrocuted by the Shadow, who

is meeting with his men at a secret headquarters. "Kruger's light has gone out," the Shadow tells them. Besides Strang, others who invite suspicion are Steinbeck, the radio room technician, who is assisted by Sparks, a big, stupid Dane; Bradley, president of the transport company; Jerome, a mysterious official of the firm; Slade, an escaped convict; a Russian countess, *et al.*

Shadow henchmen land on top of the warehouse in an autogyro and are fought off by Jack. The craft crashes into radio wires and is wrecked. Bradley is murdered by the Shadow. Slade, too, is killed. At last, after many fights and close escapes, Raymond and Jack close in on the Shadow. Jack learns that the Russian Crown jewels are hidden in the warehouse. It is revealed that Jerome is a Russian prince and Strang a high government official on the trail of the jewels. In a surprise move, Jack proves that the Whispering Shadow is the innocuous-looking Sparks, who is arrested.

Notes

The Whispering Shadow is the first of four serials in which Bela Lugosi appeared and an early instance of Mascot's use of a star name above the title. Even as a "red herring," Lugosi adds an admirably sinister note. Further substance is provided by such silent-era stars as Henry B. Walthall, Robert Warwick, Malcolm McGregor, George Lewis, Ethel Clayton, Roy D'Arcy, and Jack Perrin. Viva Tattersall (Mrs. Sidney Toler), stage actress and playwright, is lovely as Lugosi's daughter. Much of the acting, especially that of Lugosi and McGregor, is a bit heavy for the talkies. Karl Dane, a master pantomimist and comedian whose strong Danish accent brought an end to stardom when silent pictures died, had one of his last roles in this serial. He committed suicide in 1934 after a period of unemployment.

Much of the filming involved the Bekins warehouse in Hollywood. There is strategic use of a fine miniature of the building. A miniature truck crash is effective, as is depiction of the Shadow via animation.

THE VAMPIRE BAT (1933)

(Majestic Pictures Corporation)

Produced by Phil Goldstone; *directed by* Frank R. Strayer; *story, screenplay, and dialogue by* Edward T. Lowe; *photographed by* Ira Morgan; *art director,* Daniel Hall; *film editor,* Otis Garrett; *sound engineer,* Richard Tyler; *sound system,* RCA Photophone; *made at* Universal City; *running time,* 67 minutes; *released* January 21, 1933.

PLAYERS: *Otto von Neimann,* Lionel Atwill; *Ruth Bertin,* Fay Wray; *Karl Brettschneider,* Melvyn Douglas; *Gussie Schnappman,* Maude Eburne; *Kringen,* George E. Stone; *Herman Gleib,* Dwight Frye; *Emil Borst,* Robert Frazer; *Martha Mueller,* Rita Carlisle; *Gustav Schoen,* Lionel Belmore; *Sauer,* William V. Mong; *Georgiana,* Stella Adams;

Holdstadt, Paul Weigel; *Weingarten,* Harrison Greene; *Dr. Haupt,* William Humphrey; *Gertrude,* Fern Emmett; *Schmidt,* Carl Stockdale.

Synopsis

The village of Kleinschloss in Central Europe is in turmoil over a series of slayings. Townspeople are found slain in bed, their blood drained. Police Inspector Karl Brettschneider maintains the fiend is human, but he cannot gain a clue to overcome the villagers' fear of a vampire. The town has been all but overrun by huge bats.

The esteemed Dr. Otto von Neimann is ministering to old Martha. Herman Gleib, the village idiot, learns that Martha is a victim of one of the attacks. Herman displays an affection for bats, and the residents reason he must be the vampire.

Neimann's assistants, Ruth and Emil, are at work in the laboratory. Aunt Gussie joins them, complaining affably about their overwork, the clamminess of the laboratory, and the general depression of the castle in which they live. Brettschneider visits and discusses the vampire scare with the doctor. Von Neimann insists there can be such a creature.

Lionel ATWILL Fay WRAY in *The* VAMPIRE BAT
A MAJESTIC PICTURE

Paul Weigel, William V. Mong, Lionel Belmore, Melvyn Douglas, Harrison Greene.

Martha dies, and Neimann pronounces her the victim of a vampire. The villagers drive Herman to his death in a cave and pound a stake through his heart.

Von Neimann hypnotizes Emil and, after some hesitation, orders him to strangle Georgiana, a loyal servant. When the doctor has finished with the corpse, Emil returns it to the bed, unaware of his role in the crime.

Georgiana's body is found. A crucifix, which von Neimann has planted on the body, implicates Herman — but word reaches the castle that Herman is dead. Brettschneider institutes a search for the real killer. The doctor advises Brettschneider to wait until morning and gives him a quantity of pills which supposedly will quiet his nerves.

Von Neimann sends Emil to kill Brettschneider. Ruth overhears and confronts her employer, who binds her in the laboratory. The frenzied von Neimann tells Ruth what his experiments have produced:

"Life — created in the laboratory. No mere crystalline growth, but tissue — living, growing tissue. Life that moves,

Dwight Frye shows one of his pets to Maude Eburne.

pulsates, and demands food . . . You shudder in horror! So did I, the first time; but what are a few lives to be weighed in the balance against the achievements of biological science? Think of it: I have lifted the veil! I have created Life — wrested the secret of life *from* life! Now do you understand? From the lives of those who have gone before, I have created life!" (The "life" is a spongy handful.)

Brettschneider has overcome Emil, and the two go to the castle. Emil, upon realisation of what he has done while hypnotized, kills the doctor and himself. Von Neimann falls into the "life" apparatus and wrecks it.

Notes

Although the independents made many weird thrillers to cash in on a vogue, precious few of them were all-out horror films in the Universal tradition. Such a rarity is *The Vampire Bat,* a curious marriage of vampirism and science fiction — which might easily be mistaken for a Universal picture of the era. To accentuate the similarity, the show was filmed on the Universal lot on rented sets which figured in celebrated horror pictures. The town is the familiar Village Frankenstein, the von Neimann home is *The Old Dark House* (from James Whale's 1932 film of that name), furnished in part from the manse in the 1927 *The Cat and the Canary,* and the morgue is the cavernous wine cellar of Castle Frankenstein. A torchlit chase resembles the pursuit of the Monster in *Frankenstein,* although it was filmed in Bronson Canyon instead of among Universal's man-made cliffs. Even the cast includes Universal veterans — Lionel Atwill, Melvyn Douglas, Dwight Frye, and Lionel Belmore — and scripter Edward T. Lowe was scenarist of Universal's *The Hunchback of Notre Dame* (1923).

Just as Ronald Colman was the perfect Bulldog Drummond, Warner Oland the perfect Charlie Chan, Margaret Dumont the perfect foil for Groucho Marx, and Boris Karloff the perfect Frankenstein Monster, so was Lionel Atwill the definitive mad scientist. Atwill's smile could be more menacing than any scowl, his clipped English speech could substantiate the most extravagant claims about "life eternal," and his enthusiasm could convince anyone that he really believed his wildest theories. He was a handsome, personable man who seldom wore unusual makeups — a notable exception is Warners' *Mystery of the Wax Museum* (1933) — but he was frightening simply because he could project insanity with conviction. A deft moment in *The Vampire Bat* is all that is necessary to prove Atwill's belief that his discovery is so monumental as to transcend moral qualms. In this scene, Atwill's hypnotized slave steals toward a victim, a woman for whom Atwill obviously has strong affection. The killer suddenly halts as Atwill's telepathic control wavers. Atwill, staring in self-horror, gulps, falters, then mutters, "Well, she's no better than the others," and wills his slayer to strike.

Inhabitants and vistas of Faustin Wirkus' adopted land. The kneeling figure at lower right is "King Faustin I."

Fay Wray, too, was perfection as the lady in distress. Though her abilities embraced a far greater dramatic range than she was allowed to reveal in films, producers were quick to discover that red-blooded males in the audience would have given their eye-teeth to be the lucky guy who protects Miss Wray from the menaces in such epics as *The Most Dangerous Game* (1932), *King Kong* (1933), *Doctor X* (1932), *Mystery of the Wax Museum* (1933), and *Below the Sea* (1936). More than a real beauty, Miss Fay projects in films in quality of innocence that contrasts powerfully with madmen and monsters. *The Vampire Bat* was her third and last horror session with Atwill.

Melvyn Douglas, a clever and resourceful hero, is a pleasant relief from the mild leading men of most horror pictures of the time. Dwight Frye, who gained a following as a portrayer of nervous lunatics at Universal, has a meaty role here as the village idiot. George E. Stone is good in an all-too-brief part as a frightened townsman. Robert Frazer is a sympathetic menace, William V. Mong is the most sniveling of aldermen, and Lionel Belmore is again (as in *Frankenstein*) the ideal burgomeister. Maude Eburne provides some amusing scenes as Miss Wray's hypochondriac aunt and delivers the closing gag of the picture wherein she mixes some of Atwill's impressive-sounding chemicals and, after taking them, learns that they add up to epsom salts.

Frank Strayer's direction makes amends for the misfire of *The Monster Walks*. High-calibre photography by Ira Morgan, then of M-G-M, is another important factor in the film's success. Melodramatic opening music, courtesy of Meyer Synchronizing Service, comprises the widely used *mysteriosi* by Charles Dunworth and Jean de la Roche, *Stealthy Footsteps* and *The Ghost Walks*.

VOODO (1933)

(Principal Distributing Corporation)

A Principal-Adventure *production;* presented by *Sol Lesser;* produced by *Faustin Wirkus; narrative by* Frederick Shields; *film editor,* Carl Himm; *music by* Brown & Spencer; Western Electric Sound *by* Balsley & Phillips; *running time,* 36 minutes; *copyrighted* March 31, 1933.

PLAYERS: Faustin Wirkus *and* Natives of La Gonave.

Synopsis

Faustin Wirkus, a white man and former administrator of La Gonave, an island thirty miles off Haiti, returns to study the strange religious customs of the black inhabitants. He sees Voodoo ceremonials in which goats and chickens are sacrificed to the ancient African gods. Eventually he encounters a ritual in which a girl is to be sacrificed. Wirkus rescues the girl and escapes the wrath of the cult.

Notes

For three years Faustin Wirkus ruled some 10,000 black inhabitants of La Gonave, where jungle superstitions held sway just as they had in the Eighteenth Century. A Marine Corps sergeant stationed as the sole white overseer of the island in 1925, Wirkus befriended the natives and became so popular he was crowned King Faustin I. Later he returned to the island and filmed this remarkable study of Voodoo practices, released as *Voodo,* with an uncommon spelling of the word. The wild ending involving a human sacrifice was staged to make the picture something more than a travelogue. Wirkus' camerawork is surprisingly good, and his narration is less overdone than is often the case in similar films. *Voodo* was released in four reels, an arbitrary length which made for booking difficulties because it was too long to be considered a short subject and too short to be rated a feature. Even with the added dramatization, *Voodo* is a good, factual study of primitive religion. The musical score intensifies the mood of the film.

SUCKER MONEY (1933)

(Willis Kent Productions)

Produced by Willis Kent; *directed by* Dorothy Reid *and Melville Shyer;* story and screenplay by *Willis Kent; film editor,* S. Roy Luby; *photographed by* William Nobles; *produced at* Talisman Studios; *running time,* 70 minutes; *released* April 5, 1933, *by* Progressive Pictures.

PLAYERS: *Swami Yomurda,* Mischa Auer; *Claire Walton,* Phyllis Barrington; *John Walton,* Ralph Lewis; *Jimmy Reeves,* Earl McCarthy; *Mame,* Mae Busch; *Lukis,* Fletcher Norton; *and* Mona Lisa, Al Bridge, Anita Faye.

Synopsis

Swami Yomurda is a charlatan who uses phoney seances and spiritualistic paraphernalia to cheat wealthy believers. He also uses hypnosis to advance his schemes, and he has resorted to murder on at least one occasion. When John Walton, a wealthy banker from Oshkosh, arrives in the city with his pretty daughter, Claire, Yomurda uses the girl in a plot to bilk Walton of his fortune. Jimmy Reeves, who is in Yomurda's employ, actually is a newspaper reporter working under cover to expose the racket. Jimmy falls for Claire, and when Yomurda places her in a trance, Jimmy rescues her. The Swami receives his desserts at the hands of the police.

Notes

The death of silent film idol Wallace Reid, as the result of a long drug habit, was one of the most notorious Hollywood scandals of the early 'twenties. Reid's widow, Dorothy, with missionary zeal, embarked upon a campaign to expose the drug evil through motion pictures. After a decade of crusading against narcotics as actress and writer, Mrs. Reid co-directed for Willis Kent a low-budget picture exposing another evil then having a field day in Hollywood, the fake spiritualism racket. The subject had been dealt

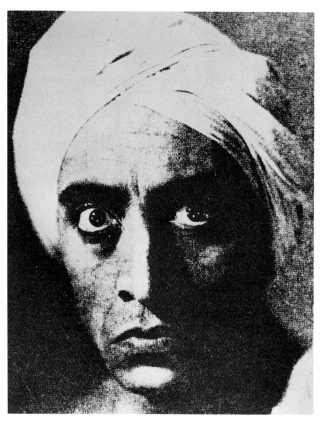

A Mischa Auer specialty – the Hindu charlatan.

with more expertly in several silent pictures such as Tod Browning's *The Mystic* (1925). *Sucker Money* suffers from clumsy writing (by the producer, Kent) and poor direction. The only bright spots are the presences of Mischa Auer in his oft-repeated role as a turbaned villain, Mae Busch in her specialty as a tough dame, and Ralph Lewis in an uncharacteristic appearance as a small-town sucker.

THE THREE MUSKETEERS (1933)

(Mascot Pictures Corporation)

"A modern version of the famous story by Alexander Dumas"; *produced by* Nat Levine; *directed by* Armand Schaefer *and* Colbert Clark; *supervising editor,* Wyndham Gittens; *story by* Norman Hall, Colbert Clark, Ben Cohen, *and* Wyndham Gittens; *dialogue by* Ella Arnold; *photographers,* Ernest Miller *and* Tom Galligan, IATSE; *music by* Lee Zahler; *film editor,* Ray Snyder; *sound engineer,* Homer Ackerman; International Film Recording Company *sound; a serial in* 12 chapters, 25 reels; *also released in* feature version, *running time,* 90 minutes; *released* April 7, 1933; *different* feature version, *70 minutes, released* 1948 *by* Favorite Films, *title,* DESERT COMMAND.

PLAYERS: *Clancy,* Jack Mulhall; *Renard,* Raymond Hatton; *Schmidt,* Francis X. Bushman, Jr.; *Tom Wayne,* John Wayne; *Elaine Corday,* Ruth Hall; *Armand Corday,* Creighton Chaney; *El Kadur,* Hooper Atchley; *Colonel Duval,* Gordon De Main; *Major Booth,* Robert Frazer;

Stubbs, Noah Beery, Jr.; *Ali,* Al Ferguson; *Ratkin,* Edward Piel; *Captain Boncour,* William Desmond; *El Maghreb,* George Magrill; *Colonel Brent,* Robert Warwick; *El Shaitan,* Wilfred Lucas; *Henchman,* Merrill McCormick; *Arab,* Ken Cooper; *Arab, Legionnaire, Stunt Double,* Yakima Cannutt.

Chapter Titles

1) The Fiery Circle; 2) One for All and All for One! 3) The Master Spy; 4) Pirates of the Desert; 5) Rebels' Rifles; 6) Death's Marathon; 7) Naked Steel; 8) The Master Strikes; 9) The Fatal Cave; 10) Trapped; 11) The Measure of a Man; 12) The Glory of Comrades.

Synopsis

El Shaitan (the Devil), mysterious leader of a band of brigands known as the Devil's Circle, has duped a young member of the Foreign Legion, Armand Corday, into joining. The band's near-massacre of a Legion detachment horrifies Armand, whose American friend, Army pilot Tom Wayne, dives his biplane into the fray and routs the Arabs with machine guns. Landing, Wayne meets the surviving legionnaires: Clancy, Renard, and Schultz, known as the Three Musketeers. Tom's fiancée, Elaine, is Armand's sister. El Shaitan forces Armand to trick Tom into delivering

contraband arms from Paris. Tom is arrested, but escapes, and flies to the Corday house. Armand, remorseful and contemplating suicide, writes a note clearing Tom and implicating El Shaitan. El Shaitan kills Armand just as Tom arrives to confront him. When Elaine and her Arab servant, Ali, rush in it seems that Tom shot Armand.

Tom escapes. Ali cuts the note so it seems to accuse Tom as the leader of the Devil's Circle and gives it to Elaine. In town, the Musketeers rescue Tom from an Arab mob. Tom soars away with his mechanic pal, Stubbs, but a Legion biplane piloted by El Shaitan forces them to land. As Arab horsemen pursue the plane along the ground, Tom leaps onto one of the riders, throws him off, and with Stubbs riding behind him tries to outdistance the Arabs. Gunfire downs the horse and kills Stubbs. Legionnaires drive off the Arabs, and Tom accompanies them to the Arabs' hideout, an old fort. Tom and the Musketeers scale a wall and open the gates. Elaine is there with El Kadur, a Shiek, and accuses Tom of murder. He is jailed, but the Musketeers help him escape. The four find El Kadur and his men at the Devil's Cauldron, a canyon combed with caves. Spying on El Kadur is the mysterious Major Booth, an American disguised as an Arab. Tom and Renard narrowly escape death, when El Kadur tries to dump them into the canyon. The Musketeers are captured and sentenced to be shot. Tom and Elaine rescue them, and Elaine realizes she has been tricked by Ali. At Ratkin's store, Tom bests Booth in a fight and retrieves the incriminating letter which, along with the excised parts, will clear him. As Tom and Elaine ride toward the fort, El Shaitan's men chase them. El Maghreb, a lieutenant of El Shaitan, leaves Tom unconscious in the desert and captures Elaine and the letter.

The Musketeers tell Colonel Duval they suspect El Kadur is El Shaitan. Tom learns that Elaine is imprisoned at an old fort, and while rescuing her he is wounded by El Shaitan. Arrested and convicted of murder, Tom faces a firing squad. In Duval's airplane, Elaine takes the letter, which El Kadur retrieved, to Colonel Foiray, who grants a reprieve. The plane is sabotaged, and Elaine must land before she reaches the fort. Tom is saved because the Musketeers loaded the rifles with blanks. Elaine delivers the reprieve, and a new trial is ordered. At El Kadur's insistence, Duval has the Musketeers arrested.

The Devil's Circle condemns El Maghreb to death. Elaine is wounded by a knife when she follows El Maghreb, who is killed by El Shaitan. Tom escapes and finds El Shaitan's garb hidden in Duval's office. Tom hides in Ratkin's store, where he is given an Arab disguise. After penetrating the cave of the Devil's Circle, Tom is believed killed in an explosion. He is discovered by Booth, who gives chase. In a fall from his horse, Booth breaks a leg. He explains to Tom that he is a Secret Service man whose suspicious behavior is the result of his attempts to identify El Shaitan. Returning to Ratkin's store, Tom sees Ratkin fighting El Shaitan, who is unmasked as Duval. Tom captures Duval, who is exposed to El Kadur and Colonel Denmoyne, whom Elaine has brought. Duval says he knows the identity of the real El Shaitan, but before he can say more he is shot by Ali. Tom chases Ali into the desert, captures him, and imprisons him in the Corday house. Ali is forced to reveal the password to the Devil's Circle meetings, "The sun rises in the east." Tom, disguised as Ali, attends a meeting. Ali escapes and warns El Shaitan. Tom fights for life when El Kadur and Colonel Demoyne arrive with their men to arrest the Circle members. El Shaitan escapes through a secret door and is tracked to Ratkin's store. Tom proves that Ratkin is El Shaitan. After a fight, Ratkin tries to shoot Tom but is shot down by the Musketeers.

Notes

This last and best of John Wayne's Mascot serials has everything a Saturday serial fan could want. There is even spectacle in this fast-moving Foreign Legion tale, with hordes of horsemen thundering across the dunes near Yuma, Arizona, and storming through desert villages yelling, "Death to the unbelievers!" Underneath the burnooses and beards are the same riding extras who appeared in scores of Westerns — a fact betrayed by their drawling voices. There is skilful photography of the riders, the desert, some vintage settings left by silent era producers, and the crags of Bronson Canyon.

Wayne's heroic aides are a doughty trio: the effervescent Jack Mulhall, Raymond Hatton (with a French accent!), and Francis X. Bushman, Jr., a genial giant who adds some comic touches by carrying large German sausages which he alternately gnaws and uses as weapons. Two other sons of famed silent stars — Creighton (Lon, Jr.) Chaney and Noah Beery, Jr. — are prominent in the first chapter, in which both are killed. Ruth Hall, Lee Garmes' pretty and athletic wife, furnishes the love interest.

The modern Musketeers are Jack Mulhall, Raymond Hatton, and Francis X. Bushman, Jr. Their D'Artagnan is John Wayne.

Mascot's insistence that the secret identity of the villain be maintained to the last, spurred the makers to new heights of subterfuge. El Shaitan is impersonated by Yakima Canutt, Robert Frazer, and Gordon De Main — who all have other roles — and by Wilfred Lucas, who does not otherwise appear. Visual and circumstantial evidence against Frazer, De Main, and Hooper Atchley is piled on until the last moments, when an innocuous and inconspicuous shopkeeper suddenly is revealed as the arch-fiend. In addition to appearances as El Shaitan and several minor characters, Canutt also doubles Wayne in numerous feats, but is not mentioned in the credits in any capacity.

The title song by Lee Zahler is the only music other than the throbbing drums of the Devil's Circle.

A SHRIEK IN THE NIGHT (1933)

(Allied Pictures Corporation)

Produced by M. H. Hoffman; *directed by* Albert Ray; *screenplay by* Frances Hyland; *story by* Kurt Kemplar; *associate producer,* M. H. Hoffman, Jr.; *production manager,* Sidney Algier; *photographed by* Harry Neumann and Tom Galligan; *film editor,* Leete R. Brown; *art director,* Gene Hornbostel; *gowns by* Alfreda; *music supervisor,* Abe Meyer; *sound recording,* Homer C. Ellmaker; *sound system,* RCA Potophone; *produced at* RKO-Pathé Studio; *running time,* 70 minutes; *released* April 15, 1933.

PLAYERS: *Patricia Morgan,* Ginger Rogers; *Ted Rand,* Lyle Talbot; *Wilfred,* Arthur Hoyt; *Inspector Russell,* Purnell Pratt; *Pete Peterson,* Harvey Clark; *Augusta,* Lillian Harmer; *Martini,* Maurice Black; *Maid,* Louise Beavers; *Editor Perkins,* Clarence Wilson.

Synopsis

A shot, followed by a scream, shatters the night at a

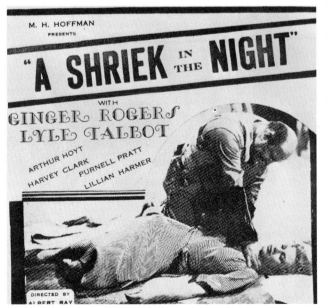

The reporters bring mobster Maurice Black to bay.

big-city hotel. Then a body hurtles from a high window to the sidewalk. Dull, sleepy Pete Peterson, the janitor, finds the corpse and identifies it as a tenant, Mr. Harker. The police arrive, headed by the dynamic Inspector Russell and his assistant, the shy and nervous Wilfred. In Harker's suite, they find Patricia Morgan, who tells them she is Harker's secretary. The frightened Harker maid, Augusta, seems to know nothing of the case. Russell finds a card bearing a crude drawing of a coiled snake and the words, "You will hear it."

A newspaperman, Ted Rand, barges into the scene and is thrown out by Russell — but not before Rand recognizes Pat as his sweetheart, a rival reporter. When Pat is able to phone in her story, Ted intercepts the call on an extension and pretends to be a rewrite man. Ted sends the story to his own newspaper, and Pat's editor, Perkins, fires her. Ted is horrified by this turn of events, but Pat continues to work on the story, gaining Russell's confidence and being on hand when a second murder is discovered. This victim is a woman who has occupied a suite under Harker's rooms. Another snake card is found. The police deduce that the woman's missing husband killed both her and Harker, but this theory is shattered when the missing man is found in the morgue. Ted follows Pat and Russell when they go to identify the body. Pat vengefully concocts a phoney story for Ted to discover, which he calls in to her newspaper in an attempt to square himself with her. When Pat repents and tells him what she has done, it is too late — the story is already on the presses.

Pat learns that the respected Harker was in cahoots with a gang headed by the infamous Martini. She searches Martini's apartment and is almost caught by him. Calling Ted, she tells him what she has discovered, but while she awaits his arrival she receives one of the serpent cards. Pat and Ted search Harker's rooms and are interrupted by Martini. A scream echoes through the halls, and another body is found in Martini's suite. Russell has Martini arrested.

The next day a thorough search of the hotel is instituted. Pat is on the verge of discovering an important clue when Pete seizes her and drags her to the basement. The janitor throws her into the furnace and turns on the flames just as Wilfred arrives, shoots Pete, and rescues Pat. It is discovered that Pete was the brother of a former member of the Martini gang, Danny Eagan, who was framed and executed by Martini's orders. Pete, driven mad by a desire for vengeance, decided to kill off all the gangsters and whomever he considered to be their associates. The serpent sounds were made by the murder weapons — steam radiators through which a deadly gas was released.

Notes

Max Hoffman was a painter, singer, lawyer, and a teacher of languages before he entered the film industry in 1910 at the age of 29. He was general manager of Universal for a while, the principal founder of both the Tiffany and Liberty companies, and, in 1931, the founder of Allied. After a brief association with Monogram, he decided to keep Allied independent and embarked on a production schedule that included a series of Hoot Gibson Westerns, several modern dress versions of literary classics, and a string of mystery and action films. Players in Allied's 1932-'33 released included some notables, such as Reginald Denny, Myrna Loy, Lila Lee, Monte Blue, Mary Nolan, and Marian Marsh.

Both Ginger Rogers and Lyle Talbot were doing well at the major studios, and it was a definite triumph for Hoffman to be able to reunite the stars of his *The Thirteenth Guest,* to which *A Shriek in the Night* is not a sequel but a close relative, utilizing the same director, screenwriter, and production crew. Scary moments are alternated with light comedy and romance in Frances Hyland's well-written and beautifully timed script. Comic elements include witty repartee between the feuding hero and girl, the mouse-like mannerisms of Arthur Hoyt, the antics of Lillian Harmer and the fine black actress, Louise Beavers, as a pair of frightened maids, and Clarence Wilson as a crochety editor. Even Harvey Clark, who plays the crazed killer, seems an amusing and likeable character until the climax, which is both unexpected and ingenious. Only Purnell Pratt and Maurice Black play it "straight," respectively as a hard-nosed detective and a gangster. Performances from all hands are well conceived.

From a production standpoint the picture is comparable to its predecessor, with the added benefit of atmospheric background music.

A STUDY IN SCARLET (1933)

(KBS Productions — World Wide Pictures)

Produced by Burt Kelly, Samuel Bischoff, *and* William Saal; *directed by* Edwin L. Marin; *based on the novel by* Sir Arthur Conan Doyle; *adaptation and screenplay by* Robert Florey; *dialogue by* Reginald Owen; *photographed by* Arthur Edeson; *film editor,* Rose Loewenger; *supervising editor,* Martin G. Cohn; *art director,* Ralph M. DeLacy; *sound recording,* Hans Weeren; *musical director,* Val Burton; *sound system,* RCA Photophone; *a KBS Production produced at the* California Tiffany Studio; *running time,* 70 minutes; *released* May 14, 1933.

PLAYERS: *Sherlock Holmes,* Reginald Owen; *Mrs. Pyke,* Anna May Wong; *Eileen Forrester,* June Clyde; *Thaddeus Merrydew,* Allan Dinehart; *John Stanford,* John Warburton; *Dr. Watson,* Warburton Gamble; *Jabez Wilson,* J. M. Kerrigan; *Inspector Lestrade,* Alan Mowbray; *Mrs. Murphy,* Doris Lloyd; *Will Swallow,* Billy Bevan; *Publican,* Hobart Cavanaugh; *Daft Dolly,* Leila Bennett; *Baker,* Cecil Reynolds; *Captain Pyke,* Wyndham Standing; *Malcolm Dearing,* Halliwell Hobbes; *Ah Yet,* Tetsu Komai; *Mrs. Hudson,* Tempe Pigott.

Synopsis

Charwomen at Victoria Station, London, are unable to open the door of a private car. Porters are likewise unable to open a high window of the coach. "I can't bulge it," says one, whereupon a co-worker corrects him; the word should be budge. They break into the car and find the corpse of a Mr. Murphy.

Next day, a notice in the newspapers carries a cryptic message comprising a sequence of numbers and the words *Scarlet* and *Limehouse.* Eileen Forrester reads the notice and goes to an address in Limehouse, joining six others in a

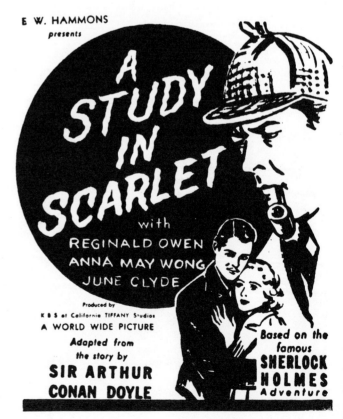

E W. HAMMONS presents

A STUDY IN SCARLET

with REGINALD OWEN ANNA MAY WONG JUNE CLYDE

Produced by K B S at California TIFFANY Studios A WORLD WIDE PICTURE

Adapted from the story by SIR ARTHUR CONAN DOYLE

Based on the famous SHERLOCK HOLMES Adventure

June Clyde, Anna May Wong, J. M. Kerrigan.

meeting at which Thaddeus Merrydew, a lawyer, presides. Others present are Jabez Wilson, Captain Pyke, Mr. Baker, Malcolm Dearing, and a mute Chinaman, Ah Yet. Merrydew explains that a second member of their organization, the Scarlet Ring, has committed suicide and that, as per custom, the legacy of the deceased will be divided among the surviving members. The first member to die was Eileen's father. She believes the death was unnatural.

The widow of Murphy comes to see Sherlock Holmes, complaining she is penniless because her husband left all his considerable fortune to his club, The Scarlet Ring. Although Mrs. Murphy cannot pay for an investigation, Holmes seizes the opportunity to take the case when he learns that Merrydew is involved. To his colleague, Dr. Watson, Holmes explains that Merrydew is "a gliding, slimy, venomous snake," whom Holmes has long wanted to bring to justice.

Merrydew calls Eileen to a meeting at the Limehouse address. He has learned that she is engaged to John Stanford, and he advises her that she should not marry.

Merrydew leaves the room just as Captain Pyke enters. Eileen hears a shot, a window breaks, and Pyke falls, bleeding. Then a mysterious figure attacks the girl, stunning her. When Merrydew returns and revives Eileen, Pyke's body has vanished.

Pyke's beautiful Chinese wife identifies a body taken from the Thames as that of Pyke. Later, Dearing is shot to death in a confrontation with a shadowy figure. Police decide the death is a suicide, but Holmes' friend and foil, Inspector Lestrade, decides to bring Holmes into the case. Holmes discerns that Dearing was shot by a large man who smokes Trichinopoli Cigars and who has small feet. It is proved moreover that the victim was shot first in the back of the head, then another shot was fired through the mouth to obliterate the first wound and make the death appear a suicide. The victim also has in his possession a verse from the children's song, "Ten Little Black Boys," of which different verses have been found on each of the slain men.

Holmes visits Merrydew — (a large man who smokes Trichinopoli Cigars and has small feet) — but he is not

89

convinced that Merrydew is the murderer. Merrydew later calls on Eileen and tells her she must come alone to the meeting place. Holmes tells John that Eileen is in danger. Holmes also deciphers the coded newspaper message after deducing that the numbers refer to pages in a book, *Whittaker's Almanac,* found in Merrydew's office. The advertisement announces a meeting of The Scarlet Ring in Limehouse.

Disguised as an old toff, Holmes visits a pub in a village near the Pyke country Grange and gets a dogcart ride to the Grange with Will Swallow, a personable, bibulous bumpkin. No one is at home but the feeble-minded maid, Dora. Having gained entry, Holmes feigns a heart attack and sends the maid to fetch a doctor. He searches the house and finds a panel leading to several hidden rooms, one of which has lately been occupied by someone who smokes Trichinopoli Cigars.

Mrs. Pyke calls on Jabez Wilson and invites him to the Grange to advise her on some financial matters, hinting that she has taken an interest in him. Merrydew calls a meeting of the surviving Scarlet Ring members. Holmes and John follow Eileen to the meeting place and wait in hiding. Later, they see everyone leave except Eileen. They break in and rescue her from a gas-filled room.

Wilson, terrified, visits Holmes and tells of an attempt on his life. Wilson also explains about The Scarlet Ring, whose members have long awaited shipment of the loot from a sizeable jewel robbery in China. Meantime, Merrydew entertains a mysterious guest, to whom he explains, "All must be finished tomorrow night, at the Grange." As Wilson leaves Holmes' rooms, the body of Baker is found at the door with a note reading, "Compliments to Sherlock Holmes," and another verse from "Ten Little Black Boys." Wilson goes to Pyke Grange to hide. Eileen also goes to the Grange after a visit from Mrs. Pyke.

Holmes, Watson, Lestrade, and a number of Scotland Yard men lie in hiding outside the Grange. After Eileen and Wilson have gone to their rooms for the night, a shadowy figure emerges from the secret rooms and tells Mrs. Pyke to use "any inducement" to lure Wilson from his locked room. The mystery man then kidnaps Eileen and carries her to his hideaway. Holmes and the detectives enter the house when they hear Wilson's cry for help. He is being attacked by a knife-wielding Ah Yet, whom Holmes kills in time to save Wilson's life. Eileen is rescued from the man in the secret rooms. The mysterious figure is Pyke, who with the connivance of his wife, Merrydew, and Ah Yet, had faked his death. Merrydew is arrested.

Notes

The KBS approach to *A Study in Scarlet* can stand practically as an original work, having little to do with Conan Doyle's novel of that name; and the Holmes-Watson team of Reginald Owen and Warburton Gamble bears small physical resemblance to the familiar book illustrations by Frederick Dorr Steele and Sidney Paget. Owen, in fact, portrayed Dr. Watson the previous year in Fox's *Sherlock Holmes!* Such discrepancies notwithstanding, the film is a highly satisfying work with capital performances from Owen, Gamble, Allan Dinehart, Alan Mowbray, June Clyde, Anna May Wong, J. M. Kerrigan, and other able actors.

The Parisian director, Robert Florey, had left Universal in anger following his removal from *Frankenstein* and his problematic encounters with management during production of *The Murders in the Rue Morgue* (1932). Florey was slated to write and direct *A Study in Scarlet.* But after completion of the *Scarlet* script, he was enticed away by a Warner Brothers offer that was too good to refuse. Edwin L. Marin, who had made a good impression with the direction of his first picture, *The Death Kiss,* replaced Florey. Marin performed with his usual competence.

In photographic terms, *A Study in Scarlet* ranks among the best of its time — which is understandable in that the great Arthur Edeson was in charge of the cameras. Edeson's exquisite studies of foggy Limehouse, eerie hidden rooms, and a menacing country mansion are wonderfully atmospheric. Ralph DeLacy's settings likewise are of major-studio calibre. One interesting sequence puts the camera in the role of the mysterious killer when he pays a visit to his accomplice.

Although the complex story strays afar from Doyle's tale, it is saturated with details from the Holmes canon. "Quick, Watson — the game is afoot!" cries Holmes at one point. The ash from a Trichinopoli Cigar figures as a clue. Dinehart is an oily villain Doyle would have relished, the sort of blackguard who warns the innocent girl that "This is a very wicked world we're living in," even as he plots her undoing. Holmes is properly nasty to Lestrade, complaining after Lestrade has stated that he has left the murder scene undisturbed for Holmes' inspection that "If a herd of buffalo came by they couldn't have made more of a mess." There is considerable cat-and-mouse byplay between Holmes and the master criminal, reminiscent of the encounters with Professor Moriarty in the stories. There is a curious error: Holmes' address is given repeatedly as 221-A Baker Street. And Lestrade's name is given an uncharacteristic pronunciation, with a long "a."

Among the smaller roles, the most winning are Billy Bevan's hard-drinking rural chap, Will Swallow, who says of the Oriental Mrs. Pyke, "You can't make English gentry out of the 'eathen Chinee, sor — at least not in these parts," and Leila Bennett's Daft Dolly, who describes Mrs. Pyke more charitably: "Such eyes! She walks like a cat. Such a figger! A nice bit o' goods."

THE FLAMING SIGNAL (1933)

(William Berke Productions — Imperial Distributing Corporation)

90

Presented by William M. Pizor; *produced by* William Berke; *directed by* C. E. Roberts *and* George Jeske; *story by* William G. Storer; *adaptation and dialogue by* C. E. Roberts *and* Thomas Hughes; *assistant director,* Charles Berner; *musical director,* Abe Meyer; *settings,* F. W. Widdowson; *produced at* Metropolitan Studios, Hollywood; *sound system,* RCA Photophone; *running time,* 64 minutes; *released* late May of 1933 *by* Imperial Distributing Corporation.

PLAYERS: *Sally James,* Marceline Day; *Jim Robbins,* John David Horsley; *Molly,* Carmelita Geraghty; *Otto von Krantz,* Noah Beery; *The Reverend Mr. James,* Henry B. Walthall; *Manu,* Mischa Auer; *Taku,* Francisco Alonso; *Rari,* Janne Olmes; *Himself,* Flash.

Synopsis

Lieutenant Jim Robbins' almost-human canine companion, Flash, must be left behind for the sake of fuel space when the celebrity pilot takes off in *The Spirit of '76* on an endurance flight from Los Angeles to Hawaii. Following a seemingly safe take-off, word leaks to the West Coast newspapers that the plane is feared lost.

Jim, who has flown off-course during a storm, swings toward an uncharted island. The tail of the plane catches fire, and Flash — a stowaway — makes his way forward to warn his master of the danger. Jim puts his parachute on Flash and drops the craft into the water. He and the dog reach the outpost known as Tabu Island, where a strange unease exists between four white settlers and the natives.

Even the white faction is divided, between missionary James and his daughter Sally, and the bestial trader von Krantz and his faded-rose companion Molly. Von Krantz is a one-man supply-and-demand system, buying the natives' pearls but then reclaiming his money in exchange for

Mischa Auer, Noah Beery, Carmelita Geraghty.

liquor, which reduces the inhabitants to an animalistic state.

Von Krantz' attack on a native girl has angered the villagers. He shoots Manu, the supposedly immortal high priest, whose followers bear him away to a shrine and proceed to work themselves into a frenzy. The natives' presence becomes increasingly threatening to the settlers.

Jim, aware that a liner is soon to arrive, seeks to buy time until the whites can reach the boat. The natives run amok, however, and Molly is their first victim. The missionary chooses to meditate and confront the mob, but the drunken von Krantz fires on the group, precipitating an attack on James. Flash, given a live brand by Jim, races to light a beacon to signal the passing ship. The high priest has been resurrected. Jim and von Krantz fight.

Flash sets the natives' sacrificial pyre ablaze and returns in time to trounce von Krantz. The natives foil Jim and Sally's escape and prepare to burn them at the stake. The ship's officers, ordered to watch for the missing pilot, spot the flames and head for shore. Flash frees Jim and Sally.

As they reach the ship, a sailor saves Flash from a shark, and the refugees are homeward bound.

Notes

Tried-and-true action ingredients with scarcely a lag — although the direction leaves something to be desired — make up *The Flaming Signal.* An intrepid pilot and his "wonder dog" encounter such perils and pleasures as an airplane crash, a native uprising, a sacrificial ritual, several killings, a high priest with seemingly supernatural powers, a fiendish German trader and his sleazy girlfriend, a beautiful dancing girl, a missionary and his lovely daughter, and a shark.

The hero is played by John David Horsely, a curly-haired juvenile lead, while the role calls for a Richard Dix or a Jack Holt. Flash, a friendly German Shepherd who has difficulty in looking as fierce as the story suggests, is no Rin Tin Tin. The professionalism of silent stars Marceline Day,

Noah Beery, and Henry B. Walthall, and of the up-and-coming Mischa Auer in the sort of parts they played best, steady action, and some pleasing pictorial effects compensate somewhat for the ineptness of much of the picture.

THE SPHINX (1933)

(Monogram Pictures Corporation)

Vice president in charge of production, Trem Carr; *directed by* Phil Rosen; *supervised by* Sid Rogell; *story and screenplay by* Albert DeMond; *photographed by* Gilbert Warrenton; *technical director,* E. R. Hickson; *musical director,* Abe Meyer; *sound recording,* John R. Stransky, Jr.; *sound system,* Western Electric *by* Balsley & Phillips; *running time,* 64 minutes; *released* June 1, 1933.

PLAYERS: *Jerome Breen,* Lionel Atwill; *Jerry Crane,* Sheila Terry; *Jack Burton,* Theodore Newton; *Terrence Hogan,* Paul Hurst; *Bacigalupi,* Luis Alberni; *Inspector Riley,* Robert Ellis; *and* Lucien Prival, Paul Fix, Lillian Leighton, George Hayes, Hooper Atchley, *and* Wilfred Lucas.

Synopsis

A janitor named Bacigalupi identifies the prominent Jerome Breen as the man he saw commit a robbery and murder. Defense attorneys put the Italian to ridicule after he testifies that Breen stopped to talk with him; it is well known that Breen is a deaf mute. Newspaper reporter Jack Burton believes Breen is guilty despite acquittal, and he suspects Breen of similar crimes in other cities. Jerry Crane, Burton's sweetheart and society editor of the newspaper, is assigned to write up Breen's life and charitable endeavors.

Burton receives a phone call from one of Breen's associates, promising information. Before the appointment can be kept, the man is murdered. The victim's mother identifies Breen as the killer and insists that Breen can hear and speak. Again Breen has the perfect alibi: He was being

interviewed by Jerry at the time of the second murder.

An investigating detective, having noticed that Breen becomes perturbed whenever police officers approach his grand piano, is murdered after confiding his suspicions. Burton's feeling that Breen is not deaf and dumb grows, but a medical examination proves him wrong. Jerry, learning of the piano clue, goes to Breen's home to continue her interviewing. While Breen is out of the room she plays a tune on the piano, and when she strikes a certain key a wall panel slides open. In the secret room, Jerry encounters Breen, who approaches her in a menacing way. When she turns to run, she finds herself facing another Breen! Burton and the police break in and find Jerry facing death at the hands of the identical men. Having rescued Jerry, the authorities learn that the man in the hidden room was Breen's twin brother, a deaf mute. The murders were necessary for Breen to be able to carry on his philanthropic works.

Notes

Lionel Atwill could always be counted on to deliver a first-rate performance whether he was working at a major studio or on Poverty Row. In a dual role in *The Sphinx* he manages to be more terrifying without makeup than most actors could be under pounds of putty. The scene in which two Atwills confront Sheila Terry provides shock without resorting to gruesomeness or undue violence. Atwill receives adequate support from Miss Terry and Theodore Newton, and there are deft comic bits by Luis Alberni and Paul Hurst. Albert DeMond's unusual yarn proves most mystifying on the screen, through strong efforts by the cast, director Phil Rosen, and photographer Gil Warrenton. Monogram remade the property ten years later as *The Phantom Killer,* with John Hamilton playing the Atwill role. The janitor of the later version was the brilliant black comedian, Mantan Moreland.

TOMORROW AT SEVEN (1933)

(Jefferson Pictures Corporation)

Produced by Joseph I. Schnitzer *and* Samuel Zierler; *directed by* Ray Enright; *screenplay and dialogue by* Ralph Spence; *photographed by* Charles Schoenbaum; *art director,* Edward Jewell; *film editor,* Rose Loewenger; *sound recording,* Lodge Cunningham; *running time,* 64 minutes; *released* June 2, 1933, *by* RKO-Radio Pictures, Incorporated.

PLAYERS: *Neil Broderick,* Chester Morris; *Martha Winters,* Vivienne Osborne; *Clancy,* Frank McHugh; *Dugan,* Allen Jenkins; *Drake,* Henry Stephenson; *Winters,* Grant Mitchell; *Simons,* Charles Middleton; *Marsden,* Oscar Apfel; *Mrs. Quincey,* Virginia Howell; *Henderson,* Cornelius Keefe; *Coroner,* Edward Le Saint; *Pompey,* Gus Robinson.

Lionel Atwill, Sheila Terry.

Death-marked victims of the mystery slayer tried to hide away at the fatal hour. But he never missed. In balloons above the clouds, in glittering halls, on speeding trains, his dagger always found them at the appointed moment!

His strength helpless to defend her against the unseen terror!

"TOMORROW AT SEVEN"

A sensational crime drama with a startling climax

CHESTER MORRIS
VIVIENNE OSBORNE

FRANK McHUGH
ALLEN JENKINS
Henry Stephenson
Grant Mitchell
Directed by Ray Enright

SOMEBODY in that group killed Winters!

It *couldn't* have been Drake, who had spent a fortune to unmask the mystery slayer.

It *couldn't* have been Martha, daughter of the murdered man.

It *couldn't* have been Broderick, who had just arrived from the West to solve the crime riddle.

It *couldn't* have been the pilot, who was driving the plane when Winters fell dead in the cabin.

It *couldn't* have been Henderson, who had an airtight alibi.

YET ONE OF THEM **DID** KILL WINTERS!

and another victim was slated for death..

"TOMORROW AT SEVEN"

A Thrilling Mystery Drama

With

CHESTER MORRIS
VIVIENNE OSBORNE
Frank McHugh · Allen Jenkins
Henry Stephenson · Grant Mitchell
Directed by Ray Enright

Synopsis

In a tender encounter with Martha Winters, writer Neil Broderick discloses his investigation of a murdering madman who has eluded the Chicago police. He learns Martha is the daughter of Winters, secretary to a businessman named Drake who has spent much money trying to track the same criminal. Martha introduces Neil to Drake, who during their discussion receives a jigsaw puzzle which yields the message, TOMORROW AT SEVEN, a warning of doom. Next afternoon, Martha has arranged for the three of them, two detectives, Winters, and two pilots to be airborne. The fatal hour finds them aloft. As Henderson passes through the passenger cabin, the lights go out and a scream is heard. Winters is found stabbed through the heart, but no weapon can be found, only an ace of spades — the killer's sign.

The detectives order a landing and herd the passengers through a swamp into a foreboding mansion. A death-warmed-over type named Simons, purportedly the Coroner, appears and finds a sealed letter in Winters' clothing. Detective Clancy reads it, the lights are snuffed, and the letter is seized. The infuriated officers herd the survivors into separate rooms; Neil sneaks into Martha's room, demanding the letter. She admits having taken it to protect her father's name; they go to fetch it from a hiding place but find only another warning from the fiend. Then the lawmen appear and accuse them.

Dugan posts Detective Drake to guard Neil, and meantime a figure in black absconds with Martha into the swamp. While taking up the trail, the detectives find the corpse of Henderson, one of the pilots. Martha learns her kidnaper is Simons, who informs her he is not the Coroner but is in cahoots with Neil, a Secret Service agent.

Neil strikes Drake in the face with a pillow and gains the

Grant Mitchell receives the dread Black Ace. Henry Stephenson, Vivienne Osborne, Chester Morris.

guard's gun. Drake knocks the firearm from Neil's grasp with a cane. They fight, and the noise attracts all the others. Amid the commotion, the murderer is revealed as Drake.

Notes

The dynamic Chester Morris heads a high-grade cast in this slick chiller from Jefferson Pictures, a company organized by Joseph Schnitzer and Samuel Zierler utilizing a crew from the foundering World Wide Pictures. Suspenseful, baffling, and well balanced with comic touches, the script is vintage Ralph Spence. The telling benefits from the direction of Ray Enright, on loan from Warners, where he made fifty-one features between 1927 and 1941. RKO-Radio acquired the film for its program, seeing fit to give it an "A" picture release including a twenty-four-sheet billboard campaign.

Identity of the villain is kept tantalizingly out of reach,

Dumb cops Frank McHugh, Allen Jenkins intimidated by Charles Middleton.

with the next logical suspect becoming the next victim. Settings — a Chicago mansion, an airliner, a dismal Louisiana swamp, and a traditional mystery house — are precisely right, and the photography is outstanding.

The unjustly forgotten Vivienne Osborne — Edward G. Robinson's Nemesis in *Two Seconds* (1932) and the murderess of Paramount's *Supernatural* (1933) — is fine as the menaced daughter of one of the victims. Charles Middleton is as hard-faced as ever, Henry Stephenson lends his usual dignity, and Grant Mitchell is convincingly frightened. The comedy duties rightfully fall to two irascible detectives, played capably by Frank McHugh and Allen Jenkins.

Gloria Shea, Wilfred Lucas, Michael Visaroff as seen by newspaper artist.

STRANGE PEOPLE (1933)

(Chesterfield Motion Picture Corporation)

Produced by George R. Batcheller; *directed by* Richard Thorpe; *screenplay by* Jack Townley; *photographed by* M. A. Anderson; *recording engineer,* Richard Tyler; *art director,* Edward C. Jewell; *assistant director,* Melville Shyer; *film editor,* Vera Wood; *musical director,* Abe Meyer: RCA Photophone *sound; produced at* Universal City; *running time,* 64 minutes; *released* June 17, 1933.

PLAYERS: *Jimmy Allen,* John Darrow; *Helen Mason,* Gloria Shea; *J. E. Burton,* Hale Hamilton; *John Davis,* Wilfred Lucas; *Crandall,* J. Frank Glendon; *Edwards,* Michael S. Visaroff; *The Plumber,* Jack Pennick; *The Barber,* Jerry Mandy; *The Insurance Agent,* Lew Kelly; *Mrs. Reed,* Jane Keckley; *The Radio Repairman,* Walter Brennan; *Mrs. Jones,* Mary Foy; *Kelly,* Frank H. LaRue; *Burke,* Stanley G. Blystone; *Guest,* Jay Wilsey; *Detective,* Gordon DeMain.

Synopsis

It is a dark and stormy night as guests arrive at a large country house. Nearby in the lashing rain, two men exhume a corpse and hide it in the barn. The guests — all tradespeople called ostensibly to perform tasks or to be interviewed for employment — include a plumber, a radio repairman, an insurance man, a barber, two elderly ladies, an auto salesman named Jimmy Allen, and his fiancée, Helen Mason. Crandall, the sinister-looking butler, admits the visitors until twelve have arrived, then locks the door. Those gathered make a startling discovery: All were members of a jury which convicted a young man of murder almost a year earlier.

The nervous guests are preparing to leave when suddenly the lights are doused. When candles are lighted it is discovered that Crandall has been killed. Now arrives J. E. Burton, purportedly the owner of the house, who calls the police. The jittery company suspects Helen, who seems to have recognized the butler. Under questioning she admits the murdered man was her former husband. All are convinced of her guilt.

Burton explains that the "murder" was a charade staged by himself, Helen, and his law partner, Crandall, to show the jurors that they could have been wrong in their verdict. The house actually is that of John Davis, the supposed victim of the condemned man. The scheme was concocted to induce the jury to sign a petition to save an innocent man from death row. It is found that Crandall actually *is* dead — shot through the heart.

Two men arrive and announce themselves as detectives. They capture Edwards, the eccentric caretaker, who is hiding in the secret passageways that honeycomb the house. A stranger, snooping outside, hides in the barn when seen by some of the inmates. A search of the barn reveals the body of the murdered man, Davis. The stranger steps forward and identifies himself as Burke, an associate of Burton. Burke says the two investigators are phoneys. One "detective," Kelly, is captured, but his partner is found murdered. Some genuine detectives arrive and question Kelly, who admits that he and his late partner were business associates of Davis, who had cheated them out of a fortune and framed them into prison. He believes that Davis is alive and that the murdered men are Davis' victims. Davis, he suspects, wanted to disappear to escape the vengeance of those he had cheated. The exhumed body in the barn is that of one of Davis' victims, buried as Davis.

A secret passage is discovered, and in it is Edwards. A chase leads to Davis. In the cellar, Davis and Edwards fight for possession of a cache of money. They are captured by Jimmy and the plumber, who turn them over to the police.

Notes

The use of some outstanding sets at Universal City gives this chiller a more imposing appearance than many of its contemporaries. Most of the action occurs in the best old house of all, the one designed by Charles D. Hall for James Whale's *The Old Dark House* (1932). Good employment is

made of the terrifying crooked staircases and forbidding nooks of the place as well as the cellar and some graveyard props from *Frankenstein* (1931). Wind, rain, menacing shadows, and unnerving sound effects add to the charm. The script — not really one of the better yarns of the genre — has some neat surprises and scares up a few thrills.

The players are a well-selected group. Just adequate are the leads, John Darrow and the petite Gloria Shea, but there is a nifty assortment of players who fit well into the atmosphere. Particularly noteworthy are the smooth-as-silk Hale Hamilton, Wilfred Lucas (here made up as a typical Scrooge), big and ugly Jack Pennick, Michael Visaroff, and Walter Brennan (still a small-parts actor at the time).

CORRUPTION (1933)

(William Berke Productions –
Imperial Distributing Corporation)

Presented by William M. Pizor; *produced by* William Berke; *written and directed by* C. Edwards Roberts; *photographed by* Robert Cline; *sound by* W. C. Smith; *edited by* H. W. deBouille *and* Finn Ulback; *assistant director,* Charles

Berner; *produced at* Western Service Studios; *sound system,* RCA Photophone; *running time,* 63 minutes; *released* June 19, 1933, *by* Imperial Distributing Corporation.

PLAYERS: *Ellen Manning,* Evalyn Knapp; *Tim Butler,* Preston Foster; *Charlie Jasper,* Charles Delaney; *Gorman,* Tully Marshall; *Sylvia Gorman,* Natalie Moorhead; *Regan,* Warner Richmond; *District Attorney Blake,* Huntley Gordon; *Assistant District Attorney King,* Lane Chandler; *Voikov,* Mischa Auer; *Police Commissioner,* Jason Robards; *Mae,* Gwen Lee; *Dr. Robbins,* Sidney Bracy; *Pat,* Kit Guard; *Bud,* Fred Kohler, Jr.; *Tony,* Nick Thompson.

Synopsis

The youthful Tim Butler has performed excellently as a lawyer and is nominated for mayor by a corrupt City Hall gang. Once cinched in office, he promises to clean up graft, starting with the machine that had him elected. As their puppet turns on them, the manipulators plot his ouster. Gorman, one of the sleaziest of the bunch, has arranged to have his daughter, Sylvia, marry Tim, but when the new mayor proves to be honest, and unwilling to take orders from the scoundrels, old man Gorman orders Sylvia to halt the relationship.

Regan, dirtiest of the tricksters, has failed to make the mayor sympathetic to the power structure's motives and threatens Tim with strong-arm tactics. Tony, an Italian who claims to have a gravely ill brother willing to disclose information against Boss Regan and the gang, lures Tim to a house in a decaying neighbourhood. In the bedroom, where Tim expects to meet the brother named Mike, a woman introduces herself as Mike's wife. As Tim approaches the bed, the woman throws off her wrap and embraces him. A burst of light indicates to Tim he has been framed; a photograph has been made of the compromising situation, and Regan and his men see to it that the newspapers print the picture. Thrown out of office by public outcry, Tim resumes his law practice and takes with him his secretary, Ellen, who has befriended him during his troubles with Gorman's daughter.

If Tim can clear himself of the accusation of immoral behavior, the Governor has promised to make him State's Attorney. Tim goes to talk with Regan, and during the conversation one of the boss' henchmen draws a gun. As Tim struggles to get the weapon, a shot is heard, and Regan falls dead. Tim is brought to trial for murder and sentenced to life imprisonment despite efforts by Ellen and another friend, Charlie, to prove his innocence.

Finally a crazed scientist named Voikov confesses his hatred for political grafters and tells the police he killed Regan with a specially prepared bullet. He threatens to kill the rest of the bunch, and as the corrupt District Attorney listens, Voikov causes the D. A.'s death. Tim is freed, and he claims both Ellen and the State's Attorney job.

Notes

A story of political chicanery with the added spice of a murderous mad scientist, *Corruption* is one of the more unusual efforts of the wiry little William Berke, veteran independent producer. C. Edwards Roberts, writer-director, put forth some intriguing characters, peppered the dialogue with colorful wisecracks and underworld slang, and contrived a novel way for the murders to be committed. His direction is not as strong as his ideas, however, and the film falls short of its promise.

Corruption is helped considerably by a worthy cast including Preston Foster, who already was making a name for himself in the major studios, and Evalyn Knapp, a Broadway actress who had just made a number of pictures for Warner Brothers. The villains, Tully Marshall, Warner Richmond, Huntley Gordon, Lane Chandler, Jason Robards, Fred Kohler Jr., Nick Thompson, and Kit Guard, are a fine lot, — and Natalie Moorhead and Gwen Lee fare well as feminine menaces. Charles Delaney adds some comedy as a nosey reporter, and Sidney Bracy is another of the few sympathetic characters. Mischa Auer adroitly steals the show, as the vengeful doctor who is ridding the city of its human vermin.

SAVAGE GOLD (1933)

(Captain Harold Auten)

Produced and photographed in Ecuador *by* Commander George M. Dyott; *film editor,* L. F. Kennedy; *dialogue written by* Burnett Hershey; *story by* Commander George M. Dyott *and* Captain Harold Auten; *adaptation by* Richard Mack; *narrated by* John Martin; *musical director,* James C. Bradford; *running time,* 67 minutes; *released* July 29, 1933. *by* Captain Harold Auten.

PLAYERS: Commander George M. Dyott *and a* native cast.

Synopsis

In a remote mountainous region of Ecuador, Command-

Evalyn Knapp, Preston Foster, Charles Delaney.

A headhunter.

A wife of the native chief.

er Dyott meets Schweitzer, a German prospector, and tells him the Jivaros have discovered gold up the Amazon. Later, Dyott receives a plea for help from Schweitzer, who has been made captive by the savages and fears for his life. Dyott and his friend, Benson, set out to attempt a rescue. Beyond a mountain pass so dangerous that even birds die trying to cross it, the party enters the almost unknown realm of the Jivaro. So frightened are the native bearers that Dyott sends them back, continuing on with Benson despite warnings of the Tundai, Jivaro signal drums. The jungle becomes so dense that they must travel by raft to the mouth of the Nangarissa. Strings of feathers across their path warn them not to enter, but next morning a drum message bids them welcome.

The Chief — a prior friendly acquaintance of Dyott — takes them to his hut, but becomes surly when Dyott asks about Schweitzer. Although the Chief says no white man is with them, Dyott and Benson try to investigate, but are warned by Shuki, the Medicine Man. During a tribal conclave, Benson at last slips away alone and searches upriver. Dyott catches the Medicine Man plying his gruesome trade of shrinking human heads.

Benson, meantime, finds a hut containing the headless body of Schweitzer. Nearby is a scribbled note to Dyott, warning him to run for it before he meets the same fate. Benson spies Shuki and kills him. One of Shuki's men spreads the alarm and in moments the Tundai sound the call to war. Hotly pursued, the explorers escape down the river after destroying all but one of the native canoes.

Adventure was an abiding sideline passion of Commander George M. Dyott, a noted engineer. By the time *Savage Gold* was assembled he had made a dozen expeditions into the uncharted regions of South America and won highest honors from the Royal Geographic Society. In 1928 he searched the Brazilian jungles for Colonel P. H. Fawcett, who had vanished three years previous. The Brazilian government was outraged by Dyott's report that Fawcett was murdered by headhunters — which is why Dyott decided to shoot his fictionalized account of a similar expedition in Ecuador. Similar in approach to the celebrated "natural dramas," *Grass* (1925) and *Chang* (1927), produced in primitive regions by Merian C. Cooper and Ernest B. Schoedsack, this film states openly that a story was added to enhance the authentic scenes. It is an exciting melodrama, far superior to most others of its kind, with exceptional photography that mirrors the beauty and the horror of the jungle. It received enthusiastic reviews: "Here is the thriller of thrillers — more exciting and ghastly than all of Hollywood's *Frankensteins* and *King Kongs* rolled into one" (New York *Journal*); "The supreme adventure thriller" (New York *Mirror*); "Couched in stunning authentic photography" (New York *World-Telegram*).

Some of its scenes are shockers: Jivaros are seen eating toasted caterpillars, making booze at a community chewing and spitting fest, indulging in drunken orgies, dragging women by the hair, and killing jungle cats with blowguns. A king snake crushes a rattlesnake and swallows it whole. The most startling sequence shows the villainous Medicine Man shrinking a human head — beginning with the careful removal of the skull, the curing of the skin, the shrinking process utilizing hot gravel and sand, and at last the intricate molding of the features. A dramatic score and a sometimes overenthusiastic narration accompany the visuals, which never lag in interest.

THE AVENGER (1933)

(Monogram Pictures Corporation)

Vice president in charge of production, Trem Carr; *directed by* Edwin L. Marin; *from the novel by* John Goodwin; *adapted by* Brown Holmes; *dialogue by* Tristram Tupper; *photographed by* Sid Hickox; *musical director,* Abe Meyer; *recorded by* John A. Stransky, Jr.; Western Electric *recording by* Balsley & Phillips; *running time,* 79 minutes; *released* August 10, 1933.

PLAYERS: *Norman Craig,* Ralph Forbes; *Ruth Knowles,* Adrienne Ames; *James Gordon,* Arthur Vinton; *Witt,* Claude Gillingwater; *Sally,* Charlotte Merriam; *Hanley,* J. Carroll Naish; *Forster,* Berton Churchill; *Cormack,* Murray Kinnell; *McCall,* Thomas Jackson; *Vickers,* Paul Fix; *Durant,* James Donlan; *Talbot,* Leonard Carey; *Ames,* Boothe Howard; *Butler,* Wilson Benge.

THREE Had PAID The Price! was he the FOURTH? What sinister power had removed these men.... and WHY? You Will Find the Answer in This Gripping Drama of Vengeance-Up-to-Date.

MONOGRAM PICTURES Presents

The AVENGER

RALPH FORBES · ADRIENNE AMES

By JOHN GOODWIN Directed by EDWIN L. MARIN

Synopsis

Norman Craig, a young assistant district attorney, comes uncomfortably close to unveiling the activities of a criminal gang led by James Gordon. The crooks frame Craig so that he is convicted circumstantially and sentenced to twenty years' imprisonment. Later, a deathbed confession from Vickers, a gang member, results in a pardon for Craig. Craig's sweetheart, Ruth Knowles, has meantime married Gordon. Although Craig knows who framed him, he cannot document their guilt. Assuming an identity as the Avenger, Craig embarks on a weird scheme, utilizing airplanes, mills bombs, and machine guns to terrorize his enemies. Gordon's henchmen disappear mysteriously, one by one.

Now only Gordon remains. Crazed with fear and the knowledge that Ruth loves Craig, the gang leader commits suicide. It is revealed that Craig has hidden away the other criminals, who have grown willing to confess their crimes.

Notes

A particularly smooth Monogram, *The Avenger* updates the theme of *The Count of Monte Cristo,* adding mystery to the machinations of a ruthless and almost villainous hero. The script, a collaboration between novelist Tristram Tupper and Brown Holmes (a leading writer on loan-out from Warner Brothers), is faithful to the novel by John Goodwin. Good reviews of this, his third picture as a

Adrienne Ames, Claude Gillingwater.

director, enhanced the prestige of Edwin Marin, who made one subsequent feature for Monogram, *The Sweetheart of Sigma Chi* (1933), and then moved up to the major lots. An important factor in the general "big-time" look of the picture is glossy photography by Sid Hickox, an outstanding cameraman from Warners' studios.

Ralph Forbes, an intelligent Englishman, whose previous Hollywood work included the role of the surviving brother in Herbert Brenon's *Beau Geste* (1926), makes convincing the grim actions of the Avenger. Stage veteran Arthur Vinton is equally right as the principal villain. Other effective chicanery is provided by J. Carroll Naish, Berton Churchill, Murray Kinnell, Jimmy Donlan, Paul Fix, and Boothe Howard. Adrienne Ames is a fascinating *femme fatale*.

TARZAN THE FEARLESS (1933)

(Principal Distributing Corporation)

Produced by Sol Lesser; *directed by* Robert S. Hill; *story by* Edgar Rice Burroughs; *story supervision,* William Lord Wright; *screenplay by* Basil Dickey, George Plympton, *and* Ford Beebe; *dialogue by* Walter Anthony; *photographed by* Harry Neumann *and* Joseph Brotherton; *film editor,* Carl Himm; *sound editor,* Charles J. Hunt; *musical supervisor,* Abe Meyer; *musical score by* Sam K. Wineland; Western Electric *recording by* Balsley & Phillips; *produced at* RKO-Pathé Studios; *a serial in* 12 chapters, 24 reels; *released* August 11, 1933.

PLAYERS: *Tarzan,* Buster Crabbe; *Mary Brooks,* Jacqueline Wells; *Dr. Brooks,* E. Alyn Warren; *Bob Hall,* Edward Woods; *Jeff Herbert,* Philo McCullough; *Nick Moran,* Mathew Betz; *Abdul,* Frank Lackteen; *Eltar,* Mischa Auer; *Priestess of Zar,* Carlotta Monti; *Arab Woman,* Symonia Boniface; *Head Bearer,* Darby Jones; *Warrior,* Al Kikume; *Guard,* George De Normand.

Chapter Titles

1) The Dive of Death; 2) The Storm God Strikes; 3) Thundering Death; 4) The Pit of Peril; 5) Blood Money; 6) Voodoo Vengeance; 7) Caught by Cannibals; 8) The Creeping Terror; 9) Eyes of Evil; 10) The Death Plunge; 11) Harvest of Hate; 12) Jungle Justice.

Synopsis

Archaeologist Brooks searches the African jungle for a lost Aryan civilization said to worship the ancient God Zar, of the Emerald Fingers. Wounded by spearmen, Brooks is taken before Eltar, the high priest, and sentenced to be sacrificed before the idol of Zar in a great vaulted room carved from the heart of a mountain. His captors are terrified when they hear the cry of Tarzan, the white man raised by apes. Tarzan carries Brooks away astride Tantor, the elephant, to Brooks' hut. Although Tarzan does not speak English, Brooks conveys the message that he wishes Tarzan to carry a letter to his daughter at the port of Durango. He gives the ape man a photo of the girl, Mary.

Mary has meantime come with her fiancé, Bob Hall, to find her father. The inexperienced pair secures as guides Jeff Herbert, an educated but unscrupulous adventurer, and Nick Moran, a former gangster. The guides have been stranded after an unsuccessful effort to find the fabled emeralds of Zar. Jeff also is aware of a large reward offered for proof of Tarzan's death in order to clear an inheritance — and he falls in love with Mary.

Tarzan rescues Mary from a crocodile and gives her the letter, fleeing when Bob and the guides arrive. Tarzan secretly follows the safari. At Brooks' hut, Mary finds her father has been kidnapped by the people of Zar. A storm wrecks the cabin. A safari boy packs Mary away to Abdul, a slave dealer. Bob, thinking the Zarians have abducted Mary, follows a map from Brooks' effects to the caves of Zar.

Nick tries to kill Bob and Jeff and steal the map but is himself killed by a lion. Bob and Jeff push on, but Eltar has an occult prescience of their approach and lures them into a

Buster Crabbe, Carlotta Monti. Tarzan's lair was the tomb of Lazarus in Cecil B. DeMille's 1927 The King of Kings.

trap. They are imprisoned with Brooks, to be devoured by lions.

Tarzan and two apes make a shambles of Abdul's camp to rescue Mary. Carrying the girl to his cave, Tarzan makes love to her. Mary makes Tarzan understand that her father is a prisoner. Tarzan goes to Zar and rescues the captives; in the escape, Jeff steals one of the emeralds from the idol's fingers. Tarzan leaves the men in safety but refuses to tell where Mary is. Jeff stalks Tarzan in an attempt to find Mary. Meantime, a giant gorilla enters Tarzan's cave, hurls aside the chimpanzee guard, and approaches the girl. Tarzan arrives in time to kill the monster and save Mary.

Jeff, infuriated over Mary's infatuation with Tarzan, reveals to her that Tarzan is of noble birth and heir to vast estates in England. The present holder of the title has offered Jeff 10,000 pounds sterling for proof of Tarzan's demise. As Tarzan approaches the cave, Jeff takes aim at Tarzan and Mary gives Jeff her promise.

Mary and Jeff reach Brooks' camp only to be captured by the savage Waziri warriors, outraged by the incantations of Eltar. The Waziri take the party to be burned. Tarzan saves Mary and returns her to the cave. Brooks, taking advantage of a solar eclipse, saves the band by pretending to control the sun. Jeff leads a party of natives to take Mary. Tarzan is shot by Jeff and left for dead. Jeff pretends to be taking Mary to her father but actually plans to take her to the coast and force her to marry him. The defeated warriors return to the village and threaten to kill Brooks and Bob, but the white men escape and are reunited with Mary and Jeff. The entire group is recaptured by the spearmen of Zar. They are freed when the emerald is returned and Bob convinces the high priest that they will never return or reveal the location of Zar. Having promised before the god, Eltar must free them.

In another attempt on Tarzan's life, Jeff is mortally wounded by his own gun. He asks forgiveness for "being a rotter," admitting he wanted the emeralds, the reward, and Mary so desperately that he could not help himself. "I tried for them all — and lost three ways," he says with his last breath.

Notes

Tarzan author Edgar Rice Burroughs signed a contract in 1929 allowing Walter Shumway and Jack Nelson to make a film titled *Tarzan the Fearless*. The pact stipulated that Burroughs would receive $10,000 in advance and that Burroughs' son-in-law, James Pierce, would portray Tarzan. Unable to obtain backing, the producers eventually relinquished the contract to Sol Lesser. In 1932, while M-G-M was making the highly successful *Tarzan the Ape Man*, Lesser completed negotiations with Burroughs to produce *Fearless*. Pierce, a muscular ex-football star who made *Tarzan and the Golden Lion* in 1926, was induced by Lesser to relinquish the role upon payment of $5,000.

Wanting a younger, slimmer Tarzan more like M-G-M's Johnny Weissmuller, Lesser signed Clarence ("Buster") Crabbe, free-style swimming champion of the 1932 Olympics and star of Paramount's excellent *King of the Jungle* (1933).

Shot in four weeks at Chatsworth and other sites in the San Fernando Valley, with interiors filmed at RKO-Pathé, *Fearless* proved highly profitable. It was released both as a conventional twelve-chapter serial and in a new form created for it by Lesser: the feature-serial. This version comprised a seventy-one-minute feature edited from the first four chapters, followed by eight weekly two-reel episodes (otherwise chapters five through twelve). The format proved successful enough to be repeated in Lesser's second and last serial and to be emulated by Mascot.

Tarzan the Fearless as a whole suffers by comparison with M-G-M's beautiful production, which is superior in both scope and smoothness of continuity. While Robert S. Hill — (who directed *The Adventures of Tarzan* in 1920 and spent years as Universal's top serial director) — achieved good individual sequences and pictorial effects, a general choppiness mars the whole. This result is surprising, in that all the writers were old hands at serial construction. Skillful staging is evident in such scenes as Tarzan's dramatic appearance during an electrical storm, his rescue of a girl from stampeding horses, and a sequence straight out of H. Rider Haggard — wherein a scientist convinces a cannibal tribe that he is responsible for an eclipse. The sets, props, and costumes of the cavernous lost city are remnants from the days of Cecil B. DeMille's reign.

Greatest asset here is Crabbe, not only the most handsome of the many screen Tarzans but also the best actor. Like Weissmuller he was muscular without being musclebound, possessing the animal-like grace and agility expected of the jungle lord. Intelligent and well educated though he was, the former law student could convey perfectly the character of a man educated only in the ways of the jungle. The delicate beauty of the blonde Jacqueline Wells (known previously at Universal as Diane Duval and later at Warners as Julie Bishop) is an ideal contrast with the bronzed hero. Mischa Auer, aided by weird lighting effects, is properly sinister as the high priest. The support is sturdy: Eddie Woods as the secondary hero, Philo McCullough as a swarthy adventurer, Mathew Betz as a dull-witted heavy, and Frank Lackteen as an Arab slaver.

Tarzan's war cry is that of Pierce, heard regularly on the *Tarzan* radio serial. A musical theme, "The Call of Tarzan," based upon the three-note cry, provides romantic scoring for occasional scenes. Silent film agitatos are employed for many action scenes, courtesy of Abe Meyer's vast library.

Buster Crabbe told us recently, "*Tarzan the Fearless* didn't have a chance against the ones Johnny Weissmuller made at M-G-M. *They* had beautiful production and a lot of great animal scenes made in Africa for *Trader Horn*. *We* shot most of ours on the backlot in six weeks, and we only had a few animals: a chimp, an old elephant, and a lion which, fortunately, didn't have a tooth in his head."

DEVIL'S MATE (1933)

(Monogram Pictures Corporation)

Produced by Ben Verschleiser; *directed by* Phil Rosen; *story and screenplay by* Leonard Fields *and* David Silverstein; *photographed by* Gilbert Warrenton, ASC; *recorded by* John A. Stransky, Jr.; *sound system,* Balsley & Phillips; Trem Carr, *vice president in charge of production; running time,* 68 minutes; *released* August 20, 1933.

PLAYERS: *Nancy Weaver,* Peggy Shannon; *Inspector O'Brien,* Preston Foster; *Natural,* Ray Walker; *Parkhurst,* Hobart Cavanaugh; *Gwen,* Barbara Barondess; *Nick,* Paul Porcasi; *Joe,* Harold Waldridge; *Clinton,* Jason Robards; *District Attorney,* Bryant Washburn; *McGee,* Harry Holman; *Collins,* George Hayes; *Warden,* James Durkin; *Butler,* Gordon DeMain; *Maloney,* Paul Fix; *Prison Doctor,* Sam Flint; *Witness,* Henry Otho; *Chaplain,* Henry Hall.

Synopsis

Silent all during the tedious march to his execution, Maloney, a convicted murderer, holds out hope for a reprieve until at last he confronts the electric chair. At this point he decides to tell the assemblage of reporters and spectators just who put him up to his crime. As he is about to reveal the name of the ringleader, Maloney drops dead. Inspector O'Brien confines all witnesses to the room and discovers Maloney has died from a poisoned dart that struck him behind the ear. The angle from which the dart was fired casts suspicion on McGee, a ward-heeler and friend of the slain convict; Natural, a reporter for the *Chronicle;* Parkhurst, a philanthropist and candidate for the Prison Board; and Clinton, a friend of Parkhurst. Finally O'Brien arrests McGee, who cannot explain why he has a cigarette holder in his possession when he has made it clear that he does not smoke.

Nancy Weaver of the *Chronicle* arrives to look for Natural and, while there, interviews Parkhurst about the murder. He gives her his card, in case she needs to contact him for further information, and they part company after a visit to a speakeasy. Nancy is not convinced that McGee is the killer. She gets O'Brien's permission to find Gwen,

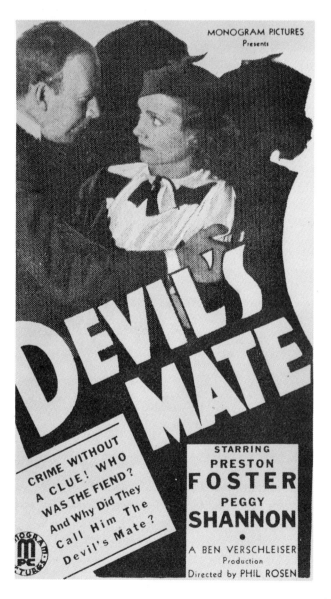

Paul Fix is led to the electric chair. Onlookers: Preston Foster, Ray Walker, Hobart Cavanaugh, Harry Holman, Jason Robards, Henry Otho, unidentified player.

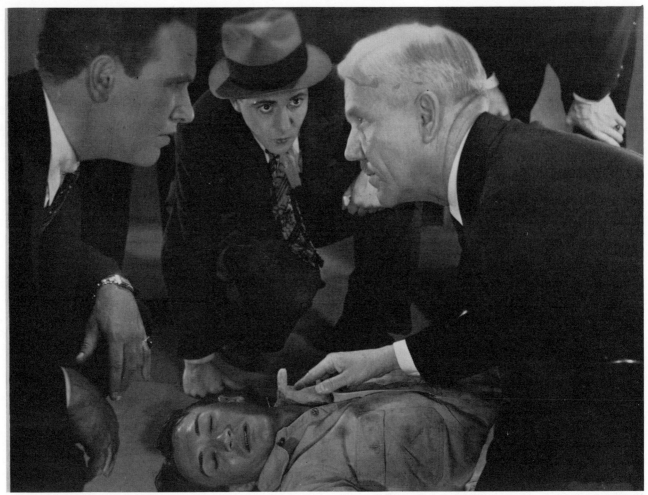

Preston Foster, Ray Walker, and Sam Flint find that Paul Fix was killed by a poisoned dart in the neck.

A clue leads Peggy Shannon to Barbara Barondess.

Purported pipsqueak Hobart Cavanaugh reveals his true nature to Peggy Shannon.

Maloney's sweetheart, and learns from her that the night before Maloney was arrested he had tried frantically to reach a telephone number that includes the digits 13-13. Gwen does not recall the prefix.

This clue leads to Parkhurst, who tells O'Brien the number belongs to his bootlegger. Gwen meantime asks Clinton to give her money to get out of town, believing that her tip to Nancy may have been a dangerous indiscretion. She prepares to drive Clinton to the bank, but when she honks the horn, she falls dead at the wheel. O'Brien discovers Gwen's death was caused by the same poison that killed Maloney, and he arrests Clinton. Nancy is still unconvinced, however, and her own deductions lead her into deadly peril. O'Brien rescues her after she has proved Parkhurst to be the real murderer.

Notes

Leonard Fields and David Silverstein delivered a highly original script in *Devil's Mate*. Intelligent direction by Phil Rosen, splendid photography by Gil Warrenton — who shot Paul Leni's classics, *The Cat and the Canary* (1927) and *The Man Who Laughs* (1927) for Universal — and thorough professionalism by the cast. brought the property to the screen as a clever, suspenseful movie. Monogram exhumed the screenplay in 1941 and remade it as *I Killed That Man* — which also was praised by critics with short memories as a highly original work.

The manner in which the first murder is committed — in the lethal chamber of a prison in the presence of numerous witnesses — sets a weird tone from the outset. A second murder is still more ingenious, with a poisoned needle concealed in an automobile horn. The identity of the killer is well hidden without cheating, the clue leading logically to perennial movie pipsqueak Hobart Cavanaugh. Interest is sustained as much from worry about the heroine's self-imposed peril as in the mystery angle.

Peggy Shannon is appealing as the reporter who solves the killings, and Preston Foster is right as the stalwart detective. There is good support from the fast-talking Ray Walker, Cavanaugh, Jason Robards, George Hayes, Paul Porcasi, Bryant Washburn, and Harry Holman. Paul Fix stands out in a brief but important appearance as the doomed convict, as does Barbara Barondess as a tough blonde.

THE DELUGE (1933)

(Admiral Productions, Incorporated)

Produced by Burt Kelly, Samuel Bischoff, *and* William Saal; *directed by* Felix E. Feist; *screenplay by* Sidney Fowler Wright; *photographed by* Norbert Brodine *and* Billy N. Williams; *special effects by* Ned Mann *and* Russell E. Lawson; *supervising film editor*, Martin G. Cohn; *film editor*, Rose Loewinger; *settings*, Ralph M. DeLacy; *musical director*, Val Burton; *sound engineer*, Corson Jowett; *musical score by* Dr. Edward Kilenyi *and* Val Burton; *assistant director*, Eric Stacy; *cameramen*, Bert Eason, Harry Davis, Johnny Eckhard, *and* Carl Guthrie; *stills*, Roman Freulich; *sound technicians*, Hans Weeren, Alf Burton, Gil Pollack, *and* Martin Jackson; *cutter*, Stanley Kolbert; *properties*, Charles Hanley *and* Robert Murphy; *electrical effects*, Al Cahen *and* Donald Donaldson; *sound system*, Western Electric; *running time*, 70 minutes; *released* September 15, 1933, by RKO-Radio Pictures, Incorporated.

PLAYERS: *Claire*, Peggy Shannon; *Martin*, Sidney Blackmer; *Helen*, Lois Wilson; *Tom*, Matt Moore; *Jephson*, Fred Kohler; *Norwood*, Ralf Harolde; *Professor Carlyle*, Edward Van Sloan; *Chief Forecaster*, Samuel S. Hinds; *Survivor*, Lane Chandler; *Renegades*, Philo McCullough *and* Harry Semels.

Synopsis

An unheralded eclipse astounds a team of scientists and meteorologists headed by Prof. Carlyle. Then the elements commence a global upheaval. Barometers drop unduly. Terrific winds rise. Seismograph needles register colossal earthquake shocks. Dispatches bespeak disaster from Southern Europe, the Mississippi Valley, the Great Lakes, Mexico, Canada, Alaska, Tibet, India, and Africa. The entire Western Coast of the North American continent sinks into the Pacific.

Several miles from New York, Martin and Helen Webster and their two infant children watch in mortal dread as a windstorm uproots trees and plucks houses from their foundations. The Websters seek shelter in an abandoned quarry near their home, and Martin returns to the cottage for food and clothing. Before he can return to the quarry, the catastrophe intensifies. Believing his family to have been destroyed, Martin wanders in search of whatever refuge can be found.

Meantime in New York, skyscrapers topple like toys. Subways drop into crevasses. Infested jailhouses, sumptuous hotels, stately office buildings all crumble. The sea engulfs the Statue of Liberty and hurls ships inland. The Empire State Building falls.

The desperate Martin has found shelter on a small island. While he rests, Claire Arlington, a debutante and long-distance swimmer who had been preparing for a swim around Manhattan Island when disaster struck, has been cast onto an island harboring two desperadoes, Norwood and Jephson. Norwood attacks Claire but is killed by Jephson. Claire swims away to the island occupied by Martin, who rescues her.

Martin and Claire set up housekeeping. Having fallen in love, they live in relative comfort until Jephson and several others outlawed by a settlement of three hundred survivors, attack the island. While Martin grapples with the savage Jephson, Claire strikes at the attacker with a heavy board. Jephson falls, dead, and Claire realizes the plank had contained a spike. The other renegades trap Claire and Martin in a cave, but a number of settlers come to their rescue.

THOUSANDS EXPECT IT TO HAPPEN!

The Destruction of Our Modern World!

CONTINENTS ARE SWEPT AWAY!

Half a hundred men . . . half a dozen women . . . survive the great flood to "start over."

TEN MEN FOR EVERY WOMAN *and no law known except desire!*

Raw passion rules the naked waste of civilization in this astounding imaginative drama!

Do you know what it means to be the last man on earth?

•

This man's story will astound you!

With

PEGGY SHANNON
LOIS WILSON
SIDNEY BLACKMER

MATT MOORE, RALF HAROLDE, EDWARD VAN SLOAN, SAMUEL HINDS. *Directed by Felix E. Feist from the book by S. Fowler Wright. Samuel Bischoff, associate producer*

A triumph of special effects.

INFORMATION INTENDED FOR EXHIBITORS ONLY!

Huge Model of   *New York City*

The producers went this captioned photo to exhibitors with instructions that it should not be published or shown.

Martin and Claire are taken to the settlement, where Martin is astonished to discover his wife and children alive. He struggles to decide whether he should give up Claire or relinquish his family to a settler, Tom, who has grown to love Helen and whom the colony leaders have chosen to become Helen's mate. He wonders whether he could claim both women.

Claire and Helen are equally self-sacrificing. Claire, however, makes the decision. She swims away from the settlement, leaving Martin with his family.

Notes

Burt Kelly, Sam Bischoff, and William Saal terminated their association with World Wide in 1933 and changed the name of their KBS Productions to Admiral Productions, Incorporated. So successful were they in the independent field that all three were offered lucrative positions at major studios. Their last venture together, *The Deluge,* was their biggest and, in some respects, their best. This remarkable fantasy, based on a popular novel by S. Fowler Wright, was among the more exciting films of its time, competing effectively with stunt films from the major companies. The timing was excellent, for the popularity of *King Kong,* which had been released several months earlier, had created a demand for spectacular trick films. *Kong's* studio, RKO-Radio, was delighted to acquire Admiral's picture for its release schedule.

The first half of *The Deluge* quite overshadows the balance, for therein are contained the superbly executed scenes in which hurricanes, earthquakes, and a tidal wave are depicted with awesome effect. These sequences dwarf the love story which follows, although some nightmarish chase episodes regain the momentum for a while. Leading roles are played with charm; Sidney Blackmer obviously relishes the opportunity to be the hero for a change, and Lois Wilson performs well as his wife. Lovely, redheaded Peggy Shannon is extremely sympathetic as the "other woman" in the romantic complications that result from the catastrophe. Miss Shannon, an alumna of Ziegfeld and Earl Carroll shows, had done leads at Paramount, Fox, and Warner Brothers and seemed a certain prospect for top stardom at the time of *The Deluge.* Her career faltered by the mid-'thirties, however, and after several years of playing small roles she killed herself.

Other effective performances come from Fred Kohler, as the brutal leader of a loathsome renegade band, and from Edward Van Sloan, Samuel S. Hinds, Ralf Harolde, and Matt Moore.

Although the special effects work has often been attributed erroneously to Willis O'Brien, chief technician of *King Kong,* it actually was the work of Ned Mann, Russell Lawson, and Billy Williams. A specialist in miniature construction, Mann supervised the preparation of a scale model of New York City and its harbor, complete with docks, ships, and the Statue of Liberty. The size of the model may be hinted at by the facts that the Empire State Building stood about twelve feet and some of the ships were as large as a man. Buildings were designed to break away on cue, and the stage was flooded for the tidal wave scenes. Billy Williams was in charge of photographing the miniatures, and his cameras captured some of the most convincing scenes of flood, earthquake, and desolation ever filmed. Although *The Deluge* seems to have vanished, the flood scenes were acquired as stock footage by Republic, which used them in *SOS Tidal Wave* (1938), *Dick Tracy vs. Crime, Inc.* (1941), and *King of the Rocketmen* (1949). Mann later conceived the effects for Alexander Korda's *The Shape of Things To Come* (1936).

Almost as impressive as the visuals is the accompanying music, which was composed by Dr. Edward Kilenyi and Val Burton. Hungarian-born Kilenyi was the father of the concert pianist of the same name, was George Gershwin's piano teacher, led the famous old Waldorf-Astoria orchestra, and scored some important silent films. Burton wrote musical revues in his native England, had been musical director of Tiffany and World Wide, wrote some hit songs ("Penthouse Serenade," "Singing a Vagabond Song"), and later wrote and produced radio dramas and movies. The film score, which was performed by a thirty-piece orchestra augmented by a huge cathedral pipe organ, is both highly original and effective. The sound recording is first-rate.

Director Felix E. Feist, son of M-G-M executive Felix F. Feist, maintains suspense during most of the picture and is responsible for a splendid dramatic scene at the climax when Peggy Shannon and Lois Wilson meet. Dialogue, wisely kept at a minimum by Warren Duff and John Goodrich, is well deployed throughout. Excellent photography, a hallmark of the KBS product, is the work of Norbert Brodine, borrowed from M-G-M. Particularly fine pictorial effects are evident in the terrifying scenes of encounters with the renegades, filmed in Bronson Canyon and its tunnels. Don Siegel much later utilized the same settings for the somewhat similar chase scenes of *Invasion of the Body Snatchers* (1956).

THE EMPEROR JONES (1933)

(John Krimsky & Gifford Cochran, Incorporated)

Produced by John Krimsky *and* Gifford Cochran; *supervised by* William C. DeMille; *directed by* Dudley Murphy; *screenplay by* DuBose Heyward; *from the play by* Eugene O'Neill; *photographed by* Ernest Haller; *settings by* Herman Rosse; *musical director,* Frank Tours; *music by* Rosamond Johnson; *sound recording,* Joseph Kane; Western Electric *sound; running time,* 80 minutes; *released* September 29, 1933, *through* United Artists.

PLAYERS: *Brutus Jones,* Paul Robeson; *Smithers,* Dudley Digges; *Jeff,* Frank Wilson; *Undine,* Fredi Washington; *Dolly,* Ruby Elzy; *Lem,* George H. Stamper; *Marcella,*

High-stakes gambling makes for drastic changes in Brutus Jones' Pullman career.

Jackie Mabley; *Treasurer,* Blueboy O'Connor; *Carrington,* Brandon Evans; *Man,* Taylor Gordon.

Synopsis

Brutus Jones stands before a mirror, admiring his uniform. The congregation of the Hezekiah Baptist Church celebrates Jones' good fortune: a new job as a Pullman porter. He sings a hymn and departs. Driven by desire for prestige and power, Jones deserts his sweetheart and romances the fiancée of his best friend, Jeff, only to abandon her as well. In a fight following a dice game he accidentally stabs Jeff fatally. He flees but is caught and sentenced to hard labor. Eventually he kills the boss of the chain gang and escapes, taking passage as a stoker on a ship. When the ship passes Haiti, he dives overboard and swims for shore.

Smithers, a ruthless English trader, makes Jones his partner. Eventually, Jones convinces the natives that he is

Paul Robeson among his "subjects." Dudley Digges in backround.

"charmed" by letting one of them shoot him with a gun Jones has loaded with blanks. "It takes a silver bullet to kill Brutus Jones," he asserts. He deposes the king and declares himself Emperor, ruling the island with an iron hand.

Revolution follows. Drums tell the story to Smithers, who informs the despot that the palace personnel have abandoned him. Jones sounds the gong to summon his entourage but finds the royal grounds deserted. Even the horses have been stolen, and Jones must flee into the jungle on foot. He gets lost in the darkness while searching for supplies he had cached for such an emergency. As the drums sound nearer he is driven to desperation, abandoning his gaudy coat and hat and firing at sounds and shadows. As he senses his approaching doom, Jones is haunted by spectres from the fatal dice game and the chain gang and tormented by faces of his victims. At last he has one bullet left — the silver one. "Don't she shine pretty?" he says, then replaces the bullet in the cylinder.

Notes

Dudley Murphy built a cinema career upon avant garde and ethnic works, his efforts including two 1929 Negro-cast shorts, *Black and Tan* and *The St. Louis Blues,* the latter boasting the only known screen performance of blues empress Bessie Smith. As early as 1928, he had discussed

Paul Robeson as a fugitive from a chain gang.

with Eugene O'Neill the prospect of filming *The Emperor Jones*. By the early 'thirties Murphy had established himself in mainstream cinema as a writer (including the *Dracula* adaptation) and was able to convince neophyte producers John Krimsky and Gifford Cochran that *Jones* would fare well on film. He was right; all the play wanted was an adaptation that would free it from its stagebound origins. With O'Neill's blessing, Murphy prepared a chronological exposition – as opposed to O'Neill's flashback monologue. In the movie, the portion presented on stage – Jones' terrified flight through the jungle – occurs during the last third of the story.

With a script by DuBose Heyward, co-author of *Porgy*, and with the brilliant William C. DeMille as supervisor, *The Emperor Jones* entered production May 25, 1933, at Eastern Service Studios on Long Island – the former Paramount Publix Studio, abandoned since March of 1932 – and saw completion late in July. Although original plans called for a location trip to Haiti, art director Herman Rosse convinced the producers that a more terrifying and dramatically effective jungle could be created in the studio.

There was but one logical choice for the title role: Paul Robeson, the celebrated singer and actor who starred in the stage version. Robeson returned from the London engagement of O'Neill's *All God's Chillun Got Wings* to give his finest screen performance. This robust portrayal of megalomania dominates the picture, although there is strong support from Dudley Digges (the only white cast member), Frank Wilson, Ruby Elzy, and the beautiful Fredi Washington. Robeson is on screen in almost every scene, conveying both menace and pathos with genuine mastery. The year after release of *Jones*, Robeson journeyed to the Soviet Union and was so accused by reactionaries of embracing the Communist system, as to gain lasting vilification in the United States. In 1949, a former Communist Party member, Manning Johnson, testified with deadly seriousness before the House Committee on Un-American Activities, "You remember the role (Robeson) played . . . of Emperor Jones. He has delusions of grandeur. He wants to be the black Stalin among Negroes." Robeson secured renewal of his passport in 1962 and the next year resettled in the United States, living in seclusion in Philadelphia, where he died at 77 in 1976. Today, a less hysterical public remembers him for his artistry.

Direction of *Jones* is excellent – (it is said that DeMille, elder brother of Cecil B., staged some of the scenes) – and the photography by Ernest Haller, one of the great pictorial stylists, is first-rate. Sets are highly imaginative, with Rosse's budgetary genius for spectacle lending a lavish appearance to the production. Rosse, who came to America from Holland, achieved fame principally as a designer for the stage, although he also was an architect, muralist, and illustrator. His occasional motion picture work included Universal's *The King of Jazz* (1930), for which he won an Academy Award; and *Dracula* (1931), *Frankenstein* (1931),

Resurrection (1931), and *Murders in the Rue Morgue* (1932) – all of which were much imitated by other designers. Jones' palace is filled with mirrors (which created many crises for Haller's cameras), and its dimensions are exaggerated by the use of columns and drapes. The jungle is an impressionistic creation of lights and shadows and simple properties. The only outdoor photography of consequence is the chain gang sequence, filmed in a stone quarry near Westchester, New York, a setting that blends in unobtrusively with the studio work.

The music – Voodoo drums, African chants, South Carolina Gullah spirituals, and jazz – is something more than accompaniment, being essential to the various milieus through which Brutus Jones passes during his rise and fall. Robeson sings three spirituals – "Now Let Me Fly," "I'm Travelin'," and "Water Boy" – in grand style.

THE WOLF DOG (1933)

(Mascot Pictures Corporation)

Produced by Nat Levine; *directed by* Colbert Clark *and* Harry Frazer; *story by* Barney Sarecky *and* Sherman Lowe; *screenplay by* Al Martin, Colbert Clark, *and* Wyndham Gittens; *supervising film editor,* Wyndham Gittens; *photographed by* Harry Neumann, William Nobles, *and* Tom Galligan; *film editor,* Earl Turner; *sound engineer,* Cliff Ruberg; *in charge of production,* Victor Zobel; *assistant directors,* George Webster, Louis Germonprez, *and* Jean Yarbrough; *production manager,* Larry Wickland; *business manager,* Albert E. Levoy; *schedules and dialogue,* Ella Arnold; *continuity clerk,* Gordon Molson; *cameramen,* Monte Steadman, Joe Lykens, *and* Jimmy Higgins; *still man,* Paul Ries; *wardrobe,* Jimmy Hertz; *grips,* Harry Horning *and* Howard Burroughs; *set decorations,* Charles Stevens *and* Jess Fleetwood; *stuntmen,* Yakima Canutt, Fred Haines, *and* Milt Cazeau; *assistants on production,* Jack Coyle, Bill Newman, Elbin Clark, *and* Art Siteman; *sound assistant,* Frank McWhorter; *sound system,* International Sound Recording Company; *a serial in* 12 chapters, 25 reels; *released* September 30, 1933.

PLAYERS: *Pal,* Rin Tin Tin, Jr.; *Frank,* Frankie Darro; *Bob,* George J. Lewis; *Irene,* Boots Mallory; *Jim Courtney,* Henry B. Walthall; *Bryan,* Hale Hamilton; *Stevens,* Fred Kohler; *and* Niles Welch, Stanley Blystone, Tom London, Sarah Padden, Max Wagner, Carroll Nye, Cornelius Keefe, Harry Northrup, Lane Chandler, Dickie Moore, Donald Reed, Gordon DeMain, George Magrill, Lionel Backus, Lew Meehan, Yakima Canutt, Leon Holmes, Jack Kenney, *and* Wes Wagner.

Chapter Titles

1) The Call of the Wilderness; 2) The Shadow of a Crime; 3) The Fugitive; 4) A Dead Man's Hand; 5) Wolf Pack Law; 6) The Gates of Mercy; 7) The Empty Room; 8) Avenging Fangs; 9) Wizard of the Wireless; 10) Accused! 11) The Broken Record; 12) Danger Lights.

Max Wagner, George J. Lewis, Fred Kohler.

Rinty, Jr., and Frankie Darro commandeer a vehicle.

Synopsis

Jim Courtney, owner of the Courtney Steamship Lines, is sent to prison when a company officer, Bryan, makes it appear Courtney is responsible for the disappearance of Frank, Courtney's orphaned nephew and heir to ownership of the line. Ten years later, pilot Jerry Patton dies when his airplane crashes in the Canadian woods. Patton's companion, a German shepherd named Pal, survives. Attacked by wolves, Pal kills the leader and joins the pack. He is found by the boy, Frank, who lives with a brutal stepfather. Frank and Pal run away and board a Courtney ship bound for Los Angeles. They befriend Bob Whitlock, the radio operator, who has invented a lightning ray that can destroy ships miles away. Bob plans to give the ray to the government, but Bryan — now president of the line — sends Brooks and Lang to steal the device. When the henchmen escape with the invention, Ray, Bob, and Pal give chase, narrowly escaping when their speedboat is blown to bits by the ray.

In Los Angeles, Bryan's men kidnap Bob and try to force him to repair the ray so they can learn its secret. The device explodes, destroying the laboratory hideout and seriously injuring Bob. As the crooks try to take Bob away in an open car, Pal attacks them and saves Bob. There are other attempts to steal the secret of the ray, to kill or kidnap Frank, and to threaten Bob's sweetheart, Irene, so that Bob will be forced to give up the secret. Attempts also are made on Courtney's life. At last Bryan is exposed and meets his death.

Notes

After the death of the great Rin Tin Tin, Mascot groomed Rin Tin Tin, Jr., as a replacement. Although a beautiful animal, Rinty, Jr., had none of the acting ability of the original and had to be doubled much of the time. His adventures in *The Wolf Dog* — a combination of science fiction, sentimental melodrama, and action on land and sea, and in the air — amount to a complex yarn in which the long arm of coincidence is stretched to the limit at times.

Most of the filming was done on locations at Lake Arrowhead, at sea, and on Mulholland Drive above Hollywood. Direction and photography are competent in light of the twenty-one-day shooting schedule. George Lewis — often a villain — is a pleasing hero, Frankie Darro an engaging juvenile (actually older than he seems here), Hale Hamilton a convincingly motivated criminal, and H. B. Walthall a sympathetic victim. There are numerous efficient heavies, some spectacular stunt work, and car and boat chases aplenty. Boots Mallory provides romantic interest.

Kazan knows who his friends are — Richard Terry, Ruth Sullivan.

JAWS OF JUSTICE (1933)

(Principal Pictures Corporation)

Produced by Sol Lesser; *directed by* Spencer Gordon Bennet; *screenplay by* Joseph Anthony Roach; *suggested by* Edgar Allan Poe's "The Gold Bug"; *running time*, 58 minutes; *released* December 4, 1933.

PLAYERS: *Kinkaid*, Richard Terry; *Judy Dean*, Ruth Sullivan; *Kickabout*, Gene Toller; *Seeker Dean*, Lafe McKee; *Boone*, Robert Walker; *Himself*, Kazan; *Kazan's Friend*, Teddy.

Synopsis

Seeker Dean, an old prospector, has a clue to the location of a gold lode and is leaving to see government authorities about rights. Boone, an author who is in love with Dean's daughter, Judy, offers to drive the old man to the train station. Dean tells his friends they all will be rich when he comes back. Boone returns with word that his car had a blowout and that Dean caught a ride with a passing motorist. The villagers grow anxious for Dean's return, not suspecting that his body lies at the bottom of a ravine.

Kickabout, a mute boy who came to the community before Dean left, is taught by Judy to read and write. The boy's constant companion is his police dog, Kazan. A Mountie named Kinkaid arrives and reveals that he sent Kickabout and Kazan down from Bear River country. The policeman falls in love with Judy, to Boone's discomfiture.

A year passes without solution of Seeker's disappearance or the secret of the lost lode. Kinkaid returns to investigate. Kickabout distrusts Boone, toward whom Kazan has developed an instinctive hatred. Boone shoots the dog after a fierce encounter. Kazan is nursed back to health.

Judy and Kickabout find a cryptogram in Seeker's desk. Judy shows the puzzle to Boone, who cannot decipher it.

Kickabout, who has read Poe's "The Gold Bug," realizes the cipher is that of the story and unravels its meaning to reveal the location of the gold. Kazan finds the remains of Dean in the ravine and brings identifying articles to Judy. Boone flees when he is caught searching Seeker's desk. Kazan tracks Boone, surprising the killer in an attempt to blow up the lost mine. The dog pulls the burning fuse and pursues Boone into the cliffs. As Boone tires to escape down a rope into the canyon, Kazan gnaws the rope in two and sends Boone falling to his doom as Kinkaid and Judy watch in horror.

Notes

Kazan, Sol Lesser's rival to Rin Tin Tin, had the advantage over most other "wonder dogs" in that he could appear as fierce as a wild wolf when the occasion demanded, while some others tended to wag their tails while chewing up the bad men. The first of a low-budget series of six Kazan pictures, *Jaws of Justice*, set the tone for all, with an offbeat story. Supporting the canine hero is Western star Jack Perrin (billed here as Richard Terry) as a romantic Mountie. Robert Walker is an effective killer, and Lafe McKee does well as an old prospector. Spencer Gordon Bennet, who directed many of the Pathé silent serials, played the story for action, his specialty. Scenery, with the Lake Tahoe region substituting for the wilds of Canada, is well photographed, and there are enough chases and fights to make up for any lack of subtlety or characterization.

1934

BIG CALIBRE (1934)

(A. W. Hackel Productions –
Supreme Pictures Corporation)
Produced by A. W. Hackel; *directed by* Robert N. Bradbury; *supervised by* Sam Katzman; *story by* Perry Murdock; *photographed by* William Hyer; *film editor,* S. Roy Luby; *a* Supreme Picture, *distributed by* William Steiner; *running time,* 54 minutes; *released* March 8, 1935.

PLAYERS: *Bob O'Neill,* Bob Steele; *June Bowers,* Peggy Campbell; *Arabella,* Georgia O'Dell; *Rusty,* Bill Quinn; *Sheriff,* Earl Dwire; *Bowers,* John Elliott; *Bentley,* Forrest Taylor; *Zenz,* Perry Murdock; *Dance Caller,* Si Jenks; *O'Neill,* Frank Ball; *and* Frank McCarroll *and* Blackie Whiteford.

Synopsis

Bob O'Neill's father is robbed and murdered at his ranchhouse by a mysterious intruder who hurls a small capsule of glass, containing a deadly, corrosive gas. Bob discovers the body and finds that acid from the capsule has eaten away part of a metal inkstand. An unbroken capsule is found outside the window alongside an oddly shaped footprint. Following these clues, Bob and the Sheriff are led to a local chemist, Zenz, whose footprint matches the one at the murder scene. Zenz escapes on horseback. Bob and the ranch foreman, Rusty, vow to hunt down the murderer. For a year they search in vain, while prospecting for a living.

At the Bowers Ranch, near Gladstone, pretty June Bowers tries in vain to dissuade her father from going into town to pay off a mortgage held by Gadski, the assayer, a hideously ugly man. On his way across the desert, Bowers is ambushed, robbed, and left for dead. The Sheriff organizes a posse to search for the missing rancher. Gadski is sending a letter to be recorded at the county seat to obtain the

change of title to the ranch. June goes to Bentley, a banker who is in love with her, to try to stall Gadski's attempt to claim the ranch.

Leaving Rusty to bring in their gear, Bob heads toward Gladstone to have some ore assayed. He sees a boot sticking out of the sand and uncovers what appears to be the skeletal remains of a man. In the clothing he finds a watch containing a photograph of June Bowers. A short time later he encounters a holdup, in which a masked bandit robs an auto-stage and escapes with a mailbag. The driver shoots the bandit's horse, and the robber is stunned in the fall. Bob rushes to the scene and finds the bandit to be June. The girl escapes on Bob's horse when Bob goes to a brook for some water. The driver finds Bob, gets the drop on him, and takes him to the Sheriff. Bob is accused of being both the bandit and — because of the watch — the slayer of the missing Bowers. A visit with Bob in his cell convinces June he did not kill her father. Rusty, drunk, is thrown into the same cell.

Perry Murdock, Bob Steele, Peggy Campbell.

Bentley and Gadski incite a mob to lynch Bob. A hand appears at the window and hurls one of Zenz's deadly capsules into the cell. Covering their faces with blankets as the capsule breaks against the cell door, Bob and Rusty escape death. The fumes weaken the door, enabling them to force it open and escape.

Next day, Bob, June, and Rusty go to the place where Bob found the supposed remains. They excavate and find the clothes to be stuffed with cattle bones. Actually, Bowers is recovering from his wounds in an Indian's hut in the hills nearby. June and Rusty return to the ranch for provisions, leaving Bob in hiding in a cave. The homely ranch cook, Arabella, discomfits Rusty with her love-making. Bob, June, and Rusty decide to attend a masquerade barn dance in Gladstone in an attempt to get evidence against Gadski and Bentley. Rusty overhears the culprits planning to rob the bank. Bob watches as Bentley and Gadski enter the bank. Inside, Bentley knocks Gadski unconscious and flees with the loot. June returns to the ranch to be confronted by Bentley, who attacks her. Bob arrives in time to overcome Bentley. Gadski has followed Bentley and is unmasked by Bob as a disguised Zenz. Bowers reveals to the Sheriff that Bentley and Gadski are the men who waylaid him.

Zenz flees, overpowering the stage driver and escaping in the auto-stage. Bob follows on horseback, leaps into the truck, and struggles with Zenz. The auto almost plunges over a precipice but balances precariously on the brink. Bob falls out but saves himself by catching hold of a wheel. Zenz takes one of the capsules from a bottle and is about to throw it at Bob, but Bob frees one hand and fires a bullet through the bottle. Doomed by his own weapon, Zenz, strangling, falls into the canyon. One of the capsules eats into the gas tank, but Bob climbs into the auto and leaps to safety as the gasoline explodes. Cleared and avenged, Bob returns to June's arms.

It is generally conceded that the weirdest Western ever made is Ken Maynard's *Smoking Guns* (1934), a study of madness and superstition which hardly fit the title and which prompted the general manager of Universal to fire the producer-writer-star. A close second for uncompromising weirdness is *Big Calibre,* directed by Robert N. Bradbury and starring his son, Bob Steele. This horror yarn disguised as an "oater" was written by Perry Murdock, veteran actor and set decorator in many outdoor films, who also appears as the grotesque, insane villain. The uncredited shooting script likely is the work of Bradbury, who usually took a hand in the writing of his films and who had a penchant for introducing unusual ideas into the Western formulae. The most constant recurring theme in the Bradbury-Steele pictures is the search by the hero for the murderer of his father — the framework for *Big Calibre.* That the killer is a mad scientist who wears a gruesome disguise and commits murder with a corrosive gas instead of a six-gun, sets the film apart from standard Saturday Western fare.

Bradbury's superb pictorial sense is well served by the work of cinematographer Bill Hyer, an underrated craftsman who never seemed able to escape Poverty Row. Directorial style and scenic beauty do much to compensate for the eccentricities of the script. Steele is at his energetic best both in action (he was seldom doubled in any of his films) and in conveying the tortured, romantic nature of the hero. Bill Quinn and Georgia O'Dell provide appropriate comic moments that mesh well with the story's basic oppressiveness; Quinn's amusing drunkenness, for example, flows nicely into horror in the jail sequence where he and Steele face the threats of a lynch mob and the madman. Murdock's crazed villain and Forrest Taylor's coldly calculating mask of respectability are menacing, although Murdock's overdone makeup probably would not have fooled anybody in real life. Peggy Campbell is an attractive romantic lead, and there are neat character portrayals by Earl Dwire, Si Jenks, and Frank Ball. The prolonged chase at the climax is suspenseful, and the literal cliffhanger ending provides as much spectacle as can be extracted from a slender budget.

Steele was no typical cowboy star. Small, wiry, and curly-haired, he projected more romance and emotion than his colleagues, particularly in the films made by his father. He was unsurpassed in staging realistic fights, and as a horseman he was second only to Ken Maynard. As Bob Bradbury, he began his film career at the age of fourteen in 1921, co-starring with his brother, Bill, in a series of adventure pictures produced by his father for Pathé. In 1927, as Bob Steele, he became a Western star for FBO, his popularity in this category lasting well into the 'forties. He gave some memorable performances as villains in "A" pictures as well, including the despicable Curly in *Of Mice* and *Men* (1940) and the hired assassins of *The Big Sleep* (1946) and *The Enforcer* (1951). More recently he gained a new following in the comedy role of Trooper Duffy in the *F Troop* television series, after which he retired.

MYSTERY LINER (1934)

(Monogram Pictures Corporation)

Vice president in charge of production, Trem Carr; *produced by* Paul Malvern; *directed by* William Nigh; *from the Saturday Evening Post novel,* THE GHOST OF JOHN HOLLING, *by* Edgar Wallace; *adaptation by* Wellyn Totman; *photographed by* Archie J. Stout; *settings by* E. R. Hickson; *sound recording,* John A. Stransky, Jr.; *musical director,* Abe Meyer; *Western Electric sound by* Balsley & Phillips; *running time,* 62 minutes; *released* March 15, 1934.

PLAYERS: *Captain Holling,* Noah Beery; *Lila,* Astrid Allyn; *Cliff,* Cornelius Keefe; *Von Kessling,* Gustav von Seyffertitz; *Major Pope,* Edwin Maxwell; *Grimson,* Ralph Lewis; *Downey,* Boothe Howard; *Watson,* John Maurice Sullivan; *Bryson,* Gordon DeMain; *Granny,* Zeffie Tilbury; *Dr. Howard,* Howard Hickman; *Edgar,* Jerry Stewart; *Wathman,* George Hayes; *Simms,* George Cleveland; *Grimson's Assistant,* Olaf Hytten; *His Excellency,* Ray Brown; *Waiter,* George Nash.

Synopsis

An invention of staggering warfare potential is the S-505

Zeffie Tilbury accuses Edwin Maxwell. Also pictured: George Hayes, Cornelius Keefe, Gustav von Seyffertitz.

tube, touted by its developer, Grimson, as a device to control ocean liners. The government arranges for a secret test with the owners of the vessel *Guthrie.* Ship's Captain Holling, taken unaccountably ill, is hospitalized and replaced by First Mate Downey. Holling does not like his removal from command any more than does Second Officer Cliff Rogers, who considers Downey his rival for the affections of nurse Lila. Grimson supervises installation of the control tube in the company of Commander Bryson, Major Pope, and Watson, owner of the *Guthrie.* Passengers include the outspoken Granny Plimpton, her nephew Edgar, and the mysterious von Kessling.

At Grimson's control laboratory, helpers find the inventor strangled by a rope tied in a sailor's knot resembling one Downey had demonstrated to a steward, Simms. Captain Holling has escaped from the hospital. Simms tells Downey he has seen Holling in Granny's cabin. Cliff is sent to search but finds no one. As Downey enters the Captain's cabin, he spots Lila peering through a bookcase. As she fumbles with an explanation, Downey tells her he plans to retire at the end of the voyage.

The laboratory puts the ship under automatic control, at length placing it on a wartime test with all lights out. Downey is throttled and discovered by Cliff. Pope investigates, and finally Cliff, having taken the captaincy, arrests von Kessling. Suddenly the vessel careens out of control in the fog; foreign agents have replaced the S-505 with a tube that scrambles the signals. Simms is startled at sight of Captain Holling.

Now Holling appears and exposes Major Pope as the villain. Pope dies when he attempts to escape by airplane.

Notes

The most prolific mystery writer of his time was Edgar

Wallace, the Englishman who died in 1932 in Hollywood while doing preliminary work on the story treatment of *King Kong*. Among the many Wallace tales purchased for filming was *The Ghost of John Holling*, the basis of *Mystery Liner*. The finished product is anything but lavish, although handling of the complicated story is adequate, and the shipboard settings are convincing. Photography, as could be expected from Archie Stout, is highly competent.

The casting avoids clichés. Noah Beery, the great villain, is here a heroic skipper. Cornelius Keefe is a romantic hero instead of his usual slick crook. Even Gustav von Seyffertitz isn't as mean as he looks. George Hayes and George Cleveland play "straight" parts instead of their usual loveable old duffer roles. Edwin Maxwell, however, is his old crooked self, Zeffie Tilbury does her specialty as a nasty old lady, and Astrid Allyn (later Allwyn) is in her element as the menaced heroine.

THE LOST JUNGLE (1934)

(Mascot Pictures Corporation)

Produced by Nat Levine; *directed by* Armand Schaefer *and* David Howard; *production manager,* Larry Wickland; *supervising editor,* Wyndham Gittens; *story by* Colbert Clark, John Rathmell, Sherman Lowe, *and* Al Martin; *screenplay by* Barney Sarecky, David Howard, Armand Schaefer, *and* Wyndham Gittens; *photographed by* Alvin Wyckoff *and* William Nobles; *film editor,* Earl Turner; *musical score,* Hal Chasnoff; *recording engineer,* Terry Kellum; International Sound Recording Company *system; a serial in* 12 *chapters,* 25 *reels; feature-serial version,* 27 *reels consisting of a* 73-*minute feature plus four two-reel chapters; released* March 22, 1934; *feature version,* 106 *minutes; released* June 13, 1934.

PLAYERS: *Himself,* Clyde Beatty; *Ruth Robinson,* Cecilia Parker; *Larry Henderson,* Syd Saylor; *Sharkey,* Warner Richmond; *Kirby,* Wheeler Oakman; *Thompson,* Maston Williams; *Explorer,* J. Crauford Kent; *Howard,* Lloyd Whitlock; *Bannister,* Lloyd Ingraham; *Captain Robinson,* Edward J. LeSaint; *Flynn,* Lew Meehan; *Slade,* Max Wagner; *Jackman,* Wes Warner; *The Cook,* Jack Carlyle; *Steve,* Jim Corey; *Sandy,* Wally Wales; *Pete,* Ernie S. Adams; *Slim,* Charles Whittaker; *Maitland,* Harry Holman; *Mickey,* Mickey Rooney; *and* The Hagenbeck-Wallace Circus Wild Animals.

Chapter Titles

1) Noah's Ark Island; 2) Nature in the Raw; 3) The Hypnotic Eye; 4) The Pit of Crocodiles; 5) Gorilla Warfare; 6) The Battle of Beasts; 7) The Tiger's Prey; 8) The Lion's Brood; 9) Eyes of the Jungle; 10) Human Hyenas; 11) The Gorilla; 12) Take Them Back Alive.

Synopsis

Clyde Beatty, star animal trainer of Maitland's Circus, accomplishes the seemingly impossible by bringing forty big cats — a mix of lions and tigers — into the same cage. Now

Clyde sets out in a dirigible to capture a new group of animals. He is accompanied by his jealous assistant, Sharkey, and press agent Larry Henderson. A terrific storm wrecks the craft in the Indian Ocean. Sharkey bails out into the jungle of an uncharted island. The aircraft crashes on the beach. It is evident that the island is the last remnant of a strip that once connected Africa and Asia; it contains wildlife of both continents. Clyde's circus tactics overcome a lion attack. He and Larry discover a stockade. Inside is the crew of a ship that months before had brought an

Clyde Beatty, Cecilia Parker.

explorer searching for the treasure of a lost city. The explorer is missing, and the crew threatens mutiny if Captain Robinson does not return to the States. Clyde promises assistance to Robinson and Ruth, the skipper's daughter.

Sharkey, meantime, finds a massive iron door leading to the buried city, whose sole inhabitant is a monster gorilla. He secures the treasure and hides it. Going to the stockade he joins the crew, planning to return with the treasure himself. He finds a willing partner in Kirby, leader of the mutineers. In protecting his friends, Beatty faces jungle cats and a bear. He survives an attempt by the heavies to throw him to crocodiles and has several near-disastrous encounters with the gorilla. Larry at one point escapes the ape by leaping to a chandelier over the crocodile pit. The fixture begins to pull free, but Clyde arrives in time to drive the gorilla away so that his friend can leap to safety.

Clyde's group is safe from the mutineers. Sharkey and Kirby pay with their lives for their treachery. Clyde hopes to capture the gorilla but is forced to kill the beast to save his friends. Clyde, Larry, and the Robinsons dig their way to safety from the buried city.

Notes

Clyde Beatty was the world's most famous wild animal trainer and proved a saleable movie commodity as well. Universal made a bundle with Beatty's first feature, *The Big Cage* (1932), although the wiry little daredevil wasn't much of an actor or the usual idea of a movie hero. That he was an authentic hero was a more important factor, and he had a likeable personality. Beatty's second picture, *The Lost Jungle,* proved both popular and profitable. Hardly polished from a production standpoint, it offers excitement aplenty, with Beatty facing death repeatedly in harrowing encounters with animals from a circus menagerie — including Hagenbeck-Wallace's highly publicized "killer lion," Sammie. A Hollywood gorilla and inmates from the alligator farm were thrown in to add to the horror. Most of the animal scenes were staged indoors on sets consisting mainly of clumps of bamboo arranged to cover walls and cages. The animal action, especially a lion-tiger fight, generates considerable audience sweat. Scenes in the temple, with a murderous gorilla lurking in shadows, build suspense. On the debit side are poorly done trick photography of the dirigible crash and repetitiousness of story and action during some episodes.

Warner Richmond and Wheeler Oakman head a fine cast of heavies. Syd Saylor — a great favorite with children, although he never caught on with adults — gets some laughs with his hyperactive Adam's apple. Cecilia Parker is a lovely, innocent-looking ingenue. The brilliant child actor, Mickey Rooney, is spotlighted in the opening scenes.

A feature-serial version of *The Lost Jungle* differs from Sol Lesser's formula in that it was edited to a seven-reel feature followed by ten chapters. The feature comprises most of the first two chapters' material, plus about twenty-four minutes of footage not used in the serial. In response to complaints from exhibitors who wanted a Beatty feature but no serial chapters, Levine had Wyndham Gittens edit an eleven-reel feature condensing the entire serial story.

THE HOUSE OF MYSTERY (1934)

(Monogram Pictures Corporation)

Trem Carr, *vice president in charge of production; supervised by* Paul Malvern; *directed by* William Nigh; *adapted by* Albert E. DeMond *from the play by* Adam Hull Shirk; *photographed by* Archie Stout; *edited by* Carl Pierson; *art director,* E. R. Hickson; *production manager,* Max Alexander; *musical director,* Abe Meyer; *recorded by* John A. Stransky, Jr.; Western Electric *sound by* Balsley & Phillips; *running time,* 62 minutes; *released* March 30, 1934.

PLAYERS: *Jack Armstrong,* Ed Lowry; *Ella Browning,* Verna Hillie (courtesy of Paramount Pictures); *Harry Smith,* John Sheehan; *Hindu Priest,* Brandon Hurst; *Chanda,* Liya Joy (Joyzelle); *Stella Walters,* Fritzi Ridgeway; *John Pren,* Clay Clement; *David Fells,* George Hayes; *Mrs. Carfax,* Dale Fuller; *Professor Potter,* Harry C. Bradley; *Ned Pickens,* Irving Bacon; *Mrs. Potter,* Mary Foy; *Ellis,* Samuel Godfrey; *Clancy,* George Cleveland; *Bartender,* Bruce Mitchell; *Hindu,* Dick Botiller; *Englishman,* James Morton.

Synopsis

The Curse of Kali seems responsible for the intrusion of a ghostly ape into the mansion of John Pren, a reclusive cripple. Pren had long ago killed the sacred ape of a Hindu temple and absconded with the jewels and a lovely dancer, Chanda. The temple priest had promised him the wealth would bring misery and the spectre of the ape would follow him. Pren has required various claimants to the fortune, which he had discovered for an investment cartel, to spend a week in his shadowy estate before he will hand over their share. Behind the foreboding exterior, Chanda holds sway as mistress before the effigy of an ape.

The party includes Ella Browning, aide to Pren; Jack Armstrong, a smart-mouthed insurance salesman; Professor Potter and his wife; Mrs. Carfax, her companion; Stella Walters; Ellis, a lawyer; David Fells, a gambler; and Harry Smith, a dull plumber. Mrs. Carfax dies in the midst of a seance. Fells is murdered while masquerading as an ape in an effort to scatter the other guests and find the jewels.

The bumbling Inspector Ned Pickens and two equally inept helpers arrive. No sooner have the bodies been carted away than Armstrong survives an attack. While Pickens accuses Armstrong of a hoax, Stella is strangled by the creature.

A Scotland Yard investigator unravels the plot just as Ellis faces death. Pren is exposed as the killer and dies at the hands of his own creation.

Notes

This picture proves Monogram to have been a pioneer. Paramount started a trend in 1938 by casting a popular radio and vaudeville comedian, Bob Hope, in a remake of the hardy Broadway comedy-thriller, *The Cat and the Canary.* This hit was followed by a string of successful features in which Hope's wisecracks alternated with scares, such as *The Ghost Breakers* (1940), *My Favorite Blonde* (1942), *Where There's Life* (1947), *My Favorite Brunette* (1947), *The Great Lover* (1949), and *My Favorite Spy* (1951). Comedy-mysteries had been popular for decades, but the early approach depended more on visual gags than on the Hope brand of verbal humor. A little-known fact is that Monogram was four years ahead of Paramount, with its selection of radio-vaudeville headliner Ed Lowry as the wisecracking hero of *The House of Mystery.* The usual formula called for a shy or innocent hero. Lowry admittedly was no Bob Hope, and Monogram's production values were below that Paramount offered, but the similarity of approach is inescapable.

In his film debut (and simultaneous farewell), Lowry comes over as reasonably good-looking and witty, well suited to play a brash smart-aleck who can rise to the occasion of heroics and romance. A young New Yorker who grew up in show business, he had twenty years' experience as a bandleader and master of ceremonies. He was appearing at Loew's State Theatre in Los Angeles when the Monogram offer came. Lowry quickly returned to stage and radio when the film failed to attract much attention. Later he could console himself with the knowledge that even such stage and radio giants as Fred Allen, Jack Benny, and Seth Parker bombed out in pictures.

A well-mounted eeriness and imaginative photography are plus factors, but direction is a bit heavy to show comedic aspects to best effect. Verna Hillie, a beauty contest winner from Michigan under Paramount contract, is a lovely leading lady. The excellent Brandon Hurst helps create the atmosphere, as does Dale Fuller, the fine player of eccentric women whose work added much to von Stroheim's *Foolish Wives* (1923) and *Greed* (1925). Various degrees of menace come from the likes of Clay Clement,

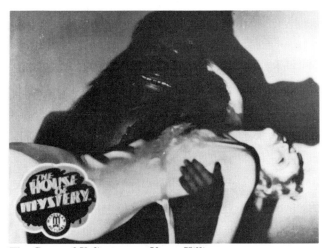
The Curse of Kali menaces Verna Hillie.

George Hayes (yes, the later beloved "Gabby"), and Mary Foy. There are additional comic bits by John Sheehan, George Cleveland, Irving Bacon, and Harry C. Bradley. Exotic dancer Liya Joy executes an eye-filling nautch dance.

PICTURE BRIDES (1934)

(Allied Pictures Corporation)

Produced by M. H. Hoffman; *associate producer,* M. H. Hoffman, Jr.; *directed by* Phil Rosen; *based on a stage play by* Charles E. *and* Harry Clay Blaney; *adaptation and dialogue,* Adele Buffington; *additional dialogue* Will Ahern; *production manager,* Ray Culley; *photographed by* Harry Neumann *and* Tom Galligan; *edited by* Mildred Johnston; *art director,* Harold H. MacArthur; *gowns by* Elizabeth Coleman; *assistant director,* J. H. McCloskey; *sound recording by* Pete Clark; *musical director,* Abe Meyer; *made at* RKO-Pathé *Studio;* RCA Victor *sound; running time,* 66 minutes; *released* April 24, 1934.

PLAYERS: *Mame,* Dorothy Mackaill; *Dave,* Regis Toomey; *Mary Lee,* Dorothy Libaire; *Von Luden,* Alan Hale; *Brownie,* Will Ahern; *Castro,* Fred Malatesta; *Dr. Rogers,* Harvey Clark; *Mateo,* Mary Kornman; *Laoma,* Gladys Ahern; *Flo,* Esther Muir; *Gwen,* Mae Busch; *Lena,* Viva Tattersall; *Steve,* Al Hill; *Pete,* Michael Visaroff; *Joe,* Brooks Benedict; *Bill,* Franklin Parker; *Tom,* Larry McGrath; *Skipper,* Jimmy Aubrey.

Synopsis

Into the Brazilian jungle comes a riverboat bearing four "picture brides" — Mame, Flo, Gwen, and Lena — sent from New Orleans to marry personnel at Lottagrasso, remote site of the Standard Diamond Mine. Also aboard is a frightened, innocent girl, Mary Lee, who is to see the mine boss, Von Luden, about a job. Knowing Von Luden's

inhuman reputation, Mame transfers the picture assigning her to Dave Hart onto Mary's card. The girls are loaded into Brownie's truck and taken to the outpost. Castro, the mail runner, meets the truck which has broken down near the settlement. One letter informs Von Luden that his partner, Hart, is wanted in the States for embezzlement. As the girls straggle into town, Von Luden shoots a native, who dies in the street. Von Luden orders the body thrown into the swamp, but Hart intervenes. Mame presents herself as the job applicant while Mary is introduced to Dave and his fellow mine supervisors, Pete, Joe, and Bill. Dave at first refuses to accept Mary, but when Von Luden invites her to his castle, Dave changes his mind and has Mary taken to his house.

Von Luden arranges the marriages that night at his residence, a veritable palace. During a wild party which follows, Von Luden lustfully watches Mary and plots with a dancing girl, Laoma. Castro, falling, rips Mary's dress, and Laoma takes her upstairs to have it mended. Alone in a bedroom, Mary is confronted by Von Luden. Hearing Mary's screams, Mame alerts Dave, who breaks in and thrashes Von Luden.

Pretty Mateo Rogers, halfbreed daughter of the camp's drunken doctor, celebrates her eighteenth birthday. Mame and Mary make the girl a dress and apply makeup, seemingly transforming the child to a glamorous woman. Von Luden lures Mateo to his castle and attacks her. Later, Dr. Rogers returns from treating a native and is unable to find his daughter. Natives find her body in the swamp.

Detectives Steve and Al, summoned by Von Luden, have come to extradite Dave. As the men gather in Von Luden's office, Rogers rushes in and empties a revolver into his daughter's slayer. Dave returns the money he embezzled

Dorothy Mackaill.

shown milking a goat, then waking her father by dousing him with the milk. An ox cart rumbles down a street. Hale is introduced as he sloppily wolfs down a meal while watching a native dancing girl. The photography is realistic.

DRUMS O' VOODOO (1934)
a.k.a. SHE DEVIL

(International Stageplay Pictures, Incorporated)

Presented by Robert Mintz; *produced by* Louis Weiss; *directed by* Arthur Hoerl; *based upon the stage play,* Louisiana, *by* J. Augustus Smith; *screenplay by* J. Augustus Smith; *photographed by* Walter Strenge *and* J. Burgi Contner; *sound technicians,* Lyman J. Wiggin *and* Verne T. Braman; *production manager,* Ben Berk; *art director,* Sam Corso; *sound system,* Blue Seal Cineglow; *produced at* Atlas Sound Studios, Long Island City, New York; *produced and distributed by* International Stageplay Pictures, Incorporated; *running time,* 70 minutes; *released* May 12, 1934.

PLAYERS: *Aunt Hagar,* Laura Bowman; *Elder Berry,* J. Augustus Smith; *Myrtle Simpson,* Edna Barr; *Ebenezer,* Lionel Monagas; *Thomas Catt,* Morris McKinney; *Deacon Dunson,* A. B. Comathiere; *Sister Knight,* Alberta Perkins; *Brother Zero,* Fred Bonny; *Deacon August,* Paul Johnson; *Sister Marguerite,* Trixie Smith; *Sister Zunan,* Carrie Huff; *Brother Zumee,* James Davis; *Sister Gaghan,* Ruth Morrison; *Sister Lauter,* Harriet Daughtry; *Bou Bouche,*

and returns with Mary to the States, where it is indicated he will be treated leniently. Brownie, now in charge of the mine, marries Mame.

Notes

An "Allied Special," *Picture Brides* represents a larger-than-usual outlay of casting and production investment. Filmed in jungle sets that are pleasingly familiar to *aficionados* of *The Most Dangerous Game* (1932) and *King Kong* (1933), it depicts a convincing and colorfully peopled Brazilian outpost. One of the inhabitants, Alan Hale's brutal sex fiend Von Luden, is reminiscent of Jean Hersholt's human beasts of *Hell Harbor* and *Mamba* (both 1930.) The overpowering Hale steals much of the thunder from top-billed Dorothy Mackaill, Regis Toomey, and Dorothy Libaire. Miss Mackaill, a silent star on the wane, is quite good, however, as a "tarnished" but sympathetic woman. Other standouts of the generally capable cast are Esther Muir, Mae Busch, and Viva Tattersall as Miss Mackaill's tough-but-decent blonde friends; Harvey Clark as a drink-sodden doctor; Gladys Ahern as a seductive dancing girl; Will Ahern as a witty truck driver, and Mary Kornman (a former *Our Gang* youngster) as a half-native girl.

Phil Rosen's direction shows admirable attention to detail in establishing the settlement's oppressively swelter-ing atmosphere. In the opening scenes Mary Kornman is

Good vs. evil in the bayou.

Bennie Small; *Marcon,* Pedro Lopez; *Members of the Flat Rock Washfoot Baptist Church,* Jennie Day, Gladys Booker, Herminie Sullivan, Lillian Exum, Edith Woodby, Mabel Grant, Marion Hughes, Madeline Smith, Theresa Harris, Dorothy St. Claire, Eleanor Hines, Pauline Freeman, Annabelle Smith, Jacquiline Ghant, Annabelle Ross, Harriet Scott; *Voodoo Dancers,* Cherokee Thornton, Arthur McLean, DeWitt Davis, Rudolph Walker, Marvin Everhart, Jimmie Cook, Irene Bagley, Sally Timmons, Beatrice James, Marie Remsen.

Synopsis

Old Aunt Hagar, last of Louisiana's Voodoo priestesses, holds a strong influence over the inhabitants of a small Negro community in the swampy lowlands outside the town of Bayou-la-fouche. The inhabitants, descendants of slaves, are still responsibe to the ancient African drums and believe in the Voodoo gods worshipped by Aunt Hagar. Elder Amos Berry, pastor of the Flat Rock Washfoot Baptist Church, tries sincerely to lead his flock in the ways of Christianity as he perceives it, but he nonetheless recognizes and respects Aunt Hagar's power to combat evil.

Into the community comes Thomas Catt, who once served time with Elder Berry on a chain gang. Catt establishes a "jook," a low dive dealing in liquor and prostitution, and so threatens to destroy the moral standards of the followers of both Aunt Hagar and Elder Berry. The preacher's niece, Myrtle Simpson, arrives home from school, and Catt decides he must have her for his "jook." To achieve his aim, he threatens to expose Berry's record as a convict. Ebenezer, grandson of Aunt Hagar, begs the conjure woman to save Myrtle from Catt. After Berry has failed to halt Catt, whom he rightly recognizes as a minion of Satan, Aunt Hagar intervenes and casts a Voodoo spell upon the villain. Blinded by a flash of lightning, Catt stumbles into the swamp and is swallowed by quicksand.

Notes

J. Augustus Smith ran away from his Florida home at fourteen to join the Rabbit's Foot Musical Comedy minstrel troupe, which presented tent shows in small Southern towns. After years of performing with minstrel shows, Smith formed small companies to stage his own one-act plays in black communities in the South, the East, and the Midwest. At last, in February of 1933, Smith hit Broadway with his one-act play, *Louisiana,* produced by George Miller for the Negro Theatre Guild. Smith's ingenuous and guileless effort at presenting a vanishing way of life of uneducated Southern blacks torn between superstition and Christianity drew high praise from some of the critics -- but not from the one who counted most, Brooks Atkinson of the *New York Times.* A vicious salvo from Atkinson helped to sink *Louisiana* after only eight performances.

A trace of Smith's play survived the sinking, however. Movie-struck, he also had written it as a film script, which he presented to Louis Weiss, the remaining active member of the old Weiss Brothers film company. With an eye to the growing market for Negro pictures, Weiss filmed the play with the original stage cast. The cost of production was negligible, because the actors already knew their lines and were in costume. These economies were unfortunately not enough for the budget-conscious producer, who put forth little effort to make a genuinely cinematic film. The sets are strictly stage-bound, and photography and lighting are devoid of the imagination such a story demands.

What makes the picture a fascinating document is the innocent sincerity of the play itself, supported by the use of authentic spirituals and Voodoo music, and by fine performances. Illinois-born singer and actress Laura Bowman, who was called "the Negro Barrymore," performed by command at Buckingham Palace before King Edward VII, starred for ten months at the Shaftsbury Theatre in London, and appeared in the theaters of Berlin, Moscow, Budapest, Vienna, Rome, Naples, Zurich, and Paris. In 1916 she joined New York's first black dramatic company, the Lafayette Players in Harlem, for which she appeared in five hundred productions. Later, for the Negro Art Theatre Company, she played in classical dramas on Broadway. Her performance in *Drums O' Voodoo* is splendid, and her makeup, achieved with varying shades of green greasepaint, is perfectly appropriate to the role of conjure woman. "Gus" Smith himself appears with admirable simplicity in another important part. Also noteworthy are Morris "Chick" McKinney, of the Broadway productions of *The Green Pastures* and *Porgy and Bess,* who plays the villain; A. B. Comathiere and Lionel Monagas, both veterans of the Lafayette Players; and Edna Barr, a musical comedy actress.

Even with recently heightened awareness of the contributions of black moviemakers, *Drums O' Voodoo* has remained virtually unknown.

THE MYSTIC HOUR (1934)

(Progressive Pictures Corporation)

Directed by Melville DeLay; *continuity and dialogue by* John Francis Nattiford; *story by* Susan Embry; *photographed by* Leon Shamroy *and* Bernard B. Ray; *length,* six reels; *released* late May of 1934.

PLAYERS: *Captain James,* Montagu Love; *Mary Marshall,* Lucille Powers; *Roger Thurston,* Charles Middleton; *Myra Marshall,* Edith Thornton; *Bradley Thurston,* Eddie Phillips; *Blinkey,* James Aubrey; *Robert Randall,* Charles Hutchison.

Synopsis

Wealthy young Bob Randall, caught up in a chase after a crafty criminal known as the Fox following an aborted bank burglary, is mistaken for a prowler in the bedroom of Mary Marshall. One of the gang is hiding behind the bed, and as Bob pounces on him the commotion rouses Mary's

No Picture Ever Held Such Drama!
No Picture Ever Held Such Thrills! as

"THE MYSTIC HOUR"

with

MONTAGUE
LOVE
LUCILLE
POWERS
CHARLES
MIDDLETON

Charles Hutchison in his serial-king days.

Eddie Phillips, Lucille Powers, Edith Thornton, Charles B. Middleton, Montagu Love.

guardian, Roger Thurston, and his brother, Bradley, who desires Mary. The Fox arranges for the henchman whom Bob has caught to be poisoned in jail.

The Fox warns a wealthy woman of his designs on her jewels. The Fox leaves his den and assumes the respectable identity of Captain James, chief of a private detective agency. James receives a call for help from the woman who received the Fox's warning. The woman proves to be Bob's aunt.

As the Fox sets out to make good his threat, he finds in the jewel box a note reading, "Put up your hands." Then Bob's voice is heard: "I mean it." The Fox escapes.

While Roger berates his brother for letting Mary see Bob, it is disclosed that Roger has been stealing from the girl. Bob and Mary enter to announce their engagement. The Fox threatens to kidnap Bob, who makes public his defiance of the warning. Roger suggests that he and his brother abduct Bob for enough ransom to cover the imbalance in Mary's funds.

At the engagement dinner, the brothers' hoodlums spy on Bob. The lights are doused, and the thugs come through a window. The Fox and an accomplice are seen leaving the estate. Mary, distraught over Bob's disappearance, calls the police and orders Roger to offer a reward. Captain James offers to find Bob without pay. Roger tells James he has been in touch with the Fox and believes Bob will be freed soon — upon payment of the ransom.

In his apartment, Bob is amused by press accounts of his abduction. A private detective reports discovery of Roger's embezzlement and attributes the kidnap attempt to the Thurstons. The detective also tells Bob that James handled the case of the attempted jewel burglary. Bob orders an investigation of James's agency. Trying to warn Mary not to put up a ransom, Bob steals into her room but startles her so, that she cries for help. Forced to leave, lest he ruin his cover, Bob is chased by two of James's detectives, but loses them by ducking between the railroad tracks as a train speeds past. Returning to explain the state of things to Mary, he overhears a conversation between James and Roger.

Bob realizes that James and the Fox are one man. He gets the drop on James and Roger and calls the law, but Bradley attacks him from behind. In the struggle, James escapes after wounding Roger. Bradley is so frightened that he frees Bob, who dashes after James, cornering him atop an oceanside cliff. The desperate criminal dives and swims for freedom. Bob follows suit and hauls James to shore, where Mary is waiting.

Notes

Little known even in its time, *The Mystic Hour* received few showings on its states'-rights release basis. The cast is surprisingly good, with two of the best villains, Montagu Love and Charles Middleton, performing in the grand manner. The inegnue role is capably set forth by blonde Lucille Powers, who had appeared for most of the major companies and was praised for her work at M-G-M in King Vidor's *Billy the Kid* (1931).

A real surprise is the presence of the famed silent era serial actor and director, Charles Hutchison, better known as "Daredevil Hutch." For some reason Hutchison's name was omitted from all advertising — despite his central role, and the screen credits list him last. Although a dozen years older than when he performed daring stunts for Pathé, Hutchison stages some rough-and-tumble fights, a hair-raising roll under a moving train, and a high dive into the ocean.

The script is by John F. Nattiford, who at the time had written almost eighty screenplays, most of them melodramas and Westerns for the independents. Director Melville DeLay was an assistant at the majors but achieved directorial status on Poverty Row. *Hour* has more action than atmosphere, but its photography surpasses the usual "quickie" standards.

MURDER IN THE MUSEUM (1934)

(Willis Kent Productions)

Presented by Willis Kent; *directed by* Melville Shyer; *story*

by E. B. Crosswhite; *edited by* S. Roy Luby; *photographed by* James Diamond, *assistant director,* George Curtner; International *sound; produced at* International Studios, Hollywood; *length,* five reels; *released* June-July of 1934 by Progressive Pictures Corporation.

PLAYERS: *Mysto,* Henry B. Walthall; *Jerry,* John Harron; *Lois,* Phyllis Barrington; *Brandon,* Joseph Girard; *Snell,* John Elliott; *Barker,* Donald Kerr; *Fortune Teller,* Symonia Boniface; *Newgate,* Sam Flint; *Judson,* Clinton Lyle; *Knife Thrower,* Steve Clemente; *King Kiku,* Albert Knight; *Carr,* Lynton Brent; *Rube,* Si Jenks; *Detective,* Al Hill.

Synopsis

Sightseers have packed the Sphere Museum of Natural & Unnatural Wonders, where a barker extols the singular physical and mental abnormalities of the various freaks. The manager, Carr, is disturbed by the arrival of three visitors: Police Commissioner Brandon, a friend named Judson, and the temperance-minded Councilman Newgate. Carr fears discovery of several cases of liquor he keeps on the grounds; he alerts his stage magician, Professor Mysto, to the identity of the three, who have just now been joined by a reporter, Jerry Ross. Brandon's niece, Lois, arrives and is introduced to Jerry and the others.

Prior to Ross's appearance, Newgate had suggested to Brandon that they postpone their contemplated raid because of the volume of onlookers. But at sight of the reporter, he whispers to Brandon that the time is right to proceed as they had planned.

Newgate approaches the rear door but falls at the sound of a gunshot. Brandon and Mysto rush to his side. The crowd stampedes toward the entrance only to be stopped by a crew of plainclothesmen whom Brandon had assigned for the intended bootleg raid. Carr, who has fled upon hearing the gunfire, is captured by two detectives. A police

surgeon pronounces Newgate dead. A search of patrons and performers yields no weapon until a .45-caliber Colt revolver is found under a platform. A concessionaire, admitting ownership of the firearm, is taken into custody. Then the back-room liquor cache comes to light; Carr, posing as the victim of a frame-up, knocks down a detective and flees through the rear doorway.

Jerry has meanwhile filed the story with his paper, and he decides to acquaint himself with Lois. Their admiration is reciprocal, but Lois tells Jerry that her uncle has no use for news reporters.

The concession manager has denied the police a confession. He is freed upon receipt of the word that the bullet that killed Newgate came from a .38-caliber weapon — not the suspect's .45.

The *Gazette,* rival newspaper to the *Times-Herald* for which Jerry works, takes Commissioner Brandon to task with a hint that one of Brandon's own men fired the fatal bullet, in view of a widely known unfriendly relationship between the commissioner and Newgate. The attack compounds Brandon's distaste for the press, and he refuses to see Jerry when the reporter calls upon the commissioner. Yet Lois admits her love for Jerry, who tells her he has been to see Professor Mysto. There is no new light, however, on the shooting, and the search for Carr goes on.

Next day Lois accompanies Jerry to a loft overlooking the museum, which has reopened for business. Jerry, considering that the slayer may return to the scene of the crime, wants to observe the crowd. As they peer through a slot left by a misplaced board, a cowled figure attacks them. Jerry is knocked unconscious, but a detective and other officers arrive just as the figure escapes. Later Jerry receives a note from Professor Mysto, advising him that Carr has arranged to meet with confederates at a desolate house outside town. Jerry enters the house that night but is captured and bound. Then Lois appears and falls into Carr's clutches.

Rival hoodlums gain entry to Carr's stronghold, and in a

gun battle Carr alone escapes unharmed. He is about to kidnap Lois when he is knifed from behind by a half-witted girl, one of the museum freaks, whom Carr has betrayed. Jerry, still seeking the identity of Newgate's killer, learns of a diabolical invention by Professor Mysto — an arrangement whereby a .45-caliber gun can be transformed to fire a .38-caliber bullet. It develops that Carr had betrayed Mysto's wife many years before and caused her death. Mysto had sworn vengeance and finally kept his word. Mysto's confession and suicide clear Brandon of suspected complicity in the murder, and Jerry and Lois are united.

Notes

Although Henry B. Walthall never regained in talking pictures the eminence he enjoyed in his early days as D. W. Griffith's finest actor, the independent producers took full advantage of his prestige and professionalism. He received top billing in this Willis Kent production, which was filmed quickly and cheaply at International Studios. Walthall applied his characteristic dignity to the effort, which boasts tolerable carnival settings and sufficient props, extras, and specialty bits (including knife-thrower Steve Clemente and some "kootchie" dancers) to create atmosphere. The photography is too straightforward for a story of this nature, where menacing shadows are sorely missed.

Most of the players, under Melville Shyer's direction, project silent-picture histrionics, although Donald Kerr, a comedian with stage experience, handles his lines amusingly in his portrayal of a sideshow barker. Newspaper advertisements mistakenly credited Gertrude Messenger as leading lady; the part actually was played by Phyllis Barrington.

FIFTEEN WIVES (1934)

(Chesterfield Motion Pictures Corporation)

Produced by Maury M Cohen; *directed by* Frank R. Strayer; *original story by* Charles S. Belden *and* Frederick Stephanie; *continuity and dialogue by* Charles S. Belden; *photographed by* M. A. Anderson; *art director,* Edward S. Jewell; *film editor,* Roland Reed; *assistant director,* Melville Shyer; *sound recording,* L. E. Clark; *sound system,* RCA Victor; *filmed at* Universal City; *running time,* 68 minutes; *released* June 1, 1934, *by* Chesterfield Motion Pictures Corporation.

PLAYERS: *Inspector Decker Dawes,* Conway Tearle; *Carol Manning,* Natalie Moorhead; *Detective Sergeant Meed,* Raymond Hatton; *Ruby Cotton,* Noel Francis; *Jason Getty,* John Wray; *Sybilla Crum,* Margaret Dumont; *The Electric Voice,* Ralf Harolde; *District Attorney Kerry,* Oscar Apfel; *Chemist,* Robert Frazer; *Davis,* Harry C. Bradley; *Connelly,* Lew Kelly; *Head Porter,* Clarence Brown; *Porter,* "Slickem"; *Thompson,* Alex Pollette; *Nurse,* Alameda Fowler; *Doctor,* John Elliott; *Butler,* Sidney Bracy; *The Boy,* Dickie Jones; *Detective,* Hal Price; *Reporter,* Lynton Brent.

John Harron is amazed at H. B. Walthall's deadly invention.

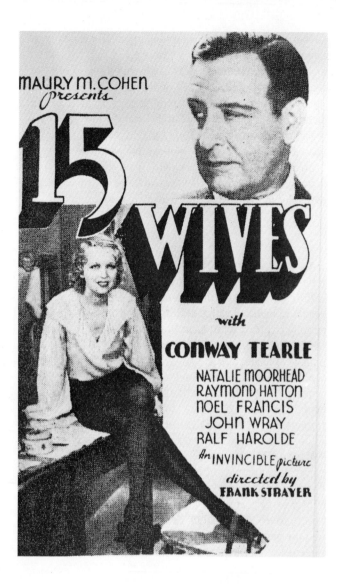

"FIFTEEN WIVES"
An INVINCIBLE PICTURE

Synopsis

A florist's messenger delivers a package for Steven Humbolt to the Savoia Hotel in New York, where Humbolt has lately arrived from South America. A bellboy, disturbed on finding that the box contains a funeral spray, goes with the manager to Humbolt's suite, where they find him dead, evidently of apoplexy. Homicide Inspector Decker Dawes, however, suspects murder, especially when it develops that Humbolt had been married fifteen times. Three of the widows are New Yorkers: evangelist Sybilla Crum; Carol Manning, now married to a Mr. Arnold; and Ruby Cotton.

Sybilla arrives and tries to stymie Dawes's arrangements for an autopsy. Florist Jason Getty discloses that the flowers had been ordered from Philadelphia, and a detective is sent there. Dawes has found several shards of glass in the suite; he reassembles these into a shape resembling a fishbowl. Mrs. Arnold reveals that she had married Humbolt five years previous, that he had disappeared with her money, and that she believed he had died in South America

— until he showed up three days before and tried to blackmail her; her present husband is unaware of the previous marriage. Mrs. Arnold has no alibi.

Examination proves hydrocyanic acid gas killed Humbolt. The glass globe was a Helmholtz resonator designed to break under certain sound-waves. The source of the fatal sound is a mystery. Dawes wins out over Sybilla's pressure to halt the investigation. Proof arrives that not only the flowers, but also the globe had been shipped from Philadelphia. Investigating a report that Mrs. Arnold maintains an apartment in her maiden name, Dawes learns she has a son unknown to her husband.

Dawes hears a radio broadcast featuring the Electric Voice, who displays his vocal ability to break glass and cause bells to ring. When the Voice emits a sound, a Helmholtz resonator on Dawes's desk breaks. Arriving at the theater where the Electric Voice is performing, Dawes finds that the Voice's associate is Ruby Cotton, the third New York wife. Sybilla is adamant about burying her husband in the traditions of her cult. Getty, the florist, goes to gloat over the body. Sybilla, observing this action, telephones Dawes to meet her at the cemetery after the funeral.

Dawes and Sergeant Meed are ignored by the heavily veiled widow at the graveyard. Dawes confronts the florist later with evidence of the visit to Humbolt's body; Getty had dropped a glove made expressly for him because of a missing finger. Dawes accuses Getty of killing both Humbolt and Mrs. Crum and then impersonating the widow at the funeral. Getty had placed Sybilla's body in the casket with her husband.

Getty, an Australian, had been crazed with grief after his wife ran away with Humbolt. He trailed the bigamist to America and contrived the murder plot. Exposed by this revelation, Getty tries to murder Dawes and Meed with the poison gas, but Dawes shoots the madman.

Mrs. Arnold's husband refuses to understand her story of the child and files for divorce. Dawes seizes the opportunity and undertakes an ocean voyage with the lady.

The script of *Fifteen Wives* is the work of Charles S. Belden, author of Warners' celebrated *Mystery of the Wax Museum* (1933), and Frederick Stephanie, director of *Flash Gordon* (1936) and later a producer at M-G-M. Almost needless to say, their imaginative collaboration is out of the ordinary, combining macabre mystery with comedy and a sophisticated love story. Although the picture is even more obscure than most other products of the Invincible-Chesterfield combine, it deserves a tip of the hat for originality — even within the restrictions imposed by the mystery genre.

Director Frank Strayer took full advantage of the contrasting elements of humor and grimness. Camera work and cutting are at times creatively employed.

An unusual touch is the use of the beloved Margaret Dumont, Groucho Marx's celebrated foil, in the half-humorous, half-serious role of an eccentric evangelist with the Marxian name Sybilla Crum. Curious, too, is the notion of having the middle-aged bachelor detective hero become romantically interested in a married woman, an angle the powerful Hays Office censorship machine would have vetoed a bit later in the year.

Conway Tearle is excellent as the efficient inspector, and Raymond Hatton adds interest as his wry partner. John Wray, as usual, steals the show whenever he appears, especially in the well-played "mad scene" at the climax. The other players provide competent characterizations.

RANDY RIDES ALONE (1934)

(Lone Star Productions — Monogram Pictures Corporation)

Produced by Paul Malvern; *vice president in charge of production,* Trem Carr; *directed by* Harry Fraser; *story and screenplay by* Lindsley Parsons; *photographed by* Archie Stout; *technical director,* E. R. Hickson; *film editor,* Carl Pierson; *sound recording by* J. R. Stransky, Jr.; *musical director,* Abe Meyer; *Western Electric Sound by Balsley & Phillips; running time,* 54 minutes; *released* June 5, 1934.

PLAYERS: *Randy Bowers,* John Wayne; *Sally Rogers,* Alberta Vaughan; *Matt the Mute,* George Hayes; *Spike,* Yakima Canutt; *Sheriff,* Earl Dwire; *Deputy,* Tex Phelps; *Henchman,* Arthur Ortega; *Henchman,* Tex Palmer; *Posse Member,* Mack V. Wright.

Synopsis

Randy Bowers's job is to ride to the Halfway House and try to get evidence on an outlaw band that has been threatening Ed Rogers and the other inhabitants. As he arrives, Randy hears the cheerful thumping of a player piano from the saloon. Smiling, he walks in — and halts at the horror he finds there. The corpses of Rogers and his several employes are strewn about the room. The sheriff and a posse arrest Randy, charging him with murder. Among the posse is a grotesque hunchback called Matt the

Mute. When Rogers's pretty niece, Sally, is brought to the jail to look at the captive, she tells him that she is the only witness to the mass killing and that Marvin Black and his gang are responsible. Sally helps Randy escape, and he promises vengeance on the slayers.

Randy trails the Black gang to a cave hidden behind a waterfall. Spike, Black's lieutenant, demands to know who Randy's employer is. "Nobody," comes the reply. "I ride alone." Randy gains the confidence of the gang and is permitted to join them. He learns that the harrassment at Halfway House stems from Black's knowledge of a large amount of money that is hidden there, but even after Rogers's murder the hiding place has not been found. The gang captures Sally in an attempt to make her tell. Randy rescues the girl, and they find a hidden vault where the money is cached. Removing the money, Randy packs the vault with dynamite.

Pursued by both the outlaws and the posse, Randy leads the bandits to the Halfway House. Black is blown to bits when he tries to take the money. Randy clears himself with the law, when he proves that Matt the Mute actually was the mysterious Black. Randy rides away with Sally.

Notes

After completing the Mascot serials, John Wayne starred in six Warner Brothers pictures sold as the Lone Star

Alberta Vaughan, John Wayne at mass-murder scene. Note the "in-joke" on the sign – a plug for director Harry Fraser.

John Wayne faces Yakima Canutt and George Hayes; "Gabby" had yet to sprout his famous beard. The henchman behind Wayne is Tex ("Squint") Palmer.

Western series and built around stock footage from Ken Maynard's silent First National productions. Wayne took Maynard's place in the closeups, and a horse named Duke (after Wayne's own nickname) substituted for Maynard's Tarzan. Once the stock shots were depleted, Wayne was at liberty again, star billing forgotten as he scrambled for jobs. Monogram's Trem Carr came to the rescue in the late summer of 1933 with an offer to revive the Lone Star series — at a rate of eight pictures a year with Wayne to receive $2,500 each. These popular and lucrative little films, released as five-reelers and made on five-day schedules for under $10,000 apiece, were still in production when Monogram became part of Republic in 1935. Sixteen Lone Star Westerns were released between September of 1933 and April of 1935.

Series producer was Paul Malvern, a muscular ex-stuntman who enjoyed making such rough-and-tumble pictures. Most were directed, and in some instances written by, Robert N. Bradbury, whose unusual pictorial style set the general tone of the pictures. This continuity of style was amplified in the stock company casting, the scenery, and the sparkling photography of Archie Stout, who shot all but two of the films. Most location work was done in the Newhall area, where there was an excellent Western town, abundant desert and mountain territory, the Kern River, and a deep lake at the foot of a cliff. The minimal interiors were filmed in Monogram's lone sound stage at Santa Monica and Van Ness. George Hayes — later the beloved Windy Halliday of the Hopalong Cassidy films and Gabby of the Roy Rogers musical-Westerns — was in most of the Monogram Lone Stars, sometimes as a villain, sometimes as the female lead's father, and often as Wayne's "old funny guy" sidekick. Yakima Canutt was another stock member, usually playing villains and always doubling Wayne in the same pictures.

Wayne described for us his work for Monogram:

"My main duty was to ride, fight, keep my hat on, and at the end of shooting still have enough strength left to kiss the girl and ride off on my horse or kiss my horse and ride off on the girl — whichever they wanted."

The seventh of the series, *Randy Rides Alone,* as written by Lindsley Parsons and directed by Harry Fraser, is perhaps the most unusual. Bradbury had introduced weird touches in earlier entries. In *West of the Divide,* for example, Wayne identifies Lloyd Whitlock as the man who murdered his father when Wayne was a child, because he recognizes Whitlock's maniacal laugh. In *Randy Rides Alone,* grotesque mystery dominates throughout, from the eerie and gruesome opening sequence to the hero's uncharacteristically ruthless destruction of the heavies. The expected action elements, however, are not sacrificed to the mystery, and there are, if anything, more of Canutt's superb stunts than usual. One picturesque setting is the outlaw hideout, a cave hidden behind a waterfall. There are riding scenes comparable to the Maynard films, and there is an exciting sequence involving diving and swimming in a rocky stream. One fine stunt has Hayes toppling a ladder from a high cliff with Wayne — actually Canutt — clinging to it. Another brilliant job of stunting has Canutt, again doubling Wayne, fall from a high cliff into a tree and then drop through the branches — a perilous bit done without resorting to dummies or camera trickery.

GREEN EYES (1934)

(Chesterfield Motion Pictures Corporation)

Produced by George R. Batcheller; *directed by* Richard Thorpe; *from* THE MURDER OF STEPHEN KESTER *by* H. Ashbrook; *continuity by* Andrew Moses; *photographed by* M. A. Anderson; *assistant director,* Melville Shyer; *recorded by* L. E. Clark; *art director,* Edward Jewell; *musical director,* Abe Meyer; RCA Victor *sound; produced at* Universal City; *running time,* 67 minutes; *released* June 15, 1934.

PLAYERS: *Jean Kester,* Shirley Grey; *Bill Tracy,* Chrles Starrett; *Stephen Kester,* Claude Gillingwater; *Inspector*

Crofton, John Wray; *Cliff,* William Bakewell; *Mrs. Pritchard,* Dorothy Revier; *Regan,* Ben Hendricks, Jr.; *Pritchard,* Alden Chase; *Hall,* Arthur Clayton; *Dora,* Aggie Herring; *Raynor,* Edward Keane; *Banker,* Edward Le Saint; *Broker,* Robert Frazer; *Chemist,* John Elliott; *Howe,* Lloyd Whitlock; *Lenox (Butler),* Elmer Ballard; *Policeman,* Frank Hagney.

Synopsis

The midnight merriment of a masquerade turns to horror when the guests find their host, Stephen Kester, stabbed to death in a closet. Kester's granddaughter, Jean, has meanwhile eloped with her fiancé, Cliff, who boasts they cannot be followed, for he has snipped all the cars' ignition wires and disconnected the telephone. The police, however, stop the couple, as suspects, and herd them back to the house. Mystery writer Bill Tracy has other ideas but cannot offer a solution. Pritchard, the victim's secretary, seems to have been the last person to see the old man alive. Pritchard explains that the mask Kester had worn is called "Green Eyes." Hall, an associate of Kester, offers an unacceptable alibi.

Jean insists she was in her room just before midnight, and Dora, the cook, bolsters this story; but Tracy and Mrs. Pritchard admit they saw Jean leave Kester's room shortly before the body was found. Lenox, the butler, discloses that Kester was widely disliked and that Hall and Kester had argued about business earlier that evening. It develops that Kester had lately disinherited Jean and had yet to sign a new will.

Hall seeks to leave, on the pretense of consulting his lawyer — who proves to be out of town. Tracy, whose meddling has angered the police, finds what he considers a solution. The next night, Hall is found dead in bed, clutching a pistol. His lawyer produces what seems to be a

Arthur Clayton, Dorothy Revier, Charles Starrett on what had been the set of Universal's Secret of the Blue Room.

suicide note and confession. This satisfies the police, but Tracy persists and traps the real murderer, Pritchard, who had spent years embezzling from his employer. Hall had meant to kill Kester, Tracy avers, but Pritchard arrived first. Jean, her inheritance intact, is now free to marry Cliff.

Notes

An unusual ending brought much attention to H. Ashbrook's novel, *The Murder of Stephen Kester.* In adapting book to screen, Chesterfield retained this strange twist, which neatly separates *Green Eyes* from the mass of mystery films that flooded the theatres in 1934. Two entirely different solutions are shown on screen and — with no cheating — prove equally consistent with the details presented. Either would seem to make for an open-and-shut case, but in the last moments one is eliminated and the other proved beyond doubt.

Such a yarn was a natural for Richard Thorpe, the highly efficient Poverty Row mystery-action director on the climb. The twists and turns are enacted by a well-chosen cast. Claude Gillingwater, then the screen's most popular grouch, dies early on, but dominates the screen until then. Thereafter the acting honors go principally to John Wray, as an efficient, hard-boiled detective. Two beautiful women have important roles. There is a stalwart hero, in former football star (and future Columbia Western star) Charles Starrett, and Chesterfield's expected highly professional supporting cast is on hand.

Most of the filming was done in one of Universal's palatial "mansion" sets. The photography is properly shadowy, and there is some humor in the battle of wits between the police and a young writer. A neatly staged "shocker" is the discovery of the body of Gillingwater, garbed in Mandarin robes and a weird Chinese mask with glowing eyes.

THE STAR PACKER (1934)

(Lone Star Productions – Monogram Pictures Corporation)

Directed by Robert N. Bradbury; *produced by* Paul Malvern; *screenplay by* R. N. Bradbury; *photographed by* Archie Stout; *technical director,* E. R. Hickson; *recorded by* John Stransky, Jr.; *film editor,* Carl Pierson; *musical director,* Abe Meyer; Western Electric Sound System *by* Balsley & Phillips; *running time,* 54 minutes; *released* July 30, 1934.

PLAYERS: *John Travers,* John Wayne; *Anita,* Verna Hillie; *Matt Matlock,* George Hayes; *Yak,* Yakima Canutt; *Mason,* Earl Dwire; *Parker,* Ed Parker; *Jake,* George Cleveland; *Pete,* William Franey; *Sheriff,* Tom Lingham; *Henchman,* Art Ortega; *Driver,* Tex Palmer; *Boy,* Davie Aldrich.

Synopsis

At a remote bend of the river, U. S. Marhsal John Travers meets with his partner, an Indian named Yak, who reports that a stagecoach is going to be robbed by members of the Shadow gang. John intercepts the couch and robs it himself. Moments later, two of the Shadow's henchmen, Mason and Parker, halt the stage and are told that it already has been robbed. The driver and guard are ruthlessly

gunned down and the coach team bolts. John overtakes the stage, saving the life of a passenger, pretty Anita Matlock. Anita's father has been murdered by the Shadow, and she is on her way to visit the ranch she has inherited. John brings the coach into town just at the conclusion of a meeting of stockmen concerned about the depredations of the mysterious Shadow.

As John tells Davis, the new sheriff, and Anita's uncle, Matt Matlock, about the robbery, a shot is heard and Davis falls dead. Yak, who has been watching the virtually deserted street, tells John, "Me hear shot, look quick, see . . only smoke." A wisp of smoke hovers over the street near the saloon. Matlock, a prominent rancher, reveals that two other sheriffs have been killed in the same way. Picking up the fallen man's badge, John says, "If it's just the same with you folks, I'll take that job of sheriff."

Mason and Parker go to a room in the rear of the saloon. The Shadow speaks to them from behind a phoney wall safe, issuing orders to kill John and scare Anita out of town. The crooks ambush John but he escapes by the old Indian trick of clutching the side of his horse and making them think he has fallen from the saddle. Later, the Shadow tells his henchmen, "Another bloop like this and you two guys keep ridin'." John and Yak trail the outlaws to their encampment, where John recognises several of the band: "Loco Frank — he'd cut a man's throat for a dollar; Slash Burden, a lifer from Walla Walla; Chuckwalla Red — he's wanted in every state on the border; Slippery Williams and Spike Morgan — what a nest of hornets!"

Mason lies in ambush as John returns from visiting Anita at the Matlock Ranch. Yak ropes the man and sends John in pursuit of another bushwhacker, Parker, who is defeated in a brutal slugfest. Having deposited their prisoners in jail after dark, John and Yak investigate the room with the false safe, where they find a trap door leading to a tunnel. They emerge inside a hollowed stump in the street. The entire north end of the street can be seen from a knothole

A bullet seemingly from nowhere fells Sheriff Tom Lingham. Onlookers: Frank Ball (in black vest), John Wayne, Verna Hillie.

in the stump. Before morning they saw off the top of the stump and replace it. During the night, several "ghosts" lurking about the ranch frighten Anita, who musters her courage and wings one with a gun John gave her. She declines Matt's offer to buy her share of the ranch.

John mobilizes all the ranchers. He forces Parker to talk to the Shadow, who orders Parker to get John out into the street. Before exiting, John forces Parker to change clothes with him. When a gun barrel emerges from the hole in the stump, Yak and several cattlemen open the top and seize the sniper, who proves to be old Pete, a town bum. Before he can identify the Shadow, Pete is killed by a shot from the saloon building. The Shadow — Matlock — escapes through another secret panel, emerging from a cave outside of town. Matlock orders his gang to attack the town. He has a secret weapon: a machine gun in a covered wagon.

Old Jake, the Matlock cook, reveals to Anita that Matlock is not her uncle but actually is the Shadow, who murdered both her father and her real uncle. Riding toward town to tell John, she is intercepted by the Shadow and his men, who take her along in the wagon to use as a shield. Meantime, John has deputized the ranchers and leads them toward a confrontation with the Shadow gang. A spectacular fight ensues, in which the gang is defeated. The Shadow, his horse shot from under him by Yak, flees in the wagon with Anita. The wagon breaks free and plunges from a cliff into the river. John dives in and rescues Anita while the Shadow tries to escape in Yak's canoe. After a chase, John ropes the Shadow and drags him ashore. Later, John and Anita marry.

Notes

An exercise in extravagance within the confines of budget — even with a running time of only 54 minutes — *The Star Packer* gave the Saturday action fans their money's worth. As suspensefully offbeat as its predecessor, *Randy Rides Alone,* this fast-paced eighth entry in the Monogram-Lone Star series emphasizes mystery and hints at the supernatural, while pitting John Wayne against a killer who leads a dual life. Monogram even loosened the purse strings sufficiently to permit a running fight sequence that can be described as spectacular, with about forty horsemen taking part. There are several Running W stunt falls, a stagecoach rescue, a wagon crash and stunt leap into the lagoon at Newhall, a beautifully staged fight between Wayne and stuntman Ed Parker, and plenty of riding and gunplay.

George Hayes is once again the villain, but another bit of casting is stranger yet: Yakima Canutt as Wayne's sidekick and comedy relief! Canutt is quite good as an otherwise solemn Indian who cries delightedly, "Hiyu skookum big fun!" whenever he anticipates a dangerous encounter with the heavies. As usual, Canutt performs extra duty stunting for Wayne, Hayes, and several of the badmen. John Wayne is — again, as usual — John Wayne, a relaxed and likeable performer. Verna Hillie is better than the usual Saturday matinee leading lady.

The Star Packer is a perfect example of the work of Robert North Bradbury, a director and writer who was ignored by critics, but whose contributions to the genre are as important as those of any director who turned to the Western. A Bradbury picture (and all of them were made on small budgets and fast schedules) is utterly distinctive in technique, as recognizable as a film by Ford or Hitchcock. He liked unusual story touches even within traditional framework and often would add mystery or even a bit of science-fiction to the basic ingredients. What appears to be a Bradbury invention is an ingenious adaptation of the swish-pan, in which the camera not only sweeps over the landscape, but also picks up the characters leaving one setting at the beginning, and arriving elsewhere, at the end of the pan. This device, found in most of Bradbury's talkies, is used several times in *The Star Packer*. When, for example, the outlaws ride out of town, the camera does a fast pan ahead of them and then picks them up as they arrive at their hideout.

John Wayne told us it was Bradbury who created the method of fighting used in films today. It is ironic that the multimillion-dollar Westerns of recent years owe so much to a technique developed for a $10,000 horse opera!

"The way we did fights in those days was to actually hit each other on the shoulders," Wayne said. "By the end of the day, Yak and I were so bruised we could hardly climb onto our horses. Yak was better at pulling his punches, so he got beat up worse than I did. Yak was complaining so much to Bob Bradbury that Bob worked out a way to photograph fights so we didn't have to really hit each other. He called it the 'pass system.' It was all in how the camera was placed, low and at a certain angle so that I could swing past Yak's face and he could react as though he'd been hit. When we saw the rushes we knew we had something. It worked so well that everybody started doing it that way. Sometimes when I'm working with a young stuntman he'll start showing me how the 'pass system' is done, not knowing that I was the first one to do it."

From 1918 to 1937 Bradbury directed at least eighty features, a couple of serials, and many short subjects. All but a handful were outdoor pictures made for the independent companies. Some of them starred his son, Bob, Jr. — Bob Steele. Bradbury had style, originality, and a genius for improvisation. One can only wonder what he might have done with substantial budgets and more generous shooting schedules.

JANE EYRE (1934)

(Monogram Pictures Corporation)

Vice president in charge of production, Trem Carr; *super-* *vised by* Ben Verschleiser; *directed by* Christy Cabanne; *adapted by* Adele Comandini *from the novel by* Charlotte Bronte; *photographed by* Robert Planck; *recorded by* Ralph Shugart; *film editor,* Carl Pierson; *musical director,* Abe Meyer; *Western Electric sound by* Balsley & Phillips; *running time,* 70 minutes; *released* August 15, 1934.

PLAYERS: *Jane Eyre,* Virginia Bruce; *Mr. Rochester,* Colin Clive; *Mrs. Fairfax,* Beryl Mercer; *Charles Craig,* Jameson Thomas; *Blanche Ingram,* Eileen Pringle; *Brocklehurst,* David Torrence; *Lord Ingram,* Lionel Belmore; *Daisy,* Joan Standing; *Adele Rochester,* Edith Fellowes; *Dr. Rivers,* Desmond Roberts; *Sam Poole,* John Rogers; *Mrs. Reed,* Clarissa Selwynne; *Bessie,* Hylda Tyson; *Miss Temple,* Gretta Gould; *Bertha Rochester,* Claire duBrey; *Grade Poole,* Ethel Griffies; *Lady Ingram,* Edith Kingdon; *Halliburton,* William Wagner; *Jeweler,* Olaf Hytten; *Minister,* William Burres; *Mary Lane,* Gail Kaye; *Young Jane,* Jean Darling; *John Reed,* Richard Quine; *Georgiana Reed,* Anne Howard.

Synopsis

Young Jane Eyre asserts herself against the sadistically bratty children of her foster parents and finds herself deposited in a Nineteenth Century public home for waifs. A friendship with Miss Temple, an instructor, sees her through the austerity of orphanage life, and when she attains young womanhood Jane secures a position with the institution. At length, however, she can no longer abide the authoritarian headmaster, Brocklehurst; she resigns and becomes governess to Adele Rochester, daughter of the English country squire Edward Rochester. She is befriended by all, but the pleasant surroundings seem shrouded in a mysterious secrecy. Jane is barred from a wing of the mansion; she hears maniacal screams from this sector at night and attributes these to a skulking servant, Grace Poole.

The source of the mystery is the confinement of Edward's hopelessly mad wife, Bertha. Solicitor Charles Craig seeks annulment of the marriage so that Rochester may wed Lord Ingram's daughter, Blanche.

The Ingrams are honored guests at the Rochester estate. During the gala proceedings, Rochester realizes he and Jane are in love. He breaks off his relationship with Blanche to marry Jane. The union is about to take place when Mrs. Rochester escapes her quarters and makes a weird appearance at the ceremony. Heartsick at this revelation, Jane leaves and takes employment with a man of God, Dr. Rivers. The insane Bertha, meantime, overpowers Grace and sets fire to the Rochester home. Rochester loses his eyesight in a futile effort to save his wife from the all-consuming flames. He takes up residence in the caretaker's cottage. Jane, ignorant of her lover's circumstances, plans now to marry Dr. Rivers and join him on a missionary trip to India.

Rochester's onetime coachman visits the mission, where

Virginia Bruce, Colin Clive.

Rochester cannot reason with his insane wife. Virginia Bruce, Colin Clive, Claire DuBrey.

The madwoman appears. Ethel Griffies, Beryl Mercer, Virginia Bruce, Claire Dubrey, William Burres, Colin Clive.

he recognizes Jane and tells her of Rochester's plight. Jane returns to Rochester, and the lovers are reunited.

Notes

Jane Eyre merits serious consideration as the *meisterwerk* of Poverty Row. It is one of those rare instances in which everyone involved seems determined to contribute only the best efforts; the result reflects an abundance of taste and skill.

Comparison is inevitable between this film and the version made in 1943 by Twentieth Century-Fox from a Selznick-International pre-production package. The later production is more sumptuously mounted, features bravura performances from a spectacular cast (Joan Fontaine, Orson Welles, Henry Daniell, Agnes Moorhead), is directed with a fine appreciation of Gothic atmosphere and horror by Robert Stevenson, and has a literate script by Aldous Huxley and John Houseman, superb production design by James Basevi, magnificent George Barnes photography, and a thundering Bernard Herrmann score. It is a film with flair, striking and highly dramatic.

Alongside such a full-blooded virtuoso work, the Monogram edition seems as pale and timid as the heroine of the story. On the other hand, it wears exceedingly well, being free of bombast and retaining more of the mood and letter of the book. Virginia Bruce is a prettier and less fluttery Jane. Colin Clive is a less weird, more explicable Rochester. Robert Planck's photography, while less dramatic than that of Barnes, carries the mystery and romance very well. The

Farewell. Colin Clive, Virginia Bruce.

settings are unspectacular when compared with Basevi's towering creations, but they carry a genuine feel of period, and it is refreshing that real exteriors (at Sherwood Forest, California) are employed for the light romantic scenes. There is no heavy music — merely a few old songs like "Sweet and Low." It seems probable that Charlotte Bronte would have preferred the more sensitive treatment Monogram accorded her masterpiece to the magnificent but overblown Twentieth Century-Fox version.

While Colin Clive and Virginia Bruce dominate the picture with their near-perfect portrayals, there are many deft performances in support: Beryl Mercer as the kindly housekeeper, Mrs. Fairfax; David Torrence (brother of Ernest Torrence) as the sadistic Brocklehurst; Lionel Belmore as an overbearing lord and Aileen Pringle as his bitchy daughter; Ethel Griffies as the mysterious Grace Poole (a role she repeated in the '43 version); Jameson Thomas as the faithful solicitor; and Claire duBrey in a brief but striking performance as the insane wife. The four children in key roles are all good, especially Richard Quine — later a distinguished director — as a spoiled brat.

Jane Eyre marks a peak in the checkered career of director Christy Cabanne (1888-1950), whose work included a 1915 version of *Enoch Arden,* many pictures for D. W. Griffith and Douglas Fairbanks, the memorable *The Last Outlaw* (1936), and that delightful B horror classic, *The Mummy's Hand* (1940). In his later years Cabanne's talents were wasted on increasingly cheap and unrewarding projects.

THE MOONSTONE (1934)

(Monogram Pictures Corporation)

Vice president in charge of production, Trem Carr; *produced by* Paul Malvern; *directed by* Reginald Barker; *screenplay by* Adele Buffington; *based on the novel by* Wilkie Collins; *photographed by* Robert Planck; *edited by* Carl Pierson; *technical director,* E. R. Hickson; *recorded by* John A. Stransky, Jr.; *musical director,* Abe Meyer; Western Electric *sound by* Balsley & Phillips; *running time,* 62 minutes; *released* August 20, 1934.

PLAYERS: *Franklin Blake,* David Manners; *Anne Verinder,* Phyllis Barry; *Godfrey Ablewhite,* Jameson Thomas; *Septimus Lucker,* Gustav von Seyffertitz; *Sir John Verinder,* Herbert Bunston; *Roseanna Spearman,* Evelyn Bostock; *Yandoo,* John Davidson; *Betteredge,* Elspeth Dudgeon; *Sir Basil Wynard,* Claude King; *Dr. Ezra Jennings,* Olaf Hytten; *Inspector Cuff,* Charles Irwin; *Henry,* Fred Walton.

Synopsis

Young Franklin Blake and his Hindu servant, Yandoo, reach gloomy Verinder Manor during a terrific storm, to deliver the Moonstone, a fabulous diamond stolen long ago from a temple in India. Now the gem has come into possession of Anne Verinder, pretty daughter of Sir John

Fred Warren drives David Manners, John Davidson to the Verinder mansion.

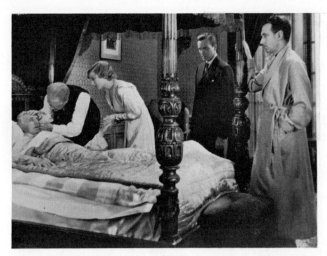

Olaf Hytton examines an injured Herbert Bunston. On-lookers: Phyllis Barry, David Manners, Jameson Thomas.

David Manners, Phyllis Barry, Gustav von Seyffertitz.

Verinder, a distinguished scientist. Guests at the house are Godfrey Ablewhite, a dealer in rare books and third cousin to Anne; and the sinister Septimus Lucker, a money-lender with a nefarious reputation. Also present is Dr. Ezra Jennings, Sir John's assistant. Servants are Betteredge, the grim housekeeper; Henry, the Cockney gardener; and Roseanna Spearman, the maid, revealed as a former thief and an acquaintance of Lucker.

Anne places the Moonstone under her pillow, despite Franklin's protests that it should be kept in a vault. Next morning the gem is gone. Scotland Yard Inspector Cuff arrives to investigate. Fear grips the household after a mysterious attacker leaves Sir John unconscious. Roseanna is murdered in the garden. At last, Ablewhite is exposed as the culprit and pays for his crimes with his life.

Notes

To Monogram's credit, the screen version condenses

Wilkie Collins' long and rambling 1868 novel — considered the cornerstone of modern detective fiction — into a suspenseful exercise in brevity. The modernizing of a classic novel was an uncharacteristic undertaking for Paul Malvern and Adele Buffington, who both specialized in Westerns and outdoor action pictures. The veteran director Reginald Barker, however, seems right at home in the Gothic setting of dread, and successfully transmits it to the audience. Barker, born in Scotland in 1886, by 1914 was directing such Thomas Ince productions as *On the Night Stage, The Typhoon, The Wrath of the Gods,* and *The Golden Claw.* Subsequently he directed several of William S. Hart's popular Westerns and action pictures with William Desmond for Triangle, and romantic dramas, such as *The Woman and the Puppet* (1920), for Goldwyn. *The Storm* (1922), a Universal picture, was a great success, and he continued directing high-budget pictures for M-G-M, Fox, First National, and Universal until 1930. After a four-year hiatus he returned with *The Moonstone.* He directed two more pictures for Monogram and one for the new Republic, before his death in 1937.

The Moonstone's predominantly British cast is quite satisfactory, with David Manners and the Australian Phyllis Barry forming a good romantic team. Herbert Bunston, like Manners a veteran of *Dracula,* is excellent as the girl's father, and Charles Irwin enacts the Scotland Yard inspector with authority. Sharp-featured Gustav von Seyffertitz, bony-faced John Davidson, the austere Jameson Thomas, cold-eyed Elspeth Dudgeon, and sneaky Olaf Hytton are an unnerving group of suspects. Photography by Robert Planck, who is better known for his work for M-G-M and Edward Small, is exemplary.

MANIAC (1934)

(Hollywood Producers & Distributors – Roadshow Attractions Company)

Produced and directed by Dwain Esper; *story and continuity by* Hildegarde Stadie; *assistant director,* J. Stuart Blackton, Jr.; *photographed by* William Thompson, ASC; *film editor,* William Austin; *length,* six reels; *running time (varies),* 67 minutes; *copyrighted* September 15, 1934.

PLAYERS: *Don Maxwell;* Bill Woods; *Dr. Meirschultz,* Horace Carpenter; *Buckley,* Ted Edwards; *Mrs. Buckley,* Phyllis Diller; *Alice Maxwell,* Thea Ramsey; *Maizie,* Jennie Dark; *Marvel,* Marvel Andre; *Jo,* Celia McGann; *Mike (Morgue Attendant),* J. P. Wade; *Neighbor,* Marion Blackton.

Synopsis

"Tonight, my dear Maxwell, I am ready to try my experiment on a human," the bearded and wild-eyed Dr. Meirschultz informs his assistant. His subject will be a suicide abiding in the City Morgue. Maxwell asks about arrangements to claim the corpse. "No! You know I do not

DWAIN ESPER'S PLATFORM

on the MAKING and SHOWING of MOTION PICTURES

(1) *Grade films as to their audience suitability before showing: A—Family; B—Adults.*

(2) *Do not inject off-color sequences into family films.*

(3) *Keep stars, who are favorites with children, in wholesome pictures.*

(4) *Eliminate scenes depicting the technic of committing crime.*

(5) *Eliminate the glorification of promiscuity.*

(6) *Parents should select the type of picture their children should see, and go with them.*

(7) *Motion picture appreciation should be made a part of the school curriculum.*

Exploitation pioneer Dwain Esper, who can take the blame for Maniac, *publicized himself as a paragon of cinematic virtue in ballyhoo for a 1936 opus,* Modern Motherhood.

Your Husband (1937, starring Elaine Barrie, wife of John Barrymore), *Maniac,* and *Marihuana,Weed with Roots in Hell* (1936) were not handled through orthodox channels but as roadshows playing at burlesque houses and other "adult entertainment" specialty theatres. In today's remarkably permissive movie industry, they would be classed as the softest of soft-core pornography because of occasional nudity and deliberate violations of taste.

For all its pains to offend, *Maniac* is in some respects a chaste and even entertaining product. Dialogue is rife with screams and ravings, and yet the language never stoops to the vulgar or profane. The limited and gratuitous nudity is subordinate to the story of a man whose phobias drive him to horrible actions. Bloodshed — a hackneyed staple in present-day films of violence — is never employed; the film's own nadir of bad taste comes when Bill Woods, as the maniac, gouges out a cat's eye and devours it. There is an offbeat humorous interlude in which a none-too-bright

neighbor explains the low overhead of his cat-raising enterprise: "Rats eat raw meat — you know, the cat carcasses . . . So the rats eat the cats, the cats eat the rats, and I get the skins!" A tolerant viewer realizes the benefits of William Thompson's photography, some ratty and eerily lighted sets, well-conceived lap dissolves, and the effective superimposition of footage from *Witchcraft Through the Ages* (Sweden, 1920) and *Siegfried* (Germany, 1923) over Woods' face to symbolise madness.

The only familiar face, sadly enough, is Horace Carpenter, onetime star of Cecil B. DeMille's company. Carpenter's presence in this granddaddy of exploitation shows parallels the more recent professional demises of such beloved actors as Lon Chaney, Jr., and J. Carroll Naish, who near the end of their careers, as an example, were given demeaning roles in the sordid *Frankenstein vs. Dracula* (1971). Supporting players serve *Maniac* in hammy fashion, notably Ted Edwards as the dangerous Buckley and J. P. Wade as the gruff morgue attendant; and no, the

137

Phyllis Diller who plays Mrs. Buckley is not the comedienne of that name.

Some prints of *Maniac* were augmented with material purported to impart an instructional value. A foreword explains the film will demonstrate mental illness, and printed narratives intercut with the action give textbook explanations of various forms of derangement. These intrusions, accompanied by inappropriate light orchestral music, only destroy suspense.

Maniac, whose bursts of quality are all the more memorable for their contrast with the overall shabbiness, is as graphic a testament as can be found to the seamier side of Poverty Row.

THE RETURN OF CHANDU (1934)

(Principal Pictures Corporation)

Produced by Sol Lesser; *directed by* Ray Taylor; *supervised by* Frank Melford; *adapted from the radio drama by* Harry A. Earnshaw, Vera M. Oldham, *and* R. R. Morgan; *adaptation and screenplay by* Barry Barrington; *story supervisor,* Harry Chandlee, *by arrangement with* Jesse L. Lasky; *production manager,* Theodore Joos; *photographed by* John Hickson, ASC: *musical director,* Abe Meyer; *art director,* Robert Ellis; *dialogue director,* Cyril Armbrister; *film editors,* Carl Himm *and* Lou Sackin; *sound recording,* Corson Jowett; *assistant director,* Harry Knight; RCA Victor *sound; filmed at* Pathé Studios; *a serial in* 12 chapters, 24 reels; *released* October 1, 1934, *by* Fox Film Corporation.

PLAYERS: *Frank Chandler (Chandu),* Bela Lugosi; *Princess Nadji,* Maria Alba; *Dorothy Regent,* Clara Kimball Young; *Vindhyan,* Lucien Prival; *Bob Regent,* Deane Benton; *Betty Regent,* Phyllis Ludwig; *Sutra,* Cyril Armbrister; *The Voice,* Murdoch MacQuarrie; *Captain Wilson,* Wilfred Lucas; *Tyba, the White Magician,* Josef Swickard; *Vitras,* Jack Clark; *Prince Andra,* Bryant Washburn; *Judy,* Peggy Montgomery; *Bara,* Elias Lazaroff; *Morta,* Dick Botiller; *Nito,* Frazer Acosta; *Tagora,* Harry Walker; *Mr. James,* Charles Meacham; *Mrs. James,* Isobel LeMall; *Reporter,* Don Brodie; *Airline Agent,* Edward Piel; *Curator,* Henry Hall; *Lady,* Beatrice Roberts; *Cat Man,* Iron Eyes Cody; *Old Man,* Elias Schaffer; *Sacrificial Aide,* Merrill McCormick.

Chapter Titles

1) The Chosen Victim; 2) The House on the Hill; 3) On the High Seas; 4) The Evil Eye; 5) The Invisible Circle; 6) Chandu's False Step; 7) The Mysterious Island; 8) The Edge of the Pit; 9) The Invisible Terror; 10) The Crushing Rock; 11) The Uplifted Knife; 12) The Knife Descends.

Synopsis

Nadji, the last Egyptian princess, is desired for sacrifice by cat-worshipping cultists of Ubasti, descended from inhabitants of the sunken continent of Lemuria. On an uncharted island in the Indian Ocean lie the remains of the once-mighty empire and the great temple of Ubasti. There the Voice of Ubasti and his priests guard the embalmed

body of their long-dead goddess, Ossana, whose resurrection requires the blood sacrifice of an Egyptian princess. Ossana, they believe, has the power to raise Lemuria from the depths. Escaping the clutches of the Ubasti in Egypt, Nadji takes refuge in the Beverly Hills home of widow Dorothy Regent, sister of Frank Chandler, Nadji's fiancé. Chandler, a master of white magic known as Chandu, is expected to arrive by plane on the night of an elaborate reception for the princess. Nito, the butler, an acolyte of the Ubasti, admits Vindhyan, high priest of the cult, and another cultist, Sutra.

Meantime, two of Vindhyan's agents attempt to waylay Chandu at the airport, but he makes himself invisible and escapes. Chandu arrives just as Nadji is about to drink a toast. At Chandu's gesture, the poisoned drink is dashed from Nadji's hand. Suspecting Nito, Chandu hypnotizes him and forces a confession. Before the man can tell the location of the secret meeting place of the Ubasti he is killed by a poison dart. Chandu narrowly averts the same fate.

Vindhyan learns that the Princess, Mrs. Regent, and her daughter, Betty, and son, Bob, are leaving at dawn for a South Seas tour. He also knows that Chandu is going to give an Egyptian mummy to the Los Angeles Museum. Ubasti

138

Wilfred Lucas, Bela Lugosi captured by the cat men of Lemuria.

agents murder the museum driver and his helper and arrive for the mummy case. A Ubasti working as a gardener has presented Nadji a drugged rose; her unconscious body is carried away in the mummy case. Chandu soon discerns what has happened, and he and Bob try desperately to find the Ubasti hideout, known only as an old house by a dead tree. At last Chandu calls upon his Yogi, who counsels him to drive blindfolded over a mountain road. Bob halts the car at the brink of a precipice overlooking the old house. Hypnotizing the guards, Chandu spirits the unconscious Nadji to the waiting yacht of his friend, Prince Andra. The craft begins its journey to the South Seas; Vindhyan is an unsuspected stowaway.

Chandu cannot revive Nadji. The Prince's aged servant, Tagora, a former Ubasti cultist, also tries in vain to remove her trance. Vindhyan waylays Tagora and impersonates him. He restores consciousness to the Princess and sabotages the yacht. Pursued by Chandu, Vindhyan tries to escape with Nadji to a motorboat which has pulled alongside, but Chandu engages him in a battle of wills. At last Vindhyan weakens, releases the girl, and escapes over the side.

It is discovered that Prince Andra has been murdered. The disabled yacht limps into the port of Suva. While Chandu reports the slaying to British government officials, Nadji and Dorothy remain with Bob and Betty. A false message delivered by a supposed policeman entices the women into a taxi to meet Chandu at the government office. They are taken instead to a shrine hidden behind a waterfront dive. Vindhyan prepares to sacrifice Dorothy to the cat god; Nadji will be taken to Lemuria to be sacrificed at the propitious time.

Chandu and Bob trail the missing women to the café. Through music accompanying a sensuous dance, Chandu hears the distinctive drums of a Ubasti ceremonial. Sending Bob for the police, Chandu takes the place of a robed acolyte and gains entrance. Just as Vindhyan is about to

strike Dorothy with his scimitar, Chandu leaps upon him. Before the others can overpower Chandu, the police arrive and rout the worshippers. Chandu overtakes Vindhyan on a high balcony above the altar. A railing gives way, and both men fall toward the sacrificial fire. Chandu saves himself, and Vindhyan is devoured by the flames.

The Voice sends Vitras, great black magician of Lemuria, to bring back Nadji. At Suva there is a confrontation between Vitras' forces and Chandu, but Vitras is able to transport Nadji away to Lemuria by invoking the Magic Circle, which can be used but once during a magician's lifetime. Nadji is imprisoned until the proper time for the sacrifice, "when the rays of the North Star fall within the temple." Securing a ship commanded by Captain Wilson, Chandu and his friends set out to search for the lost island. The Ubasti bewitch the ship's compass. A Ubasti spy foments a mutiny and scuttles the ship. Chandu, the Regents, and Captain Wilson escape on an improvised raft and reach the shores of Lemuria. When Chandu goes searching for the temple, the others are attacked by the Cat People, cannibalistic savages of the jungle. Wilson is killed, and the others are captured. Chandu, meantime, is swallowed up by the earth, falling into a winding passageway underground. Vitras places Nadji inside the Invisible Circle to thwart rescue and makes plans for the Cat People to feast on the other prisoners. Chandu, lost in the caves, calls

Bela Lugosi rescues Maria Alba from the Ubasti Temple on the Isle of Suva.

Bela Lugosi denounces the priests of Ubasti on their own ground as Maria Alba watches.

upon the highest powers for aid. He discovers and releases Tyba, the White Yogi, who has been imprisoned by the Ubasti. As both men hurry toward the temple, Chandu is plunged into a pit with a tiger. With the Yogi's aid he escapes. Chandu is given the power of invisibility for a brief period of time, and in this form he can rescue Bob from a sword pendulum. When Chandu's time of invisibility runs out, he is captured and placed under a great rock which is lowered on a chain. Bob rescues Chandu, who proceeds to the temple where Nadji faces the assembled throng of the Ubasti. Tyba urges Chandu to use "the highest power" against the Ubasti, but it carries a fearsome penalty if used selfishly. The Voice tells Nadji that if she will forswear Chandu and his love and dedicate her body as a sacrifice to Ossana, her friends will be spared. Nadji makes the promise, which frees Chandu from the curse of using the "power." Chandu exchanges the sleeping Nadji and the body of Ossana, and it is Ossana who is plunged into the sacrificial fire. In a fierce battle of wills, Chandu defeats the Ubasti and now calls upon "the highest power" to destroy the cult. Chandu, Nadji, and the Regents escape as the temple collapses.

Notes

Fox Film Corporation in 1932 adapted a popular radio serial, *Chandu the Magician,* into a highly imaginative stunt film with Edmund Lowe as Chandu and Bela Lugosi as the arch villain, Baron Roxor. Sol Lesser, who had a releasing agreement with Fox, leaped at the chance to produce a second *Chandu.* Rescuing Lugosi from villainy for a time, Lesser gave him the title role, to which Lugosi actually was better suited than the debonair, but hardly mysterious, Lowe.

The Lesser *Chandu* was made at the Pathé lot and on locations north of Hollywood during the summer of 1934. It was first released in two forms, as a twelve-chapter serial and as a "feature-serial," a format created by Lesser in which a seven-reel first episode edited from the first four chapters is followed by a weekly release of the eight concluding chapters. The feature was conceived as a complete entity, ending with the death of principal villain Lucien Prival — but with a tag scene showing the Ubasti still plotting. The feature also offered a smoothness of continuity because of some clever advance considerations lacking in most other serial condensations. Lesser had the "cliff-hangers" that close each chapter and the "take-outs" that open subsequent episodes re-shot with less emphasis on peril for use in the feature. Lesser at first insisted that theatres must book the final eight chapters to get the feature, but later he relented and released the feature alone. As a sequel, he also had Carl Himm edit a feature from the balance of the serial; this was released as *Chandu on the Magic Island.*

The Return of Chandu is not comparable artistically to the Fox original, which was directed by William Cameron Menzies and Marcel Varnel. It is a good action piece, however, with many supernatural overtones that are not explained away by any attempts at "logic." Director Robert Hill and cameraman John Hickson were secured from Universal's serial department. The work of these craftsmen, plus the use of some spectacular standing sets and exciting background music, imbues *Return* with desirable factors not found in the work of Mascot and the other independent makers of serials. In the matter of stunts and fast action, though, it must take a back seat to the Mascot product.

The Lemurian exteriors were filmed on the Skull Island village set from *King Kong,* erected by RKO at Pathé in 1932 over the ruins of some of Cecil B. DeMille sets for *The King of Kings* (1927). Here it is possible to see *Kong's* Great Wall, as photographed in broad-daylight detail. Some of the scenes representing Suva were staged in the Port of Dakang sets from *The Son of Kong* (1933). Two temples of Ubasti are impressive, both dominated by cat idols.

Lugosi obviously relished the chance to play hero. He beams with unaccustomed benevolence when addressed as "Uncle Frank." The dramatic moments involving hypnotism and "battles of wills" are infused with the same intensity he lavished on his portrayals of Count Dracula. Lucien Prival, Jack Clark, and Murdoch MacQuarrie are splendid menaces, and Josef Swickard makes the great Yogi as believable as possible. Maria Alba of Barcelona, Castilian accent and all, is charming and beautiful as Chandu's Egyptian sweetheart. Cyril Armbrister, who was in charge of dialogue during production and who glowers effectively on screen as a cultist, was producer of the *Chandu* radio adventures.

THE RETURN OF CHANDU (1934)

(Principal Pictures Corporation)

Running time, 65 minutes; feature presentation.

Notes

Two features prepared from the serial, *The Return of Chandu,* are sufficiently original works to merit individual consideration. In this first condensation, installments one through four were trimmed into a seven-reel feature to be followed by the weekly release of chapters five through eight. The feature is complete as a story, ending with the death of Vindhyan, and many theatres played it without the subsequent chapters. By planning in advance for a dual production, Sol Lesser was assured of a smoother-running feature than was the case with the earlier condensation of *Tarzan the Fearless.* Smoothness was achieved by re-filming the "cliff-hanger" at the close of each chapter, "cooling down" the instances of dire peril for use in the feature.

CHANDU ON THE MAGIC ISLAND (1934)

(Principal Pictures Corporation)

Film editor, Carl Himm; running time, 60 minutes.

Notes

This feature was edited from chapters five through eight of the serial, *The Return of Chandu,* prepared for use by theatres that did not carry serials. Although it was trimmed to less than half the length of the original sixteen reels, a fairly smooth continuity is maintained.

THE GHOST WALKS (1934)

(Invincible Pictures Corporation)

Presented by Maury M. Cohen; *directed by* Frank R. Strayer; *photographed by* M. A. Anderson, ASC; *assistant director,* Melville Shyer; *recording engineer,* L. E. Clark; *film editor,* Roland D. Reed; *art director,* Edward Jewell; *musical director,* Abe Meyer; *sound system,* RCA Victor; *filmed at* Pathé Studio; *running time,* 66 minutes; *released* December 1, 1934, *by* Chesterfield Motion Pictures Corporation.

PLAYERS: *Prescott Ames,* John Miljan; *Gloria Shaw,* June

Collyer; *Herman Wood,* Richard Carle; *The Professor,* Spencer Charters; *Erskine,* Johnny Arthur; *Dr. Kent,* Henry Kolker; *Terry,* Donald Kirke; *Beatrice,* Eve Southern; *Carroway,* Douglas Gerrard; *Jarvis,* Wilson Benge; *Head Guard,* Jack Shutta; *Guard,* Harry Strang.

Synopsis

Broadway producer Herman Wood accepts an invitation to visit the country home of playwright Prescott Ames. Buffeted by a rainstorm, the auto carrying Ames and Wood is halted short of its destination by a huge fallen tree. Ames suggests they seek shelter at a large house nearby. They are met by Dr. Kent, who invites them to spend the night. Wood eagerly accepts and retires to a bedroom to dress for dinner. He is startled by a woman's scream. At dinner, he is told to disregard the cries, which are attributed to one of Dr. Kent's mental patients. A moment later, the patient, a beautiful girl called Beatrice, enters. It is revealed that

Harry Strang, Johnny Arthur, Jack Shutta, John Miljan.

John Miljan, June Collyer, Wilson Benge, Donald Kirke, Henry Kolker, Douglas Gerrard.

Beatrice's husband was murdered in the dining room three years ago, and Beatrice speaks of her ability to communicate with the dead man. Suddenly the room is plunged into darkness, and a ghostly hand materializes over the table. Beatrice screams, and when the lights come on, it is found that she has disappeared. Wood asks to be excused and retreats to the quiet of his room.

Ames now congratulates the household members on their convincing performances, and it develops that they are actors who have just staged the first act of Ames' new play, *The Ghost Walks*, which Ames hopes Wood will buy: They go to call Beatrice back and find, to their horror, that she has been murdered. Ames reveals the true situation to Wood, who by now refuses to believe he is not seeing the balance of the play. The actors are terror-stricken, engulfed in a real mystery. After a series of strange happenings, the company learns that a madman known as the Professor has intruded upon the premises and is responsible for the weird events.

Notes

Although plausibility is not a virtue of Invincible's farce-mystery, *The Ghost Walks*, the film boasts some good gags and suspenseful moments. The "play within a play" idea, while old stuff on Broadway, is an unusual surprise element for a movie of the 'thirties. Tricky lighting effects are applied well to the old house setting — complete with sliding panels and secret passages — to deepen the mystery.

John Miljan, given a respite from his usual villainous roles, is convincing as the playwright-hero, and June Collyer is a beautiful and competent love interest. Henry Kolker lends dignity to the scene, and Johnny Arthur contributes his specialty, as a frightened milquetoast. Even these

seasoned performers are easily upstaged by the raspy-voiced Richard Carle as the harried producer, and he in turn is upstaged toward the finish by Spencer Charters' comical, and yet frightening, maniac.

MYSTERY MOUNTAIN (1934)

(Mascot Pictures Corporation)

Produced by Nat Levine; *directed by* Otto Brower *and* B. Reeves Eason; *supervised by* Armand Schaefer *and* Victor Zobel; *original story by* Sherman Lowe, Barney Sarecky, *and* B. Reeves Eason; *continuity by* Ben Cohen *and* Armand Schaefer; *photographed by* Ernest Miller *and* Willian Nobles; *supervising editor,* Wyndham Gittens; *film editors,* Earl Turner *and* Walter Thompson; *sound supervisor,* Terry Kellum; *musical director,* Abe Meyer; *filmed at* Universal City *and* Mack Sennett Studio; International Sound Recording Company *system; a serial in* 12 chapters, 25 reels; *released* December 1, 1934.

PLAYERS: *Ken Williams,* Ken Maynard; *Tarzan,* Himself; *Jane Corwin,* Verna Hillie; *Blayden,* Edward Earle; *The Rattler,* Edmund Cobb; *Matthews,* Lynton Brent; *Breezy,* Syd Saylor; *Little Jane,* Carmencita Johnson; *Corwin,* Lafe McKee; *Henderson,* Al Bridge; *Lake,* Ed Hearne; *Hank,* Bob Kortman; *and* Wally Wales, George Chesebro, Hooper Atchley, Gene Autry, Smiley Burnette, Jack Kirk, Lew Meehan, Jack Rockwell, William Gould, Tom London, Philo McCullough, Frank Ellis, James Mason, Steve Clark, Cliff Lyons, Art Mix, *and* Curly Dresden.

Chapter Titles

1) The Rattler; 2)The Man Nobody Knows; 3) The Eye That Never Sleeps; 4) The Human Target; 5) Phantom Outlaws; 6) The Perfect Crime; 7) Tarzan the Cunning; 8) The Enemy's Stronghold; 9) The Fatal Warning; 10) The Secret of the Mountain; 11) Behind the Mask; 12) The Judgment of Tarzan.

Synopsis

Blayden, in charge of his railroad's Westward expansion, suspects stagecoach executive Corwin is the Rattler, a mysterious bandit leader responsible for murderous raids on the rail crews. When Corwin is murdered, his daughter,

IN MASCOT'S "MYSTERY MOUNTAIN"

endangered by an explosive trap. Ken and Breezy recapture Henderson, who is about to reveal the Rattler's identity when he is killed by one of the warning darts.

The Rattler gang captures Ken, and the Rattler puts on a face mask that makes him exactly resemble Ken. In this disguise, the Rattler lures Lake's wagon train into an ambush. Ken, escaping, rides to the wagon train and barely misses being killed by the defenders. Ken is imprisoned. Breezy, seeking to clear Ken, trails the Rattler to his cave and, in disguise as one of the heavies, sees the Rattler's collection of lifelike head masks. Wearing a Blayden mask, the Rattler and two "deputies" take Ken into custody. Breezy helps Ken escape, and together they capture a number of the Rattler's men.

Jane, meantime, becomes suspicious of Matthews (actually the Rattler in disguise) and, with Blayden, trails him. Blayden is knocked out by Rattler men, and Jane is chased into the cave hideout, where she meets Ken in the Rattler's disguise. Ken finds there is a producing gold mine in the mountain. He is unmasked by the Rattler himself and locked up along with Breezy. Jane and Blayden release Ken and Breezy in time to save them from poison gas, taking them to a hospital to recover. Jane has taken some of the Rattler's masks, and the Rattler is wounded in the left arm when he tries to retrieve them. Matthews is revealed to have a bullet wound in the left arm, but when he escapes it proves that the Rattler was wearing a Matthews mask, and the real Matthews is not wounded. Dr. Edwards also has a wounded left arm, but he tells Ken he was shot by one of the Rattler's men after being forced to minister to the Rattler.

Ken is about to descend a cliff to the Rattler's hideout when he meets the Rattler face-to-face. Ken unmasks the Rattler but is shoved over the edge. Saved by hanging onto a rope, Ken reveals the Rattler is Dr. Edwards. Ken finds his horse, Tarzan, bleeding from a beating administered by the Rattler. Breezy learns that the Rattler was wearing an

Jane, tells Blayden she will carry on her father's fight. Ken Williams, a railroad sleuth, retrieves a wrench with which the Rattler struck a construction worker. He believes that fingerprints on the tool will implicate Dr. Edwards, who owns land the rail system needs for right-of-way. The Rattler sends Hank and his henchmen to kill Ken and get the wrench, but Ken captures Hank. Meantime, the Rattler kills the injured worker and leaves a dart bearing a warning to Ken. Hank escapes and is traced to the Corwin Transportation Company. Chasing the Rattler in a stagecoach, Ken and Jane narrowly escape death when their coach crashes over a cliff. Jane is wounded when Hank shoots at Ken. Ken's friend Breezy Baker, a newspaper reporter, is slightly injured in an encounter with the gang members, who think he has the wrench. Ken has placed the evidence in Blayden's safe, which is dynamited by the Rattler, destroying the fingerprints. Ken unmasks a man wearing the Rattler's disguise, revealing Henderson, who claims he donned the garb to get next to the gang. Henderson shows Ken a secret cave used by the Rattler, and Ken is

Ken Maynard accuses Al Bridge of malfeasance. Onlookers: Syd Saylor, Verna Hillie, Wally Wales, unidentified player.

143

Edwards mask. Believing that Tarzan will be able to identify the man who beat him, Ken gathers the suspects together at the mine camp. Tarzan tries to attack Blayden, who escapes with Ken pursuing. Riding to the mine, the Rattler is killed in an explosion of his own making.

Notes

Upon learning that Ken Maynard had been fired at Universal, Nat Levine immediately telephoned the strong-willed Westerner and arranged to star him in a feature, *In Old Santa Fe* (1934), and two serials, *Mystery Mountain* and *The Phantom Empire*. Levine offered Maynard the unprecedented (by Mascot, at least) salary of $10,000 a week, knowing that the tremendous popularity of Maynard – then vacationing in Europe – would justify an increase in budget. The feature turned out well, and *Mystery Mountain* proved Mascot's largest grosser to date, to be surpassed only by the Tom Mix fifteen-chapter serial, *The Miracle Rider* (1935). *Mystery Mountain* cost $80,000 – double the amount spent on most previous Mascots, with Maynard's salary accounting for half the cost. Maynard was difficult to handle, insisting upon making the film his way as he had done when he had his own producing unit at Universal, and browbeating Levine into renting the Western town at Universal rather than using the less imposing set at Mascot's home lot, the Mack Sennett Studio. Before the shooting was over, Levine was beset by mixed emotions – anxious to shed himself of Maynard and yet aware that it was Maynard's presence that made this serial outstanding. A weirdly prophetic note occurs at the end of *Mystery Mountain's* sixth chapter: Maynard is shot from the saddle by a seedy-looking bit player named Gene Autry.

The story, deriving from *The Hurricane Express,* repeats the idea of having the unknown villain able to disguise himself as any of the other male cast members. Another familiar bit of Mascot deception is employed, with Edmund Cobb, who is not otherwise in the cast, appearing in false nose, dark glasses, and moustache as the Rattler. Viewers with long memories may have noted after the denoument in Chapter Twelve that Edward Earle, unmasked as the Rattler, appeared with the arch villain several times in earlier episodes. Mascot gave the customers more than their money's worth in the way of escapist excitement – but seldom played fair in the matter of letting them solve mysteries.

Most of the outdoor sequences were shot at Bronson Canyon, one end of the quarry being used for the railroad camp and the other for the Rattler's secret domain, and at Chatsworth. Much of the photography is striking. Maynard and Tarzan are fascinating to watch, and there are a number of dependable character actors. Verna Hillie is highly decorative, and Syd Saylor adds some peppy comedy. The action scenes are well managed, which is not surprising in that both Otto Brower and "Breezy" Eason were noted for their direction of spectacular second-unit sequences in epic productions.

MURDER ON THE CAMPUS (1934)

(Chesterfield Motion Pictures Corporation)

Produced by George R. Batcheller; *directed by* Richard Thorpe; *adapted from* THE CAMPANILE MURDERS *by* Whitman Chambers; *continuity by* Andrew Moses; *photographed by* M. A. Anderson; *assistant director,* Melville Shyer; *art director,* Edward Jewell; *sound recording,* L. E. Clark; *musical director,* Abe Meyer; *produced at* Universal City; RCA Victor *sound; running time,* 73 minutes; *released* December 27, 1934.

PLAYERS: *Lillian Voyne,* Shirley Grey; *Bill Bartlett,* Charles Starrett; *Captain Ed Kyne,* J. Farrell MacDonald; *Ann Michaels,* Ruth Hall; *Professor Hawley,* Edward Van Sloan; *Blackie Atwater,* Maurice Black; *Reporter,* Harry Bowen; *Charlie Lorrimer,* Dewey Robinson; *Hilda Lund,* Jane Keckley; *Brock,* Harrison Greene.

Synopsis

Co-eds working their way through college are the subject of a feature series by Bill Bartlett of the *Times-Star.* His affections lead him first to nightclub singer Lillian Voyne, who refuses to consent to an interview. Her boss, a hoodlum called Blackie, is angered by Bill's presence. Driving to the campus one night, Bill accuses Lillian of loving Malcolm Jennings, a notorious college athlete who has the soft job of playing the Campanile chimes. Leaving Lillian just before nine o'clock, Bill hears the chimes commence to ring and wanders toward the Campanile. A shot is heard, and the chimes halt. Bill guards the only exit until Captain Kyne arrives with the police. Jennings is found shot through the head; suicide is ruled out, but the killer is not in the building. Lillian, found to have been waiting for Jennings, is strangely silent. Another co-ed, Ann, who has been intimate with Jennings, is questioned without result.

Kyne finds Bill at Lillian's apartment. He also turns up a .32-caliber pistol – the sort that killed Jennings – which implicates Lillian. Lillian insists she is innocent. Bill leaves on learning of the murder of a lawyer, Smythe, with the same sort of weapon. The killer is nowhere to be found.

Bill consults Professor Hawley, a chemist and respected amateur sleuth. Bill, who has light-fingered both murder bullets and a slug from Lillian's revolver, presents them to Hawley, who asserts all three were fired from the same weapon. Blackie disappears. Lillian is arrested. A new development adds to Bill's confusion: Hawley shows him the body of Brock, who has purportedly committed suicide.

Having sorted evidence against suspects, Bill confronts Hawley with a detailed explanation of how all the slayings were committed: The professor used delayed recordings of

Presenting in stirring drama a ridiculously simple solution of the mystery of three seemingly impossible murders

GEORGE R. BATCHELLER presents

MURDER on the CAMPUS

with
SHIRLEY GREY
CHARLES STARRETT
J. FARRELL Mac DONALD

DIRECTED BY
RICHARD THORPE

Charles Starrett, Shirley Grey, J. Farrell MacDonald.

pistol shots and applications of poison gas in establishing alibis for his near-perfect crimes. Hawley confesses and abruptly tries to kill Bill with poison gas. The police, who have been trailing Bill in secret, rescue the reporter and nab Hawley. Bill gets a warmer-than-usual greeting when next he meets Lillian.

Notes

A good novel as its basis — Whitman Chambers knew how to spin a mystifying yarn — elevates *Murder on the Campus* from the run-of-the-mill. Suspense and several scares enliven the telling on screen. Old-timers J. Farrell MacDonald and Edward Van Sloan steal the honors from the rest of a satisfactory cast.

1935

MYSTERIOUS MR. WONG (1935)

(Monogram Pictures Corporation)

Vice president in charge of production, Trem Carr; *directed by* William Nigh; *supervised by* George Yohalem; *from* THE TWELVE COINS OF CONFUCIUS *by* Harry Stephen Keeler; *adapted by* Nina Howatt; *continuity by* Lew Levinson; *additional dialogue by* James Herbuveaux; *photographed by* Harry Neuman, ASC; *film editor,* Jack Ogilvie; *settings by* E. R. Hickson; *recorded by* John A. Stransky, Jr.; *musical director,* Abe Meyer; *sound system,* Western Electric *by* Balsley & Phillips; *running time,* 68 minutes; *released* January 25, 1935..

PLAYERS: *Mr. Wong,* Bela Lugosi; *Jason Barton,* Wallace Ford; *Peg,* Arline Judge; *Tsung,* Fred Warren; *Moonflower,* Lotus Long; *McGillicuddy,* Robert Emmett O'Connor; *Jen Yu,* Edward Peil, *Chan Fu,* Luke Chan; *Brandon,* Lee Shumway; *and* Etta Lee, Ernest F. Young, Theodore Lorch, James B. Leong, *and* Chester Gan.

Synopsis

To the possessor of the twelve Coins of Confucius, according to legend, comes the right of rule over the Chinese Province of Keelat. San Francisco's Chinatown becomes the scene of a series of strange crimes, as the ruthless Mandarin Wong begins a quest for the fabled coins. Men are struck down in the shadowy streets, shopkeepers are murdered, and unsuspecting victims are beheaded at their dinner tables. The newspapers are slow to grasp the significance of the murders, which are regarded as merely another tong war — until the *Globe's* city editor, Brandon, decides there is a distinct pattern to the killings. Jason Barton, a respected feature writer, is assigned to investigate.

Beside the body of a victim in a Chinese laundry, Barton discovers a scrap of paper bearing writing in Chinese. When he takes it to a Chinese scholar for translation, Jason unwittingly reveals that he knows too much and is marked for death. Jason persuades Peg, his fiancée, to dine with him at a restaurant in Chinatown. A man is murdered in an adjacent booth, and one of the twelve coins falls into Jason's booth. When Jason and Peg try to leave Chinatown, they narrowly escape a strangler's noose. Seeking refuge in a little shop, they meet the beautiful Moonflower, Wong's neice. They have stumbled upon the entrance to Mr. Wong's underground den. Seized by Wong's hatchetmen, they are taken to a torture chamber where Wong is torturing Tsung, the legal representative of the Province of Keelat. Jason has managed to hide the coin in a passageway leading to Wong's headquarters.

Unable to persuade Jason to tell where the coin is hidden, Wong has Jason and Peg chained and is about to subject them to torture. When Wong is called from the

In the torture chamber with E. Allyn Warren, Bela Lugosi, Wallace Ford, unidentified player, Arline Judge, Edward Piel.

146

DEAD MEN TELL NO TALES

Out of the Night Creeps a Shadow Striking Terror into the Heart of Chinatown

MONOGRAM PICTURES present

MYSTERIOUS Mr. WONG

WITH

BELA (DRACULA) LUGOSI
WALLACE FORD · ARLINE JUDGE

Directed by WILLIAM NIGH · A GEORGE YOHALEM Production
Suggested by the story "The 12 Coins of Confucius"
by Harry Stephen Keeler · Screen play Nina Howatt

Adaptation by Lew Levinson

room, Jason manages to dislodge the receiver of a telephone and issue a call for help to his newspaper. The police arrive just as the ordeal is about to begin. Wong is shot to death when he tries to escape.

Notes

Little remembered today, Harry Stephen Keeler was one of the outstanding mystery writers at the time Monogram purchased film rights to *The Twelve Coins of Confucius*. Nina Howatt's screen adaptation hardly does justice to Keeler's excellent novel, although the picture does combine old-time melodramatics and comedy pretty well. The leading players are bigger "names" than usually were found in combination in Monogram's product. Bela Lugosi was still a great audience favorite despite his having appeared in several "turkeys," and Wallace Ford and Arline Judge had built solid reputations at RKO-Radio. William Nigh, a top director at M-G-M in the pre-sound era, doubtless found *Mr. Wong* quite a comedown from his famous *Mr. Wu* (1927), in which Lon Chaney scored a great success. Curiously, Nigh — who never strayed long from Poverty Row during the remainder of his career — several years later directed the six *Mr. Wong* detective pictures, five of which starred Boris Karloff as James Lee Wong. As *Mysterious Mr. Wong's* malicious mandarin, Lugosi performs with demonic relish, although his Hungarian accent is hardly in concert with his Oriental makeup. Ford and Miss Judge handle the wise-cracks in typical 1930s style.

The sets and props are effective in establishing the Oriental milieu, and Harry Neumann's lighting effects add to the implied menace. Unusual in Monogram products of the time is the use of some spooky music during some of the murder scenes. One sequence is so charged with terror as to stand out from the rest of the film. It opens in a Chinatown restaurant, where hands appear suddenly over the back of Wallace Ford's booth and, with a dying shudder, drop one of the coveted coins. As Ford and Miss Judge attempt to flee, they barely escape such hazards as a strangling cord descending from the darkness, a dropping ceramic vase, and Chinese daggers.

The dialogue is categorically unkind to Orientals. When another Chinatown killing is reported the hero says, "What do I care about another laundryman? The world is full of 'em." A cop, asked if he knows a Chinese named Wong, replies, "I haven't run into one yet that ain't named Wong." He also notes that "Them Chinamen is jabberin' like monkeys . . . There's nothin' noisier than a Chinaman." And as for encountering some murdered Chinese, "Better dead ones than live ones."

QUEEN OF THE JUNGLE (1935)

(Screen Attractions Corporation)

Directed by Robert Hill; *supervised by* Herman A. Wohl;

original story and screenplay by J. Griffin Jay; *photographed by* William Hyer; *technical director,* Fred Preble; *assistant director,* Glenn Cook; *musical director,* Hal Chasnoff; *sound engineer,* Herbert Eicke; *film editor,* Carl Himm; *a serial in* 12 chapters, 24 reels; *released* February 1, 1935; also released as a feature in 6 reels.

IT BEGINS WHERE
"TRADER HORN" LEFT OFF!
•
Screen Attractions Corporation
presents
"QUEEN
OF THE
JUNGLE"
with
REED HOWES
MARY KORNMAN
Directed by ROBERT HILL
•
12 Amazing Chapters of
Adventure & Romance

148

PLAYERS: *David Worth,* Reed Howes; *Joan Lawrence,* Mary Kornman; *David Worth (as a child),* Dickie Jones; *Joan Lawrence (as a child),* Marilyn Spinner; *John Lawrence,* William Walsh; *Kali,* Lafe McKee; *Ken Roberts,* George Chesebro; *Rocco,* Eddie Foster; *Captain Blake,* Robert Borman; *Abdullah,* Barney Furey.

Chapter Titles

1) Lost in the Clouds; 2) Radium Rays; 3) The Hand of Death; 4) The Native's Revenge; 5) Black Magic; 6) The Death Vine; 7) The Leopard Leaps; 8) The Doom Ship; 9) Death Rides the Waves; 10) The Temple of Mu; 11) Fangs in the Dark; 12) The Pit of the Lions.

Synopsis

John Lawrence and Frank Worth prepare to launch the balloon in which they plan to search out the legendary elephants' graveyard in a remote African jungle. When their small children, Joan Lawrence and David Worth, are menaced by marauding lions, the girl takes refuge in the gondola and is carried away when the balloon takes off accidentally. Kali, the white high priest of Mu, a lost kingdom, orders one of the blacks, Gura, to prepare a sacrifice of an infant to the god Rad, represented by a gigantic stone image. Thom, a tribesman, tries to halt the ceremony, saying the white god will soon come to rule over them and destroy the tribe for its sins. Spotting the balloon, Thom brings it down with a flaming arrow. Joan is brought into the sacred enclosure, where Gura demands her sacrifice. Thom says she is the daughter of the white god. Joan, still clutching a music box and a string of firecrackers David had given her, is placed at the feet of the idol. Gura releases lions which race toward Joan. Igniting the fireworks in an incense burner, Joan frightens the beasts away. Now Thom's prophecy is believed, and the girl becomes Queen of Mu and Priestess of Rad.

Our Gang alumna Mary Kornman, Reed Howes.

David, grown by now to manhood, reports to Lawrence that he has found the balloon gondola and the doll Joan had carried when she was lost so many years before. Gathering a safari, David goes in search of Joan. David and his headman, Talbo, are captured by the lion men and dragged before Joan, who has become cruel and ruthless. The natives hold a celebration to be climaxed by a double sacrifice. Talbo is strapped to a rock before the idol and is burned to death by rays of radium emanating from the eyes of Rad. David next is bound to the idol, but before the rays can destroy him he is saved by Joan, who has seen a locket taken from David containing her picture.

In the council chamber, David explains who Joan is. Gura, spying, sends a message to Kali, who orders Joan to be sacrificed. David and Joan are placed on the lap of the god and the lions are released. The beasts force Joan back into the hand of the god, which begins to close about her.

A 1922 tradepaper advertisement for The Jungle Goddess, source of much footage for Queen of the Jungle.

Joan has called the elephants, which arrive in time to save her and David. Thom convinces the natives that Gura has lied. Gura is branded and cast out. Kali goes into hiding. David finds a hoard of pure radium inside the idol, and Thom shows him the radium mine. As Joan and David try to return to her family, Gura sends the Leopard Woman and her cats to stop them. They face other perils, including a murderous ape, an evil Tree Man, and lions. Through Gura's treachery, Joan is blinded by a poisoned drink and Thom is killed in a lion pit. Gura tries to send Joan over a high waterfall, but she is rescued by a chimpanzee. Joan is caught by Kali, who ties her next to a pit of crocodiles. David saves her but is caught by Fish Men. The Fish Men's chief gives David a magic plant with which he cures Joan's blindness.

Rocco, a gangster, and Blake, an unscrupulous sea captain, come in search of the radium. These men conspire with Kali. Rocco kills a native who catches him ransacking the temple. Later he and the captain kidnap David and Joan, taking them aboard ship and attempting to force them to tell the location of the mine. By freeing captive animals on the ship, Joan and David escape. Kali recaptures them. Escaping a tiger pit, they find a band of friendly Arabs helping Joan's father, who has lost his reason. The Leopard Woman turns against Kali, and one of her cats kills him. Joan is taken to the temple to be sacrificed. A masked man, who proves to be Lawrence, tries to save her, but Gura has him thrown to the lions. The Arabs arrive, and Abdullah, their leader, kills Gura. Lawrence is saved and recovers his wits. David rides in on an elephant and rescues Joan.

Notes

Queen of the Jungle, Screen Attractions' "Triumphant Wild Animal Spectacle," does indeed have some spectacular scenes — but they are extracts from Colonel Selig's 1922 serial, The Jungle Goddess. Reed Howes, Mary Kornman, and others of the cast are shown in the dialogue scenes and close shots, with most of the real action being silent shots featuring Vonda Phelps and Truman Van Dyke. The faster cranking speed at which the Selig original was shot gives the game away. The animal action is quite good otherwise, and the setting with the huge idol, which moves in an uncanny fashion, is exceptional. The partial sets used for matching in the new footage work pretty well. Howes and Mary Kornman look good in the leads, but acting and direction are generally uninspired. Lafe McKee, who played likeable old gents in scores of films, does surprisingly well as the evil high priest.

A SHOT IN THE DARK (1935)

(Chesterfield Motion Pictures Corporation)
Produced by George R. Batcheller; directed by Charles Lamont; supervised by Lon Young; from the novel and

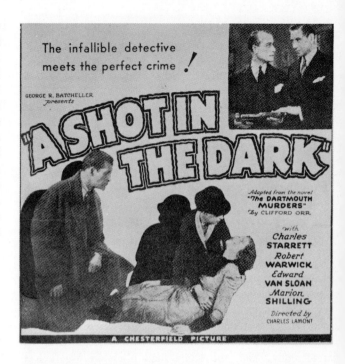

COLLEGE HUMOR serial, THE DARTMOUTH MURDERS, by Clifford Orr; adaptation and screenplay by Charles Belden; photographed by M.A. Anderson, ASC; assistant director, Melville Shyer; sound engineer, L. E. Clark; art director, Edward C. Jewell; film editor, Roland Reed; musical director, Abe Meyer; RCA Victor sound; produced at RKO-Pathé Studios; running time, 65 minutes; released February 1, 1935.

PLAYERS: Ken Harris, Charles Starrett; Joseph Harris, Robert Warwick; Professor Bostwick, Edward Van Sloan; Jean Coates, Marion Shilling; Byron Coates and John Mesereux, James Bush; Charlie Penlon, Julian Madison; Sam Anderson, Ralph Brooks; Bill Smart, Eddie Tamblyn; Sheriff, Robert McKenzie; Deputy, George Morrell; College President, Herbert Bunston; Dr. Howell, Broderick O'Farrell; Professor Brand, John Davidson; Housekeeper, Jane Keckley.

Synopsis

Student Ken Harris, a guest at Professor Bostwick's football victory party for Cornwall College, receives a telephoned request to meet his father, Joseph, at the close-by town of Barrington. Jean Coates, sister of Ken's roommate Byron, declines to accompany the youth. Arriving late back at Cornwall, Ken drops his father at a hotel and returns to his dormitory room only to find he cannot get inside. He beds down instead on a couch in Charlie Penlon's room downstairs.

Ken wakes to find Byron's body suspended outside a window. Investigation proves the boy was murdered and then hanged to appear a suicide. Jean is at a loss to suggest a suspect. Ken's father leads the investigation, learning that another student, Sam Anderson, knows who was in Byron's room but will tell only Ken, Joseph, or the authorities. Before the information can be divulged, Sam is murdered.

Marion Shilling and masked killer.

The murder weapon proves to be an unusual industrial device which Byron had borrowed from a class demonstration: a cattle-slaughtering instrument, propelled by an air pistol, which causes the insertion of a sharp object under the skull. Then comes a third slaying; John Mesereux is shot to death in a deserted house. Ken's father deduces Professor Bostwick to be the murderer, the man who had deserted Mesereux' mother in Paris.

Notes

Wittily directed and scripted, *A Shot in the Dark* gets a shot in the arm from top-drawer character portrayals by Edward Van Sloan, Robert Warwick, Doris Lloyd, Herbert Bunston, and John Davidson. The juvenile leads also are well cast, with the necessary romance handled by Charles Starrett — shortly to become Columbia's leading Western star — and Marion Shilling, an alumna of Max Reinhardt's stage productions.

The use of a compressed air gun designed for killing livestock as a murder weapon is perhaps a "first" for mystery films. The secret of the killer's identity is well kept. Pathé sets are put to good use, and the photography adds to the mood of dark doings at old Cornwall.

THE LOST CITY (1935)

(Regal Pictures – Super Serial Productions, Incorporated)

Produced by Sherman S. Krellberg; *directed by* Harry C. Revier; *general production manager,* George M. Merrick; *story by* Zelma Carroll, George M. Merrick, *and* Robert Dillon; *screenplay by* Perley Poore Sheehan, Eddie Graneman, *and* Leon d'Usseau; *dialogue director,* Zelma Carroll; *assistant directors,* William Nolte *and* Richard L'Estrange; *sound by* Clifford Ruberg; *photographed by* Eddie Linden *and* Roland C. Price; *technician,* James Altweis; *special effects,* Norman Dawn; *electrical effects,* Kenneth Strickfaden; *film editor,* Holbrook N. Todd; *art director,* Ralph Berger; *music by* Lee Zahler; *filmed at* Mack Sennett Studio; *distributed by* Super Serial Productions; *a serial in* 12 chapters, 25 reels; *two feature versions,* 108 minutes *and* 74 minutes; *released* February 14, 1935, *by* Principal Distributing Corporation.

PLAYERS: *Zolok,* William (Stage) Boyd; *Bruce Gordon,* Kane Richmond; *Natcha,* Claudia Dell; *Dr. Manyus,* Josef Swickard; *Butterfield,* George F. Hayes; *Reynolds,* Ralph Lewis; *Gorzo,* William Bletcher; *Jerry,* Eddie Featherstone; *Andrews,* Milburn Morante; *Queen Rama;* Margo D'Use; *Appolyn,* Jerry Frank; *Colton,* William Millman; *Ben Ali,* Gino Corrado; *Hugo,* Sam Baker; *Giant,* Everett Brown; *Officer,* Henry Hall; *Arab,* Curly Dresden; *"and a cast of more than 500 featured players."*

Chapter Titles

1) Living Dead Men; 2) Tunnel of Death; 3) Dagger Rock; 4) Doomed; 5) Tiger Prey; 6) Human Beasts; 7) Spider Men; 8) Human Targets; 9) Jungle Vengeance; 10) The Lion Pit; 11) The Death Ray; 12) The Mad Scientist.

Synopsis

An invention by Bruce Gordon shows promise of tracking the source of electrical disturbances which are causing worldwide chaos. The device directs Gordon to Central Africa, accompanied by his friend, Jerry, and two engineer-colleagues, Colton and Reynolds. At a remote outpost they find Butterfield, a renegade trader in slaves and ivory, and a derelict named Andrews. Following Andrews' clues, they investigate "Magnetic Mountain," wherein lies the unknown city of Liguria. Once the home of a race of master scientists, Liguria now is the domain of Zolok, who proclaims that he is "carrying on the electromagnetic traditions of my people." Zolok is served by the muscular Appolyn and a hunchbacked dwarf, Gorzo. His unwilling partner is Dr. Manyus, a scientific genius held prisoner, along with his daughter, Natcha. Zolok also commands a corps of giant, black zombies. On his television device Zolok watches every move of Gordon's expedition.

SHERMAN S. KRELLBERG
presents
THE LOST CITY

EPISODE 2 "TUNNEL OF FLAME"

Eddie Featherstone, Jerry Frank, Sam Baker and Kane Richmond.

As Gordon and Jerry approach a native hut, Zolok forces Natcha to scream into a microphone. Hearing the cry, Bruce and Jerry dash into the shack. They are plunged into a trap, and a long slide carries them to Zolok's prison quarters.

Bruce and Jerry see the wonders of Liguria. A native is captured by two of Zolok's giants. One machine destroys the victim's mind, and another changes him into one of the zombies. The giants capture Colton and Reynolds, who develop a sinister plot of their own: to force Manyus to make them wealthy with his inventions. As the scientists flee with Manyus through a cave, Natcha helps Bruce and Jerry escape by tricking Zolok into one of his own dungeons. A giant, Hugo, seizes Bruce outside the Tunnel of Flame, but Bruce manages to push Hugo into the flames. Zolok sends Gorzo, Appolyn, and several giants in pursuit. Manyus falls into the hands of some of Butterfield's natives, who try to sacrifice Manyus to a gigantic spiked boulder which is lowered from the treetops. Bruce and Jerry rescue the doctor, incurring the hatred of Butterfield, who wants

to force from Manyus the secret of creating an army of giants.

Natcha and Jerry fall into the hands of Ben Ali, an Arab slaver, while Colton and Manyus are captured by Gorzo and Hugo, who has survived the Tunnel of Flame. Ben Ali's men seize this group as well. Ben Ali sees in Hugo the possibility of giant slaves for the market. Colton suggests a partnership with Ben Ali in exploiting Manyus' inventions, but Ben Ali has Colton executed. Seeing a rival in Butterfield, the Arab has him imprisoned with the others. At Gorzo's command, Hugo breaks free and releases Gorzo. Natcha also escapes and is reunited with Bruce in the jungle. Bruce frees Jerry, Manyus, and Butterfield. When Ben Ali comes after them, his forces are routed by Butterfield troops. Butterfield tries to capture the others, so he can force Manyus to aid him, but his natives will not follow the fugitives across the Path of Skulls. Manyus leads his friends to the village of the Spider Men, a tribe of once-black pygmies whom Manyus has turned white. A black tribesman begs Manyus to make him white, and Manyus does so as the others watch in awe.

Butterfield makes a deal with Queen Rama, a power in the slave industry, to capture Manyus, then leads Rama's

Billy Bletcher commands Sam Baker to kill an Arab guard.

The Spider King plots with Billy Bletcher while Sam Baker awaits orders.

Margo D'use and George Hayes plot to rule Africa. "Gabby" was less loveable in those days.

Renegade Milburn Morante threatens Kane Richmond, Eddie Featherstone, Claudia Dell.

tribe, the Wangas, into the Spider Men's territory. Gorzo, meantime, plots with some of the Spider Men to sacrifice Bruce and Jerry, and force Manyus to make him into a normal-size man worthy to marry Natcha. As the execution is about to take place, the tribesmen arrive, defeat the Spider Men, and bring back the prisoners. Rama is smitten by Bruce and invites him to dinner, also ordering that Butterfield be staked out in the jungle to die. Rama wants Bruce as her mate, but Bruce refuses. After angrily lashing a servant girl, Rama puts a drug in Bruce's wine that causes blindness. Natcha is cast into a lion pit. The native servant helps Bruce rescue Natcha. Manyus also escapes and frees Butterfield, who promises to help Manyus and his friends. Butterfield restores Bruce's sight with a native remedy.

Hugo seizes Bruce but is killed by Natcha, who employs a death-ray pistol invented by Manyus. Leaving Manyus and Natcha in a cave, Bruce and Butterfield go back to try to recapture the trading post from Rama. They find that Rama has been stabbed to death. Zolok's television reveals the hiding place of Manyus and Natcha, who are soon recaptured by Appolyn. Bruce goes to search for the scientist and his daughter and also is captured. Jerry goes to Butterfield for help. Gorzo also has turned against Zolok and shows Butterfield and Jerry the entrance to the lost city. The horde descends upon Zolok's refuge just as Bruce is about to be killed by a destroying ray. Zolok is imprisoned. Bruce considers destroying the laboratory, but Manyus convinces him it can be used to benefit mankind. By means of a vial of acid, Zolok escapes and returns to the laboratory and, in his insanity, turns on all of the electrical equipment, including his secret "Ray Number Seven." As Bruce and his friends flee through the cave, the lost city is blown to atoms.

Crude, old-fashioned, and overdone, *The Lost City* piles horror upon horror in a manner undreamed of since the days of Pearl White. Its twelve chapters contain enough plot elements and cliffhangers for three times as much film. Members of the large cast, under direction of old-timer Harry Revier, perform in a wild-eyed manner more suited to silent pictures or Italian opera than to a mid-'thirties movie, as one scene after another stretches credulity to the limit. This affront to culture, this paean to *kitsch,* is great entertainment; it keeps the spectator, mouth agape, wondering just what in hell can happen next. There is nary a dull stretch.

The mad monarch of the dead city can destroy distant cities, cause storms and earthquakes, reverse the flow of tides and the course of rivers, make men into giants, destroy the will of anybody, view past and present on television, freeze electricity, change black men into white, and read minds from afar. Augmenting these mad machinations against the few sympathetic characters are an evil hunchback, a race of Spider Men (hardly as benevolent as the present day's popular comics character), Arab slavers, a ruthless jungle queen, giant zombies, a greed-driven trader, and assorted jungle beasts. Needless to say, this is one of the few serials in which no padding is evident.

There are some surprises among names in the technical staff. Eddie Linden, chief cameraman of *King Kong,* and Roland Price, the expeditionary photographer, handled the cameras. The sets are the work of Ralph Berger, famed for *Flash Gordon* (1936). Kenneth Strickfaden, designer of the electrical effects for Universal's *Frankenstein* and *Flash Gordon* pictures, created the laboratory equipment. Some special effects are quite striking, such as one in which Zolok causes a diminutive native to grow into a giant — all in plain sight. Some of the sets are impressive.

"Stage" Boyd (who died shortly after the film was completed) gives an unusual interpretation of the mad scientist, more as a tough guy than the usual bemused fanatic. Josef Swickard, as the wild-haired, captive assistant, is more the expected type, somewhat reminiscent of Ernest Thesiger's Pretorius in *Bride of Frankenstein* (1935). Kane Richmond, one of the more popular serial heroes, is an ideal Nemesis. George Hayes, as the renegade trader, hides his usually benevolent character behind a mask of villainy until late in the game, when he shamefacedly admits he's been "an awful rotter" and joins the good guys. Billy Bletcher, the little man with the big voice, cackles maniacally as the hunchback.

The Lost City was also released as a long feature and as a seven-reel feature to be followed by eight chapters. The feature version also was released as *City of Lost Men.* The Five Star Library issued a novelization in 1935, and during the nineteen-forties a comic book series was adapted from the serial.

SECRETS OF CHINATOWN (1935)

*(Northern Films, Limited –
Producers Laboratories, Incorporated)*

Produced and supervised by Kenneth J. Bishop; *directed by* Fred Newmeyer; *screen story and continuity by* Guy Morton *from his novel; photographed by* William Beckway; *technical director,* Li-Young; *sound engineer,* Wallie Hamilton; *film editor,* William Austin; *running time,* 63 minutes; *released (U. S.),* February 20, 1935, *by* Syndicate Pictures.

PLAYERS: *Robert Rand,* Nick Stuart, *Zenobia,* Lucile Browne; *Donegal Dawn,* Raymond Lawrence; *Brandhma,* James Flavin; *Chan Tow Ling,* Harry Hewitson; *Commissioner,* James McGrath; *Dr. Franklin,* Reginald Hincks; *Doverscourt,* John Barnard; *Yogi of Madrada,* Arthur Legge-Willis.

Synopsis

The police commissioner, desperate to solve a chain of Chinatown crimes, calls in a famed private detective, Donegal Dawn. Dawn scoffs at the official view of tong killings.

Dawn's young friend, Robert Rand, is interested in the

Nick Stuart.

blonde and beautiful Zenobia, an employee at Chan Tow Ling's curio shop. Zenobia tells Robert that they would be doomed should he try to spirit her away from Chinatown. A knife is thrown from above, but Bob can find no sign of the assailant. Zenobia vanishes. That night, Robert steals into the cellar of the shop, where he hears strange music and voices. He spies upon a weird ceremony in which Zenobia, elaborately gowned and jeweled, officiates as high priestess. The robed and hooded worshippers capture Bob. Zenobia seems entranced; she either cannot or will not help him.

Dawn tracks the mysterious Order of the Black Robe, but he is too late to rescue his friend. The strange temple and its worshippers have disappeared. Then Dawn discovers the new location of the temple in a mountainous area. Leading the police, he is able to rescue Robert and the mesmerised Zenobia. The cultists responsible for the crime wave are captured or killed.

Notes

Although it was filmed in Canada, *Secrets of Chinatown* differs little from the productions of Los Angeles' Poverty Row. It was directed by Fred Newmeyer, who in better days was associated with Harold Lloyd, and features three

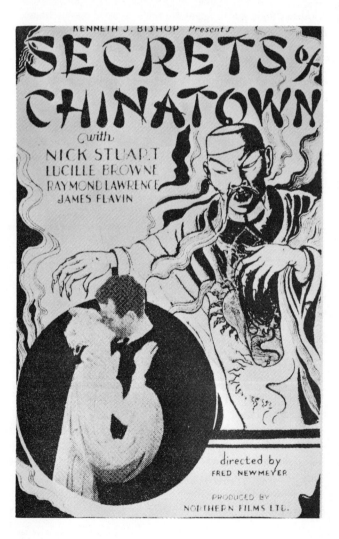

Lucile Browne, Nick Stuart in a Canadian Chinatown.

young players well known in Hollywood: Nick Stuart, Lucile Browne, and her husband, James Flavin. Stuart and Miss Browne are natural and attractive in the leads, and Flavin does a good job of villainy. The detective hero, Donegal Dawn, is a pompous intellectual, overplayed by Raymond Lawrence. The sets aren't up to Hollywood standards, but there are interesting exteriors in the climactic fight scenes, including an unfamiliar cliff from which a couple of villains are toppled.

Producers Laboratories of New York City and Kenneth Bishop's Commonwealth Productions studios at Willow Park, Victoria, B. C., were linked in this low-budget production, which captured little attention on either side of the border. The same company also teamed Miss Browne and Stuart in a romantic comedy, *The Fighting Playboy.*

BEAST OF BORNEO (1935)

(Du World Pictures, Incorporated)

Produced and directed by Harry Garson; *story by* Alfred Hustwick *and* Frank J. Murray; *filmed in* Borneo; RCA Photophone *sound; running time,* 65 minutes; *released* March 1, 1935.

PLAYERS: *Bob Ward,* John Preston; *Alma Thorne,* Mae Stuart; *Dr. Boris Borodoff,* Eugene Sigaloff; *Nahnda,* Doris Brook; *Darmo,* Val Durran; *Derrik Van De Mark,* Alexander Schonberg; *Kruger,* John S. Peters; *Borneo Joe,* Himself, *and* Dyak Natives of Borneo.

Synopsis

A giant orangutan escapes the nets of hunter Bob Ward during a trek through the jungles of Borneo, but the party captures an affectionate baby orang, who receives the name "Little Joe."

Meantime, in London, Dr. Boris Borodoff is infuriated at his failure to draw a "human" reaction from a brain removed from the skull of a still-alive beast. Borodoff determines to search the green hell of Borneo for a huge male orang in an insane zeal to plumb the mysteries of evolution. His colleague, Alma, agrees to accompany him.

The capture of Borneo Joe.

Upon reaching Moejoeb, the party is referred by Van De Mark, the overseer, to Bob Ward. Bob, however, refuses to help Bordoff, on learning that the scientist wants the orang for vivisection. Alma sways Bob.

After eight days' treacherous travel upriver, Borodoff develops a hatred for Bob — quite the opposite with Alma, who has come to depend on Bob's guidance. Borodoff is weakening under the jungle hardships, but success comes suddenly. A huge orang is treed and after ten days descends to take food which the trappers have doctored with gin. Netted, the beast struggles, and Borodoff becomes entangled with the natives. The scientist hurls Darmo, Bob's aide, into the embrace of the ape. Darmo is fatally injured before Bob can free him.

Borodoff's actions have caused desertion by the natives. The scientist makes ready to perform his experiment, but Bob intervenes and in a violent confrontation Borodoff fells Bob with a stalk of bamboo. The orang breaks from its cage and drags Bob away. Borodoff reports the abduction back at camp, and Alma makes a futile search for Bob. Now Borodoff proposes to use his scalpel on Little Joe. The young ape breaks free and takes to the jungle, where he finds Bob, helpless. Elsewhere in the jungle, Borodoff is looking for Joe. Alma wanders aimlessly into the jungle, finally dropping from exhaustion. Little Joe manages to reunite Bob and Alma, but soon the lovers are confronted by Borodoff, gun in hand.

Abruptly, though, Borodoff cringes in terror and commences to retreat. Bob and Alma turn and see the great ape, which crushes Borodoff. Bob, Alma, and Little Joe seek the river but are too exhausted to cover much ground. Then Little Joe hears native drumming — a message that rescue awaits them on Wild Mountain nearby.

Notes

Harry Garson in 1930 led an expedition to Borneo and the Straits settlements to film the second-unit work for Universal's *East of Borneo* (1931). Later, Garson returned to the same jungles to make his own picture, *Beast of Borneo*. The similarity ends with the title and setting, for the later film lacks the polish of the Universal picture, which George Melford completed at the studio.

The cast comprises virtual unknowns. John Preston, a flashing-eyed hero of the old school, had the lead in a series of Northwest Mounted Police films. Eugene Sigaloff had played minor villains at M-G-M. John S. Peters was one of Erich von Stroheim's Teutonic associates and did a notable parody of Stroheim in the Laurel & Hardy comedy, *Double Whoopee* (1929). The biggest scene-stealer is a baby orangutan, and the most photogenic character is a large orang which snuffs out the lives of a native and the villain. Some of the jungle footage is impressive.

CIRCUMSTANTIAL EVIDENCE (1935)

(Chesterfield Motion Picture Corporation)

Produced by George R. Batcheller; *directed by* Charles Lamont; *screenplay by* Ewart Adamson; *based on a story by* Tom Terriss; *photographed by* M. A. Anderson; *sound supervisor,* L. E. Clark; *art director,* Edward C. Jewell; *film editor,* Roland D. Reed; *assistant director,* Melville Shyer; *production manager,* Lon Young; *musical director,* Abe Meyer; *sound system,* RCA Victor; *running time,* 68 minutes; *released* March 30, 1935.

PLAYERS: *Jim Baldwin,* Chick Chandler; *Adrian Grey,* Shirley Grey; *Fred Stevens,* Arthur Vinton; *Ralph Winters,* Claude King; *Mrs. Winters,* Dorothy Revier; *Spike,* Lee Moran; *District Attorney,* Robert Frazer; *Cassidy,* Al Bridge; *and* Eddie Phillips, Carl Stockdale, Robert Elliott, Edward Keane, Lafe McKee, Lew Kelly, Lloyd Ingraham, *and* Henry Hall.

Synopsis

Newspaper reporter Jim Baldwin, covering the murder trial of Cassidy, is horrified when the man is condemned to death on evidence that is purely circumstantial. Sickened by the public's frenzied reaction, Baldwin determines to expose such trials as being uncivilized. He enlists aid in this campaign from Adrian, his fianceé, and Spike, his reporter pal. His sympathetic publisher, Ralph Winters, encourages the plan.

Fred Stevens, a wealthy gossip columnist for the same newspaper, feigns friendship, but in fact hates Jim and covets Adrian. Stevens is, in the words of one acquaintance, "a Jekyll-Hyde character," outwardly charming but secretly a morbid pervert who keeps skeletons and mummies in his study, and seeks to compromise the wives of other men.

Jim and Stevens concoct a scheme to put circumstantial evidence to the test and prove to the public that it should be outlawed. First they stage a fake brawl; then Stevens stages a drinking party which Jim angrily and publicly refuses to attend. Jim is seen skulking about the grounds

Dorothy Revier.

principal workhorse of the Chesterfield-Invincible outfit, did a neat job of directing this topical mystery. A heated controversy had been stirred up because the accused kidnapper of Charles A. Lindberg's infant son was convicted on circumstantial evidence. (Bruno Richard Hauptmann, the convicted kidnapper, was executed in April 1936 without ever confessing his guilt.) The provocative nature of the story and the depravity of one of the characters give the film its interesting aspects.

The cast, as was usual with Chesterfield, consists of seasoned professionals who are a pleasure to watch. Chick Chandler, usually seen as a light comedian, is surprisingly good in a straight hero role. Shirley Grey, formerly of Paramount and Universal, proves an appealing heroine. Arthur Vinton is especially effective as an outwardly charming villain, Dorothy Revier is convincing as the beautiful wayward wife, Claude King brings dignity to the role of a sympathetic murderer, and Robert Frazer is excellent as the flashy and ambitious district attorney. Adequate technical aspects showcase the players to good effect.

Lamont, typical of the Chesterfield directors, graduated to the major studios and became much in demand as a comedy director, among other projects presiding over many of the adventures of Abbott and Costello, Ma and Pa Kettle, and Francis, the Talking Mule.

during the party. Later a skeleton is planted and a fire set with evidence arranged to make it appear Jim killed Stevens and set the fire. Stevens is supposed to go to San Francisco and hide until Jim is brought to trial. Actually, Stevens intends to see that Jim hangs for the "murder." Under an alias, Stevens has secured a passport and steamer tickets to Europe.

In the ruins, police find both the skeleton and a charred body which proves to be Stevens. Jim is speedily tried, convicted, and sentenced to die. Shortly before the execution is to take place a phoney guard smuggles Jim to safety. Jim is taken to Winters' penthouse, where he learns that the publisher arranged his rescue. The "guard," captured by police as he tries to leave town, confesses that Winters hired him. The police go to the penthouse where they find Winters with his young wife and Jim, Adrian, and Spike. When Jim attempts to escape, Winters tries to stop the police from shooting Jim and is himself gunned down. Dying, Winters confesses that he murdered Stevens when he learned that the columnist had victimized Winters' wife. Mrs. Winters corroborates the confession and Jim is freed, his argument against circumstantial evidence dramatically proved to the world.

Notes

Charles Lamont, successor to Richard Thorpe as the

ON PROBATION (1935)

(Peerless Pictures Corporation)

Produced by Sam Efrus; *directed by* Charles Hutchison; *story by* Crane Wilbur; *screenplay and adaptation by* Sherman L. Lowe; *photographed by* Henry Kruse; *sound technician,* J. F. Westmoreland; *set dressing by* Jennett; *film editor,* Fred Bain; *assistant director,* Melville DeLay; *running time,* 71 minutes; *released* April 17, 1935

PLAYERS: *Al Murray,* Monte Blue; *Jane Murray,* Lucile Browne; *Bill Coleman,* William Bakewell; *Mable Gordon,* Barbara Bedford; *Dan,* Mathew Betz; *Judge,* Edward J. LeSaint; *Jane at Age Twelve,* Betty Jane Graham; *Benson,* Arthur Loft; *Lambert,* Henry Rocquemore; *Horne,* Lloyd Ingraham; *Clarence,* King Kennedy; *Negro Lad,* James ("Hambone") Robinson; *District Attorney,* Henry Hall; *Fagan Woman,* Margaret Fealy; *Detectives,* John Webb Dillon *and* Roy Rice; *Housekeeper,* Marie Werner; *Waiter,* Gino Corrado; *Man at Station,* Charles Hutchison.

Synopsis

When Al Murray, a crooked contractor and politician, becomes the guardian of an orphaned little girl who has been placed on probation as a pickpocket, he incurs the wrath of an old hag fortune-teller who has been using the child. The woman curses Murray: He will be killed by a lion, she decrees, at the time he has the most to live for.

Murray, who feels that the child will counteract some of the unfavorable publicity he has received, shrugs off the curse and in the ensuing years grows more wealthy and powerful. When Jane, now grown to beautiful womanhood, returns from finishing school, Murray is inflamed with desire. At a party in her honor, Jane meets Bill Coleman, a well-to-do Pasadena bachelor. When Bill kisses Jane, Murray strikes him. Bill apologises. Later that evening, Murray proposes to Jane, who is taken aback by the offer and says

'ON PROBATION'

Arthur Loft, Henry Roquemore, Monte Blue, Mathew Betz.

she would like to finish her studies in interior decorating in Europe. Murray agrees.

Bill follows Jane across Europe but fails to impress her. One of Murray's spies reports Bill's actions, and Murray orders Jane home. In Paris, however, Jane admits her love for Bill, who asks her to marry him. She refuses, fearful he will learn of her past. On returning from Europe, the youngsters tell Murray they are in love. Murray, meantime, faces arrest and plans to flee the country with Jane. Pretending friendship, Murray tells Bill of Jane's background but fails to change the youth's mind. Some of Murray's thugs attack Bill later that night, but Bill escapes. Murray attacks Jane, who strikes him over the head with a bronze lion, apparently fulfilling the old woman's prophecy.

Fleeing, Jane meets Bill and confesses the deed. Bill leaves her in his car and hurries upstairs to find Dan, Murray's henchman, who says he has stuffed his employer's body into a trunk. Bill takes the trunk, thinking to dispose of the body. He and Jane board a train, shadowed by detectives. Jane tries to go to the police to confess. Bill struggles with her when suddenly the train collides head-on with another train. Bill and Jane reach safety, thinking the resulting fire will dispose of Murray's corpse. Then Dan emerges from another car to reveal that Murray is alive inside the trunk. Bill makes a daring rescue. The detectives arrest Murray as Dan explains that Murray was only stunned by Jane's blow and had hit on the idea of escaping the law by pretending to be dead.

Notes

Peerless's product seldom rose above the morass of "off-brand" films, but *On Probation* is an exception. Suspenseful, beautifully photographed, and boasting a spectacular climax, the picture has the look of a major studio effort. The screenplay has freshness (symbolic

'ON PROBATION'

Barbara Bedford, Lucille Browne, William Bakewell, Mathew Betz, Monte Blue.

fulfillment of a curse promising death by a lion was the basis of Paramount's excellent *The Night Has a Thousand Eyes* thirteen years later), and the direction shows a skill not apparent in some of Charles Hutchison's earlier work. The career of the former serial daredevil was unfortunately nearing its end. "Hurricane Hutch" doubled William Bakewell in the climactic rescue scene.

Monte Blue, in one of his last leading roles, creates an almost likeable blackguard. Lucile Browne gains sympathy as the frightened heroine, as does Betty Jane Graham in portraying the character as a child. Mathew Betz as a loyal henchman and Margaret Fealy, seen briefly as a female Fagan, do much to make the fanciful story convincing.

ONE FRIGHTENED NIGHT (1935)

(Mascot Pictures Corporation)

Produced by Nat Levine; *directed by* Christy Cabanne; *supervised by* George Yohalem; *story by* Stuart Palmer; *screenplay by* Wellyn Totman; *supervising film editor,* Joseph H. Lewis; *directors of photography,* Ernest Miller *and* William Nobles; *film editor,* Edward Curtiss; *sound by* Terry Kellum; *musical director,* Arthur Kay; *horror mask by* Markoff; *special effects by* Jack Coyle and Howard Lydecker; International Sound Recording Company *sound; running time,* 66 minutes; *released* April 20, 1935.

PLAYERS: *Jasper Whyte,* Charles Grapewin; *Doris Waverly,* Mary Carlisle; *Tom Dean,* Regis Toomey; *Joe Luvalle,* Wallace Ford; *First Doris,* Evalyn Knapp, *Arthur Proctor,* Arthur Hohl; *Laura Proctor,* Hedda Hopper; *Jenks,* Fred Kelsey; *Felix,* Clarence H. Wilson; *Deputy Sheriff,* Adrian Morris; *Elvira,* Rafaela Ottiano; *Dr. Denham,* Lucien Littlefield.

Synopsis

Old Jasper Whyte arranges for a group of conniving friends and relatives to hear a reading of his will. They stand to divide a large inheritance provided Jasper's long-lost granddaughter is not found. Lawyer Felix arrives with a blonde supposed to be the missing Doris Waverly. Then a vaudeville magician, Joe Luvalle, brings in another blonde who claims to be Doris. Jasper sends for the Sheriff. Tom Dean, Jasper's great-nephew, shows up. The first Doris is found dead.

The Sheriff and a deputy find the girl was poisoned by cyanide in coffee. The relatives hurl accusations. Then a shrouded, seemingly invulnerable apparition in a hideous mask tries to kill the second Doris with a blowgun from the library. The attempt fails, and the monster fells Joe and escapes. Doris barely escapes a dagger. The killer's mask is found. Tom becomes a suspect. Then another of the party, Arthur Proctor, becomes the logical suspect when a shortage in his bank account comes to light. The killer drags Doris into a hidden passageway. After a fight with Tom, he is unmasked as another guest, Dr. Denham.

Notes

Although Mascot's primary interest was serials — of which it released thirty-one between January 1927 and December 1935 — Nat Levine also produced an occasional feature. Having leased the Mack Sennett Studio in 1935, Levine stepped up feature efforts, turning out nine features (exclusive of serial cutdowns) during the year. One of the better of these is *One Frightened Night,* a mystery-farce along the lines of *The Cat and the Canary,* written by Stuart Palmer, author of the Hildegarde Withers detective novels. Because the heavier schedule dictated against Levine's continuing personal supervision of each project, he brought in Monogram executive George Yohalem. Yohalem brought along Christy Cabanne and Wellyn Totman, respectively Monogram's top director and scenario editor.

The picture opens impressively with an excellent miniature of a storm-battered old house. Credit titles — including

Mary Carlisle, Charles Grapewin, Regis Toomey.

Reeves Eason; *supervised by* Armand Schaefer; *story by* Wallace MacDonald, Gerald Geraghty, *and* Harry Friedman; *continuity by* John Rathmell *and* Armand Schaefer; *photographed by* Ernest Miller *and* William Nobles; *film editors,* Earl Turner *and* Walter Thompson; *sound recording,* Terry Kellum; *musical director,* Arthur Kay; *songs,* "In My Vine-Covered Cottage," "Just Come On In," "Uncle Noah's Ark," "I'm Oscar," "Moon-eye View of the World," *and* "No Need To Worry" *by* Gene Autry *and* Smiley Burnette; *settings by* Mack D'Agostino, Jack Coyle, *and* Ralph M. DeLacy; *photographic effects;* Ellis ("Bud") Thackery; *special properties,* Howard Lydecker, Theodore Lydecker, *and* Billy Gilbert; *costumes,* Iris Burns; *produced at* Studio City; *cameraman,* William Bradford; *assistant director,* William Witney; *International Sound Recording system; a serial in* 12 chapters, *running time,* 230 minutes; *released* June 29, 1935; feature version, RADIO RANCH, *running time,* 71 minutes, *released* 1940 by Nat Levine.

PLAYERS: *Gene,* Gene Autry; *Frankie,* Frankie Darro; *Betsy,* Betsy King Ross; *Queen Tika,* Dorothy Christy; *Argo,* Wheeler Oakman; *Mal,* Charles K. French; *Rab,* Warner Richmond; *Professor Beetson,* Frank Glendon; *Oscar,* Smiley Burnette; *Pete,* William Moore; *Dr. Cooper,* Edward Piel, Sr.; *Frankie,* Frankie Marvin; *Saunders,* Jack Carlyle; *Muranians,* Wally Wales, Fred Burns, Jay Wilsey, Stanley G. Blystone, Richard Talmadge, Frank Ellis, Henry Hall, *and* Jim Corey.

Chapter Titles

1) The Singing Cowboy; 2) The Thunder Riders; 3) The Lightning Chamber; 4) The Phantom Broadcast; 5) Beneath the Earth; 6) Disaster from the Skies; 7) From Death to Life; 8) Jaws of Jeopardy; 9) Prisoners of the Ray; 10) The Rebellion; 11) A Queen in Chains; 12) The End of Murania.

photographs of the principal actors — appear behind flapping shutters; the Dunworth-de la Roche misterioso theme that also opened *The Vampire Bat* is heard between peals of thunder. Photography maintains this forbidding atmosphere throughout, and the effect is heightened by startling bursts of venerable music. Among a thoroughly professional cast, top honors go to Charley Grapewin's eccentric oldster and Wallace Ford's wisecracking vaudeville ham. None of the expected occupants is overlooked: the beautiful heiress, the stalwart hero, the hatchet-faced housekeeper, the crooked lawyer, the fidgety relative with the overbearing wife, the shifty doctor, and the dumb cop with the even dumber assistant. As always in any Mascot mystery, the identity of the villain is a secret well kept until the last moments.

Unlike previous Mascot pictures, *One Frightened Night* contains a great deal of dramatic music. The score features compositions by in addition to Charles Dunworth and Jean de la Roche, Josiah Zuro, Francis Gromon, Milan Roder, Rex Bassett, Rudolph Friml, Oscar Potoker, and Constantin Bakaleinikoff.

THE PHANTOM EMPIRE (1935)

(Mascot Pictures Corporation)

Produced by Nat Levine; *directed by* Otto Brower *and* B.

Thunder Riders.

Wally Wales and an unidentified player fight with Gene Autry. Onlookers: Wheeler Oakman, Dorothy Christy, Stanley Blystone.

Synopsis

Gene Autry and Tom Baxter own Radio Ranch, a resort famed for its musical broadcasts. Tom's children, Frankie and Betsy, see a weirdly masked band of horsemen who make a noise like thunder as they ride. Professor Beetson and his associates arrive by airplane, shoot Gene, and leave him for dead. In a search for radium deposits, Beetson's party shoots a Thunder Rider, puncturing his "mask" — actually a breathing apparatus. Other riders take their fallen comrade into a secret cave and down 25,000 feet in an elevator to the futuristic city of Murania, where the beautiful Queen Tika rules. Frankie and Betsy find Gene, and the three are pursued by Thunder Riders. They fall from a cliff but hang onto a bush and are rescued by the Junior Thunder Riders, a group of youngsters organized by Frankie. Back at headquarters, Gene is accused of the murder of Tom, actually killed by Beetson. Gene escapes and is pursued by the Sheriff in Beetson's airplane. Eluding both the law and a party of Thunder Riders, Gene flees in an auto which, when brakes fail, crashes over a cliff and

163

Gene Autry does battle on a catwalk in this Episode Seven scene. Backround is projected miniature.

Gene Autry, Betsy Ross King, Frankie Darro menaced by Wheeler Oakman, Jay Wilsey in Episode Ten.

burns. The posse thinks Gene is dead, but in fact he gets back to the ranch in time to stage his radio show. After an encounter with Beetson's thugs, Gene falls into the hands of the Muranians. Argo, the disloyal Prime Minister conspiring for the throne, saves Gene from a death chamber. After surviving fights with robots and rebel soldiers, Gene dies in a radium explosion.

Gene is brought back to life by Muranian scientists. He fights his way to the surface and frees Betsy and Frankie, who have been captured. Escaping in Beetson's airplane, the three narrowly escape death when Queen Tika disables the craft with a ray. Gene is seized by Beetson's gang while the kids are taken to a Muranian dungeon. Pete and Oscar, two of Gene's cowhands, save him. The children evade the Queen's radium ray, but Gene is caught when he tries to help them. Pete and Oscar, disguised as robots, enter Murania. When Argo's revolt begins, Gene and his friends side with Tika, who is captured by Argo. Gene saves her at the last minute from the disintegrating ray. The ray gets out of control and commences to melt the city. Tika elects to remain on her throne as Murania is destroyed. Gene and his group return to the ranch and force a confession from Beetson.

Notes

Ken Maynard originally was advertised as the star of *The Phantom Empire,* a wild fantasy dreamed up by Wallace MacDonald while he was under anasthesia in a dentist's chair. Nat Levine changed his mind after experiencing difficulties with the volatile cowboy while making *Mystery Mountain* and a feature, *In Old Santa Fe* (1934). In both of these, small roles were played by Gene Autry, a radio singing cowboy from Texas, whom Levine had under contract for $100 a week. Autry's pals, Smiley Burnette and Frankie Marvin, also were contracted for $75 and $60

weekly. In a rare gamble, Levine switched Autry for Maynard; threw in Burnette and William Moore as comic relief; added Frankie Darro and a trick rider named Betsy King Ross, from Alamo, Texas, as a pair of daredevil youngsters; and made what proved to be one of his more successful serials. Produced for $70,000, *The Phantom Empire* laid the foundation of a multimillion-dollar career for Autry, popularized the musical Western, and established a vogue for science fiction serials that had great influence in this curious sector of the industry.

Autry's sudden success is puzzling. He had a pleasing personality but little acting ability. As a horseman, he was no compensation for Maynard. He wrote good ballads and had a pleasant, but bland, singing style. Compared to huskies like Maynard, he hardly seemed the type for violent action. His surge to two decades of stardom is proof that "star quality" cannot be defined.

Exteriors for *Empire* were filmed at the Mack Sennett lot in the San Fernando Valley and in Bronson Canyon. The impressive throne room was set up in an unfinished solar observatory. The miniatures of Murania, used alone and in rear projection, are a vast improvement over the special effects of earlier Mascots. Also effective are scenes of the city's destruction, achieved by the melting of a special thick film emulsion. The robots are laughably unconvincing; they remained so when resurrected for Republic and Columbia serials nearly twenty years later.

The picture carries two sub-plots: a standard horse-opera formula of crooks seeking control of a ranch, and a ridiculous cliffhanger in which Autry periodically must interrupt the chases and fights to get back to the ranch in time to do a radio show. Several of the songs became Western standards. The comedy is elementary. The two youngsters all but steal the show from the grown-ups, but there is a formidable group of villains, led by Wheeler Oakman, Warner Richmond, and Frank Glendon. Blonde Dorothy Christy — best known as Stan Laurel's shrewish wife in *Sons of the Desert* (1933) — is an attractive Queen

Tika, although not as exotic a type as one might expect in such a role.

Aside from the Autry-Burnette songs, there is some stirring chase music by Henry Hadley, a theme for the underground kingdom by Hugo Riesenfeld, and some use of classical music, such as Herold's *Zampa Overture.*

CAPTURED IN CHINATOWN
A POLICE MELODRAMA (1935)

(Consolidated Pictures Corporation)

Presented by Bert Sternbach; *a* Weiss *production;directed by* Elmer Clifton; *continuity and dialogue by* Elmer Clifton *and* Arthur Durlam; *photographed by* Harry Forbes; *sound engineer,* Cliff Ruberg; *produced by* Consolidated Pictures Corporation *and distributed by* Stage & Screen Productions, Incorporated; *running time,* 50 minutes; *released* July of 1935 by Superior Pictures Corporation.

PLAYERS: *Himself,* Tarzan, the Police Dog; *Ann,* Marion Shilling; *Bob,* Charles Delaney; *Raymond,* Philo McCullough; *Zamboni,* Robert Ellis; *Harry,* Robert Walker; *Newsboy,* Bobby Nelson; *City Editor,* John Elliott; *Joy Ling,* Bo Ling; *Wong,* James B. Leong; *Tom Wong,* Wing Foo; *Ling,* Paul C. Fong.

Synopsis

Reporters Ann Parker and Bob Martin of the *Daily Chronicle* are sent to Chinatown to cover a story about the wedding of Joy Ling and Tom Wong. The story is important because the marriage is expected to end the hatred that has plagued the Wong and Ling families for generations. Bob is called away from the Ling house, leaving Ann to cover the story. Tom Wong presents to his bride at the ceremony a jade-and-diamond necklace valued at $50,000. When the girl goes to her room, the necklace is snatched from her throat by a man who has gained entrance to the house by posing as a recording engineer. Actually, the thief is Zamboni, a murderer and jewel robber who has garbed himself in clothing stolen from the Ling family. When Tom Wong rushes to the aid of Joy Ling, he is fatally stabbed by Zamboni. Tom's father sees the killer escaping and, fooled by the clothing, thinks it is one of the Lings. Wong declares a tong war, demanding the deaths of all members of the Ling family.

Ann, who knows too much, is imprisoned in the Ling home by Zamboni and his henchmen, Raymond and Harry. Her police dog friend, Tarzan, finds her. He goes to Bob and brings him to the Ling house. The dog attacks Zamboni and reveals the hiding place of the necklace. In a pitched battle, the gang is overcome and the plot exposed. The tong war is halted, and peace is restored between the families.

Notes

Bert Sternbach, one of the most penurious of indepen-

BERT STERNBACH presents

"Captured In Chinatown"
A POLICE MELODRAMA

Police dog Tarzan joins Charles Delaney and Marion Shilling for the happy ending.

dent producers, presented in the early 'thirties a series of action pictures featuring Tarzan, a German police dog. Each of the several films was subtitled, *A Police Melodrama.* Tarzan does a good imitation of the great Rin Tin Tin in *Captured in Chinatown,* the most unusual of the series.

Some good players appear in support, notably Marion Shilling, Philo McCullough, Robert Walker, and Robert Ellis — the latter being a particularly slimy murderer. Elmer Clifton, director and co-author, was a protégé of D. W. Griffith. Clifton suffered from the same problem as the Master — an inability to adjust to the different acting styles demanded by talking pictures. Its old-fashioned histrionics notwithstanding, *Captured in Chinatown* delivers some agreeable mystery and action. The rented sets are effective, and reasonably authentic.

CONDEMNED TO LIVE (1935)

(Invincible Pictures Corporation)

Directed by Frank R. Strayer; *produced by* Maury M. Cohen; *production manager,* Lon Young; *story and screenplay by* Karen DeWolf; *photographed by* M.A. Anderson; *art director,* Edward C. Jewell; *recording engineer,* Richard Tyler; *film editor,* Roland D. Reed; *assistant director,* Melville Shyer; *musical director,* Abe Meyer; RCA Victor *sound; filmed at* Universal City; *running time,* 65 minutes; *released* September 15, 1935, *by* Chesterfield Motion Pictures Corporation.

PLAYERS: *Paul Kristan,* Ralph Morgan; *Margurite Mane,* Maxine Doyle; *David,* Russell Gleason; *Dr. Anders Bizet,* Pedro de Cordoba; *Zan,* Mischa Auer; *Mother Molly,* Lucy Beaumont; *John Mane,* Carl Stockdale; *Anna,* Hedi Shope; *Maria,* Marilyn Knowlden; *Old Doctor,* Paul Weigel; *Manservant,* Edward Cecil; *Bell Ringer,* Ted Billings; *Villagers:* Harold Goodwin, Charles ("Slim") Whittaker, Dick Curtis, Frank Brownlee, Horace B. Carpenter; IN THE PROLOGUE: *Woman,* Barbara Bedford; *Doctor,* Robert Frazer; *Father,* Ferdinand Schumann-Heinck.

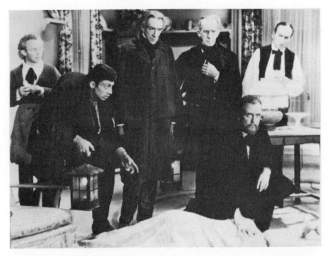

Another vampire murder. Mischa Auer, Pedro de Cordoba, Carlton Stockdale, Ralph Morgan. Players at background left and right are unidentified.

The climactic scene in the cave. Russell Gleason (in opera hat), Mischa Auer, Ralph Morgan, Pedro de Cordoba. Among bit players are Harold Goodwin and Horace Carpenter (left) and Dick Curtis (right).

Synopsis

Unknown even to himself, the kindly Professor Paul Kristan is the vampire terrorizing a European village early in the Twentieth Century. Asleep in his darkened library and bathed in the full moon's beams, Kristan is transformed. An attack on a pretty girl follows. Then Kristan's hunchbacked servant, Zan, carries the body to a cave and disposes of it in a pit. Later, Kristan and a group of townsmen find the pit containing the bodies of a number of victims.

Kristan sends for an old friend, Dr. Anders Bizet, to investigate. Bizet determines that Kristan's fiancée, Margurite, loves the professor only platonically and plans to marry him to please her father, who has a short time to live.

Bizet believes Margurite will fall in love with a younger man.

A young villager, David, advances an unpopular theory that the killer is actually a human who plays on the superstitions of the country folk. David is in love with Margurite.

Advised by Bizet not to marry Margurite, Kristan goes for a walk at night in the woods. Buffeted by winds, Kristan drops to the ground, his lantern extinguished. Without the light, he becomes the vampire once more, and goes to Margurite's home. There he kills a pretty, blonde servant. Bizet and Zan find Kristan in the woods, himself again. The villagers suspect Zan is the killer. In a confrontation with Zan, Bizet learns the hunchback has been disposing of evidence that might lead to Kristan.

Bizet goes after Kristan, who has gone to tell Margurite of his fears about himself. Meantime, a mob searches for Zan. Kristan tells Margurite he has spells of unconsciousness and loss of memory and that he is releasing her from their bethrothal. When Margurite sees that the light hurts his eyes, she turns some of them out. One by one the lights go off and then clouds obscure the moon, plunging the room into darkness. Margurite catches a glimpse of Zan's face as he comes in through a window. She struggles with someone. Bizet and the villagers arrive to find Margurite and Kristan unconscious and Zan fleeing. The mob pursues Zan, who has purposely led them away.

When Kristan recovers, Bizet tells him the truth: Kristan's mother was attacked by a giant bat in Africa shortly before Kristan was born, and a French doctor learned the child had vampiric tendencies. Kristan and Bizet rush to save Zan from the mob. They find Zan at bay in the cave. Kristan tells the villagers he knows now that he is himself the monster. Tearing away Zan's shirt, he reveals his mark. The villagers grow sympathetic. Kristan leaps into the pit. Zan, stricken with grief, follows before the townspeople can stop him.

Notes

Pretentious in its class, *Condemned To Live* is one of the few thirties independent pictures to address vampirism. The concept of prenatal influence is a daring theme and apparently a "first." The only picture to which *Condemned* bears much likeness if Majestic's *The Vampire Bat* of 1933, which also presented variations on the theme and which utilized the same director, musical scoring, and settings. The finished portrayal of a sympathetic vampire in *Condemned* is the work of Ralph Morgan, a fine actor best remembered as the tragic husband of M-G-M's *Strange Interlude* (1932), but whose fame was overshadowed by that of his brother, Frank. Also memorable are Mischa Auer, sympathetic as a grotesque hunchback; Pedro de

Cordoba as the pragmatic "Van Helsing" type essential to vampire tales; and the silent star, Barbara Bedford, seen briefly in a prologue as the mother of the vampire child. Maxine Doyle is a beautiful and convincingly innocent leading lady.

Filming at Universal City involved sets that include the European street, still dressed for the just-completed *The Bride of Frankenstein;* the exterior of Castle Frankenstein; the bell tower from *The Hunchback of Notre Dame* (1923), with Ted Billings — in his costume from *The Bride of Frankenstein* — ringing one of the great bells; and several European home interiors and some peasant huts. The cliffs and caves are those at Bronson Canyon, which are made to seem part of a seascape by the clever cutting-in of a coastal shot and use of the sounds of breakers. Costumes from Universal's two Charles Dickens films, *Great Expectations* (1934) and *Mystery of Edwin Drood* (1935) are in evidence.

The pervading sense of period is aided by rather lofty dialogue that never seems too stilted. The night-lighting effects are excellent, and the suspense is well conceived in Morgan's climactic scenes with Miss Doyle.

Compositions for the main and end titles are the work of David Broekman, former musical director of Universal, and the Dunworth-de la Roche *Stealthy Footsteps* (probably the most popular mystery theme in Abe Meyer's repertoire) is heard during the establishing scenes.

HONG KONG NIGHTS (1935)

(Futter Productions – WAFilms)

Produced by Walter Futter *and* Fenn Kimball; *directed by* E. Mason Hopper; *adaptation and dialogue by* Norman Houston; *story by* Roger Allman; *photographed by* Arthur Reed, ASC; *art director,* Charles Gardner; *filmed at* Mack Sennett Studios; *running time,* 62 minutes; *released* September 15, 1935, *by* First Division Exchanges.

PLAYERS: *Tom,* Tom Keene; *Trina,* Wera Engels; *Wally,* Warren Hymer; *Wong,* Tetsu Komai; *Burris,* Cornelius Keefe; *Captain Evans;* Freeman Lang; *Blake,* Tom London.

Synopsis

Tom and Wally, Customs agents who are trailing gun runners, are sent from Nanking to Hong Kong to receive secret orders. Trina, a Viennese girl, is being romanced by a slicker named Burris, who purports to be a businessman but is in fact an ex-convict involved with Chinese criminals. Burris decamps abruptly for Macao, an island off Hong Kong where crime is rampant. Wally warns Trina not to go to Macao, but she is adamant. A consul assigns Tom to halt Burris' activities.

Wong, who has observed Tom's activities, prepares to follow him to Macao. On arrival in Macao with Wally, Tom spots Burris with Trina. Wong summons Burris and tells him

hides him. At the destination, Tein Chau, Burris locks Trina aboard and goes ashore. Tom comes out of hiding, releases Trina, and goes ashore to prevent delivery of the weaponry. He arrives in time to see Burris accept a chest of silver in exchange for the guns and ammunition. Tom fires on the village and retreats toward the boat but is captured by Burris.

Back at the yacht, Burris declares he will keep the silver and sell the bulk of the munitions elsewhere. Wong overhears the plot and vows revenge against Burris for having tricked his people. The boat docks at Langow Island, a deserted atoll, where Burris hides the weapons and several barrels of oil and then announces his plan to dispose of Trina and Tom, by leaving them in a cavern which will be submerged at high tide.

Back at the beach, Wong has ordered the weapons returned to the boat. Burris arrives and starts to protest, but the yacht starts back to Tien Chau. Burris shoots Wong, and Wong stabs Burris to death.

Wong, again repaying his debt of life to Tom, fires the oil drums even as he dies from Burris' gunshot. The blaze is seen by a passing patrol ship, and Tom and Trina are rescued.

that Tom is on Burris' trail. Burris orders Wong to go to a waiting boat. Tom overhears and follows with Wally.

Aboard the boat, Trina, having overheard Wong and Burris planning to dispose of Tom, quarrels with Burris. She warns Tom of the plot. Tom lodges her in his and Wally's cabin and as he prepares to sleep in a deck-chair Wong attacks him. Tom overpowers the Chinaman and escapes. Next day, back in Hong Kong, Tom invites Trina to a polo match to try to learn what he can of the gun runners' plot. Trina tries to convince Tom that Burris is trying to "go straight" and urges Tom to visit Burris' waterfront office following the game. He agrees.

Wally meantime follows Burris and Wong to a warehouse on the waterfront. He sneaks a look at some crates and finds a sizeable supply of lethal weapons. Elsewhere, Burris and a henchman plot to kill Tom. When Tom and Trina arrive at the warehouse, Burris asks Trina to wait outside and sets out to bribe Tom.

While waiting, Trina investigates the warehouse and finds Wally, who proceeds to show her the stockpiled munitions. The sounds of a terrific battle emanate from the office. Tom has done away with Burris' henchman and is preparing to attack the ringleader when Wong arrives with a boatload of coolies. Tom is captured, and Wong is ordered to kill him, once the weapons are loaded aboard the boat.

One of the bombs which Wally has been examining is touched off, and Wally tosses it out of the warehouse. The coolies hasten to load the boat. Wong raises his gun and fires into the air, explaining to Tom that he is repaying the debt of his life — (Tom could have killed him earlier in the shipboard attack) — by sparing Tom's life.

The police arrive to investigate the explosion just as the boat surges away. Trina is taken aboard with Burris. Tom leaps to a dory behind the boat and climbs aboard. Trina

Notes

Although the "yellow peril" had ceased to interest the major studios, the independents continued to exploit Oriental mystery throughout the 'thirties. Walter Futter decided the tong war was passé, opting instead for a tale of "smugglers' bullets and Chinese knives." Futter made his film at the Mack Sennett Studio and locations in Los Angeles' Chinatown and on Catalina Island. While working in Chinatown, the company became embroiled in a tong war, which erupted on the third day of filming. The On Leong Tong had interested itself in helping one of its

Wera Engels, Tom Keene, Warren Hymer.

members to get back his money after a wife (purchased from her father, an elderly Chinese extra in the film) deserted him. After some threats, knife-brandishing, and rock-throwing, the matter was settled.

Hong Kong Nights is not, by any standard, a slick production, but it contains a spectacular sequence in which a fair-size village, covering more than an acre of the Sennett backlot, is burned to the ground. There is also a highly suspenseful climax in which the romantic leads, Tom Keene and Wera Engels, are trapped in a cave on an island being inundated by high tide. The romantic aspects are more sophisticated than in the usual independent melodrama, and the comedy relief is handled with competence.

The director, E. Mason Hopper, was a stage veteran who began directing films for Essanay in 1911. By 1930 he had directed approximately 350 pictures and written some 400 scripts, most of his work being done for the majors. His specialty, preceding the talkie era and his demotion to the independents, was romantic comedy, *e. g.*, *Up in Mabel's Room* and *Paris at Midnight* (both 1926).

The cast is of singular interest. Star Tom Keene was a New York stage actor who, as George Duryea, played romantic leads in early talkies — before RKO changed his name and starred him in a series of good Westerns. Just before making *Hong Kong Nights,* he won critical acclaim as the hero of King Vidor's *Our Daily Bread* (1935). Later, he returned to Westerns for several years and, in the 'forties, changed his name to Richard Powers in an effort to launch himself as a dramatic actor. His death occurred before his fourth career could gain much momentum. Wera Engels, an unusual beauty from Vienna, had appeared with Edmund Lowe in Universal's *The Great Impersonation* (1935) but failed to catch on in American films. The comedy lead, Warren Hymer, was the leading portrayer of tough but stupid sidekicks (as in *The Unholy Garden*). He was so adept in the role, that film scripts of the period often referred to a character as "a Warren Hymer type." Hymer is also celebrated as the actor who dramatized the termination of his Columbia contract by urinating on Harry Cohn's desk. Cornelius Keefe is in his element as a handsome but despicable crook, and Tetsu Komai, the Japanese actor, efficiently repeats his specialty as a *Chinese* menace.

MURDER BY TELEVISION (1935)

(Cameo Productions, Incorporated — Imperial Distributing Corporation)

Produced by Cameo Productions, Incorporated; *presented by* William M. Pizor; *directed by* Clifford Sanforth; *associate producer,* Edward M. Spitz; *story and screenplay by* Joseph O'Donnell; *from ideas suggested by* Clarence Hennecke *and* Carl Coolidge; *television technician,* Milton M. Stern; *technical supervisor,* Henry Spitz; *art direction,* Louis Racmil; *songs, music, and lyrics by* Oliver Wallace;

film editor, Lester Wilder; *production manager,* Melville Delay; *photographed by* James Brown, ASC, *and* Arthur Reed; *running time,* 60 minutes; *released* October of 1935 *by* Imperial Distributing Corporation.

PLAYERS: *Arthur Perry*, Bela Lugosi; *June Houghland,* June Collyer; *Dr. Scofield, ASBS,* Huntley Gordon; *Richard Grayson,* George Meeker; *Nelson, Chief of Police,* Henry Mowbray; *and* Charles Hill Mailes, Charles K. French, Claire McDowell, Larry Francis, Hattie McDaniel, Henry Hall, Allan Jung, William ("Billy") Sullivan, *and* William Tooker.

Synopsis

Having at last perfected television — a revolutionary communications concept — Professor Houghland rejects all corporate offers to buy his inventions. Promoters eschew scruples to get them. Several prominent experts gather at Houghland's home to witness a demonstration. The first test is patently a success, but as the second broadcast

commences Houghland drops dead. Chief Nelson and his officers arrive to find a number of suspects. Houghland's assistant, Perry, was away from the room after the murder. Jordan had sought to gain the plans by bribing Perry. Grayson had promised his company he would get the inventions. Dr. Scofield refuses to explain a phone call he made before Houghland's death.

Houghland's plans have been stolen, along with a tube device which contained the secret. A servant, Ah Ling, blames Perry, who disappears and is found dead after a search, his heart pierced by Ah Ling's knife. Perry then appears to have returned from the dead. Finally it develops that Perry's twin has come to investigate. Perry proves Dr. Scofield killed Houghland with an infernal machine, of his own making, which created "the interstellar frequency that is the death ray."

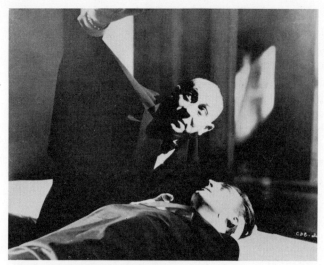

Erich von Stroheim, John Bohn.

Notes

We are hard-put to imagine a film of less merit than *Murder by Television*, which was filmed during the summer of 1935, released briefly in October, shelved, then released again about two years later. Never widely shown, it disappointed patrons who were intrigued by the Lugosi name and a dandy title. (Television was then a dozen years away from commercial acceptance and was regarded by the public as science fiction.) A dull script, plodding direction, and poor performances by normally dependable players add up to a lifeless, dreary picture. Technically and histrionically, it resembles some of the earliest talkies from 1928, with cameras firmly anchored and actors seemingly ill at ease with dialogue.

Erich von Stroheim.

THE CRIME OF DR. CRESPI (1935)

(Liberty Pictures Corporation – Republic Pictures Corporation)

Produced and directed by John H. Auer; *based on* "The Premature Burial" *by* Edgar Allan Poe; *story by* John H. Auer; *adaption by* Lewis Graham *and* Edwin Olmstead; *photographed by* Larry Williams; *art director,* William Saulter; *film editor,* Leonard Wheeler; *musical director,* Milton Schwartzwald; *makeup artist,* Fred Ryle; *production supervisor,* W. J. O'Sullivan; *produced at* Biograph Studio, New York; *sound system,* RCA Victor; *running time,* 63 minutes; *released* October 21, 1935, *by* Republic Pictures Corporation.

PLAYERS: *Dr. Andre Crespi,* Erich von Stroheim; *Dr. Thomas,* Dwight Frye; *Dr. Arnold,* Paul Guilfoyle; *Mrs. Ross,* Harriet Russell; *The "Dead" Man,* John Bohn; *Miss Rexford,* Geraldine Kay; *Miss Gordon,* Jeanne Kelly; *Jeanne,* Patsy Bertin; *DiAngelo,* Joe Verdi; *Minister,* Dean Raymond.

Synopsis

Festering within the mind of the eminent Dr. Andre

Crespi is a desire for revenge against Ross, the man who married Crespi's onetime enamorata. When Ross must have a major operation and Crespi's surgical skills are needed, the doctor seizes the opportunity for vengeance. After the operation, Ross apparently dies. Actually, Crespi has administered a powerful drug that places Ross in a deathlike trance, yet leaves him capable of thought and in possession of his senses. The drug will wear off in a few days. Crespi declares the man dead and arranges to bypass the embalming process as burial arrangements are made. Crespi comes to the morgue to gloat over his victim and taunt him about his fate. His triumph is complete when he sees Ross lowered into the grave.

Dr. Arnold, one of Crespi's colleagues, becomes suspicious of the supposed death and enlists the aid of Dr. Thomas in investigating the matter. The doctors exhume Ross's body on their own, intending to perform an autopsy. Their blades, however, draw circulating blood, and Ross, at

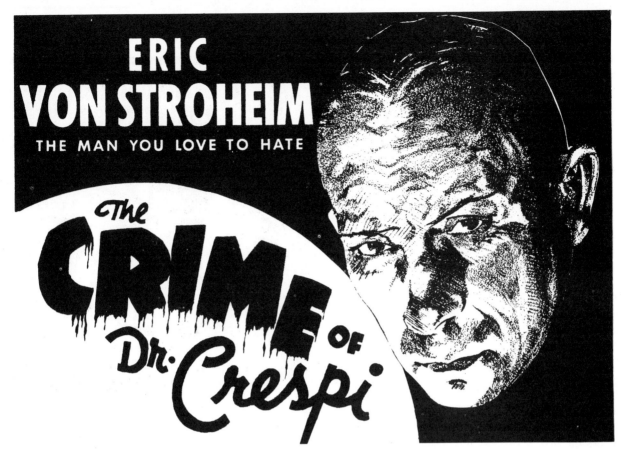

ERIC VON STROHEIM
THE MAN YOU LOVE TO HATE

THE CRIME OF Dr. Crespi

Republic's ad-men got the Stroheim slogan right but mispelled Erich.

Erich von Stroheim, Harriet Russell.

Dwight Frye, John Bohn, Paul Guilfoyle.

length, is revived — a terror-stricken, ghostly figure who stalks the corridors of the hospital in his madness. Ross is led to a confrontation with Dr. Crespi. The surgeon's violent response before witnesses fails to gain him any quarter, and he commits sucide.

Notes

His career as a director destroyed because of budgetary extravagances which the major studios found intolerable, Erich von Stroheim continued to appear as an actor. His first talkie effort without directorial authority was *The Great Gabbo* (1930), a portrait of a ventriloquist emotionally bound to his mannequin. The role of Gabbo was patently not von Stroheim's only contribution to that film, which bears such Stroheim trademarks as a nosey man and wife whose eavesdropping helps advance the story, plus the pivotal character's own pompous formality. Moreover, the producer-director of *Gabbo*, James Cruze, made a practice of assembling creative suggestions from what he termed a "community council" of all cast and crew members.

Acting was not a task von Stroheim enjoyed, for he had difficulty remembering lines and was frustrated at not being able to take charge. He was, however, an immensely effective actor who dominated any scene. Shortly before his return to Europe, where his genius was better appreciated, von Stroheim went to New York and worked for just over a week at the old Biograph Studio in the Bronx. The result was *The Crime of Dr. Crespi*, a delightful Poe inspired chiller masterminded by the up-and-coming John H. Auer, a young director from Budapest who had worked on Spanish-language films for several years.

When Herbert J. Yates, the principal stockholder in Biograph, assembled the independent producers who formed Republic Pictures Corporation, the combine decided to purchase the completed product of the faltering Liberty and Majestic companies. *Crespi* was made for M. H. Hoffman's Liberty Pictures but went into release under the Republic brand as the "SCREEN'S SUPER-THRILLER ... AN EPIC OF HORROR!" Typically enthusiastic, publicists asserted that *Crespi* "starts where 'Frankenstein' left off!"

Hardly the first or last film to fall short of its publicity. *Crespi* nonetheless turned out rather well, in view of the limitations of time and money. Auer, as producer, director, and author, maintained an oppressive mood of death and evil surrounding a dominant chracter who lacks redeeming qualities. He put the mood on an effective tangent with a man driven to madness by imprisonment in the grave. There is a minimum of comedy and romantic byplay.

Stroheim — advertised here as Universal had touted him in *Blind Husbands* (1919), "The man you love to hate" — is beyond critical reproach as the sadistic and lecherous Dr. Crespi. When brooding in his laboratory office, wreathed in tobacco smoke as he glares balefully at a dwarf's skeleton on his desk, and when gloating over his victim in the morgue, he comes across as the most utterly despicable bad man since Bela Lugosi's sorcerer in *White Zombie*. Paul Guifoyle, Dwight Frye, and John Bohn provide excellent support, with Frye displaying the nervous mannerisms which so perfectly served the moods of *Dracula, Frankenstein,* and *The Bride of Frankenstein* (1935); and with Bohn appearing both frightened and frightening in his "resurrection" sequences.

The music includes only an orchestral version of Anton Rubenstein's *Kamenoi Oistrow,* a *Dramatic Lamento* by an unknown composer, and Josef Pasternak's "Sometime, Somehow, Somewhere." The lights and shadows are in the right places to suggest the spirit, if not the letter, of Poe in this underrated little drama.

THE FIGHTING MARINES (1935)

(Mascot Pictures Corporation)

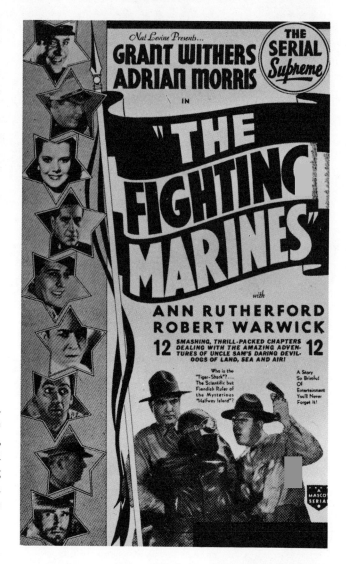

Produced by Nat Levine; *directed by* B. Reeves Eason *and* Joseph Kane; *supervised by* Barney Sarecky; *story by* Wallace MacDonald, Maurice Geraghty, *and* Ray Trampe; *screenplay by* Barney Sarecky *and* Sherman Lowe; *supervising editor,* Joseph H. Lewis; *film editor,* Richard Fantl; *sound technician,* Roy Granville; *photographed by* William Nobles *and* Jack Marta; *musical director,* Arthur Kay; *sound engineer,* Terry Kellum; *Settings by* Mack D'Agostino, Jack Coyle, *and* Ralph M. DeLacy; *photographic effects,* Ellis ("Bud") Thackery; *special properties,* Howard Lydecker, Theodore Lydecker, *and* Billy Gilbert; *costumes,* Iris Burns; *produced at* Studio City.

PLAYERS: *Lawrence,* Grant Withers; *McGowan,* Adrian Morris; *Frances,* Ann Rutherford; *Colonel Bennett,* Robert Warwick; *Schiller,* George J. Lewis; *Kota,* Jason Robards; *Captain Grayson,* Pat O'Malley; *Metcalf,* Warner Richmond; *Steinbeck,* Frank Reicher; *Douglas,* Robert Frazer; *Buchanan,* Frank Glendon; *Ivan,* Richard Alexander; *Pedro,* Donald Reed; *Miller,* Tom London; *Gibson,* Stanley Blystone; *Red,* Milburn Stone; *Captain Holmes,* Lieutenant Franklin Adreon; *Captain Henderson,* Billy Arnold; *Captain Drake,* Lee Shumway; *Miss Martin,* Grace Durkin.

172

1)Human Targets; 2)Isle of Missing Men; 3)The Savage Horde; 4)The Mark of the Tiger Shark; 5)The Gauntlet of Grief; 6)Robber's Roost; 7)Jungle Terrors; 8)Siege of Halfway Island; 9)Death from the Sky; 10)Wheels of Destruction; 11)Behind the Mask; 12)Two Against the Horde.

Marine Sergeant Schiller is held on a tropical island by crooks bent upon learning the secret of his invention, a gyro-compass. Corporal Larry Lawrence and Sergeant Mac McGowan, Schiller's buddies, lead a raiding party and free him. From San Diego, Schiller flies to Halfway Island in mid-Pacific to test the compass, but the aircraft is brought down by a death ray manipulated by minions of a mysterious crime overlord known as the Tiger Shark. Steinbeck, an unscrupulous scientist, and a ruffian named Metcalf are in charge of the gang, which has headquarters in a "dead spot" near where the Marines are building an airstrip. Schiller's sister, Frances, learns the compass is in the hands of Douglas, an industrialist, who she suspects may be the Tiger Shark. Escaping death from the gang, Larry and Mac trail a henchman to a warehouse and learn the hoodlums are using a death ray on Halfway Island to wreck ships for looting. Overpowering a gangster who is about to fly to Halfway, they steal his plane and head for the island to look for Schiller. Saved from the death ray by Schiller's intervention, the leathernecks land and begin searching.

They have a close escape from a dump-cart full of dynamite, and the crooks, thinking them dead, turn Schiller over to a savage tribe. Larry and Mac save the unconcious Schiller from a fire and escape to San Diego in the airplane, foiling the death ray by hiding in the clouds.

In San Diego hospital, a Shark agent disguised as an intern tricks Larry and Mac into leaving Schiller's room. The underling strangles Schiller, leaving on his neck the stamp of the Tiger Shark, and escapes, his auto hotly pursued by Larry and Mac on a motorcycle. Larry leaps to the car's running board but is thrown to the roadway. Mac wrecks the 'cycle to avoid running over Larry, but both men emerge relatively unhurt. Frances telephones Colonel Bennett to say she has found papers among her brother's effects that may yield valuable clues. Larry and Mac, sent to fetch the papers, are intercepted by two Shark henchmen. Eluding the heavies in a wild chase, the Marines arrive only to see other men escaping with the papers. Larry catches hold of a fire escape. As the Marines head back to base with their prisoner, they are attacked and overcome by other gang members. Hanging onto the back of the car as the crooks flee, Larry is taken to an old warehouse where, he learns, the Tiger Shark soon will arrive. Colonel Bennett, meantime, has come to suspect Buchanan, a transportation executive, of being the arch villian. Mac is sent to tail Buchanan but loses him near the warehouse. The Shark, disguised in mask and goggles, arrives in an autogyro and tries to shoot both Marines. A gun battle ensues, and all the gang members escape.

Larry, Mac, and four other Marines elude the death ray and land safely on Halfway Island. The outlaws send the savages after the Marines, who escape and return to the Marine encampment. The island gang receives the Shark's orders to dispose of Larry and Mac. In an ambush, the gangsters capture Mac and leave Larry for dead. Mac is bound in a cave. Larry arrives, and a fight takes place. The Marines are trapped in a chamber when the Tiger Shark arrives and orders an attack on the Marine camp. Larry and Mac escape and alert the camp. The Tiger Shark flies over and bombs the ammunition pit, then heads back to the mainland in the mistaken belief he has killed all the Marines. The Marines lure the gang into a trap, capturing them after a skirmish. Larry and Mac fly after the Shark. At the Marine Base in San Diego,they find Colonel Bennett accusing Buchanan of being the Tiger Shark. The gang members abduct Buchanan. Larry and Mac give chase, but a smokescreen from the gangster car causes them to crash over a cliff. They are thrown free.

The Marines recover Buchanan who, with Douglas, is interrogated in Bennett's office. Buchanan says he saw the Tiger Shark's face, but a mysterious bullet kills him before he can reveal the villian's name. Douglas leaps out a window and is caught by Larry. Douglas says he saw the Tiger Shark drop a gun which, recovered, proves to be the Colonel's weapon. Later, Larry and Mac track the Shark to the old warehouse where Steinbeck has his laboratory. The Marines are trapped in a corridor where the doors suddenly close and the walls push in on them. They stop the walls with a crowbar, smash down a door, and escape.

Larry and Mac corner the Tiger Shark in his cave on Halfway Island. After a fight the gang boss is unmasked: He is Kota, Colonel Bennett's mess boy. Kota attempts to escape but is killed in the explosion of a can of nitroglycerine.

Notes

This last serial to bear the Mascot brand was made after the Republic amalgamation and was released through Republic exchanges. The Nat Levine serials that followed were released under Republic's aegis. In production terms *The Fighting Marines* is vastly better than the Mascots of a year or so earlier, sparkling with the slickness and swift development that became characteristic of the sixty-six official Republic chapter plays to come. A less tense budget, a longer shooting schedule, and greatly improved special effects do wonders when applied with Levine's knowledge of this specialised kind of production.

The show opens and closes to the stirring strains of *Semper Fidelis* with worthy excitement in between. There is sufficient menace for a dozen melodramas: South Sea savages who sacrifice intruders to a stone idol; death rays, a mad scientist; and a spectacular assortment of heavies led by a mysterious masked pilot; and yet the plot avoids the over-complexities that packed many Mascots. Another science-fictional treat is that the Tiger Shark commutes in a futuristic — for the time — flying wing, later used in Republic's *Dick Tracy* (1937) and *Fighting Devil Dogs* (1938). It's a safe bet that very few viewers guessed the identity of the Shark, whose voice is definitely not that of the guilty native boy, Jason Robards! Suspicion is heaped upon Robert Frazer and Frank Glendon, who are shown to make phone calls just before the Tiger Shark telephones instructions, and who are otherwise circumstantially incriminated. Robert Warwick's Marine officer also becomes a target of suspicion.

Heroes Grant Withers and Adrian Morris (Chester Morris' brother) are husky and athletic enough to make their derring-do believable. The ingenue is a Levine "discovery," Ann Rutherford, a charming actress who graduated to fame at M-G-M, RKO, and Twentieth Century-Fox. Frank Reicher is a high-class mad scientist, and the unusually large collection of henchmen includes many of the best in the business. A minor heavy is Milburn Stone, the beloved "Doc" Adams of television's long-running *Gunsmoke*.

William Nobles and Jack Marta photographed *Marines* in the grand style for which their many Republic serials are famous.

SCREAM IN THE NIGHT (1935)
a.k.a. MURDER IN MOROCCO
[Announced as SCREAM IN THE DARK]

(Ray Kirkwood Productions, Incorporated)

Produced by Ray Kirkwood; *directed by* Fred Newmeyer; *photographed by* Bert Longenecker; *story by* Norman Springer; *production manager*, Dick L'Estrange; *technical director*, Zarah Tazil; *length*, six reels; *scheduled for release in* December of 1935 *by* Commodore Pictures; *released as a new product in* 1943 *by* Astor Pictures Corporation.

PLAYERS: *Jack Wilson* and *Butch Curtain*, Lon Chaney, Jr.; *Edith Bentley*, Sheila Terry; *Inspector Green*, Richard Cramer; *Mora*, Zarah Tazil; *Wu Ting*, Philson Ahn; *Johnny Fly*, Manuel Lopez; *Bentley*, John Ince; *Arab*, Merrill McCormick.

Synopsis

Inspector Green and detectives Jack Wilson and Wu Ting meet in a Singapore café to plot the downfall of Johnny Fly, an international jewel thief and sadistic killer. Jack renews a long friendship with Edith Bentley, just arrived in Singapore with her wealthy uncle. Bentley has bought a ruby of fabulous worth and is concerned that Johnny Fly might try to steal it. Later, Bentley is attacked in his room by the ruthless thief, who leaves him for dead with a strangling noose around his neck. Bentley survives, however, and Jack takes out after the elusive criminal.

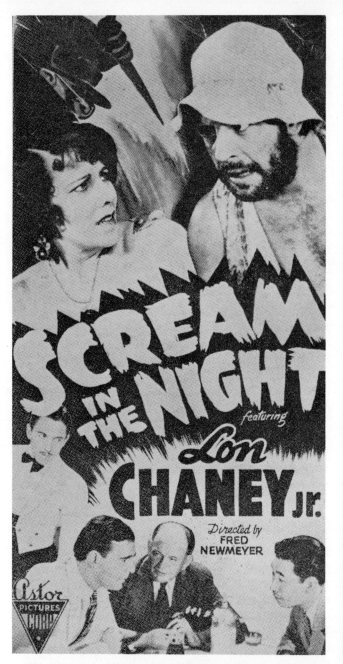

Lon Chaney, Jr., Zarah Tazil, Manuel Lopez.

174

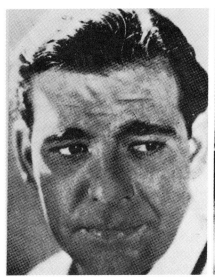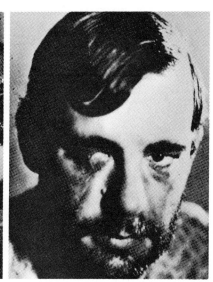

Lon Chaney, Jr., in character studies that display his haunted features to fine effect.

Wu Ting, masquerading as a coolie, meets Butch Curtain, owner of the Half Moon Cafe and an employee of Fly. Fly informs Curtain that Wu Ting is a government agent, and Curtain murders the Chinese detective with a thrown knife. Fly's treacherous mistress, Mora, is carrying on an affair with the grotesque Curtain in the hope of getting some stolen gems from Fly. Meantime, Fly has become interested in the lovely Edith Bentley. Fly's agents kidnap Edith, and he makes her a prisoner in the back rooms of the Half Moon, intending to force her uncle to surrender the ruby.

Following a clue left by Wu Ting, Jack and Green capture Curtain. Through skillful makeup, Jack is able to impersonate Curtain and thereby meet Johnny Fly and his cohorts. When she kisses him, Mora penetrates Jack's disguise. A fight ensues in which Jack overwhelms Fly. Inspector Green arrives in time to kill a knife-throwing Chinese henchman and save Jack's life. Edith is rescued, a large cache of stolen jewels is recovered, and a wealthy merchant Fly had marked for death is spared.

Notes

Ray Kirkwood headed another of the companies that dealt in "quickie" Westerns but made occasional "indoor" pictures — in this instance, one with a sinister Oriental setting. The modest production hardly does justice to its provocative title, but it does have worthwhile elements.

Lon Chaney, Jr., then playing small parts at the major studios under his real name, Creighton Chaney, received here his first opportunity to go into the kind of heavy makeup that later became his stock-in-trade. In a dual role he plays both handsome hero and deformed villain, with the appearance of the latter being strikingly similar to that of the elder Lon Chaney in *The Road to Mandalay* (1926). Publicity for *Scream,* in fact, sought to imbue Chaney Jr. with his father's reputation, billing him as "the man with a 1,000 faces" *(sic).*

The supporting cast is adequate, with Richard Cramer, surprisingly, playing a sympathetic cop instead of his usual blackguard and Sheila Terry quite competent in the feminine lead.

Director Fred Newmeyer had been a top silent director, whose work included Harold Lloyd's classic *Grandma's Boy* (1922), *Safety Last* (1923), *Why Worry?* (1923), and *The Freshman* (1925). His fortunes nose-dived with the talkies' advent, and for two decades he labored on Poverty Row.

The settings are colorful and well peopled with extras. Bert Longenecker, a cameraman usually assigned to outdoor melodramas, provided some well-conceived low-key photography. Such qualities as these — not to mention the opportunity to "discover" Chaney well before his emergence as a major horror actor — were enjoyed by only a random few contemporary moviegoers. *Scream in the Night* is a drastic example of Poverty Row's sporadic marketing trends, for it was never copyrighted, its makers seem never to have released it in the accepted sense of the word, and the only generally reliable indicator of its public distribution is that an unrelated company, Astor, had it in release during the early 'forties.

OUANGA (1935)
a.k.a. CRIME OF VOODOO

(George Terwilliger)

Produced, written, and directed by George Terwilliger; *assistant director,* Phil Brandon; *photographed by* Carl Berger; *running time,* 63 minutes; *foreign release by* Paramount Pictures, 1935; *United States release by* J. H. Hoffberg, July 1, 1936.

PLAYERS: Fredi Washington, Sheldon Leonard, Philip Brandon, Marie Paxton, *and* Winifred Harris.

Synopsis

The character portrayed by Fredi Washington, seemingly

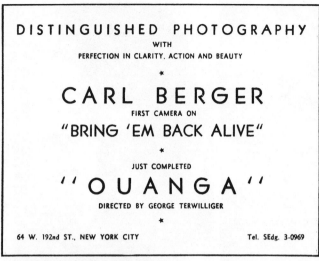
Tradebook advertisement.

Fredi Washington, trapped by Sheldon Leonard at the Voodoo Tree.

a civilized member of Haitian society, is in fact a Voodoo priestess, officiating over native rituals that sometimes include human sacrifice. Through her mastery of hypnosis, she is able to gain whatever ends she wishes, excepting the love of a young, white plantation owner (Sheldon Leonard). The sorceress plans to destroy the planter's fiancée (Marie Paxton) through Voodoo. She formulates a curse — an *ouanga* — against the girl and frightens the plantation servants into helping her in the plot. The victim is drugged and taken to the hills, where the sacrificial dance begins. The planter learns of the plot and, with a loyal servant, interrupts the ceremony. The servant destroys the *ouanga*, and the sorceress, pursued by her intended lover, flees to her death in the jungle.

Notes

George Terwilliger, pioneer writer-director who first gained prominence as a scenarist for D. W. Griffith, set out for the West Indies aboard the S. S. *Haiti* in 1933, intent upon filming his screenplay, *Drums of the Night,* in an appropriate Haitian setting. With him was Carl Berger (who photographed Frank Buck's *Bring 'Em Back Alive* [1933] in Africa), a small technical crew, several truckloads of equipment, and the principal actors. At Port au Prince, despite warnings that he was heading for trouble, Terwilliger drove into the backwoods with a guide to find authentic Voodoo dancers, drummers, and worshippers for his film. Friendly at first, the papaloi and his flock became angry when the subject of recreating their ceremonies for the camera was approached. An *ouanga,* an object symbolic of a curse, was placed in the seat of the director's car, a tire was punctured, and a royal palm tree was felled in the auto's path. Returning to the city, Terwilliger spent several days recruiting dancers, drummers, and extras there. After a week of warnings, "accidents," and other unnerving occurrences, he arranged to transport everybody, including his native supporting cast, on the *Columbia* to Jamaica. On the morning of departure, he found that the dancers had disappeared and the drummers and extras were in jail. Putting together another company as Kingston, Terwilliger began shooting in the nearby jungles and hills. The tropic heat proved too much for the cast and crew, so it became necessary to shoot everything at night under the floodlights. A tropical rainstorm drowned two of the natives and a cyclone destroyed the sets, one of the American crew members became ill and died, and insects made life miserable for the entire company. After two months, the company returned to America with the film.

Such hard-earned footage deserved better fate. Paramount bought the picture but only released it outside the United States in 1935, under the title *Ouanga.* The following year it was taken over for states'-rights distribution by J. H. Hoffberg, but bookings were spotty indeed. It is almost impossible to find anybody who saw the picture, although the stills are fascinating enough to suggest a UFA fantasy of the 'twenties. The story also bears a resemblance to Clements Ripley's novel, *Black Moon,* which Columbia filmed in 1934.

The leading role of the Voodoo priestess was performed by Fredi Washington, a beautiful black actress who gained critical acclaim as a tragic girl attempting to "pass for white" in Universal's *Imitation of Life* (1933) and who is prominent in *The Emperor Jones.* The Sheldon Leonard who portrays the hero is not the well-known gangster player and later television producer of that name.

Terwilliger revamped the script, which Arthur Leonard filmed in Jamaica in 1939 as *Pocomania,* later shown as *The Devil's Daughter,* with an all-black cast headed by Nina Mae McKinney and Hamtree Harrington.

1936-1937

JAWS OF THE JUNGLE (1936)
a.k.a. JUNGLE VIRGIN

(Jay Dee Kay Productions)

Produced by J. D. Kendis; *story narrative by* Eddy Graneman; *storyteller,* Clif Howell; *edited by* Holbrook N. Todd; *recording engineer,* Cliff Ruberg; *length,* six reels; *released* following previews during 1936.

PLAYERS: *The Boy,* Teeto; *The Girl,* Minta; *The Rejected Suitor,* Gukar; *The Ape,* Walla; *The Honey Bear,* Agena.

Synopsis

In a small village in Ceylon, Teeto and Minta invoke the blessing of the sacred peacock for their betrothal. Walla, Teeto's pet orangutan, cries a warning as a horde of giant vampire bats clouds the sky. The monsters swarm down, gorging themselves on man and beast. Teeto leads the villagers into the dark jungle, where they face new dangers: leopards kills a nursing mother, and a giant python crushes a tribal patriarch.

Gukar, who desires Minta, causes dissent and demands to be declared leader. A council is held, and Teeto proposes a sacrifice. An old man and a boy are placed in a cart and pushed over a cliff in a ritual which supposedly will gain the tribe the welcome of the valley gods. Gukar, repulsed by Minta, narrowly escapes death twice in his efforts to destroy Teeto. At last he attacks Minta, whose cries bring Teeto. After a savage fight, Gukar tries to escape and is killed by a tiger. The tribe treks onward and finds a hidden valley where they will be safe from the vampires.

Notes

Authentic footage from Ceylon, probably the work of foreign cameramen, forms the basis of J. D. Kendis's tale of

177

The tattooed but lovely heroine.

jungle horror. Scenes of hordes of giant bats are cleverly edited to make it seem some unknown species of vampire is attacking. It's not exactly true to nature, but it's much more convincing than the hijinks of 1930's *Ingagi*. The expedition photography is quite good, and the story sustains interest throughout — although *Jaws of the Jungle* is not, as its advertisements proclaim, "the greatest jungle picture ever produced." Like most talkies of this sort, the film is overburdened with narration.

THE DARK HOUR (1936)

(Chesterfield Motion Pictures Corporation)

Produced by George R. Batcheller; *directed by* Charles Lamont; *production executive,* Lon Young; *adapted by* Ewart Adamson *from* "The Last Trap" *by* Sinclair Gluck; *photographed by* M. A. Anderson, ASC; *sound recording,* Richard Tyler; *art director,* Edward C. Jewell; *film editor,* Roland D. Reed; *assistant director,* Mellville Shyer; RCA Victor *sound; running time,* 64 minutes; *released* January 15, 1936.

PLAYERS: *Jim Landis,* Ray Walker; *Elsa Carson,* Irene Ware; *Paul Bernard,* Berton Churchill; *Mrs. Tallman,* Hedda Hopper; *Charles Carson,* Hobart Bosworth; *Foot,* E. E. Clive; *Henry Carson,* William V. Mong; *Blake,* Harold Goodwin; *Mrs. Dubbin,* Aggie Herring; *Helen Smith,* Katherine Sheldon; *Mrs. Murphy,* Rose Allen; *Choong,* Miki Morita; *Dr. Munro,* John St. Polis; *Watson,* Fred Kelsey; *Dr. Bruce,* Lloyd Whitlock; *Policeman,* Harry Strang.

Synopsis

Detective Jim Landis and a retired colleague, Paul Bernard, are consulted by Elsa Carson, who fears danger will befall her eccentric uncles, Henry and Charles. Henry

orders Jim away from the Carson mansion. Later that night, Henry is found starved to death in his study. The detectives find Elsa evasive. Foot, the butler who found the body, gives a confused account. Other suspects are Blake, a boarder; Choong, an Oriental butler; Dr. Munro, the family physician; Mrs. Tallman, the victim's sister-in-law; and Mesdames Dubbin, Smith, and Murphy. Jim, smitten by Elsa, is upset at the apparent guilt of her aunt. Bernard suspects Foot.

The discovery of a dress of Mrs. Tallman's size hidden among Elsa's clothing causes Bernard to change his mind. Jim is less certain and concentrates on Blake, an experimental chemist. Then Foot is slain in the same manner and place as Henry. It is learned that incendiary fires have broken out in Carson-owned properties in various parts of town. Arthur Bell, victim of one of the fires, seems a likely suspect for the killings.

Bernard sets a trap and nabs Charles, who is disguised as a woman. The authorities determine that Charles killed his brother to gain control of his money, set the fires to collect on insurance, and killed Foot because he knew too much. Elsa now admits she saw what she thought was Mrs. Tallman enter the study on the night of the first murder, but has kept silent to shield her aunt. Jim is not convinced of Charles' guilt. He proves that Henry was killed by carbon monoxide gas, made in Blake's laboratory, before he was stabbed. Guilt now points to Bernard, but the old detective clears himself by proving who the killer is.

Notes

Here is Chesterfield's stock-in-trade: a murder yarn from

Ray Walker, Irene Ware, Hedda Hopper.

a published novel, with suspicious characters gathered in a big, dark house. Director Charles Lamont fails to extract the full measure of suspense, but weird moments accrue as a killer in drag stalks the mansion. Shadowy photography and good rental sets are tangible assets.

Irene Ware, a former Miss America who had just appeared with Karloff and Lugosi in *The Raven* (1935), is welll showcased as a frightened inmate. Ray Walker, usually seen as a fast-talking reporter, slows down to a walk as a detective and seems rather out of his element. Berton Churchill, as the wise old sleuth, is quite adequate in a respite from his usual pompous con-man portrayals. Sturdy old Hobart Bosworth and the Scrooge-like William V. Mong provide good support as the wealthy, eccentric brothers. Fred Kelsey brings in some comedy relief in his oft-repeated role of a befuddled detective.

A FACE IN THE FOG (1936)

(Victory Pictures Corporation)

Produced by Sam Katzman; *directed by* Bob Hill; *from* "The Great Mono Miracle" *by* Peter B. Kyne; *screenplay by* Al Martin; *photographed by* Bill Hyer; *film editor,* Earl Turner; *sound recording,* Josh Westmoreland; *settings by* Fred Preble; *running time,* 66 minutes; *released* February 1, 1936.

PLAYERS: *Jean Monroe,* June Collyer; *Frank Gordon,* Lloyd Hughes; *Peter Fortune,* Lawrence Gray; *Elmer,* Al St John; *Reardon,* Jack Mulhall; *Wilson,* Jack Cowell; *Davis,* John Elliott; *Harrison,* Sam Flint; *Cromwell,* Forrest Taylor; *Detective,* Edward Cassidy; *Policeman,* Robert Williams.

Synopsis

Drama editor Jean Monroe of the *Daily Journal* pulls a typographical indiscretion: She opines in print that she knows the identity of a mad hunchback known as the Fiend, whose murderous attacks have been directed at the cast of *Satan's Bride,* now playing at the Alden Theatre. Reporter Frank Gordon saves Jean from the Fiend's revenge attempt, and the two set out to solve the sequence of slayings. The victims have been poisoned by an untraceable substance. A bumbling photographer, Elmer, joins Frank and Jean to interview Ted Wallington, stage star, who has summoned them to the theatre. The invitation, however, proves to have been a ruse, and while Jean and Wallington visit, there is a blackout. Wallington becomes the Fiend's latest victim. Playwright Peter Fortune, who has assisted the law with previous mysteries, offers his help but demands autonomy.

Frank and Jean take rooms at the Globe Hotel, residence of Reardon, an actor. Frank gets a 'phone message—a trick, in fact, to lure him from the hotel. Reardon pretends to put in a call to the police, depressing the hook on Frank's telephone while dialing. Meantime, a call from Elmer comes through on Frank's 'phone. Reardon escapes following a scuffle with Frank. The hunchback steals into Frank's suite, but Frank returns as the Fiend tries the door to Jean's rooms. The Fiend takes a shot at Frank but misses.

Fortune, investigating a hideway, takes snapshots of Reardon getting into the guise of the Fiend. Following Reardon's arrest, a re-enactment of the Wallington slaying is staged, during which the actor is murdered.

Frank finds a cigarette case, Fortune's property, at the scene of the last Fiend attack. This clue leads to the revelation that Fortune's brother had died in flames which ruined a theatre owned by show producers Cooke and Baker. Fortune, searching for his cigarette case, inquiries of Frank, who keeps mum about the discovery. Now Fortune hints that he is going to visit Sanchi, a hunchback suspect: this ruse leads Frank into a trap, and he learns too late that Fortune is the Fiend. Elmer, however, has snooped enough to lead the police to the murderer's hideout. Frank, meantime, watches Fortune load his devilish murder gun with grozen bullets from the cigarette case. As Fortune takes aim at Frank, Elmer shows up with the police, and Fortune is gunned down.

Notes

One of several Victory features based upon short stories by a popular novelist, Peter B. Kyne, *A Face in the Fog* has an unusual plotline and a pleasing cast in its favor. On the debit side is the expected cheapness of production (Sam Katzman's specialty) and sound reproduction approximating the 1928 standard. Katzman, who in 1914 entered the film industry as a prop boy (he was thirteen), worked his way up to production manager and assistant producer during the 'twenties. In 1931 he produced some pictures for Screencraft (a short-lived company sponsored by Universal), and he assisted A. W. Hackel in production of

Singer-murderer Lawrence Gray in a production number. Sam Katzman was no Flo Ziegfeld.

a series of Bob Steele Westerns in the mid-thirties. In 1936 he commenced production as Victory Pictures, making over a two-year period a string of feature melodramas and two serials. Katzman had a knack for stretching a minute budget to cover a marketable product. The production staff of the entire Victory output remained relatively unchanged, being the same crew that made most of the Puritan Pictures product. Casting also was consistent, with a stock company atmosphere prevailing. Lloyd Hughes, Lawrence Gray, Jack Mulhall, John Elliott, Herman Brix, Sam Flint, Forrest Taylor, Jack Cowell, and several others were employed in most of the Victory releases. After shutting down the Victory company in 1937, Katzman continued making his cheap but profitable independent pictures for Monogram, then Columbia, and, eventually, even M-G-M.

A Face in the Fog has an interesting show-biz setting, somewhat along the lines of Universal's classic mystery of 1928, *The Last Warning,* on which Bob Hill was associate director to the German Paul Leni. Universal's top serial director during the silent era, Hill suffered a seige of ill health during the early 'thirties, and his career faltered. Acting and direction here are a bit old-fashioned for the period, and the lack of budget limits the possibilities of attaining any spectacular qualities. There are plenty of mysterious characters and a surprise ending that makes sense.

DARKEST AFRICA (1936)

(Republic Pictures Corporation)

Produced by Nat Levine; *directed by* B. Reeves Eason *and* Joseph Kane; *supervised by* Barney Sarecky; *original story by* John Rathmell *and* Tracy Knight; *screenplay by* John Rathmell, Barney Sarecky, *and* Ted Parsons; *photograph by* William Nobles *and* Edgar Lyons; *supervising editor,* Joseph H. Lewis; *film editor,* Richard Fantl; *sound engineer,* Terry Kellum; *sound effects by* Roy Granville; *special effects by* Jack Coyle, Ellis Thackery, Howard Lydecker, *and* Theodore Lydecker; *RCA sound; a serial in* 15 chapters, 31 reels; *feature version,* seven reels; *released* February 15, 1936; *serial reissued* 1948 *as* KING OF JUNGLELAND; *different feature version, running time,* 100 minutes, *released* 1966 *as* BAT MEN OF AFRICA.

PLAYERS: *Clyde,* Clyde Beatty; *Baru,* Manuel King; *Valerie,* Elaine Shepard; *Dagna,* Lucien Prival; *Bonga,* Naba; *Samabe,* Ray Benard; *Durkin,* Wheeler Oakmen; *Gorn,* Edward McWade; *Craddock,* Edmund Cobb; *Hambone,* Ray Turner; *Negus,* Donald Reed; *Driscoll,* Harrison Greene; *Tomlin,* Henry Sylvester; *Nagga,* Joseph Boyd; *Tiger Chief,* Prince Modupe; *Slave,* Joseph Delacruz; *Bat Man,* Edwin Parker.

Chapter Titles

1) Baru, Son of the Jungle; 2) The Tiger-Men's God; 3) Bat

The airborne batman is a seven-foot-tall dummy designed by Howard Lydecker.

served by an army of flying Bat Men. Clyde, Baru, and the boy's gorilla, Bonga, lead a safari toward Joba in the Valley of Lost Souls. They are trailed by Durkin and Craddock, unscrupulous traders who seek the diamond mines of Joba. Clyde's bearers flee at sight of the Bat Man leader, Samabi, overhead. Knowing Samabi will report to Dagna, Baru leads Clyde via a secret route where they must cross a gorge hand-over-hand by rope. They survive an earthquake. Beyond, they are attacked by the Tiger Men, who worship the only tigers in Africa. Beatty hides Baru but is thrown into a pit with a tiger. He masters the tiger, and Bonga routs the natives.

Samabi takes Durkin and Craddock to Dagna. Faced with the sentence of death, the traders tell Dagna of Clyde and Baru's approach. Bat Men are sent to attack the outlanders as they enter the secret passage of the ruined temple. Menaced by Bat Men and by trained hunting lions, Clyde and Baru escape through the palace and the diamond mines into the jungle, taking Valerie. Hordes of Bat Men give chase, and Clyde shoots down several of them. Bonga buards Valerie but is seriously wounded by a Bat Man's spear, and Valerie is recaptured. Clyde and Baru are imprisoned.

Hambone, Clyde's faithful servant, comes to Joba in search of his boss. Valerie steals the keys to the dungeon and leads Clyde and Baru through a passage, but they encounter the hunter lions. Clyde and Bary hold off the lions and flee with Valerie to the sanctuary of Gorn, the Wizier and Keeper of the Law. Dagna fears to enter, lest the populace turn against him. Meantime, Durkin and Craddock have brought guns and ammunition to Dagna in exchange for diamonds. After further encounters with the traders and with Bat Men, Clyde and Baru fall captive again but are rescued by Hambone. Durkin and Craddock align themselves with Negus, a slave leader in fomenting revolt. Valerie and Clyde are caught by the slaves but escape when

Men of Joba; 4) Hunter Lions of Joba; 5) Bonga's Courage; 6) Prisoners of the High Priest; 7) Swing for Life; 8) Jaws of the Tiger; 9) When Birdmen Strike; 10) Trial by Thunder Rods; 11) Jars of Death; 12) Revolt of Slaves; 13) Gaunlet of Destruction; 14) The Divine Sacrifice; 15) Prophecy of Gorn.

Synopsis

Baru, a jungle-raised white boy, seeks out the famed animal trainer, Clyde Beatty, to rescue his sister, Valerie. The girl is a captive in the hidden city of Joba, built by Solomon in ancient times, where the high priest, Dagna, has established her as Goddess of the Golden Bat. Dagna is

In the Palace of Solomon with villians Eddie Cobb, Wheeler Oakman; batmen Eddie Parker, Ray Bernard (Corrigan); and Robert McWade, Clyde Beatty, Manuel King, Elaine Shepard, Lucien Prival.

In Episode Fifteen, Clyde Beatty, Manuel King and Elaine Shepard see Gorn's prophecy fulfilled.

the hunter lions are released into the mines. Clyde overcomes Durkin and Craddock but is seized by Bat Men and taken before Dagna. Clyde and Baru are sentenced to death, but Valerie elects to sacrifice herself in a leap from Pinnacle Rock; as Gorn interprets the law, she may have any last request before making such a sacrifice. She demands that Clyde and Baru be freed. As Dagna watches the white-robed figure leap from the rock, he is forced to release the prisoners. Clyde and Baru hurry to the base of the rock and find that it was Gorn who leaped, wearing Valerie's robes. As he dies, Gorn places a curse on Joba. A gigantic volcanic eruption follows, destroying the city and with it Dagna, Durkin and Craddock. Clyde and his friends return home, where Clyde and Valerie announce wedding plans.

Notes

This first of sixty-six serials to bear the Republic brand was an enormous success and the harbinger of great things to come during the next two decades. Originally planned as a Mascot sequel to *The Lost Jungle*, it was produced under Nat Levine's supervision, for the negative cost of $119,343 (the fee for the negative film)—quite a sum compared to the Mascot budgets. Parts of the picture were filmed during two weeks' location work at W. A. King's Jungleland near Brownsville, Texas, in October-November of 1935. Another month was spent shooting action at the studio and among the rocks at Chatsworth. The Texas location enabled utilization of a menagerie of jungle beasts gathered by King (known as the Snake King because of his dealership specialty), several experienced animal trainers and handlers, good tropical scenery (augmented with artificial boulders hauled from Hollywood), and especially King's twelve-year-old son, Manuel—"the world's youngest wild animal trainer." The chubby youngster could handle twenty lions at a time as though they were kittens and thus

proved an ideal companion in companion in adventure for Beatty.

Even more fantastic in theme than the trend-setting *The Phantom Empire,* the story provides opportunity for a great variety of photographic effects, presented with an expertise well beyond Mastoc's capabilities. The soaring Bat Men are convincing even in close-up, being in many scenes seven-foot figures of balsa wood gliding along invisible wires. Large flocks of the flying men, made of rubber to various scales, sail realistically over the miniature city of Joba. A spectacular upheaval in the final chapter is very well done, except for some shots of bubbling lava that would have been better served by overcranking of the camera. There is a fine assortment of explosions, landslides, and fires.

The directional pace set by "Breezy" Eason and Joseph Kane (a former film editor who became one of Republic's most dependable action directors) seldom lags. The acting of the principals is barely adequate, although Beatty and King's feats compensate for histrionic shortcomings. Lucien Prival, hampered during filming by a bad cold, walks through a role that could have been his best. Both a Bat Man leader and the gorilla "hero" are portrayed by Ray Benard, who as Ray Corrigan was destined to star in Republic's second serial, *The Undersea Kingdom.* Corrigan's ape is calculated to alternate between amusing and frightening moves, and both come off very well. Ray Turner's Hambone adds good comedy, Edward McWade is an impressive law-giver, and the villainy of Wheeler Oakman and Ed Cobb is well conceived. The animal scenes (with stock footage from *The Lost Jungle* interpolated) are excitingly staged and photographed.

One great step forward from previous serials is the use of elaborate musical scoring, which became a hallmark of Republic's product. This quality set an industrial standard; in fact, one of the greatest improvements in serial production that may be credited to Republic is the utilization in heroic proportions of exciting, mood-building music. Republic's first musical director was Harry Grey, later a producer, who received sole music credit on the films. The augmentation of original scoring with library music resulted in sound tracks superior to most of those being made at the major studios. Most of the original music in *Darkest Africa* was the work of Arthur Kay, a German-trained composer and conductor who formerly headed the music department at Fox Film Company. Works by Jean Beghon, Heinz Roemheld, Milan Roder, and Charles Dunworth and Jean de la Roche also are heard in action sequences. The wild chant of the Tiger Men was composed by director "Breezy" Eason.

THE ROGUES TAVERN (1936)

(Mercury Pictures)

Directed by Bob Hill; *screenplay by* Al Martin; *production manager,* Ed W. Rote; *photographed by* Bill

Hyer; *film editor,* Dan Milner; *recording,* Josh Westmoreland; *settings by* Fred Preble; *musical director,* Abe Meyer; *running time,* 67 minutes; *released* March 1, 1936, *by* Puritan Pictures Corporation.

PLAYERS: *Jimmy Flavin,* Wallace Ford; *Marjorie,* Barbara Pepper; *Gloria Rohloff,* Joan Woodbury; *Mrs. Jamison,* Clara Kimball Young; *Bill,* Jack Mulhall; *Mr. Jamison,* John Elliott; *Morgan,* Earl Dwire; *Bert,* John W. Cowell; *Hughes,* Vincent Dennis; *Wentworth,* Arthur Loft; *Harrison,* Ivo Henderson; *Mason,* Ed Cassidy; *Dog,* Silver Wolf.

Palatial Pathé interiors lend dignity to Poverty Row. (Frame enlargement from a sequence in which camera makes a rapid pan of the room.)

Synopsis

"The person that killed those two men used a set of false dog teeth!" detective Jimmy Flavin confides to his fiancée Marjorie, as they investigate weird happenings at the isolated Red Rock Tavern, their marriage site. Instead of the Justice of the Peace they expected to meet, they have found themselves ensnared in complications involving members of a jewel-smuggling gang—Bill, Mason, Harrison, Hughes, and the exotic Gloria—who await the arrival of their boss, Wentworth. It is "the kind o'night that gives me the willies," Bert, the stupid handyman, tells Mrs. Jamison, the innkeeper. Mrs. Jamison's husband, confined to a wheelchair, fidgets with a pair of hand-exercisers.

Blame for the murders of Harrison and Hughes is laid at first on the Jamisons' part-wolf police dog; the victims' throats are torn. Wentworth arrives, and the smugglers realize they have been lured to the tavern by forged letters. Jimmy has the dog, a friendly animal, in tow when Mason is murdered. Bert has been sent to bring the police and the Coroner, for the killer has disconnected the phones. Bars close over the windows, and the desperate gangsters seek Jimmy's protection. While Jimmy interviews the Jamisons and the guests, Marjorie—who has seen the cripple leave his wheelchair—prowls through a bureau in the Jamisons' room and finds a hand-operated device shaped like a dog's head and equipped with fangs. Confronted with this discovery, Mr. Jamison confesses that is the killer, although he cannot articulate a motive, and is narrowly restrained from using the murder weapon on himself.

Morgan, a scientist who owns the tavern and who has a grievance against the smugglers, steals into the basement.

Barbara Pepper, Wallace Ford, Ivo Henderson, Edward Cassidy.

Barbara Pepper risks terminal dogbite. (Frame enlargement.)

183

Clara Kimball Young handles an uncharacteristic role – the mad killer – with relish if not conviction. (Frame enlargement.)

The trapped inmates trace a mysterious warning voice to a phonograph in the basement, where Morgan holds them at gunpoint. He obviously wants to do away with the gang but is surprised to learn of the murders. Jimmy has sneaked upstairs.

Now a secret panel opens onto the basement, revealing the motherly Mrs. Jamison, tranformed into a cackling fiend. "Say your prayers," she warns, announcing her plan to drop poison gas onto the party, in revenge for the Wentworth gang's having caused her sister's suicide through a frame-up. Jimmy pounces upon her from hiding and foils the plot. Bert arrives with the police and a Justice of the Peace, who marries Jimmy and Marjorie.

Notes

The most popular prop at the RKO-Pathé Studio was a fireplace that cost RKO $1,000 in 1932, when it was built for a Constance Bennett picture. After Pathé became a leasing lot, studio manager G. B. Howe often had to referee disputes between independent producers who wanted to use the mantle in their pictures. This elegant prop is an eye-catching part of the handsome set of the Red Rock Tavern, which the crew for *The Rogues Tavern* assembled from the scene dock at Pathé. It was at the time a real coup for a little company like Mercury Pictures to obtain a berth at Pathé because Selznick-International, Sol Lesser, Reliance, and Chesterfield—all well-established companies—had leased space at the lot, and the studio had barred the doors to most of the smaller companies by demanding minimum budgets of $25,000 to $40,000. That *The Rogues Tavern* is a more attractive production than most other Puritan Pictures releases may in part be credited to its settings.

There are other good things. The script contains a number of surprises, not the least being the denoument in which the gentle Clara Kimball Young is revealed (not too convincingly) as a mass murderess. The method used in the

killings is unusual, perhaps unique, in films. While Wallace Ford and Barbara Pepper aren't exactly William Powell and Myrna Loy, they give lively performances patterned after those of the protagonists in M-G-M's highly successful *The Thin Man* (1934). Miss Pepper's portrayal of street-wise innocence—not to mention her physical appearance—is remarkably similar to Sally Struthers' interpretation of the daughter on television's *All in the Family;* many years and many additional pounds later, Miss Pepper proved popular to television audiences as a hefty regular on the comedy serial *Green Acres.*

The luscious Joan Woodbury lends a touch of sinister allure to *Tavern,* clad in an exquisitely seductive dress that somehow eluded the sensitive bluenoses of the Production Code Administration. Among the heavies and red herrings are the competent Jack Mulhall, John Elliott, Earl Dwire (seen briefly in thick spectacles as a most Karloffian vengeful scientist), and Arthur Loft. Unusual in low-budget production is the mobility of the camerawork, in which fluid dolly and lateral tracking shots enhance many scenes.

The dialogue has treats galore for lovers of wisecracking arrogance and lowbrow comedy. As suspicion focuses upon the "wolf-dog," Ford observes the animal must be "very clever...After he kills his victims, he cuts the telephone wires." When Ford discloses he is a detective "travelling incognito," the hotel's dim-witted bellman stutters, "I thought you came in a bus!"

THE HOUSE OF A THOUSAND CANDLES (1936)

(Republic Pictures Corporation)

Produced by Nat Levine; *directed by* Arthur Lubin; *supervised by* Mrs Wallace Reid; *based on the novel by* Meredith Nicholson; *screenplay by* H. W. Hannemann *and* Endre Bohem; *musical director,* Arthur Kay; *photographed by* Jack Marta *and* Ernest Miller; *art director,* Ralph Oberg; *film editor,* Ralph Dixon; *special effects,* Ellis Thackery *and* Howard Lydecker; RCA Victor *sound; running time,* 71 minutes; *released* April 6, 1936.

PLAYERS: *Tony Carleton,* Phillips Holmes; *Carol Vincent,* Mae Clarke; *Sebastian,* Irving Pichel; *Raquel,* Rosita Moreno; *Alf,* Fred Walton; *Marta,* Hedwiga Reicher; *Sir Andrew MacIntire,* Lawrence Grant; *Travers,* Fredrik Vogeding; *Barrie,* Michael Fitzmaurice; *Jules,* Rafael Storm; *Dimitrios,* Mischa Auer; *Agent,* Paul Ellis; *Steward,* Keith Daniels; *and* Olaf Hytten, Charles De Ravenne, Lal Chand Mehra, Charles Martin, Max Wagner, *and* Count Stepanelli.

Synopsis

World peace hangs on the secrecy of a message which the British governmint has entrusted to Tony Carleton for delivery to Geneva. On the train from Paris, Raquel, a famous dancer, charms Tony into taking a drugged drink.

Rosita Moreno as a seductive spy.

Awakening to find the message gone, Tony seeks out Raquel at a fabulous hotel and casino, the House of a Thousand Candles. Raquel's boss, Sebastian, not only runs the house but is a master spy. He is unable to find the message, which is written in invisible ink on a ticket envelope. Carol, Tony's sweetheart, spies on Sebastian in hopes of helping Tony.

Sebastian murders Raquel and captures Tony, plotting him lose heavily at the gaming tables and apparently commit suicide. When Carol's life is threatened, Tony agrees to show Sebastian the secret message. Carol tries to burn the envelope, and the flame reveals the writing: "England votes yes. Enforce 4-32 May First." Sebastian orders his henchmen to expedite Tony's "suicide" and to arrange an "accident" for Carol in a mountain crevasse. Sebastian leaves with the message.

Tony is rescued by his valet, Alf, and the casino orchestra leader, Keith Barrie. Carol is released. A search reveals a code book and Sebastian's communications method, through radio commercials. Pursued by Tony and Carol, Sebastian is killed when a runaway truck knocks his white Mercedes over a cliff. Tony gets the message to Geneva in the nick of time.

Notes

The general picture of Nat Levine is that of a maker of crude but exhilarating thrillers in view of his fast-and-cheap Mascot productions. Some of the pictures he made during his brief stay with Republic—where he did not personally have to scratch up every dime he spent—were an entirely different matter. *The House of a Thousand Candles,* for example, is so slick as to pass muster as an M-G-M picture of the period. It won unstinting praise from even the New

York critics, who compared it favorably to Alfred Hitchcock's *The 39 Steps,* the critics' darling of several months earlier. It deserved every kind word; the pace is brisk, the dialogue has snap, there is a first-rate musical score, the sets are elaborately luxurious, and the photography sparkles. Nowhere in evidence is the hurried, harried quality of the Mascot shows. The direction by Arthur Lubin, best known for the 1943 classic *The Phantom of the Opera,* is highly competent.

Phillips Holmes and Mae Clarke, notables from the major studios, do splendid work in the romantic roles, and Fred Walton is amusing as a light-fingered valet. It's the villians, though, who are tops. Irving Pichel, sepulchral-voiced and voluptuous-featured, etches a perfect portrait of suave, polite evil. The forces of wrong have a field day, with the beautiful Spanish dancer Rosita Moreno to do the vamping, and such expert spine-chillers on hand as Mischa Auer, Hedwiga Reicher, Fredrik Vogeding, and Paul Ellis.

This is the only talkie version of Meredith Nicholson's popular old novel, which was adapted for silent films at least twice. It was modernized beyond recognition for the talkies and possibility is the first of the many American films to show the influence of Hitchcock's then-recent English films, *The Man Who Knew Too Much* and *The 39 Steps.* The nebulous "maguffin" (a cryptic message that is never explained in detail but is the reason for what happens), the terror of being in danger in a public place but unable to seek help, and the advent of both menace and assistance from unexpected quarters are all "pure Hitchcock" vintage.

THE AMAZING EXPLOITS OF THE CLUTCHING HAND (1936)

(Weiss Productions, Incorporated)

Presented by George M. Merrick; *directed by* Albert Herman; *supervised by* Louis Weiss; *from a novel by* Arthur B. Reeve; *adaptation by* George M. Merrick *and* Eddy Graneman; *screenplay by* Leon D'Usseau *and* Dallas Fitzgerald; *photographed by* James Diamond, ASC; *assistant director,* Gordon S. Griffith; *sound engineer,,* Cliff Ruberg; *musical director,* Lee Zahler; *electrical effects,* Kenneth Strickfaden; *edited by* Earl Turner; *production manager,* Adrian Weiss; *sound recording by* International Film Corporation, Ltd.; *a* Weiss-Mintz *serial, distributed by* Stage & Screen Productions, Incorporated; *in 15 episodes totalling* 31 reels; *also released in a* featured version *of* seven reels; released April 18, 1936.

PLAYERS: *Craig Kennedy,* Jack Mulhall; *Shirley McMillan,* Ruth Mix; *Verna Gironda,* Marion Shilling; *Gordon Gaunt,* William Farnum; *Number Eight,* Yakima Canutt; *Walter Jameson,* Rex Lease; *Sullivan,* Reed Howes; *Mrs. Gironda,* Mae Busch; *Denton,* Bryant Washburn; *Dr. Gironda,* Robert Frazer; *Louis Bouchard,* Gaston Glass; *Montgomery,* Mahlon Hamilton; *Mitchell,* Robert Walker; *Cromwell,* Joseph W. Girard; *Wickham,* Frank Leigh; *Hobart,* Charles

Locher; Nicky, Franklyn Farnum; *Captain Hansen,* Knute Erickson; *Olaf,* Richard Alexander; *Marty,* Milburn Morante; *Mr. White,* John Elliott; *Warden,* Henry Hall; *Snub,* Snub Pollard; *Guard,* Olin Francis; *Trusty,* Robert Russell; *Bartender,* William Desmond; *Maid,* Artemus Nigolian; *Margaret,* Ethel Grove; *Hamick,* Gordon S. Griffith; *Ali,* Roger Williams; *Jenkins,* George Morrell; *Secretary,* Vera Steadman; *Board of Directors Members,* Art Howard, Eugene Burr, Bert Howard, Gil Patrick, *and* Willard Kent; *Henchmen,* Bob Kortman *and* Roy Cardona; *Sailors,* Bull Montana, Slim Whittaker, Tom London, Art Felix, *and* George Allen; *Policemen,* John Cowell *and* John Ince.

Chapter Titles

1)Who Is the Clutching Hand? 2)Shadow; 3)House of Mystery; 4)The Phantom Car; 5)The Double Trap; 6)Steps of Doom; 7)The Invisible Enemy; 8)A Cry in the Night; 9)Evil Eyes; 10)A Desperate Chance; 11)The Ship of Peril; 12)Hidden Danger; 13)The Mystic Menace; 14)The Silent Spectre; 15)The Lone Hand.

Synopsis

Directors of the International Research Foundation

gather for a demonstration of Dr. Paul Gironda's formula for making synthetic gold. Cries are heard from Gironda's laboratory, and it is found that he has been kidnapped by the Clutching Hand. Walter Jameson, newspaper reporter and fiancé of Gironda's daughter, Verna, calls in the famed scientific detective, Craig Kennedy. The dective is almost killed when the Clutching Hand sets fire to the laboratory. Kennedy escapes through a trap door, but his pursuit of the masked villain is thwarted by the intervention of a truck driver. Kennedy and Jameson later have to bail out of a taxicab which the driver, a Clutching Hand henchman, sends over a precipice.

Mrs. Gironda is menaced by Mitchell, an extortionist who Kennedy suspects may be the Clutching Hand. Another clue takes Kennedy, disguised as a rough seaman, to the Harbor Hotel, where he is attacked by minions of the Hand. With Jameson's help, Kennedy escapes and goes to the aid of Shirley, Gironda's secretary, who is abducted by the Clutching Hand. Kennedy and Jameson are lured into a barn, which explodes. Eluding the trap, the men trace Shirley to the Sacred Temple. Kennedy sends Shirley to a waterfront house suspected of being a hideout of the Clutching Hand, having his partner, Sullivan, guard the place. Gangsters, mistaking Sullivan for Kennedy, capture him. Kennedy, disguised as the Clutching Hand, goes to Help Shirley but is foiled.

Verna receives a call from Shirley to bring certain papers to the temple and place them on the altar. Verna does so and finds there the murdered body of Montgomery, one of the Research Foundation directors. Kennedy finds Shirley in the temple, but he and the girl are trapped by poison gas. Jameson breaks in and saves them. Kennedy suspects the high priest of the temple, Hamid, who is able to prove his innocence.

Kennedy and White, Gironda's lawyer, are attacked by the Clutching Hand and his henchmen, who seize important

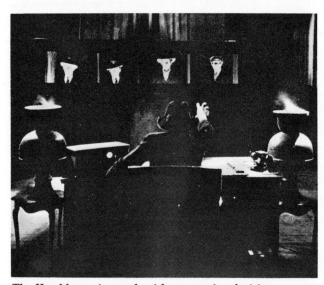

The Hand keeps in touch with agents via television.

186

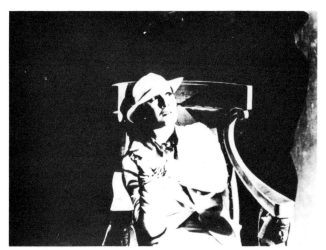

Ruth Mix.

papers, leaving a warning pinned with a valuable jewelled dagger. This throws suspicion upon Bouchard, a board member from whose collection the dagger was taken. Bouchard's valet, Felix, reveals that he stole the dagger and gave it to Mitchell as part of a gambling debt. With Felix as a decoy, Kennedy sets a trap for Mitchell, but Felix is killed and Kennedy is saved only by his bulletproof vest.

Kennedy thwarts a plot by Hamid and his assistant, Ali, to steal Mrs. Gironda's jewels during a ceremony at the temple. Kennedy again traces the Hand, this time to a freighter, the *Nellie D.* Nick (Dr. Gironda's assistant) has had Mitchell shanghaied aboard the ship. Kennedy wins out in a fight with Olaf, the giant first mate, and finds Mitchell. The two men escape. Later, at his hotel, Mitchell calls Mrs. Gironda, who arrives just as Mitchell is shot to death by a supposed friend, Hobart. Kennedy pursues Hobart's car but is lured into a crash. Returning to Mrs. Gironda, Kennedy is told that Mitchell, her ex-husband, was blackmailing her.

Kennedy rescues Gironda from the *Nellie D.*, but Gironda is seized again by kidnappers in the employ of Hobart and Denton, another Foundation board member. After exposing and capturing the culprits, Kennedy calls a meeting of the directors and reveals that Gironda is the Clutching Hand. Actually Verna's guardian and not her real father, Gironda had misappropriated vast sums belonging to her. He faked the gold formula and created the Clutching Hand to remove suspicion from himself, intending to make a fortune and leave the country. Gironda flees to his laboratory and commits suicide.

Notes

Weiss and Mintz announced an ambitious program of serials for 1936-'37, but the company was dissolved after the making of three, *Custer's Last Stand, The Clutching Hand,* and *The Black Coin.* Devoid of production slickness and hampered by overly complex scripts, these old-fashioned chapter plays are nonetheless a joy to watch because of their many veteran performers. In the most famous of the three, *The Clutching Hand,* any movie fan of 1936 possessed of a "whatever became of...?" turn of mind could have encountered fifteen stars of silent and early talking pictures: Jack Mulhall, Yakima Canutt, Reed Howes, William Farnum, Rex Lease, Mae Busch, Bryant Washburn, Robert Frazer, Gaston Glass, Mahlon Hamilton, Franklyn Farnum, Snub Pollard, Milburn Morante, William Desmond, and Bull Montana! There's also a star of the future, Charles Locher, who within a year became a Goldwyn discovery, Jon Hall.

The picture harks back to the Pearl White serial of 1916, *The Exploits of Elaine,* in which Arthur B. Reeve's then-popular detective, Craig Kennedy, was played by Arnold Daly and Lionel Barrymore and the Clutching Hand was Sheldon Lewis. Here, Mulhall makes Kennedy a high-spirited sleuth; Rex Lease is a pleasing secondary hero. There is great variety of locations, and interesting lighting effects are put to good use on one of Kenneth Strickfaden's well-equipped laboratory sets. Stunting is vintage Yakima Canutt, who is seen as the Clutching Hand's right-hand man. The solution to the mystery is surprising, yet not as great a strain on the credulity as the serial denouments of Mascot. Direction is old-fashioned but fast-paced.

DEATH FROM A DISTANCE (1936)

(Invincible Pictures Corporation)

Produced by Maury M. Cohen; *directed by* Frank R. Strayer; *production manager,* Lon Young; *story and screenplay by* John W. Krafft; *photographed by* M. A. Anderson, ASC; *special effects by* Jack Cosgrove; *art director,* Edward C. Jewell; *film editor,* Roland Reed; *assistant director,* Melville Shyer; *recording director,* L. E. Clark; *musical director,* Abe Meyer; RCA Victor *sound; produced at* Universal City; *running time,* 68 minutes; *released* April 30, 1936, *by* Chesterfield Motion Pictures Corporation.

PLAYERS: *Detective Lieutenant Ted Mallory,* Russell Hopton; *Kay Palmer,* Lola Lane; *Jim Gray,* George Marion, Sr.; *Professor Trowbridge,* John St. Polis; *Professor Ernst Einfeld,* Lee Kohlmar; *Detective Regan,* Lew Kelly; *Langsdale,* Wheeler Oakman; *Morgan,* Robert Frazer; *Gorman,* Cornelius Keefe; *District Attorney,* Captain E. H. Calvert; *Ahmad Haidru,* John Davidson; *City Editor McConnell,* John Dilson; *Medical Examiner,* Henry Hall; *Witnesses,* Creighton Hale, Jane Keckley, *and* Eric Mayne; *Photographer,* Herbert Vigran; *Fingerprint Expert,* Charles West; *Reporters,* Lynton Brent, Ralph Brooks, *and* Joel Lyon; *Desk Sergeant,* Frank LaRue; *Detective,* Hal Price.

Synopsis

The eminent Professor Ernst Einfeld, a comically eccentric genius, is delivering a lecture to a select, invited audience at the Trowbridge Planetarium when a gunshot is

Lon Young, former magician (The Great Lorenzo), was listed as production manager on most of the Invincible-Chesterfield pictures. Actually, he was the producer, staying on the set constanly and supervising every aspect of each production. One of Young's personal favorites was *Death From a Distance,* for which he stretched the budget sufficiently to employ one of the greatest special effects men in Hollywood, Jack Cosgrove. This extra touch, along with the utilization of some of Universal's spectacular properties from the just-completed Karloff-Lugosi film, *The Invisible Ray,* gives the picture an aura of "class." Cosgrove's perfect matte shots, simulating planetarium projection, are of the same high quality as the work he turned out for David O. Selznick, Walter Wanger, and other big-time moviemakers.

There are other good things about the picture, such as firm direction by Frank Strayer and pleasant performances by Russell Hopton and Lola Lane. George Marion, Sr., is highly satisfactory as a crazed killer, and Lee Kohlmar has some neat comic scenes as a slightly loopy scientist. There is a fine collection of suspects, including such perennial culprits as Wheeler Oakman, John Davidson, John St. Polis, and Cornelius Keefe. The story develops with less suspense than one might hope, but the mystery angles are worked out with some ingenious touches, and the spooky ending avoids the almost inevitable letdown suffered by many murder yarns.

heard in the darkness. When the lights go up, it is found that Dr. Stone, a wealthy drug manufacturer, has been shot to death. Lieutenant Ted Mallory of the Homicide Squad soon arrives with a crew of investigators.

Witnesses disagree as to where the gunfire originated. It is finally established that it came from the back of the room. Newspaper reporter Kay Palmer, sent to cover the lecture, is excited to be on top of a big story. She becomes furious when Mallory refuses to let her leave the room to phone in her report. Finally, by a ruse, Kay gets past the guards and calls in the story, spicing it with a blast against Mallory and the inefficiency of the police in handling the case.

Kay's newspaper continues the vitriolic attacks, putting Mallory on the spot with the District Attorney. Actually, Mallory has made headway in the case and believes he knows the identity of the murderer, but fears to reveal too much until he has more evidence. As the questioning of suspects continues, it becomes evident that many persons had motives for killing Stone. Kay's articles have placed Professor Einfeld's life in jeopardy, and in trying to make amends she draws the conclusion that Mallory is really a brilliant detecteve. Mallory and Day combine their efforts and learn that the fatal bullet was fired through a clever device connected to the planetarium equipment.

During another lecture, Professor Einfeld becomes the prey of the crazed killer. It is announced that the professor is dead, but later, in the darkness, the supposed corpse makes a dramatic appearance. The killer, Jim Gray, thinking he is seeing the ghost of his victim, breaks down and confesses. Mallory reveals that Einfeld is alive and that the hoax was staged to make the criminal reveal himself.

Wheeler Oakman.

THE MINE WITH THE IRON DOOR (1936)

(Sol Lesser Productions)

Produced by Sol Lesser; *directed by* David Howard; *screenplay by* Don Swift *and* Daniel Jarrett; *based on the novel by* Harold Bell Wright; *photographed by* Frank B. Good, ASC; *art directors*, Ben Carre *and* Lewis J. Rachmil; *Film Editor*, Arthur Hilton; *sound engineer*, Earl Crain; *assistant director*, Geroge Sherman; *musical director*, Abe Meyer; *sound system*, RCA Victor; *running time*, 66 minutes; *released* May 6, 1936, *by* Columbia Pictures Corporation.

PLAYERS: *Bob Harvey*, Richard Arlen; *Marta Hill*, Cecilia Parker; *David Burton*, Henry B. Walthall; *Dempsey*, Stanley Fields; *Thad Hill*, Spencer Charters; *Pitkins*, Charles Wilson; *Secretary*, Barbara Bedford; *Garage Man*, Horace Murphy.

Synopsis

A slick land promoter sells some Arizona property to Bob Harvey, a young salesman. Dempsey, a detective,

In the mine with Cecilia Parker and mad killer H. B. Walthall.

Taking Marta to the well-hidden mine, Burton tries to murder her. Bob breaks in, overcomes Burton, and rescues Marta. The lovers find the iron door and, behind it, the treasure which has remained intact for three centuries.

comes to arrest the promoter and reveals to Bob that the legendary Mine with the Iron Door, a cache of mission gold, is repured to be hidden on the property. Bob and Dempsey decide to search for the fabled mine. In Arizona they meet Marta Hill and her grandfather, Thad, who live on Bob's land. They also meet a nearby resident, Professor Burton, an archaeologist. The elderly scientist, quite insane and in love with Marta, conceals his jealous hatred of Bob.

Marta and Bob fall in love and search together for the mine, which the fanatical Burton has long discovered.

The madman vanquished. Richard Arlen, Cecilia Parker, H. B. Walthall.

Harold Bell Wright's immensely popular novel, *The Mine with the Iron Door,* has fascinated millions of readers since its publication in 1923. The romantic but convincing tale derives from an enduring legend of a fabulous treasure somewhere in the Santa Catalina Mountains of Arizona. A successful silent film of the subject was produced in 1924 by Sol Lesser. Lesser's talkie was purchased by Columbia for its 1936 program and merited a Columbia reissue in 1952.

This unspectacular production fails to get out of the story what a larger budget and more imaginative handling could have yielded. It is, however, a pleasing melodrama whose weird and comic elements lift it above the ordinary. David Howard, director of some fine outdoor dramas for Fox and RKO-Radio and formerly principal director of Fox's foreign-language releases, contributed skillful work.

There are smooth performances by star Richard Arlen, ingenue Cecilia Parker, character comedian Spencer Charters, and the former boxer Stanley Fields, a tough-guy comedian in the Wallace Beery mold. Henry B. Walthall, seen here in one of his last appearances, adds finesse, with a finely shaded portrayal of madness. Photography is exceptional, and set design blends in well with the outdoor scenery. The use of some of Abe Meyer's stock soundtrack music — including the venerable chase accompaniment by Joseph Carl Briel from *The Birth of a Nation* (1915) — imparts an old-fashioned quality.

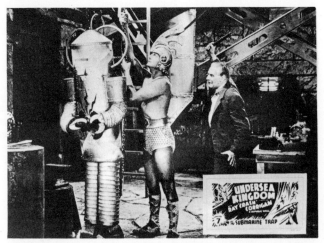

Two-legged water heater, Ray Corrigan, C. Montague Shaw.

Monte Blue and Boothe Howard watch Ray Corrigan and Lane Chandler on "reflectoplate."

THE UNDERSEA KINGDOM (1936)

(Republic Pictures Corporation)

Produced by Nat Levine; *directed by* B. Reeves Eason *and* Joseph Kane; *supervised by* Barney Sarecky; *screenplay by*

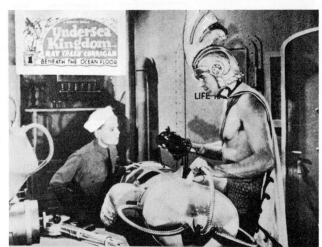

Lee Van Atta, Ray Corrigan.

John Rathmell, Maurice Geraghty, *and* Oliver Drake; *original story* by Tracy Knight *and* John Rathmell; *supervising editor,* Joseph H. Lewis; *photographed by* William Nobles *and* Edgar Lyons; *film editors,* Dick Fantl *and* Helene Turner; *sound supervision,* Terry Kellum; *musical supervision,* Harry Grey; *musical score by* Arthur Kay *and* Jacques Aubran; *special effects by* Ellis Thackery *and* Howard *and* Theodore Lydecker; RCA *sound;* a *serial in* 12 chapters, 25 reels; *released* May 30, 1936; *feature version,* SHARAD OF ATLANTIS, *running time,* 100 minutes, *released* 1966.

PLAYERS: *Crash Corrigan,* Ray Corrigan; *Diana Compton,* Lois Wilde; *Unga Khan,* Monte Blue; *Sharad,* William Farnum; *Ditmar,* Boothe Howard; *Gasspom,* Raymond Hatton; *Norton,* C. Montague Shaw; *Billy,* Lee Van Atta; *Briny,* Smiley Burnette; *Salty,* Frankie Marvin; *Hakur,* Lon Chaney, Jr.; *Darius,* Lane Chandler; *Andrews,* Jack Mulhall; *Joe,* John Bradford; *Zogg,* Malcolm McGregor, *Martos,* Ralph Holmes; *Moloch,* John Merton; *Gourck,* Ernie Smith, *Clinton,* Lloyd Whitlock; *Antony,* Everett Gibbons; *Doctor,* Kenneth Lawton; *and* Bill Yrigoyen, Eddie Parker, George de Normand, Alan Curtis, Tom Steele, Wes Warner, Don Rowan, Rube Schaeffer, David Horsley, Jack Ingram, Tracy Layne, Millard McGowan, William Stahl, Kenneth Lawton, *and* Al Seymour.

Chapter Titles

1)Beneath the Ocean Floor; 2)The Undersea City; 3)Arena of Death; 4)Revenge of the Volkites; 5)Prisoners of Atlantis; 6)The Juggernaut Strikes; 7)The Submarine Trap; 8)Into the Metal Tower; 9)Death in the Air; 10)Atlantis Destroyed; 11)Flaming Death; 12)Ascent to the Upper World.

Synopsis

Professor Norton tells newspaper reporter Diane Compton and Navy Lieutenant Crash Corrigan about his invention, a device that predicts earthquakes and, he hopes, can transmit a regulatory ray. The machinery has gathered evidence that a destructive series of quakes originated from the sea bottom where the lost continent of Atlantis is thought to have been. Norton has dredged a statuette made of Orichalum, a fusion of gold and copper known only to the Atlanteans. Norton proposes to go to Atlantis in his rocket submarine and halt the tremors. Crash, Diana, and sailors Joe, Salty, and Briny go with Norton to the ocean floor. Billy, Norton's young son, stows away.

Atlantis does, indeed, exist, ten thousand feet below the surface, protected from the sea for centuries by a dome of Orichalum. Two factions are in a continual state of war, the White Robes under the kindly King Sharad, and the Black Robes of the power-crazed Unga Khan. Khan, from his enclosed metal tower, sends forces against the Sacred City where Sharad rules. Khan's scientists have augmented his army with an armored juggernaut, robots known as Volkites, atomic guns, a disintegrating ray, and radio-con-

In Sharad's prison with Ray Corrigan, Rube Schaeffer, Ernie Smith, John Merton.

trolled aircraft called Volplanes. The earthquakes that plague the upper world are caused by Khan, whose ambition is to conquer the earth. His tower is designed as a giant rocket, but his scientists have been unable to devise a propulsion system powerful enough to raise the tower.

On his Reflectoplate (a television apparatus), Khan and his assistant, Ditmar, observe the approach of the submarine. Khan's magnetic ray draws the sub into a cave. The ship surfaces in a lake in Atlantis, and Khan sends Captain Hakur with the Imperial Guards to capture the invaders. Joe fires ineffectually on the Volkites, then tries to flee — only to be destroyed by an atom blast from a robot. Crash and Billy narrowly escape a similar fate.

Norton, Diana, and the sailors are taken before Khan. Billy and Crash are caught by White Robes led by Darius, but Crash overcomes the guard, leaves Billy in hiding, and goes to the tower to try to rescue his friends. Failing in this, he returns to find that Billy has been taken to the Sacred

John Merton and Ray Corrigan are sentenced to be dragged to death. Lee Van Atta, in sailor hat, watches helplessly.

City. Crash is captured when he tries to rescue Billy and is accused of being a Khan agent. Sentenced to the arena, Crash defeats several Black Robes. When Sharad hands Crash the Sacred Sword of Victory to be used on his last opponent, Moloch, Crash breaks the weapon. For this sacrilege, Crash is sentenced to be dragged to death behind a chariot. Gourck and Magna, two prisoners, seize Sharad and escape in the chariot, and overpowers the Black Robes, rescuing Sharad. Moloch assists in the rescue. Crash is made Commander of the White Robes, with Moloch as his aide.

Norton, his mind warped by Khan's fiendish transformation machine, willingly builds rocket engines for his new master. Khan sends his army against Sharad again. During a terrific battle, Crash and Moloch fall outside of the wall. Taking a Black Robe uniform, Crash impersonates Hakur and tricks the Black Robes into retreating. Later, Crash gets inside Khan's tower but has difficulty rescuing his friends because of Norton's treachery. After many narrow escapes, Crash, Norton, and Billy flee in a Volplane, only to crash while dodging Khan's aerial torpedoes. All survive, but Norton is still under the spell, and returns to the tower.

Khan's rocket fire at last destroys Sharad and his city. Moloch dies protecting his friends. Diana, Billy, and the sailors escape and return to the outer world in the sub. Crash gets inside the tower, returns Norton to normalcy, and tries to sabotage Khan's rocket engines. Khan fires the tower through the dome. The sea rushes in, and the tower rises. Adapting a Reflectoplate, Crash warns the U. S. Navy. When the tower surfaces, warships open fire but cannot penetrate an invisible atom ray shield surrounding it. Crash and Norton smash the machines that create the rays. Now Navy guns wreak havoc with the tower. Crash and Norton encounter Khan and Ditmar about to escape in the last Volplane. Crash knocks both men unconscious, and he and Norton escape in the craft an instant before the tower explodes.

Notes

Darkest Africa's success plunged Republic back into fantasy for its second serial, *The Undersea Kingdom.* This original screenplay likely owes as much to the *Flash Gordon* newspaper cartoon (which was being adapted on film at Universal at the time *Kingdom* was in the planning stage) as to any literary work about the fabled sunken continent. Here, as in Alex Raymond's inspired comic strip, is beheld an athletic hero thrown into an alien world where swords and chariots are pitted against robots, death rays, rocket ships, and other futuristic devices. Even the hero's name, Cash Corrigan, has a familiar ring. Filmed in twenty-five days at a cost of $99,222, *The Undersea Kingdom* generally bears comparison with the Universal *magnum opus,* which cost more than three times as much. Coincidentally, Ray Corrigan worked in his gorilla suit as Flash Gordon's opponent in the Tournament of Death

episodes (unbilled, as per his Republic contract) a couple of weeks before beginning his stint as star of *Kingdom.*

Retaining most of the production staff of *Darkest Africa,* this serial maintains the same high quality in photography, special effects, settings, and almost non-stop musical accompanient. The seige of the city in Chapter Four is staged with great skill. In an economy move, the sequence is repeated in Chapter Ten, altered slightly by being printed down as a night effect. Some of the "take-outs" following the cliffhangers that end the first eleven episodes cheat in Mascot tradition. The most notorious such incident occurs at the end of Chapter Eight, when Crash is strapped to the front of the juggernaut (an armored car), which is used to crash through the gates of the city. Although the gates are shown splintering in this chapter, in the next episode they are quickly opened to allow the juggernaut to pass through. There are occasional plot inconsistencies, typical of the multi-author serial idiom.

Corrigan proved a fine serial and Western star whose stunting skills and breezy personality won him a devoted following. He also ran Corriganville, the famed movie location ranch at Chatsworth, and he continued his unbilled work as gorillas and other monsters for many years. He died in 1976 at the age of 72. Monte Blue is well cast as the mad tyrant, and William Farnum gains sympathy as good King Sharad. Lee Van Atta, a plucky youngster, has greater appeal than most other Hollywood moppets. Lois Wilde overplays the heroine role. Raymond Hatton and Lon Chaney, Jr., are the best of the supporting heavies. Veteran "bad guy" John Merton is a pleasant surprise in a secondary hero role.

The robots look a bit like water heaters on accordion legs, but they are a vast improvement over their counterparts in *The Phantom Empire.*

Once more, as with *Darkest Africa,* much of the clout of this serial lies in the extensive use of excellent music by musical director Harry Grey. Most of the compositions are by Arthur Kay, arranged by Jacques Aubran. Published dramatic music by Leon Rosebrook, Meredith Willson, Rex Bassett, Charles Dunworth, and Joseph Carl Breil also is utilized.

REVOLT OF THE ZOMBIES (1936)

(Academy Pictures Corporation)

Produced by Edward Halperin; *directed by* Victor Halperin; *written by* Howard Higgin, Rollo Lloyd, **and** Victor Halperin; *art and technical direction,* Leigh Smith; *director of photography,* Arthur Martinelli, ASC; *operative cameraman,* J. Arthur Feindel; *film editor,* Douglas Biggs; *Sound technician,* G. P. Costello; *musical director,* Abe Meyer; *production manager,* John M. Hicks; *coiffeurs by* Phillip Scheer; *special effects,* Ray Mercer; *studio executive,* Leon D'Usseau; *filmed at* Talisman Studio; *running time,* 65 minutes; *released* June 4, 1936, *by* Academy Pictures Distributing Corporation.

PLAYERS: *Claire Duval,* Dorothy Stone; *Armand Loque,* Dean Jagger; *Colonel Mazovia,* Roy D'Arcy; *Clifford Grayson,* Robert Noland; *General Duval,* George Cleveland; *Dr. Trevissant,* Fred Warren; *Ignacio Mcdonald,* Carl Stockdale; *Buna,* Teru Shimada; *Hsiang,* William Crowell; *Officer,* Selmer Jackson; *German Soldier,* Hans Schumm.

Synopsis

Living dead men rout a German detachment on the Franco-Austrian frontier during World War I. An Oriental priest, chaplain of a French regiment, is imprisoned for life because of his power to create zombies attuned to his will. As the captive priest prepares to burn a parchment revealing the location of his secret formula, the wily Colonel Mazovia steps in kills the priest, and steals the charred document.

193

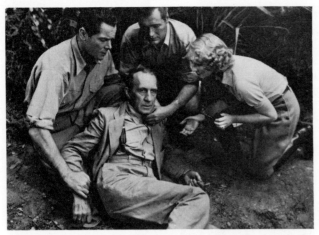

Dean Jagger, Robert Noland, and Dorothy Stone go to the aid of Carl Stockdale.

After the war, an Allied expedition is sent to the ruins of Angkor in Cambodia to destroy the secret of the zombies. The party includes General Duval and his daughter, Claire; Armand Loque, a brilliant but shy student of dead languages; Clifford Grayson, an Englishman; Dr. Trevissant and Ignacio McDonald, scientists; and the enigmatic Mazovia. Claire accepts Armand's marriage proposal after an argument with her real love, Clifford. When a high temple scaffolding collapses and drops two men to their deaths, Claire instinctively runs to Cliff for protection. Armand, heartbroken, releases Claire from their engagement.

Mazovia had plotted the fall of the scaffolding and other "accidents" affecting the expedition. Native workers rebel, and the party returns to the base at Pnom Penh. Armand, after a clue, steals back to Angkor against orders. There he views an ancient ceremony. A native is sent from the temple bearing a bronze tablet. Armand follows the man through a swamp to a hidden building with a bronze doorway. When the native has gone, Armand enters and finds a room panelled in bronze. In the center is a multi-limbed idol holding a gong. When Armand accidentally strikes the gong, a wall panel opens, revealing the tablet — the source of the sought-after secret.

Armand is dismissed for insubordination. With the secret power he turns his servant, Buna, into a zombie. The power transforms the scholar into a ruthless despot, bending all the expeditioners to his will. The natives are turned into a small army of zombies. With threats on the life of Clifford, Armand forces Claire to consent to marry him, but his triumph is destroyed by the realization that Claire will never love him. Armand relinquishes his power and liberates the zombies, who descend upon him. Destroying the ancient secret, Armand turns to face Buna, who puts a bullet through his heart.

Notes

The Halperins, in a long-planned effort to repeat their *White Zombie* success, amplified a legend that the great Cambodian city of Angkor was built in the year 900 with a labor force of animated corpses. In spite of careful preparation and good ideas, *Revolt of the Zombies* proved almost a total disappointment. Silent-era directorial methods, which marred but did not destroy *White Zombie*, are fatal to a picture made after four more years' evolution of acting and directing styles. Even so fine a performer as Dean Jagger cannot overcome the handicap, and the other players — including Dorothy Stone, daughter of stage star Fred Stone — perform in an even more outmoded way. The story lacks the simple strength of the 1932 film and has little of its virtuosity in the matters of set design, photography, and cutting.

Establishing shots of Angkor Wat are intercut with studio settings comprising drops and back-projection of the ruins. The rebellion is staged in a beautiful Oriental garden in Los Angeles. The Cambodian zombies, alas, are not nearly so frightening as the Haitian variety. Again, the Halperins became embroiled in a lawsuit involving their use of the word *zombie*. Release was delayed when Amusement Securities Corporation, which was enjoying a national reissue on the strength of its financier status and ownership of *White Zombie*, brought suit complaining that a second zombie picture constituted unfair competition!

THE NEW ADVENTURES OF TARZAN (1936)

(Burroughs-Tarzan Pictures, Incorporated)

Presented by Ashton Dearholt, George W. Stout, and Ben S. Cohen; An Ashton Dearholt Expedition Picture; directed by Edward Kull; adapted by Charles F. Royal and Edwin F. Blum from the novels by Edgar Rice Burroughs; screenplay by Charles F. Royal; photographed by Edward Kull, ASC, and Ernest F. Smith; art director, Charles Clague; sound recording, Earl N. Crain; film editor, Edward Schroeder; assistant director, Wilbur F. McGaugh; special effects by Ray Mercer and Howard Anderson; musical director, Abe Meyer; sound by Lyle E. Willey & Associates; filmed in Guatemala and at the Selig Zoo; a serial in 12 chapters; complete feature, 75 minutes; released June 10, 1936.

PLAYERS: *Tarzan,* Herman Brix; *Ula Vale,* Ula Holt; *Major Martling,* Frank Baker; *Alice Martling,* Dale Walsh; *Gordon Hamilton,* Harry Ernest; *Raglan,* Don Castello (*and* Ashton Dearholt); *George,* Lewis Sargent; *Bouchart,* Merrill McCormick; *Nkima (Chimpanzee),* Jiggs; *Renegade,* Earl Dwire; *Queen Maya,* Mrs. Gentry.

Chapter Titles

1) The New Adventures of Tarzan; 2) Crossed Trails; 3)The

Devil's Noose; 4) River Perils; 5) Unseen Hands; 6) Fatal Fangs; 7) Flaming Waters; 8) Angry Gods; 9) Doom's Brink; 10) Secret Signals; 11) Death's Fireworks; 12) Operator 17.

Synopsis

In Africa, Tarzan rescues Bouchart from a lion and is informed that Tarzan's best friend, the French pilot Lieutenant D'Arnot, is a captive of the Monster Men of a lost city in Guatemala. Aboard the S. S. *Corinthian* to South America, Tarzan meets Major Martling, a distinguished archaeologist going to search for the Green Goddess (a priceless Mayan monolith containing a fortune in jewels); Alice, Marling's daughter, and her fiancé, Gordon Hamilton; George, a comical chap who has stowed away with Nkima, Tarzan's chimpanzee friend; Ula Holt, a beautiful woman of mystery; and Raglan, an unscrupulous soldier of fortune. Raglan attacks Martling in an attempt to learn the

whereabouts of a document divulging the location of the statue. Tarzan rescues Martling, and Raglan escapes without his identity being revealed.

In Guatemala City, while Martling and Tarzan visit President Ubico, Raglan steals the document and sets out into the jungle. Tarzan and Martling's party give chase. Raglan uncovers a bat-infested passage to the lost city, home of the Green Goddess. When Tarzan and company arrive, they are seized by the Monster Men and taken before Queen Maya, who reigns in a ruined temple containing a pool of crocodiles. D'Arnot is being held captive there. Maya decrees death for all but Tarzan, whom she wants for her consort. So great is her desire for Tarzan that she is unable to plunge the sacrificial dagger into his heart. The enraged monsters threaten to kill Maya, but they are distracted when Raglan is seen hauling the Goddess up through a hole in the roof. In the confusion, Tarzan seizes a club and clears a part for his friends. George mows down the natives with a portable machine gun. Raglan lays an explosive trap that nearly kills Tarzan and his companions. Hiding the Goddess, Raglan returns to try to get a notebook from Martling that holds the secret of the

AT LAST! A Tarzan thriller in a natural setting with Herman Brix the greatest Tarzan of all time! Filmed in Guatemala where the story was laid. SEE the perilous trek into unknown jungle wilds— Tarzan in a death battle with a ferocious Numidian Lion - - a terrific fight with the Monster Men in the City of The Green Goddess - - hair-raising adventure and breathtaking escapes!

DEARHOLT - STOUT and COHEN *PRESENT*
EDGAR RICE BURROUGHS' THRILLING NEW PICTURE
THE NEW ADVENTURES OF TARZAN
FEATURING HERMAN BRIX
WORLD'S GREATEST ATHLETE

THE GREATEST TARZAN OF ALL TIME!
HERMAN BRIX
WORLD FAMOUS ATHLETE and OLYMPIC GAMES CHAMPION
in EDGAR RICE BURROUGHS' THRILLING NEW PICTURE
THE NEW ADVENTURES OF TARZAN
with ULA HOLT FRANK BAKER LEWIS SARGENT and a Tremendous Supporting Cast a BURROUGHS-TARZAN ENTERPRISE
CHAPTER 11. DEATH'S FIREWORKS
FILMED IN GUATEMALA BY THE ASHTON-DEARHOLT EXPEDITION

The NEW ADVENTURES OF TARZAN
CHAPTER 4
RIVER PERILS
Herman BRIX WORLD FAMOUS ATHLETE and OLYMPIC GAMES CHAMPION
A BURROUGHS-TARZAN ENTERPRISE
filmed by The ASHTON-DEARHOLT EXPEDITION

Goddess. Shocked to find everybody alive, he feigns friendship and joins the group.

Ula Vale, meantime, finds the Goddess and has two aides carry it away. After placing D'Arnot, Alice, and Gordon on a boat to Puerto Barrios, Tarzan scouts for Ula. Garcia, one of Ula's men, sets a noose trap which whips Tarzan into the air feet first. The ape man feigns unconciousness and when Garcia lowers him to search for the notebook Tarzan overcomes him and frees himself. George and Martling almost die in quicksand, but Tarzan returns to save them. Raglan tries to crush Tarzan under a boulder and attempts to shoot Nkima, but his treachery remains undetected. Paco, Raglan's henchmen, almost destroys Tarzan, Martling, and George, when he sets their river launch afire. Discovering that Raglan has the crucial pages from Martling's notebook, Tarzan and his friends pursue and barely escape death at the hands of the savages. They proceed and rescue Ula and her aide, Garcia, from a burning hut. After a boat crash and an encounter with crocodiles in which Garcia is killed, Tarzan overtakes the boat on which Raglan is attempting to escape with the help of Captain Melville, a smuggler. While fighting with Tarzan, Melville accidentally causes an explosion. Tarzan retrieves the Goddess but is arrested along with Raglan, Melville, and the Martling party. Ula has Raglan arrested, revealing that she is a government secret agent. Martling presents the Green Goddess to the people of Guatemala.

Notes

Edgar Rice Burroughs was invariably dissatisfied with the movies based upon his Tarzan character, because of the producers' insistence upon changing his concept of the ape man. In September of 1934, Burroughs entered the movie business himself in partnership with an old friend, Lee Ashton Dearholt, who had worked as an RKO-Radio representative in Guatemala, and several others who had been active in independent production.

The short-lived Burroughs-Tarzan Enterprises, Incorporated, established for the production of features and serials adapted from Burroughs' novels, embarked upon its first and most ambitious project, *Tarzan in Guatemala,* almost immediately. In October, Olympics decathlon champion Herman Brix was signed as Tarzan (at $75 per week!) after attempts to borrow Johnny Weissmuller and Buster Crabbe failed. Some excellent wild animal scenes — including a fight with a lion — were filmed at the Selig Zoo in Los Angeles during November. Early in December the Ashton Dearholt Expedition of twenty-nine persons, a famous trained chimpanzee named Jiggs, cameras, and a four-ton sound truck, arrived in Guatemala during a storm which seemed to set the tone of the venture. Don Castello, the actor playing the villian, was stricken ill almost immediately, and Dearholt took over, appearing in the role

throughout (although Castello's name appears on the titles).

Much danger and difficulty was encountered in getting the heavy equipment over mountains and through jungles, everybody was blotched with insect bites, and a sound technician barely survived a bite from a poisonous snake. Thy problems of recording in the tropics proved overwhelming. The natives' fear of Jiggs (with good reason) created labor disputes. The weather often refused to cooperate. The company spent four months in the jungle. Most of the filming was done in Guatemala City, at the ancient Spanish capital of Antigua, at the Mayan ruins at Tikal, and along the Rio Dulce River. Shooting was completed by March of 1935.

There were emotional complications as well. Dearholt and the leading lady, Ula Holt, fell in love. Meantime, Burroughs became seperated from his wife and was comforted by Mrs. Dearholt — an attractive woman about half his age — who later became Mrs. Burroughs. Through it all, Dearholt and Burroughs remained good friends. They continued the operation of Burroughs-Tarzan until the money ran out in 1937, making several features, of which one, *Tundra,* filmed in Alaska, gained high praise.

The New Adventures of Tarzan, while it has its moments of excellence, is a crude effort when compared to the M-G-M pictures. The poor sound recording is annoying; an apology for its quality actually appears in the credit titles. Years later the entire soundtrack of the feature version was rerecorded, which improved the picture enormously. The story fails to provide the swift development and charm of the better Tarzan films, and the direction and acting lack the sharpness an adventure film needs. Tarzan's fights with both men and animals are in many cases more convincing than the choreographed encounters at M—G—M, with Brix obviously getting roughed up in some of them. The scenics are splendid, with some spectacular waterfall scenes and photogenic ruins in particular coming off well in sequences involving as many as 650 natives.

The story was developed further in a so-called sequel, a feature called *Tarzan and the Green Goddess* (1938), which was made after the production firm folded, utilizing footage from the original expedition, plus added material. The ending improves the dull close of the serial, by having Raglan murdered aboard a sailing ship by the evil Captain Blade (Jack Mower), who in turn perishes in a storm at sea.

Brix, after appearing in other features and serials under his own name, later began a long second career as Bruce Bennett.

KELLY OF THE SECRET SERVICE (1936)

(Victory Pictures Corporation)

Produced by Sam Katzman; *directed by* Bob Hill; *screenplay by* Al Martin; *adapted from the story,* ON IRISH HILL, *by* Peter B. Kyne; *production manager,* Ed W. Rote;

photographed by Bill Hyer; *film editor,* Dan Milner; *recording,* Hans Weeren; *settings by* Fred Preble; *lighting effects by* Otto H. Buhner; *running time,* 69 minutes; *released* June 15, 1936.

PLAYERS: *Ted Kelly,* Lloyd Hughes; *Sally Flint,* Sheila Manors; *Lefty Hogan,* Fuzzy Knight; *Red,* Syd Saylor; *George Lesserman,* Jack Mulhall; *Dr. Marston,* Forrest Taylor; *Dr. Walsh,* John Elliott; *Ylon,* Miki Morita; *Chief Wilson,* Jack Cowell.

Synopsis

Dr. Marston, developer of a radio-controlled bomb accurate within 200 miles, hires a prizefighter and his manager to guard the laboratory, pending government testing. A tear gas bomb is hurled into the laboratory where Marston and his helper, George, are conferring. The boxer, Lefty, and his manager, Red, are kayoed in a sneak attack. Operative Kelly arrives after the bomb plans have been stolen. Kelly spots an Oriental hurrying away, but a shattering sound keeps him at the lab site. George is unconscious, and the inventor's apparatus has been demolished.

Kelly tracks Sally Flint, Marston's secretary, to a Chinese restaurant and eavesdrops on her conversation with an Oriental. Meantime, the incompetent laboratory guards are overwhelmed with fear. Kelly discerns that Sally's uncle, Howard Walsh, was replaced by George as Marston's aide. He also links the prior murder of a Secret Service agent

Principals of Kelly of the Secret Service include Lloyd Hughes, Sheila Mannors, Forrest Taylor, Miki Morita, Syd Saylor, Fuzzy Knight.

197

is an efficient heroine. The low-comedy routines by Fuzzy Knight and Syd Saylor contrast nicely with the mysterious elements. Thin, pale-eyed Forrest Taylor makes nice work of his villain portrayal. Robert Hill's direction is well paced.

I COVER CHINATOWN (1936)

(Banner Pictures Corporation)

Produced by Fenn Kimball; *directed by* Norman Foster; *story and screenplay by* Harry Hamilton; *photographed by* Art Reed *and* James V. Murray; *art director,* Ralph Berger; *film editor,* Carl Pierson; *musical director,* Abe Meyer; *produced at* RKO-Pathé Studio; RCA *recording; running time,* 65 minutes; *distributed by* William Steiner, Commodore Pictures Corporation; *released* August of 1936.

PLAYERS: *Barton,* Norman Foster; *Gloria,* Elaine Shepard; *Clark,* Theodore von Eltz; *Myra,* Polly Ann Young; *Agent,* Arthur Lake; *Detective,* Bruce Mitchell; *Policeman,* Robert Love; *Trucker,* Eddie Gribbon; *Head Waiter,* George Hackathorne; *Puss,* Vince Barnett; *Victor,* Edward Emerson; *Woman,* Cherita Alden Ray.

Lloyd Hughes

named Hendricks, with the early stages of development on the bomb. Now becoming enamored of Sally, Kelly broadens his investigation to find the Walsh home honeycombed with secret passageways.

Sally disappears via a hidden panel. Kelly bursts into the adjoining room and finds Marston, who attempts to hypnotize him. Kelly affects a mesmerized condition until he can get the drop on Marston. It is revealed that Walsh conceived the bomb; Marston stole the concept, then hypnotized Walsh to murder Hendricks.

Notes

A combination of themes dear to the hearts of mystery lovers — spies, science-fiction, and murder by hypnotism — makes *Kelly of the Secret Service* a most entertaining entry in Victory's series of Peter B. Kyne adaptations. Almost inconceivably, the concept of an explosive missile that will travel 200 miles *was* science-fiction only forty years ago!

Photography and lighting effects are better in this instance that in any other Victory films (all of which were made with virtually the same production staff), leaving the impression that Sam Katzman may have given the company an extra couple of hours shooting time. Lloyd Hughes is a snappy hero despite old-fashioned acting techniques and Shiela Manors (a. k. a. Shiela Manners and Sheila Bromley)

Norman Foster, Elaine Shepard, Theodore von Eltz.

Danger stalks Norman Foster and Elaine Shepard.

Synopsis

Barton, who drives a sight-seeing bus in San Francisco's Chinatown, Becomes involved innocently in the machinations of a pair of dealers in stolen jewels, Clark and Victor. Clark viciously murders a girl, Myra, who knows too much, and hides the body in a trunk. Barton falls under the suspicion of the police and, aided by Gloria, sets out to get evidence against Clark. They narrowly escape death several times in the secret byways of Chinatown. The police come to the rescue, and Clark and his gang are brought to justice after a harrowing chase and fight.

Notes

During several years as a Fox contract player, Norman Foster established himself as a likeable leading man of the easy-going variety. By the mid-thirties, however, Henry Fonda was getting the better roles of the type at Fox while Foster's career was bogging down baldly. Foster jumped at the chance to direct as well as star in a film for the newly organized Banner Productions, *I Cover Chinatown*. It was a wise move, leading to a long string of directorial jobs that included some of the more memorable *Charlie Chan* and *Mr. Moto* films at Twentieth Century-Fox, an association with Orson Welles as director of *Journey Into Fear* (1943), plus such noteworthy items as *Rachel and the Stranger* (1948), *Kiss the Blood off My Hands* (1948), *Woman on the Run* (1950), and many Walt Disney projects.

Foster's initial effort as director is a well-done little picture, strong on atmosphere and peopled with talented players. There is a grim murder sequence, considerable chase action, and some comedy interludes by Arthur Lake (remembered as Dagwood Bumstead in the Columbia *Blondie* pictures), Eddie Gribbon, and Vince Barnett.

Foster and Theodore von Eltz are dominant as whimsical hero and slick villain, respectively. The deft mixing of humor and chills seems, in retrospect, to provide a blueprint for Foster's handling of the *Chan* and *Moto* pictures. The sets and camerawork are a cut above the average independent standard.

GHOST PATROL (1936)

(Excelsior Pictures Corporation)

Produced by Sigmund Neufeld *and* Leslie Simmonds; *directed by* Sam Newfield; *story and continuity by* Wyndham Gittens; *original story by* Joseph O'Donnell; *production manager,* William O'Conner; *electrical effects by* Kenneth Strickfaden; *produced at* Talisman Studios; *running time,* 60 minutes; *released* August 3, 1936, *by* Puritan Pictures Corporation.
PLAYERS:*Tim,*Tim McCoy; *Natalie Brent,* Claudia Dell; *Dawson,* Walter Miller; *Kincaid,* Wheeler Oakman; *Henry,* Jim Burtis; *Charlie,*Dick Curtis; *Professor Brent,* Lloyd Ingraham; *Mac,* Jack Casey; *Frank,* Slim Whitaker; *Ramon,* Artie Ortego; *Shorty,* Art Dillard; *Bill,* Fargo Bussey.

Kenneth Strickfaden's fantastic machinery surrounds Claudia Dell, Lloyd Ingraham, and Tim McCoy.

Unaccountable hijackings of cargo have followed the mysterious crashes of two mail planes crossing the desert. Tim McCoy, an agent of the Federal Bureau of Investigation — and an ex-cowboy — is sent to investigate. On horseback and garbed in chaps and sombrero, Tim looks into a suspicious gang which hides out in a deserted ghost town, once a thriving gold-mining center. Posing as a desperado, Tim insinuates himself into the gang. He learns that the aircraft have been brought down by use of a death ray invented by Professor Brent, whom the gang leaders, Dawson and Kincaid, have imprisoned in the ghost town. Brent's pretty daughter, Natalie, also is held by the gang and used as a method of coercing Brent into cooperating with the scheme. Tim survives a spate of exciting and frightening adventures to prevent the destruction of another airplane. He rescues the girl and her father and brings about the demise of the killers.

Notes

Col. Tim McCoy, formerly a Western star at M-G-M, Universal, and Columbia, was during the mid-thirties the most distinguished of the film cowboys to labor on Poverty Row. He wound up at Excelsior Pictures Corporation on a fluke — Columbia had delayed picking up the option on McCoy's contract, and just before the company decided to renew him, he signed with Sigmund Neufeld and Leslie Simmons to do a series of ten pictures. On the surface it wasn't a bad deal — he received $4,000 per picture, with each film being shot in one week — but it was a move that kept McCoy out of the major-league studios for the balance of his career.

Director Sam Newfield actually was Sam Neufeld, the co-producer's brother, a prolific director of small-scale Westerns and melodramas; he also used the *noms-de-plume* of Sherman Scott and Peter Stewart. As written by serial specialists Wyndham Gittens and Joseph O'Donnell, *Ghost Patrol* has elements of science fiction and mystery to an extent seldom encountered in Western films. The action is well staged (in view of the fast production schedule) in California desert settings, with dialogue kept to a minimum and with plenty of emphasis on adventure and gunplay. Claudia Dell and Lloyd Ingraham are good as the imperiled girl and her father, Walter Miller and Wheeler Oakman bring characteristic expertise to the "brains-heavy" roles, Jim Burtis supplies some comic touches, and there are such menacing "dog-heavies" as Dick Curtis and Slim Whitaker to add danger to the action.

SHADOW OF CHINATOWN (1836)

(Victory Pictures Corporation)

Produced by Sam Katzman; *directed by* Robert S. Hill;

story by Rock Hawkey; *continuity by* Isadore Bernstein and Basil Dickey; *special dialogue by* William Buchanan; *photographed by* William Hyer; *production manager,* Ed W. Rote; *film editor,* Charles Henkel; *settings by* Fred Preble; *sound recording,* Hans Weeren; *a serial in* 15 chapters, 31 reels; feature version, *running time,* 65 minutes; *released* October 10, 1936.

PLAYERS: *Victor Poten,* Bela Lugosi; *Martin Andrews,* Herman Brix; *Sonya,* Luana Walters; *Joan Barclay;* Willy Fu *Maurice Liu;* Grogan, Charles King; *Healy,* William Buchanan; *Captain Walters,* Forrest Taylor; *Wong,* James B. Leong; *Dr. Wu,* Henry F. Tung; *Tom Chu,* Paul Fung; *Old Luee,* George Chan; *Captain,* John Elliot; *Wong's Brother,* Moy Ming; *White Chink,* Jack Cowell; *and* Lester Dorr, Henry Hall, Roger Williams.

Chapter Titles

1)The Arms of the God; 2)The Crushing Walls; 3)13 Ferguson Alley; 4)Death on the Wire; 5)The Sinister Ray; 6)The Sword Thrower; 7)The Noose; 8)Midnight; 9)The Last Warning; 10)The Bomb; 11)Thundering Doom; 12) Invisible Gas; 13)The Brink of Disaster; 14)The Fatal Trap; 15)The Avenging Powers.

Thrills and Chills and Shivering Shocks as a Crazed Scientist Terrorizes the Underworld!

VICTORY PICTURES SAM KATZMAN *presents* Bela LUGOSI *in* SHADOW OF CHINATOWN *with* HERMAN BRIX LUANA WALTERS JOAN BARCLAY MAURICE LIU Directed by BOB HILL SUPERVISED BY SAM KATZMAN 15 THRILLING CHAPTERS

Sonya Rokoff, a beautiful Eurasian, is engaged by European promoters to close the West Coast Chinatowns to tourists. In San Francisco she hires Victor Poten, a Eurasian scientist who hates both the white and yellow races, to help her. After several disturbances, Chinese merchants led by Dr. Wu go to Sonya for help. Joan Whiting, newspaperwoman, interests novelist Martin Andrews in helping her look into the problem. Poten learns through his tele-audient machine of Martin's involvement and orders the abduction of Martin's servant, Willy Fu, who is thrown into a pit at Poten's den by "the God," a hypnotized man disguised as an idol. Martin and Joan search for Willy and are menaced by Grogan, Poten's henchman, and the God. They escape both and rescue Willy and an old Chinese.

Poten and Sonya spy on a Chinese merchants' meeting via the tele-audient device and decide upon Tom Chu as the next victim. Joan sees this abduction and follows them to Poten's den, only to be trapped in a hydraulic room whose walls begin closing together. Martin and Willy Fu are about to force their way into the shrinking room when Grogan throws a sword at them. The sword severs wires which control the walls, and the three escape.

Disguised as telephone repairman, Poten prepares to insert a poisoned needle in the receiver of Martin's telephone. Martin is saved by a warning from the conscience-striken Sonya. Later, Martin escapes a bomb planted in a manhole by Poten. Joan saves Dr. Wu from a telephone trap, and Willy similarly saves Martin. Joan is captured while two henchmen overpower Martin at his home, leaving him unconscious under an improvised death ray—a goldfish bowl concentrating rays of the sun. A detective, Wong, saves Martin. Police Captain Walters now suspects Martin as the perpetrator of the Chinatown troubles because the incidents have emulated occurrences related in one of Martin's books. Martin and Walters go to Chinatown to look for Joan. Joan has written H-E-L-P in lipstick on a mirror and flashes the message on a wall opposite her upstairs prison. Martin tries to reach the window by crossing on telephone wires. The wires break, and Martin is precipitated through a window below, where he overpowers a Poten gangster, rescues Joan, and informs Walters, who has the den closed.

Willy Fu learns that Poten is taking a ship to Los Angeles. Martin, Wong, and Willy also board the ship. Grogan, infatuated with Sonya, tries to kill Poten with a wire noose. Poten, hypnotizing Martin, arranges that Grogan will mistake Martin for Poten, but Martin is saved by Wong. Poten informs Grogan he will die at midnight. Grogan goes to the captain for protection while Poten, disguised as an old man, plots his destruction. Martin guards Grogan in the captain's cabin, but Poten has drilled a hole in the wall and strikes Grogan down with a poisoned dart. The ship's doctor saves Grogan. Sonya is aboard, and

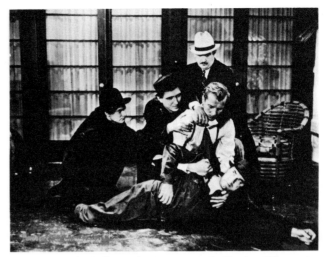

Jack Cowell, William Buchanan, and Charles King seize Herman Brix, who has attacked crime chief Bela Lugosi.

Martin and Joan go to question her. Poten tries to kill them all with a gas bomb, but Wong and the doctor save them. Poten abducts Sonya to his cabin, throwing a dummy overboard so it will appear she has drowned. Poten disguises himself, Sonya, and the hypnotized Grogan and disembarks at Wilmington.

In Los Angeles' Chinatown, Martin and Wong escape a bomb and save Sonya and Grogan. Sonya is sent to a specialist in San Francisco, and Grogan is hospitalized in Los Angeles. En route to San Francisco, Joan and Martin narrowly escape death when Poten causes their car to crash over a cliff.

Released from Poten's spell, Sonya agrees to help end the terrorism. Poten learns of an impending raid and fills his den with an undetectable gas. As the party enters, a gardenia on Joan's coat wilts, warning them of the trap. Poten hides out at Sonya's apartment. When Martin and Willy come after him, Poten leaves the mesmerized Grogan to face them and, with another henchman, Healy, slips over the roof to another building. Martin grapples on the roof with Grogan until both fall over the edge. They strike a fire escape platform, and one plunges over the rail to his death. Joan and Sonya find the dead man to be Grogan. Martin is not seriousy injured.

Sonya, Joan, and Willy wait at Martin's house, while Martin searches for Poten. Poten and Healy capture and bind Joan and Willy while Sonya sleeps. Poten rigs a chandelier to fall at the opening of the front door. Sonya wakes and sees the trap just as Martin enters. Rushing forward as the chandelier falls, Sonya is killed. Martin captures Healy as police go after Poten, who apparently drowns in the bay. The Chinese merchants celebrate with a ceremonial dinner. Martin recognizes Poten as one of the waiters and seizes him just as he is poisoning the wine. Walters takes the venal criminal in charge.

For his first of many serials, Sam Katzman acquired the biggest name his stringent budgets ever allowed: Bela Lugosi. He also pitted Lugosi against Victory Pictures' best leading man, Herman Brix, former Olympics decathlon champ and cinematic Tarzan, who at the time was starrring in a series of romantic sports features for Katzman. More extravagant in plot than production, the serial gave Lugosi freedom to create one of his more evil characters, a paranoiac Eurasian who admits of no prejudice — he hates Orientals and Caucasians equally. It's a good performance of the lay-it-on-thick variety. Also worth watching is the extraordinarily beautiful Lauana Walters as a half-caste Dragon Lady. Joan Barclay, leading lady in many Westerns of the time, is the ingenue, and the principal "dog-heavy" is Western favorite Charles King.

The plot gets overly complicated, particularly in the shipboard episodes, and fifteen chapters stretch it beyond its potential. Lugosi's lethal devices stand out among the interesting gimmicks, but there is a dearth of the elaborate stunt and effects work of the better serials. It is noteworthy that the screenplay is by Isadore Bernstein, author of *Our People* and a former managing director of Universal, and Basil Dickey, author of some of the earliest silent serials.

The feature version is interesting, in that it ends with Lugosi's apparent death; whereas in the serial he survives to be captured later.

A guest at "The House of Secrets"... an adventurer finds plenty of excitement when Death plays host.

Directed by
ROLAND REED
Produced by
GEORGE R.
BATCHELLER

THE HOUSE OF SECRETS (1936)

(Chesterfield Motion Picture Corporation)

[cf THE HOUSE OF SECRETS (1929)]

Produced by George R. Batcheller; *directed by* Roland D. Reed; *from the novel and play by* Sydney Horler; *adapted by* John W. Krafft; *business manager,* Melville Shyer; *photographed by* M. A. Anderson, ASC; *film editor,* Dan Milner; *recording engineer,* Richard Tyler; *musical director,* Abe Meyer; *sound system,* RCA High Fidelity; *produced at* RKO-Pathé Studio; *running time,* 64 minutes; *released* October 26, 1936.

PLAYERS: *Barry Wilding,* Leslie Fenton; *Julie Kenmore* Muriel Evans; *Dan Wharton,* Noel Madison; *Tom Starr,* Sidney Blackmer; *Dr. Kenmore,* Morgan Wallace; *Sir Bertram Evans,* Holmes Herbert; *Commissioner Cross,* Ian MacLaren; *Coventry,* Jameson Thomas; *Jumpy,* Matty Fain; *Ed,* Syd Saylor; *Hector Munson,* George Rosener; *Mrs. Shippam,* Rita Carlyle; *Peters,* Tom Ricketts; *Man on Ship,* Matty Kemp; *Gregory,* David Thursby; *English Policeman,* R. Lancaster; *Police Inspector,* Ramsey Hill.

Synopsis

While crossing the English Channel, Barry Wilding, an

Muriel Evans, Leslie Fenton.

American, saves an English girl from a masher. The girl refuses to tell who she is. Once in London, Barry learns he has inherited *The Hawk's Nest,* a large estate near London, on condition that he never sell the property. When Barry goes to see his estate, trespassers roughly put him off the grounds. He receives several offers to sell the place — along with warnings to leave England — but he obstinately refuses these.

Barry learns the girl he met on the ship is Julie Kenmore, who lives at *The Hawk's Nest.* Julie asks him to allow her and her father to remain on the property for at least six months, but she declines to explain the request. She also tells Barry he can not visit her, to which he replies that he will come to his estate whenever he pleases. Later, on the property, he is set upon by three American gangsters. Barry escapes and tries to enlist the aid of Scotland Yard, but the authorities refuse to help him; he is similarly spurned by Sir Betram Evans, the Home Secretary. At last, with the aid of detective Tom Starr, Barry penetrates the mystery. He rescues Julie and her father, a distinguished scientist working in secret for the British government, from a band of criminals headed by Dan Wharton. The crooks have been trying to find a treasure hidden on the estate. Barry finds the treasure and looks forward to a pleasant future with Julie.

Notes

Chesterfield, near the end of its existence, remade its early talkie, *The House of Secrets*. One of the company's better efforts, the 1936 version benefitted from improvements in sound recording and photographic tecniques as well as the work of a strong cast. Substantial sets, and the use of such eerie effects as the howling of dogs and the cries of a maniac, give the new setting a more unnerving atmosphere than was achieved in 1929. Leslie Fenton and Sidney Blackmer, usually seen as villains, are good offbeat heroes. Morgan Wallace and George Rosener add greatly to the mystery, and the principal villainy is in the capable hands of Noel Madison, Matty Fain, and the serio-comic Syd Saylor. Muriel Evans is a pretty, but not at all English, heroine. The well-paced direction is executed by Roland Reed, a former film editor and future television pioneer.

THE PENITENTE MURDER CASE (1936)
a.k.a. THE LASH OF THE PENITENTES (1937)
Spanish-language version,

EL ASASENATO DE LOS PENITENTES

(Telepictures; The Stewart Productions, Incorporated; Kinotrade)

Photographed by The Vagabond Cameraman, Roland C. Price; *directed by* Harry J. Revier; *story by* Roland C. Price; *screenplay by* Zelma Carroll; *music by* Lee Zahler; *running time,* 70 minutes; *released by* Telepictures, 1936; *Spanish version released* December 17, 1936, *by* Kinotrade; distributed by Mike J. Levinson, 1937.

PLAYERS: *Dr. Robert Taylor,* José Swickard; *Raquel,* Marie de Forest; *Manuel,* William Marcos; *Chico, Jose* Rubio.

Synopsis

Amidst scenes of mountain village life near Taos, New Mexico, the history is told of the Penitentes, a worship cult that practices torture, flagellation, and crucifixion. To this strange setting comes George Mack, feature writer for a magazine, to research a series about the Penitentes. He rents a cabin and hires a Penitente youth, Chico, as his houseboy. He then tours the village of Morado, a known center of Penitente activity.

Dr. Robert Taylor, a missionary, visits Raquel, a former cult member and a childhood sweetheart of Chico. The young woman is frightened because of gossip among the

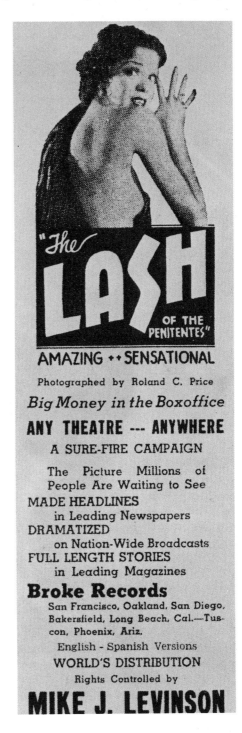

"The chosen one."

cultists, who deem immoral her work for Manuel, a well-to-do artist. Dr. Taylor explains that the Penitentes are in most respects a gentle people and will not harm her. Raquel and Manuel have fallen in love, and Chico is crazed with jealousy. Learning Raquel is posing in the nude, Chico threatens her, but she tells him she and Manuel soon will marry.

Mack bribes Chico to take him to the secret ceremony in which a man is initiated into the cult. Mack watches the rite from hiding. Chico later goes to the church council and tells malicious lies about Raquel, demanding that she be punished. Mack induces Chico to take him to the hills to see the secret Good Friday procession, in which a chosen member is scourged and crucified. While Mack is writing his story, Chico is summoned before the council and informed that his duplicity in guiding Mack has been discovered. He is given no choice but to carry out the council's orders. Acccordingly, he shoots the journalist in the back as he sits at his typewriter.

Cultists that night kidnap Raquel from her bed and drag her to the hills, where she is stripped naked, suspended by the arms from a wooden yoke, and given twenty lashes with a leather whip. Her brother, Felipe, runs to Manuel's home with the news. Manuel finds the girl unconscious and takes her to Dr. Taylor's home. Under Taylor's care, Raquel soon recovers. Chico, meantime, is arrested by the Sheriff and confesses to the murder.

Notes

Los Hermanos Penitentes (The Penitent Brothers) is a secretive religious society descended from the Third Order of St. Francis, which espoused flagellation as a form of atonement. During the Thirteenth Century the *Disciplinati de Gesu Cristo* and similar large *flagellante* cults flourished in Italy, Spain, and other countries. Later, The Black Death descended upon Europe and left in its wake many apostles of exaggerated forms of penance, the largest group being the Brotherhood of the Cross. Public scourgings and torture were encouraged by Pope Leo XIII, Henry III and Louis IX of France, and Elizabeth of Thuringia among others.

The Spanish conquest spread the influence of the flagellantes to the Philippines, the Near East, and the Americas. Don Juan de Onate, founder of the San Juan Pueblo, introduced the order to New Mexico, where several thousand Penitentes still live in isolated villages in the foothills of the Sangre de Cristo Mountains near Taos, Santa Fe, Abiquiu, and Mora.

On the night of Good Friday, Penitentes scourge themselves with whips and follow the honored local Cristo, a member chosen after a long competition of torture and self-denial, as he drags a heavy log cross to a New World Golgotha. The man is masked in black and swathed in white. The eerie procession is accompanied by the sounds of shepherd's flute, hymns cries of agony, and the thudding of whips. Riflemen surround the site to guard against spies. The beaten and exhausted Cristo is stripped, bound to the cross with rawhide thongs, and elevated. (The brotherhood long ago gave up the use of nails because of a high mortality rate among Cristos.) After forty-five minutes the crucified one is taken down, ever after to be a subject of veneration. Should a Cristo die during the ordeal, he is buried secretly, and his tombstone and honors are held in abeyance for a year.

Early in 1936 a globe-trotting free-lance writer, Carl Taylor, who studied torture cults in the Philippines, went to New Mexico to research a first-hand report of the Penitentes for Vincent Astor's magazine, *Today*. Shortly after he had mailed to editor Raymond Moley a first article in which he expressed a sympathetic view toward the faith of the brotherhood, Taylor was murdered by his houseboy, Modesto Trujillo. Taylor had written that "The boy who chops wood for me . . . I think secretly cherishes an ambition someday to be elected the village Cristo . . ." The official view was that robbery was the motive, but Moley felt certain Taylor was killed for intruding into Penitente affairs.

Some months before Taylor's death, a Penitente ceremony was filmed near Taos by Roland C. Price, a tough pioneer cinematographer known as "the vagabond cameraman." Undaunted by the fate of his predecessor, Charles F. Lummus, who had escaped alive with a bullet in his neck when he tried to photograph a ritual in the same area, Price returned to Hollywood with a great deal of authentic footage. One of the present writers once met Price on location and was surprised to see him cranking the camera by hand in true silent picture tradition, even though all but the upper palm of his right hand was missing. The similarly maimed "Three-finger Harry" Revier, a veteran director of Westerns, sparked by the notoriety given the Taylor case, got the idea of expanding Price's documentary into a dramatic feature. Revier and Price made the finished picture for something over $15,000.

Needless to say, no Production Code member would touch a picture about bizarre religious practices, especially one involving a Catholic group. Unable to release the picture through normal channels because of refusal by the Hays Office to grant a purity seal, Revier roadshowed it during the spring and summer of 1936 under the title, *The Penitente Murder Case.* Revier made several attempts to edit the film so that it would meet Hays Office standards, cutting scenes of nudity involving actress Marie de Forest, but approval never came. Independent distributor Mike J. Levinson took it over later and kept it circulating profitably for years. Despite mostly amateurish performances and general production crudity, this cruel and rough-hewn film has points of interest that in some degree compensate for its faults.

The dialogue sequences of *The Penitente Murder Case* were filmed also in Spanish with the same cast. Some of the scenes removed from the English-language edition remain in the Spanish version, *El Asasenato de los Penitentes.*

RIDERS OF THE WHISTLING SKULL
(1937 [made 1936])

(Republic Pictures Corporation)

Produced by Nat Levine; *directed by* Mack V. Wright; *supervised by* Sol C. Siegel; *based on* RIDERS OF THE WHISTLING SKULL *and* THE SINGING SCORPION *by* William Colt MacDonald; *story by* Oliver Drake *and* Bernard McConville; *screenplay by* Oliver Drake *and* John Rathmell; *photographed by* Jack Marta; *supervising editor,* Murray Seldeen; *film editor,* Tony Martinelli; *musical supervisor,* Harry Grey; RCA *sound; running time,* 58 minutes; *released* January 4, 1937.

PLAYERS: *Stony Brooke,* Bob Livingston; *Tucson Smith,* Ray Corrigan; *Lullaby Joslin,* Max Terhune; *Betty Marsh,* Mary Russell; *Otah,* Yakima Canutt; *Rutledge,* Roger Williams; *Henrietta,* Fern Emmett; *Professor Cleary,* Earle Ross; *High Priest,* Chief Thundercloud; *Professor Marsh,* John Van Pelt; *Indian,* Iron Eyes Cody; *Henchman,* Tracy Layne; *Sheriff,* Edward Peil; *Deputy,* Jack Kirk; *and* Tom Steele, Wally West, Eddie Boland, Ken Cooper.

Synopsis

An archaeological expedition consisting of Professors Flaxon, Brewster, Frone, and Cleary goes to a remote wasteland in search of the fabled lost city of Lukachuke and the missing Professor Marsh. Their guides are three adventurous ranchers, Tucson Smith, Stony Brooke, and Lullaby Joslin. Smith and Brooke become rivals for the attention of Marsh's daughter, Betty, who accompanies the

Ray Corrigan, Max Terhune and Elmer, Bob Livingston, Mary Russell, Fern Emmett.

party. They find the city in the Valley of the Skull, which lies beneath a gigantic, skull-shaped rock formation through which the winds whistle mournfully. It is evident from the beating of tom-toms that the city is occupied by descendants of its original inhabitants.

Rutledge, a ruthless highbinder who has been stealing treasure from the lost city, inflames the natives against the expeditioners. But the ranchers — known as the Mesquiteers — and the scientists earn the natives' friendship and rescue Marsh, who has been imprisoned in a cave. Rutledge and his gang attack in force, but are wiped out in a fierce battle as the Mesquiteers lead the Indians to victory.

Notes

Three features from different studios had been adapted from the Western novels of William Colt MacDonald before Nat Levine arranged to produce *The Three Mesquiteers* in 1936. Seeing the makings of a successful series in MacDonald's robust trio of ranchers, Levine arranged for Republic to buy rights to make other films utilizing the characters. Levine's judgement was typically sound, and the result was fifty-one popular and lucrative features starring The Three Mesquiteers. Ray ("Crash") Corrigan, Bob Livingston, and Syd Saylor were Republic's original Mesquiteers, and after the first film Saylor was replaced with ventriloquist Max Terhune, who appeared with Corrigan and Livingston in many of the films. Later Mesquiteers were John Wayne, Raymond Hatton, Duncan Renaldo, Bob Steele, Rufe Davis, Tom Tyler, and Jimmie Dodd. The stories were off-trail melodramas laced with humor and romance. The good-natured performances of the principals successfully covered up the incompatibility between Corrigan and Livingston.

The fourth of the series, *Riders of the Whistling Skull,* is substantially an original story suggested by two MacDonald books. In addition to the pleasing lead performances, the picture offers an imaginative and suspenseful tale, beautifully photographed locations (near St. George, Utah), plenty of good action music, and a large helping of Yakima Canutt's great stunt work. The mysterious members of the lost tribe are initially introduced through ominous drumming and by glimpses of distorted shadows moving along the rocks. Although the Indians are eventually perceived as sympathetic characters, they are, for a time, a more dramatic menace than Roger Williams and his conventional heavies. In addition to his stunting, Canutt does a nice job as a tribal leader. Scoring adds to the excitement, incorporating music by Hugo Riesenfeld, Karl Hajos, Arthur Kay, Leon Rosebrook, J. S. Zamecnik, Jacques Aubran, and Sidney Cutner.

The story of *Riders* was remade by Monogram as a *Charlie Chan* picture, *The Feathered Serpent* (1949), again written for the screen by Oliver Drake — but with Bob Livingston appearing this time as the villian!

DICK TRACY (1937 [made 1936])

(Republic Pictures Corporation)

Produced by Nat Levine; *associate producer,* J. Laurence Wickland; *directed by* Ray Taylor *and* Alan James; *based on the cartoon strip by* Chester Gould; *screenplay by* Barry Shipman *and* Winston Miller; *original story by* Morgan Cox *and* George Morgan; *photographed by* William Nobles *and* Edgar Lyons; *supervising editor,* Murray Seldeen; *film editors,* Helene Turner, Edward Todd, *and* Bill Witney; *sound engineer,* Terry Kellum; *musical supervision,* Harry Grey; *original music by* Alberto Colombo; *special effects by* Howard Lydecker; *RCA recording; a serial in* 15 chapters; *running time,* 290 minutes; *released* February 20, 1937.

PLAYERS: *Dick Tracy,* Ralph Byrd; *Gwen Andrews,* Kay Hughes; *Mike McGurk,* Smiley Burnette; *Junior,* Lee Van Atta; *Moloch,* John Picorri; *Gordon Tracy (after),* Carleton Young; *Steve Lockwood,* Fred Hamilton; *Clive Anderson,* Francis X. Bushman; *Ellery Brewster,* John Dilson; *Gordon Tracy (before),* Richard Beach; *H. T. Clayton,* Wedgewood Nowell; *Patorno,* Theodore Lorch; *Walter Odette,* Edwin Stanley; *Cloggerstein* (also *Durston*) Harrison Greene; *Martino,* Herbert Weber; *Burke* (also *Whitney* and *Henchman),* Buddy Roosevelt; *Flynn* (also *Max* and *Destino),* George DeNormand; *Korvitch,* Byron K. Foulger; *Oscar,* Ed Platt; *Elmer,* Lou Fulton; *Death Valley Johnny,* Milburn Morante; *Brandon,* Bruce Mitchell; *Brock,* Sam Flint; *Carter,* John Holland; *Clancy,* Monte Montague; *Coulter,* Forbes Murray; *Farley,* Kit Guard; *Governer,* Edward Le Saint; *Intern,* I. Stanford Jolley; *Moffett,* Harry Strang; *Henderson,* Al Ferguson; *Pilot,* Brooks Benedict; *Henchman,* Roy Barcroft; *Wickland,* Burr Caruth; *Whitney,* Walter Long; *Tony,* Loren Raker; *Vance,* Wilfred Lucas; *Teacher,* Alice Fleming; *Reporters,* Jack Ingram, Donald Kerr, *and* Charley Phillips; *Renee,* Andre Cheron; *Watchman,* Roscoe Gerall; *Officer,* Bob Reeves; *Announcer,* Kernan Cripps; *Pete,* Harry Hall; *Potter,* Louis Morrell; *Betty Clayton,* Ann Ainslee; *Georgetta,* Mary Kelley; *Crane,* Hal Price; *Costain,* Al Taylor; *Commander,* Henry Sylvester; *Peters* (also *Henchman* and *Riveter*), Loren Riebe; *Stevens* (also *Dock*

Official), Leander de Cordova; *Doctor,* John Ward; *Fox,* William Stahl; *Kraft* (also *Harry*), Wally West; *Mrs. Henkin,* Jane Keckley; *Joe,* John Bradford; *James,* William Humphrey; *Morris,* Jack Cheatham; *Mills,* Jack Gardner; *Noble,* John Butler; *Cop,* Jack Stewart; *teacher,* Eva Mackenzie; *and* John Mills, Harold De Garro, Edgar Allan, Buddy Williams, Philip Mason, *and* Henry Guttman.

Chapter Titles

The Spider Strikes; 2)The Bridge of Terror; 3)The Fur Pirates; 4)Death Rides the Sky; 5)Brother Against Brother; 6)Dangerous Waters; 7)The Ghost Town Mystery; 8)Battle in the Clouds; 9)The Stratosphere Adventure; 10)The Gold Ship; 11)Harbor Pursuit; 12)The Trail of the Spider; 13)The Fire Trap; 14)The Devil in White; 15)Brothers United.

Synopsis

Five notorious criminals wanted by the Federal Bureau of Investigation gather in a private car on a speeding train

Ralph Byrd (center) in the hands of the enemy. At foreground are John Picorri and the Lame One/Spider. Henchman are Buddy Roosevelt, Carleton Young, Loren Riebe, Al Taylor.

to meet with their leader, known to them only as the Lame One. The five speak of rebellion but become silent when the Lame One's dragging footsteps are heard and they are confronted by his grotesque silhouette. One of them, Korvitch, defies his boss and fires on the silhouette. The Lame One only laughs. Later, walking at night down a deserted street, Korvitch hears the footsteps of the Lame One. Running until he is exhausted, Korvitch stops to rest, then sees the Lame One's shadow. The luminous shape of a spider appears on Korvitch's forehead. Korvitch is found shot to death. At the Western Division of the FBI, San Francisco, operative Dick Tracy discusses the murders of Korvitch and six other wanted criminals with his partner, Steve Lockwood, his secretary, Gwen Andrews, and an assistant, Mike McGurk. The killings have occured in various parts of the United States, and each victim bears the spider mark.

Dick's birthday is celebrated with a party at the estate of millionaire philanthropist Elliott Brewster, secretly one of the rebellious members of the Lame One's gang, which the FBI knows as the Spider Gang. Guests include Dick's orphaned ward, twelve-year-old Junior; Gordon, Dick's brother, an attorney; and two philanthropists, Potter and Odette. While Martino and Andrea are presenting a puppet show, Brewster becomes the latest spider victim. With Junior's help, Dick proves that Martino killed Brewster while a recording performed his part in the puppet show. Gordon reveals that Brewster gave him a sealed envelope to be opened in case Brewster's death. Gordon heads for his office to get the envelope. A car forces Gordon off an embankment, and he is taken, unconscious, to Cragg's Head, hideout of the Spider gang. Moloch, a crazed medical genius, tells the Lame One that by "a simple altering of certain glands" he can make Gordon "unable to distinguish between right and wrong." After Gordon's disappearance, FBI Division Director Clive Anderson gives Dick permission

to work full time on the Spider case. Martino is convicted of Brewster's murder and sentenced to die.

The Governor of California tells Dick that he has been warned that unless he stays the execution of Martino the newly built Bay Bridge will be destroyed at noon on the day of its opening. Meantime, the Lame One demonstrates a miniature model of his disintegrating ray which destroys objects by use of high-frequency sound waves. Gordon Tracy — his features as well as his mind altered by Moloch's genius — is put in charge of the project. Gordon and his men fly toward the bridge in the wing, a sophisticated and powerful aircraft which contains the sonic device.

Dick, having successfully tracked the typewriter on which the threatening letter was written, finds a chart which states that steel will crystallize at 36,000 cycles. Deducing that the Spider gang plans to use sound to destroy the bridge, Dick has a fleet of trucks driven onto the bridge to destroy the effectiveness of the sonic weapon. Clearing a Spider truck out of the way, Dick narrowly escapes death when girders break away and fall toward him. The bridge is saved by Dick's ruse, but the wing easily outdistances the pursuing patrol planes and vanishes.

A clue leads Dick to the abandoned plant of the Sierra Pacific Power Company, hiding place of the wing. Pole-vaulting over an electrically charged fence, Dick engages in a gun battle with members of the gang. Dick finds the wing and destroys the disintegrator. Steve joins him, and they commandeer a small airplane to escape overwhelming numbers of Spider men. Disabled by gunfire, the craft crashes, but Steve and Dick are unhurt and reach safety. Gordon and his henchmen escape in the wing.

The Spider gang plans to steal a million dollars worth of furs off the SS *Morovania*. Dick allows Burke, a captured Spider henchman, to escape, following him to an abandoned steamship. Gordon captures Dick and leaves him tied on the ship, while attacking the *Morovania* with a smoke screen. Dick escapes, turns off the smoke machine, and commandeers a motor launch in order to chase Gordon and a henchman. As his boat passes between two ships, the huge vessels come together and crush the launch. Dick dives under the ships just in time.

Dick and Steve board the dirigible *Pacific Queen*, bound for San Francisco, to guard the fabulous Mogra Necklace. It has already been stolen by a passenger, a supposed hunchback named Mills. The "hump" is a parachute; Mills escapes. Using an imitation necklace as bait, Dick has the newspapers announce that the stolen necklace was a phoney and the owner, M. Renee, is going home in a private airplane. The plane is actually radio-controlled by Dick and Steve from another plane, in hope of luring the wing out of hiding. Junior, examining the robot plane, is inside when it takes off. Dick manages a mid-air transfer from his plane to the robot craft, but the plane is shot down by the wing. Escaping via parachute, Dick and Junior plant an imitation necklace in the wreckage. When Spider gangsters pick up the necklace, Dick follows them to a hideout, the Beechwood Hotel. Gordon captures Dick, who is taken before the Lame One. Pretending to have in his possession a vial of nitroglycerine, Dick escapes with the necklace. The gang flees in the wing.

The Lame One arranges to deliver the secret of nickolanium, an alloy of great importance, to a foreign government. At a supposedly deserted waterfront warehouse, Gordon is about to hand the formula to Killian, a foreign agent who has arrived by submarine, when Dick grabs it. A fight follows and Killian escapes in the sub, almost drowning Dick, whose foot is entangled in a mooring line.

The Lame One next tries to steal a hoard of gold from Death Valley Johnny, a venerable prospector. Dick and Gordon tangle at the ghost town where the gold is hidden. Dick falls into an abandoned mine shaft but is saved from the guns of the Spider gang when Steve arrives.

Gordon is dispatched to obtain a speed plane to be test-piloted by Betty Clayton, daughter of the inventor. Dick accompanies Betty on the test flight and overpowers a stowaway who tries to hijack the craft. Gordon kidnaps Clayton away on the airplane. The craft is shot down by the wing, but Dick and Clayton bail out before it explodes. Gordon tries to shoot the men as they float down, but Steve's airplane arrives and drives the wing away. Gordon flies to the site of the crash and retrieves the secret motors, then guides the wing toward a high-altitude rendezvous at sea with a foreign dirigible. Dick, meantime, has waylaid one of the gang and taken his place aboard the wing. The wing hovers over the dirigible and the motors are transferred. Dick gets aboard the dirigible before the wing separates. Covering Durston, the enemy agent, and the crew, Dick orders them to head for the mainland. Steve, unaware that Dick is aboard, machine-guns the dirigible. Dick is knocked unconcious just before the dirigible explodes. Dick escapes by grabbing Durston as he bails out. Detective and spy are rescued from the ocean.

Dick next foils a Spider gang plot to steal a million dollars in gold from the SS *Atlantis,* narrowly escaping being crushed beneath a falling armor plate. He also rescues Coulter, a government engraver, from the Lame One's clutches , with the aid of the Coast Guard. The Lame One's personal attempt to assassinate Dick in his office is foiled and leads Dick to the latest hideout, a derelict ship. Dick covers the Lame One, Moloch, Gordon, and Kraft, but is trapped by the arrival of other henchmen. During a struggle the ship is set afire, and Tracy is knocked unconscious. He awakens to find himself tied up on the doomed ship but manages to free his feet and jump overboard.

Believing the Lame One will try again to kidnap Coulter, Dick takes the injured Coulter's place in hospital and is spirited away in an ambulance to Cragg's Head, the main hideout. The Lame One's men lose the G-Men who try to follow. Dick gets the drop on Moloch and Gordon but is surprised and disarmed by the Lame One, who emerges from

a secret panel. Moloch gleefully anaesthetises Dick, preparatory to performing the same operation suffered by Gordon. Steve and Mike capture a henchman and learn where Dick is being held. The G-Men are discovered as they approach the hideout. The Lame One and his men flee through a secret passageway, but Moloch remains behind, determined to use his scalpel on Dick. Dick overcomes Moloch, who falls under a dripping can of ether. Moloch's black cat lies down by its master. Dick, Steve, and Mike enter the secret tunnel just as the house explodes. They overtake the Lame One and his henchmen, who are reaching the nearby Sierra Power plant. As Dick struggles with Gordon, the Lame One tries to hit Dick with a pistol but strikes Gordon instead. Dick grapples with the Lame One and accidentally tears away a mask, revealing the features of Odette. Odette covers the G-Men and orders the dazed Gordon to drive the car. Rounding a curve, Gordon sees Gwen and Junior in the road ahead. Recognizing them, he swerves the car, which crashes over a cliff. The Lame One is killed and Gordon, dying, tells his brother, "It's all like a horrible nightmare . . . I can't seem to remember anything . . . I think I'm going places."

Notes

Universal's success with serial adaptations of cartoon strips, particularly *Flash Gordon,* led Republic to pay the Chicago Tribune Syndicate $10,000 for rights to produce *Dick Tracy,* a serial based upon Chester Gould's popular feature. Although the hero of the newspaper strip was a city police detective, Republic made him an FBI agent as part of an initial plan to star Melvin Purvis, the famous G-Man who hounded John Dillinger and other infamous public enemies to their doom. For the film version, the writers deleted all the other characters from the cartoon except Junior, Tracy's ward, replacing them with characters of their own creation. Shortly before production began, the deal with Purvis fell through and a bit-player, Ralph Byrd, was selected to play the sharp-featured Tracy. The casting proved ideal; Byrd starred as Tracy in three more Republic serials, two RKO features, and thirty-nine television shows, the latter being filmed just before his death in 1952. Byrd received $150 a week during the twenty-five days *Dick Tracy* was in production. As was usually the case with serial favorites, Byrd's feature assignments were unworthy of his talents.

Photography was completed on Christmas Eve of 1936 at a cost of $127,640. Extensive use of unusual locations around Los Angeles and San Pedro, second-unit photography at San Francisco, spectacular miniature effects, and an unusually large cast give the picture an expensive appearance seldom seen in previous serials. Music is plentiful and exciting. *Tracy* was a fittingly impressive serial swan-song for Nat Levine, who a short time later sold his interest in Republic to Herbert J. Yates. Levine next worked briefly for M-G-M and then retired from film production.

The criminal mastermind is a grotesque character fully as

strange as Gould's comic-strip villains. His face hidden throughout by shadows or camera angles, the gang lord is discovered only in the last chapter to be another character in disguise; decades later, this classic Levine technique proved useful for the handling of the chief of S.P.E.C.T.R.E. in the *James Bond* films. The Lame One's hunchbacked mad scientist assistant, payed by John Picorri, is equally weird and is usually seen with a black cat . A distinctly unusual touch is the portrayal of Tracy's brother briefly by Richard Beach as a mild-mannered youth, then by Carleton Young as a hard-faced, mechanical-voiced villian. So good is Young, a radio actor, in the part that it should have led to more important roles, but he never rose above the status of a supporting player.

Cast size notwithstanding, some of the players may be seen doing extra duty in the course of fifteen weekly installments. Buddy Roosevelt, George De Normand, Loren Riebe, and Al Taylor are each seen in three roles, with De Normand also appearing as Byrd's stunt double. Leander de Cordova, Harrison Greene, Wally West, and Henry Sylvester each have two roles.

The story construction differs from previous serials in that it is built upon a series of almost self-contained plots within the framework of the major premise, each continuity being resolved in about two or three reels. This is made possible by the various machinations of the Lame One, who moves from scheme to scheme, each of which is frustrated by FBI interference. This formula was adhered to thereafter in most of Republic's mystery-type serials and was imitated often by Universal and Columbia. Some episodes defy logic, but all are exciting and imaginative. Such trick effects as the flying wing — (which is strikingly similar in design to ones developed a decade later by the U. S. Air Force) — a flaming dirigible crash, a burning ship, a collapsing bridge, airplane crashes, and explosions are accomplished with the unsurpassed realism and artistry for which Republic serials became famous. The splendid musical scoring which Republic pioneered in this specialized genre is fully evident in *Dick Tracy*. Original music by Alberto Colombo is augmented by previously published works of Karl Hajos, Arthur Kay, Hugo Riesinfeld, William Frederick Peters, and Jean Beghon.

The flying wing.

Index